The Annotated Marx Brothers

To My FABULOUS FRIEND
MARIE —

Hope You ENJOY IT!

WITH THANKS AND
MY VERY BEST WISHES —

Marie

The Annotated
Marx Brothers

*A Filmgoer's Guide to
In-Jokes, Obscure References
and Sly Details*

MATTHEW CONIAM

McFarland & Company, Inc., Publishers

Jefferson, North Carolina

LIBRARY OF CONGRESS CATALOGUING-IN-PUBLICATION DATA

Coniam, Matthew, 1973–
The annotated Marx Brothers : a filmgoer's guide to in-jokes,
obscure references and sly details / Matthew Coniam.
p.   cm.
Includes bibliographical references and index.

ISBN 978-0-7864-9705-8 (softcover : acid free paper) ∞
ISBN 978-1-4766-1876-0 (ebook)

1. Marx Brothers films—History and criticism.   I. Title.

PN1995.9.M33C66 2015   791.4302'80922—dc23   2015001183

BRITISH LIBRARY CATALOGUING DATA ARE AVAILABLE

On the cover: 1930 publicity photo for *Animal Crackers*.
Left to right: Chico, Groucho, Harpo, Zeppo.

Printed in the United States of America

*McFarland & Company, Inc., Publishers
Box 611, Jefferson, North Carolina 28640
www.mcfarlandpub.com*

For Edward

Table of Contents

Acknowledgments

I wrote my first book on the Marx Brothers around Christmas 1983. I was ten years old and had been aware of the Brothers for a few days. At sixteen pages it was a little light on information, and somewhat sketchy in its factual authority (I thought Zeppo was the one who played the piano). Looking at it now, it is all too obvious that its author had not yet read Bergson's *Laughter* (*Essai sur la signification du comique*). But what it lacked in research it more than made up for in vague felt-tipped pen illustrations.

Now, at long last, here is the second edition.

And because I *have* read Bergson by now, I can't help but recall his assertion that "cranks of the same kind are drawn, by a secret attraction, to seek each other's company" as I take this opportunity to express my gratitude to the many cranks without whom this book would have been the merest shadow of its present self:

First and especially to Glenn Mitchell, author of the invaluable-is-putting-it-too-mildly *Marx Brothers Encyclopedia*, for the generosity with which he has volunteered time, insight and rare Thelma Todd movies; to Anthony Blampied, who as well as being my man on the inside at the Cinémathèque Royale de Belgique has long offered professional encouragement and personal friendship in unique and irreplaceable union; to Grouch McGummo (a.k.a. Simon Louvish), Scott Saternye and Trudy Marshall, who read early drafts and made helpful suggestions; to Chuck Harter, who pulled superb research finds out of his hat in Los Angeles; to Randy Skretvedt, who couldn't be a nicer guy (scientific fact); to Steven R. Wright, who kindly allowed me to make use of his work on the two versions of *Love Happy*; to David A. Cory, who generously donated his essay on "Lydia" for use as an appendix; to my editor, Dylan Lightfoot, who sounds like he should be a 1930s private eye, and to Richard Larcombe, who has been all four of the Three Musketeers for two and a half decades.

Further invaluable assistance or information was provided by Joe Adamson, Richard J. Anobile, Patrick Barr, George Bettinger, Noah Diamond, Allen Eyles, Meg Farrell, Steve Garland, Steven Kurtz, Annette D'Agostino Lloyd, Ian McLagan, Jim Marx, Damian O'Hara, Robert Moulton, Thomas Rácz, Ben Robinson, Jenny Romero (Margaret Herrick Library), Michael J.C. Taylor, Mikael Uhlin, Raymond White and Tighe Zimmers.

The readers of my blog "The Marx Brothers Council of Britain" and the members of its spin-off Facebook group have been unendingly helpful in providing plausible solutions to the many conundrums I have placed before them; my gratitude to them all, and especially to Bill Andres, Annie Bones, Jay Brennan, Marjie Cardwell, Eugene Conniff, Geno Cuddy,

Kevin Jon Davies, Glenn F, Billy Frolick, Bill Groves, Jason Hyde, Ginger Ingénue, Lotten Kalenius, Debra MacLaughlan-Dumes, Jessica Martin, Josh Max, Steve Miller, Alice Mulconry, Mary O'Benar, Scott T. Rivers, Tom Rogers, Stefan Timphus and Bluejay Young.

And thanks above all to my behind the scenes research team and sounding board for their inexhaustible energy, enthusiasm, efficiency and good company. They are: Ed Watz, pre-eminent expert on all things comedic, whose faith in this project, and the help and encouragement he has given at every stage, go way beyond generosity and into the sort of eccentricity that gets people asked to leave early at parties; Rodney Stewart Hillel Tryster, a man who gives polymathy a good name (well, a better one than Rodney, anyway), and a master of archival research who saved the day time and again with his supernatural ability to find exactly the right 80-year-old one-inch newspaper clipping at exactly the most helpful moment; Andrew Smith, author of the definitive *Flywheel* guide *Marx and Re-Marx*, and an invaluably free-thinking influence on the *Love Happy* chapter in particular; W. Gary Wetstein, a constant force of both encouragement and restraint, and a shrewd judge of relevance and tone (whose advice I should have ignored far less frequently), and Bob Gassel, whose occult gift for suggesting new avenues of interpretation, couched in some deceptively casual asides, has enriched the book in countless ways, and led directly to the complete rewriting of at least three chapters.

Finally I would like to thank my parents for letting me stay up and watch these films when I was ten years old, my sister Helen for putting up with the consequences, my wonderful wife, Angela, for accompanying me to all of them at the National Film Theatre when we'd only been going out a couple of months and *still* letting me marry her afterwards, and our baby son, Edward, for graciously consenting to sleep occasionally so I could get the book written.

Introduction

Between 1885 and 1901, Minnie Marx and her husband Samuel produced six sons. The first, Manfred, tragically died at the age of just seven months. But the other five, who had sensible names too, but remain better known as Chico, Harpo, Groucho, Gummo and Zeppo, grew up to become the Marx Brothers.

Spurred on by the aspirations of their stage-struck mother, they grew from a boy act to one of the top comedy turns of vaudeville. Gummo, who was never comfortable under the lights, used the First World War as the excuse he needed to duck out. With Zeppo in his place they went on to conquer Broadway.

And after that, they made a bunch of films that still provoke helpless laughter to this day.

And what happened after *that* is that a whole bunch of writers wrote a whole bunch of very good books about those films. So doubtless you are wondering why I'm expecting you to care about the fact that I've come along and written another one.

Well, rest assured that this is not an attempt to tell you what you already know, nor to supplant the work of those esteemed Marxian scribes who have gone before me. This is not a history, nor a biography, nor a series of reviews, but a viewer's guide to the films themselves.

What does that mean? Well, it means that each chapter focuses on a different movie and, after a general introduction, takes the form of a running commentary, discussing points raised by the film as and when they appear, filling in background detail, pointing out things you might just have missed, and explaining a few of the more obscure jokes and references. Every section referred to is precisely located in the running time, with the time code given for both PAL and NTSC DVD, so you can quickly look it up to refresh your memory. Or, you can keep the book by your side as you watch the movies in full, to be referred to whenever the mood strikes. Sometimes what I have to offer will be a mere nugget, other times a lengthy digression, but always, I hope, something that adds to your enjoyment. Think of it as a travelling companion as you ramble through the landscape of these remarkable comedies, both a newcomer's guide and an addict's resource, a source of contention and of illumination, a mire of speculation and an oasis of confirmation, and all of these things at one and the same time.

Now, you may have heard an internal alarm bell ringing when you read that bit about "explaining jokes." Too much analysis, you may feel, is the death of comedy. Take a joke apart to see how it works, you may want to add parenthetically, and you'll never get it back together again. And you'd have a point. Don't worry: I've never been a great one for reading stuff into the Marx Brothers' films that isn't really there. It seems to me there's more than enough that *is* really there, and it's usually a good deal funnier too.

But answer me this: have you ever been watching a Marx Brothers movie and wondered what "habeas Irish rose" is? What is the trial of Mary Dugan with sound? What is a college widow? Who are those five kids up in Canada? Exactly when did Don Ameche invent the telephone?

The films of the Marx Brothers are full of these in-jokes and obscure theatrical, literary and topical references that can baffle modern audiences. This book will, in part, strive to explain such mysteries, as well as offer all the other obscure or interesting trivia and background information relevant to each film that it is in my power to provide. If it is aimed a little more (but I hope by no means exclusively) at the confirmed enthusiast than the novice, that's simply because I can't really be bothered to repeat all those well-known anecdotes you find in every other book on the Marx Brothers. But if you want to know the *real* secret of Abie the Fish Man, which film exists in two versions with two completely different songs, or exactly how many Frenchmen can't be wrong, you've come to the right place.

The book is not solely an assembly of facts, however. And given that personal assessment must inevitably intrude, I doubtless owe you an honest account of my prejudices before proceeding further.

Well, I was introduced to the Marx Brothers at the age of ten, over the Christmas of 1983. In those days Britain only had four television channels, and that year, BBC-2 was offering a season of five Marx Brothers films. I know many people who forged an obsession with the team from the most unlikely first encounters, including *Room Service* and *Go West*. Even so, I thank my stars for having been offered so perfect an introduction: all the Paramount titles bar *Cocoanuts* (I had to wait till the following year to catch up with that one) plus *A Night in Casablanca*. My first taste was *Monkey Business,* which I actually tuned into halfway through, just in time to see funnier humans than I had ever seen in my life doing ridiculous impressions of a man I had never heard of, called Maurice Chevalier. One of them didn't speak, and so performed his impersonation with a wind-up gramophone strapped to his back. I hadn't realised it was *possible* for people to be *that* hilarious. By the time Groucho interrupted a party to announce that a diamond earring had been lost, so was I. A lifelong love affair had started.

But I don't think it's anything to do with that formative experience to say that, in common with most fans, I prefer greatly the Brothers in that Paramount incarnation to the later movies made at MGM. Neither is it simply because I find these films generally faster and funnier. I'm also in love with the whole world of pre–Code Hollywood, those movies made up until the rigid implementation of the Hays Code in 1934.

There is a tendency to credit the shift in tone that occurs after *Duck Soup* solely to the innovations of Irving Thalberg, who deliberately softened their style to broaden their appeal, and to MGM generally, who seemed, especially after Thalberg's death, to have little understanding of their style at all, and diluted their comedy with musical fluff and distracting production values. All fair enough, but it is not entirely MGM's fault that after 1934 the Brothers stop playing their satires against backgrounds like the Florida land boom or society parties and start hanging round circuses: the transition between studios also coincided with the beginning of the Code era. The manner in which they become harmless "zanies" at MGM would not have been entirely avoided elsewhere. Even if they had stayed at Paramount, a general taming and domestication would have been obvious.

So what defines the difference? First, the satire is inevitably blunted: if the world being deflated is not recognisable, real and modern, then the Marx Brothers have lost a huge part of their comedic edge: who cares if they are set in the old west or some boring department store, insulting crooks and cowboys instead of society matrons and pretentious art critics? Even the joyous *A Night at the Opera* (1935) is in this sense as much a portent of what is to come as a last hurrah. The fun of seeing them take on grand opera is far cosier and more remote from the everyday experience of most cinemagoers, and panders to their prejudices. Far better have them satirise inane, popular genre cinema (as they do in *Monkey Business*, *Horse Feathers* and *Duck Soup*, parodies of society gangster films, college pictures and Ruritanian fantasies respectively) or take on the Long Island set in a spirit of genuine anarchy. They are not anarchists at MGM, merely crazies. But in *The Cocoanuts* and *Animal Crackers* they really are dangerous to be around. The Code era takes the danger away.

Similarly, MGM is not entirely to blame for the lesser quality of their final three films for the studio. Even with sympathetic producers and better writing, the times were simply out of joint. Something I have noticed many times (particularly but by no means exclusively with television comedians) is that when a comedy act is hip, and riding a wave of fashionable credibility, there is an energy to what they do that goes beyond the innate excellence of their performances and material. There is something far more: a supremely confident bravado and a kind of understood rapport with the audience that conveys itself like an electric charge. They almost crackle. This is especially obvious with the Marx Brothers, because they had been the Broadway darlings of an extremely sophisticated and literary set, and because so much of their act is about being daring and confrontational and breaking social rules in the first place. You can see this mad energy, this kind of disregard for all the safeguards with which comedians usually strive to ingratiate themselves, *and* how it further ignites the artistic potential of the raw materials, very keenly in the Paramount films. You can see it especially in *Animal Crackers*, and again just as fiercely in *Horse Feathers*, once they had been assured the Hollywood gamble had paid off. Decline almost always follows when this quality of hipness is taken away. It's not the loss of popularity per se: the act may still make profits and retain a following, but they are no longer *the latest thing*, no more the guys that everyone's talking about. The evidence of many, many other comedians (that it would be instructive but churlish to name) is that the adjustment is next to impossible. In a few cases the withdrawal proved literally fatal, but even if they still produce quality work, with any number of redeeming moments, the loss of spirit is always obvious, and you *can't* fake it.

We see this with the Marxes in their final MGM films, and while it is unquestionably true that Louis B. Mayer had no interest in their doing anything other than fulfilling their contract as quickly as possible, it was simply the dawn of the forties, as much as anything one man could do or the Brothers' own advancing years and declining interest, that cast a gloom over the work.

The 1940s was one of those annoying "new broom" decades, when fashion dictates that the popular entertainments of the previous generation are not only of the past but also explicitly passé. The Marxes could never have avoided that: some newspaper ads for *At the Circus* actually opted for the tagline: "A New Marx Bros Type of Picture Because It Is Their Old Time Comedy!" The meaning is all too clear, even if it does appear to have been translated from the original Greek in a bit of a hurry. The Marx Brothers are *so* last decade, and the way to enjoy them is *nostalgically*. Anyone who watches, say, *The Big Store* wondering why it lacks the confidence and zip of *A Night at the Opera* would do well to remind themselves of the year it was made. It's a sweet enough film, but it is obsolete: it is the work of a team that belonged to an earlier time. The "Road" films are happening now; Abbott and Costello are happening now. Comedy is broader and brasher; it's timed to the beat of Glenn Miller rather than Fred Waring's Pennsylvanians, and it's much, much less cerebral and confrontational than the Brothers at their peak.

And there wasn't really a place for the Marxes anymore, because the tradition they had started had been re-routed, leaving them stranded. Now, you only have to look at a film like *Road to Utopia* to see where the Marx tradition had actually ended up. It's a very funny movie, but it's different in a way the Brothers could never have competed with. The fact that it has everything *The Big Store* most pointedly lacks and needs—irreverence, pace, rat-a-tat jokes, energy, a sense of purpose and a feeling of relevance—does not mean that if you took all those jokes and gave them to the Marxes they would have had another smash hit. It would feel odd and forced (as would giving them the material of *Hellzapoppin'*, perhaps the clearest display of what was intrinsically different between the absurdist humour of the two decades and, try as I might, a film I've never been able to warm to at all). Bing and Bob and Dottie, of course, were riding on just that wave of hipness, of being perfectly in tune with the zeitgeist, which the Marxes had enjoyed the decade before, and *that* is what the film conveys in their hands.

I suspect that if the Brothers *had* continued in the early forties, not even new Kaufman scripts could arrest the decline. As it is, the rest did them good, and when they did come back with *A Night in Casablanca*, it was a smaller production, and audiences had been given time to miss them and, perhaps, revise a few of their more frivolous and ephemeral commitments. Either way, it's a new Marx Brothers again that we see in it, a Marx Brothers Mark Three, older and no longer attempting to hold on to stardom, but relaxed again and doing what they do as if unscrutinised, and uncaring of the result. As a consequence, the film represents a small but certain renaissance.

The finer points of my personal position will doubtless announce themselves as we go along; that, I think, covers the bases in as much detail as necessary at the outset. But if there's one thing I want to make absolutely certain it's that, just as it must be distinctly understood from the outset that Marley is dead, so it must be made clear now that if you ever catch me talking about "a lesser Marx Brothers movie" or "a disappointing Marx Brothers movie," or even "a poor Marx Brothers movie" I mean BY THE STANDARDS OF OTHER MARX BROTHERS MOVIES. As James Agee once observed, "the worst they might ever make would be better worth seeing than most other things I can think of." And I'll sign my name to that without demur.

I would hate to know for definite that I had just seen any one of them for the last time.

A Word About Time Codes

There's no one single way this book has to be read. You can, if you wish, read it from cover to cover. Or you can keep it by your bedside, to be opened at random and dipped into. If, however, you intend using it while watching the films, please bear in mind the following:

Time codes are shown in both NTSC and PAL format. These are unavoidably approximate, and various factors may result in my timings being slightly different to yours. Different releases may contain imperceptible irregularities in speed, or minute mastering flaws that result in seconds being lost or gained.

Wherever possible I have used the best official materials available in the UK, specifically the 2006 Universal "Marx Brothers 8 Movie Collection" box set for the Paramount titles and *Room Service*, and the 2004 Warner Brothers "Marx Brothers Collection" box set for the MGM titles and *A Night in Casablanca*.

In the case of *Love Happy,* rather than the shorter cut in the Universal set, I opted to refer to the 91 minute version. For this I used an NTSC import as the long cut does not seem to be available in PAL format. For *The Incredible Jewel Robbery* I referenced the NTSC set *The Marx Brothers TV Collection* from Shout Factory. Thus all the timings were taken in PAL and converted for NTSC, with the exception of *Love Happy* and *The Incredible Jewel Robbery*, to which the opposite applies. (Please note that the fact that I have included PAL timings for the last two titles should not be taken to suggest that they exist in official PAL editions: to the best of my knowledge at time of writing they do not. I include PAL timings, however, in the interests of uniformity, and in the hope that such editions will be made available in the future, in which case the timings should hold good.)

Finally, please note that I start my times from the beginning of the original film. I do include the studio logos from the original print, but not the added video logos which, on some of the Universal discs, start at 0:00 on the disc's counter. My 0:00 for *The Cocoanuts*, for example, is 0:21 on my DVD counter, i.e. when the actual film starts. Basically, if it's authentic and original, I include it. This goes for the NRA logo preceding *Duck Soup* and the Production Code certificate at the top of *Monkey Business*.

There may be a bit of trial and error at first, but whether you're watching the film and trying to look something up in the book, or reading the book and trying to find the relevant point in the film, allow a leeway of twenty seconds or so in both directions and you should find what you're looking for soon enough.

1

The Cocoanuts (1929)

> Think of the opportunities here in Florida! Three years ago I came to Florida
> without a nickel in my pocket. Now I've got a nickel in my pocket.
> —Mr. Hammer (Groucho Marx)

In *Film Daily* on November 27, 1929, under the heading "Timely Topics: A Digest of
Current Opinion," the following letter was published:

> I am beginning to believe that the talkies are a step backward in the development of the screen.
> A silent comedy had to be fairly funny to make an audience laugh, but the comedy dialog shorts
> they are displaying now are in the main just a re-hash of the stalest, nastiest and most inane bits
> culled from the Mutual Wheel Shows of Nineteen Ten. Well, there is no use getting angry about
> it. There must be a market for this goulash or it wouldn't be made.

The letter is signed "Groucho Marx, comedian."

It's far from the last time we'll encounter this most iconoclastic of all the great screen
comedians devaluing his art (though the explicit reference to shorts may perhaps be taken
as a vague attempt at personal disassociation). Even so, it remains as eye-opening a gesture
as it is typical, given that it was published the very year the Marx Brothers began their magnificent assault upon the codes and conventions of the talking screen.

But then, we have to remember that to the Marx Brothers in 1929, making a talking
picture may not have seemed all that big a deal. They had been performers of one sort or
another since boyhood, and edging into their forties as established superstars of Broadway,
they would have no reason to suppose they were only now arriving at the most significant
turning point of their entire careers.

Recall also that *The Cocoanuts* was not quite their first film as a team. In the early twenties they made a short, self-financed silent, punningly titled *Humor Risk*, in which they
played roles bearing no resemblance to their stage personae. (Groucho was the villain.) It
was deemed a failure and almost immediately lost, perhaps even destroyed. The chances of
it showing up now are vanishingly slender—which is no bad thing, Groucho might be
expected to add. (Though in later life he did express a yearning to see it again, while in the
mid-forties, recognizing its sentimental and archival, if not, perhaps, artistic value, Harpo
offered a reward of $10,000 for a print.)

And there were other near-misses on the road to *Cocoanuts* too: an offer from First
National to make a starring silent comedy got as far as an announcement in *Variety* in 1926;
the same sheet had MGM courting them (for "a series" of comedies, presumably meaning

History is made in the lobby: (left to right) Groucho, Chico and Harpo commence their assault on screen history in *The Cocoanuts*.

screen originals) as close to the wire as 1928. United Artists expressed their interest in shooting *The Cocoanuts* a year before Paramount took them up: had they done so it would almost certainly have been largely if not entirely silent.

Finally shot at Long Island in early 1929, while *Animal Crackers* was still cutting up Broadway, *The Cocoanuts* enjoyed a rapturous reception from critics and audiences both. It's "the most enjoyable musical show yet to come to the talking screen," the *Palm Beach Post* reckons. "Praising *The Cocoanuts* is like giving an endorsement to June sunshine," offers the *Sarasota Herald-Tribune*. "Beyond question it represents one of the greatest accomplishments of the talking screen." By the end, "one's ribs are aching and one's cheek muscles exhausted by almost constant laughter," says the *Free Lance-Star*. The *Berkeley Daily Gazette* is calling it "the most unique and entertaining screen presentation yet perfected." And in common with the rest, they single out the music, chorus, supporting cast and "unique camera angles" for special commendation too. "Talking pictures are getting more vigorous and sprightly all the time," Monta Bell, producer in charge of Paramount's Long Island studios, told *Film Daily* magazine in 1929. "We have made already a big musical comedy, *The Cocoanuts*, starring the Four Marx Brothers. It presented difficulties for which there was no guiding precedent. It was the first attempt to put a first class musical show from the stage, preserving the musical comedy technique, into talking pictures. We learned much from the experiment, and in some ways it represents our most difficult accomplishment."

A sense of just how difficult is ably conveyed in this shooting report from *Variety* (and note also its more sober contemporary perspective on the legend that the Marxes were untamed dervishes on the set):

All the stages of the upper floor are in use, with one length of the studio given over to an enormous sweep of beach scene, complete with ocean effects. Besides the principals, show girls and chorus, there are four dancing troupes scattered around the studio. But the personnel to whip the picture into shape is the amazing thing. First there's Joe Santley to direct dialog and rehearse over and over again until the scene is perfect for shooting. And this, with those ad-libbing Marxes on the set is no small task. Then there's Morrie Ryskind to arrange the dialog should any changes be necessary, and Robert Florey to supervise photography and work out picture angles. George Folsey, head photographer under Florey, commands the battery of cameras, four or five being used for each big scene. It is his job to watch the lighting and keep the scenes in original composition. Sound supervisor attends to the placing of the microphones, his particular problem being to hang them where they'll get the best reception and yet be outside the camera. He works in close association with the recorder in the sound booth who regulates sound levels, intensifying or diminishing as the recording requires. Vocal sequences are "played back" after they have been taken, with corrections given to the cast. Then there is Frank Tours to supervise the 35-piece orchestra, and the four dancing directors to watch for lack of precision in the dance numbers; and Jimmy Cowan, head producer, to watch everything. It's amazing mechanical activity, taking hours of preparation for perhaps three minutes of actual shooting. Under the weight of all this high-powered production are the Marxes—four somewhat quelled spirits, feeling a trifle strange in an atmosphere not conducive to wisecracking. They are four bad boys trying to act like "little gentlemen." Occasionally, during the heated conferences of the supervisors, the Marx madness breaks out and Chico dashes to the piano, Groucho sings a melancholy ballad as only Groucho can sing a melancholy ballad, and Harpo dashes around the studio testing knee reflexes. But for the most part, they're pretty orderly.

But flash forward a few decades, and the film would find itself in a somewhat paradoxical position. It remained one of the most popular and regularly revived of all the early talkies, but its critical standing seemed to have gone into reverse at high speed. Where once it had inspired awe and wonder, now it was dismissed as hopelessly primitive, dramatically static, gracelessly photographed, undermined by cramped and unrealistic sets and bewilderingly imprecise sound recording. Paul D. Zimmerman wrote that the camerawork "showed all the mobility of a concrete fire hydrant caught in a winter freeze." (Thank God, then, that the Marx Brothers were in front of it at the time, being hilarious. Otherwise that could have caused a few problems.) Surely there was no mention of fire hydrants in the *Evening Independent* on June 5, 1929. I know standards are relative, and cynicism loves looking backwards to see what it missed out on, but still, the contrast is striking:

There's a camera shot in *The Cocoanuts* ... in which a group of shadows within a circle opens up like a six-pointed star—just as you might see by gazing through a kaleidoscope. It turns out to be a ring of beautiful girls extending their arms with hands clasped together, as viewed from a camera swung on a scaffolding 40 feet overhead. There is a formation of 40 chorus girls, some of them rigged out fantastically to suggest fluffy and cuddly pets, the "Monkey Doodle" dance in which the camera seems to float through a wide arc to pick fresh points of view. The music and song are continuous, but the picture now appears from a level with their feet, now from a hilltop. It makes the dance rather fascinating. The studio got that effect by a skyscraper placement of cameras in their sound-proof booths, three of them piled on one another, all turning at the same time. A trifle dangerous for the topmost operators, but nothing happened and the result was obtained....

There are many bits of effective and novel camera work in *The Cocoanuts*.... The sequence in which two adjoining hotel rooms are shown together, with the hilarious comedy mix-up of characters chasing from one to another, affords an example of camera work taking on almost a mathematical precision and the rhythm of a drum beat.... In obtaining such effects, [Robert] Florey worked with George Folsey, veteran cameraman who was in charge of the photography, to pack the greatest possible wallop into his visual film.

As the visuals, so the sound recording. Gilbert Seldes wrote in *The New Republic:* "Groucho's is the first voice I have heard from the screen in swift chatter—not as swift, not as crisp as his wisecracking on the stage, but better in these respects than all the other deliveries I have encountered."

Elsewhere, though, Seldes (highbrow that he is) anticipates the more familiar and enduring view of the production (along with one less familiar one about Harpo: the concern that "the semiclose-ups take away some of the mystery of his expression"):

> Apart from that, it should be noted that the director never made up his mind whether he was making a movie or photographing a musical show; for the most part the production might as well have been a moving picture of what took place on the stage. The movie added nothing; the talking was exactly what it had been. All the virtues of the offering are due to G.S. Kaufman, Irving Berlin, the Marxes, and the other collaborators in the original stage show.

As for the show itself, Allen Eyles notes "its silly plot and dated musical elements," while Simon Louvish observes that "a rendition of 'the skies will all be blue / When my dreams come true' is enough to convince us that the 1920s had their down side."

The inauthenticity of almost anything in a Marx Brothers film except the Marx Brothers is so accepted now it has taken on the status of empirical fact. To this consensus, the Marx Brothers are *defined by opposition*, in permanent revolt not merely against the straight world they encounter in their plots, nor even the system in which their films are being made, but also against the very fabric of those films themselves. They are enemies within, artists as agent provocateurs. Whatever it is, they're against every little bit of it.

Advocates of this consensus adhere (albeit not always knowingly) to that very specific set of attitudes through which the work was filtered by the generation that hailed them as counterculture heroes in the 1960s and '70s. (For instance, Andrew Sarris writing in 1969: "They were a welcome relief not only from the badness of their own movies but also from the badness of most of the movies around them.") Through this prism the Marxes become not wonderful examples *of* 30s culture but wonderful *in spite* of being examples of 30s culture. Any audience thus attuned soon learns the necessity of resenting the intrusion of extraneous elements, even the harp and piano solos. Still, de rigueur as it may now be to snort derisively through the subplots, supporting players and songs, I doubt it's anything the brothers themselves would have endorsed.

It is important to locate the Marx Brothers leaping to life here (as opposed to the vaudeville Marx Brothers, now lost to us and surely a broader, less distinctive force than the one here preserved) in the current of twenties New York humor that pulsed through the pages of *The New Yorker,* and, via the Broadway stage, created the rhythms and cadence of talking pictures. Into the world of Dorothy Parker and Robert Benchley and Alexander Woollcott and, most luckily, the great playwright George S. Kaufman, came a wild, unpretentious but uncommonly talented comedy team. This team was then taken under the collective wing of the wits and sophisticates there assembled. Something about the unrestrained anarchy of the Marx Brothers' comic tornado appealed to their delight in disrupting propriety, and it was they who gave them the impetus, opportunity and *material* necessary to become the fashionable darlings of high-class Broadway audiences.

The success that first got them into that orbit was a revue called *I'll Say She Is*, a loosely constructed amalgam of sketches, specialties and songs, some of it dating back to their earliest days in vaudeville, assembled primarily by a talented, traditional writer (and no mean cartoonist) called Will B. Johnstone. (Johnstone would return to the fold when they made their first two Hollywood movies, *Monkey Business* and *Horse Feathers*.) But it would be Kaufman's writing with Morrie Ryskind here and in *Animal Crackers* that gave them true definition as an act.

Kaufman saw an act with one foot on Broadway and the other still happily, even defiantly, in vaudeville, and he was astute enough to see that it was this very mix—of raw vaudeville energy and smart Broadway style—that made them seem so fresh and daring. Accordingly, he and Ryskind set about creating vehicles that preserved their maniac spirit and love of sheer nonsense, but integrated a seam of verbal sophistication that was intricately structured and often dense with allusions and cross-references. As such, he could be said to have been the chief architect of the Marx Brothers as we now know them, as well as providing the basic template for all their other writers to come. (And his astute recall for *A Night at the Opera* is probably the deciding reason why that film is as unexpectedly good as it is.)

Kaufman inherited a team too well defined to reinvent, but working with what he was given he added surprising new layers, and marginalized their more generic aspects. (It was in the transition from vaudeville to Broadway that Chico in particular developed his unique comic persona, so that its roots in stock ethnic humor could eventually blur, leading to all manner of later confusion as to whether he is or isn't supposed to be a "real" Italian.) He also supplied them with the finest wordplay, wildest ideas and most sustained flights of insanity, where absurdist argument develops rigidly by its own internal form of anti-logic. The "why a duck?" sequence, first and most quintessential of the great Groucho-Chico duologues, is justly famous, but even funnier for me is the auction scene to which it serves as prelude, with Chico's maddening refusal to stop bidding up, and Groucho's exasperated attempts to maintain enthusiasm:

> What am I offered for Lot 25? Come on, folks, you know you're all allowed to bid, this is a free country. What am I offered for Lot 25? What am I offered for Lot 25 and a year's subscription to *Youth's Companion?* Will somebody take a year's subscription? I'm trying to work my way through college. Will somebody take a six months' subscription? I'll go to high school. Does anybody want to buy a lead pencil? I'll wrestle anybody in the crowd for five dollars.

The script, like all early Marx material, is also keenly alert to its historical moment. The setting is the Florida land boom, and the invention strikes me as classic Kaufman: given an act whose comic persona in large part revolves around conning and duplicity, and with pretensions to affluence, status and power entirely at odds with the reality of their situation, it is both natural and inspired that Kaufman should find the perfect contemporary setting with which to transform them from sketch artists in revues to characters in musical comedy. (Sorry that was such a long sentence, but it's all over now.)

Florida in the mid-twenties was a huckster's paradise, with trainloads of suckers pouring in to purchase lots that in many cases turned out to be worthless or even non-existent: Simon Louvish notes one development being described as "not more than three-fourths of a mile from the prosperous and fast-growing city of Nettie." It's on its way to sounding like a Groucho line already, the true Marxian twist being that there was of course no such city, prosperous and fast-growing or otherwise: Nettie was an abandoned turpentine camp. (That it was not more than three-fourths of a mile away was doubtless perfectly true.)

It takes no effort at all to imagine Groucho thriving in such a milieu, with his aggressive if absurd badgering of Margaret Dumont to observe the type of sewer pipes used in the new construction, the description of the condominiums as "only a stone's throw from the station" instantly qualified in the film by the disclaimer "as soon as they throw enough stones we're going to build a station," and, above all, his proudly announced "personal guarantee": "If these lots don't double in value in a year, I don't know what you can do about it."

Then, into this hive of duplicity and scheming come the only people Groucho cannot outwit: Harpo and Chico, the latter making no secret of his desire to fleece the fleecer while the former steals the cutlery that Groucho has himself stolen from other hotels. (Look out, too, for a fourth brother, Zeppo, occasionally to be spotted hiding behind the desk in the hotel lobby. And make the most of him. He has even less screen time in *Animal Crackers*.)

It's often eye-opening to compare the original playscript of *The Cocoanuts* to the film version, not least because the former lacks "why a duck?" entirely. (In fact it was worked out by Kaufman, Chico and Groucho during the run: these were clever fellows.) It also shows how shrewdly they shaped material in performance: dozens of familiar jokes are to be found here in forms a fraction as effective as we know them from the film. Consider these:

> "Think of the opportunities here in Florida. I came here with a shoe string, and now I've got three pair of buttoned shoes."
> "Do you know the population of Cocoanut Beach has doubled in the past week? Three horses were born."
> "Every lot is a stone's throw from the station. The only reason we haven't got any station is because we haven't got any stones."
> "No, my friends, money is not everything. And everything's not money. For all I know that's an epigram."

The Cocoanuts is a great moment in Broadway history, and I've always thought it was to the film's credit how well it retains the original's structure, artificiality and design, allowing us to at least pretend we are settling down to enjoy it live. From *Monkey Business* on we have plenty of opportunities to enjoy the Marx Brothers at the movies—but for the time being, let's enjoy them on stage. Besides, *Educational Screen* ("the only magazine devoted to the new influence in national education") finds it "genuinely funny at times ... but touching rather frequently on the cheap and vulgar." That's good enough for me.

0:36 (NTSC)/0:38 (PAL)—The lovely land of Florida

I like this opening sequence for several reasons. First, considering the film's reputation for visual inertia, there are some stylish ideas here and in later fill-ins that play very well, especially if you are a devotee of Deco and Jazz Age iconography. The opening shot of the woman's face taken through the fabric of a twirling parasol is a gem. I also find the estab-

Harpo and Chico rob the rich to help themselves in *The Cocoanuts*.

lishing shots of verdant Florida beach land, swarming with frolicking extras crammed like sardines into the tiny sets, irresistibly suggestive of what it must have been like to see the curtain rise on this thing on Broadway. Thank heaven director Robert Florey's desire to shoot second unit cut-ins on genuine locations was rebuffed by the studio brass with what still seems to me to be the perfect dismissal of all those whose enjoyment is compromised by the artificial nature of the production: "Why are you so concerned with having real backgrounds when one of the leading characters wears an obviously false moustache?" ("With that kind of logic, what could I say?" Florey explained in *The Marx Brothers Scrapbook*, adding: "I did prevail upon him to powder it a bit. If you look at the film closely, you'll notice that the moustache shines in a couple of reels more than others.")

4:01/4:12—"Remember there is nothing like liberty, except *Collier's* and the *Saturday Evening Post*...."

Liberty, first published in 1924, was a magazine known as "a weekly for everybody." At one time second only to the *Saturday Evening Post* in circulation, it was accordingly known as "the second greatest magazine in America." Contributors included Robert Benchley and

F. Scott Fitzgerald. It folded in 1950. This line was written expressly for the film, replacing the play's slightly nearer-the-knuckle version: "Remember, there's nothing like liberty. That is, there's nothing like it in this country."

4:27/4:39—"Couple of telegrams for you, Mr. Hammer...."

As well as a rare chance to see Zeppo Marx come out from behind the hotel's reception desk, this moment gives us our first sighting of another of the most endearing features of *The Cocoanuts:* wet paper. Because of the undiscriminating sound recording technology, ordinary paper crackled so obtrusively on the soundtrack that dialogue was completely drowned out. The ingenious solution was to liberally douse all the paper, giving it the weird, limp quality of decaying lettuce leaves. The inevitable problems caused by this solution to a different problem are especially enjoyable to witness in the "why a duck?" scene, where the map Groucho is referring to visibly and repeatedly tears as he attempts to manipulate the sodden mess.

5:08/5:21—"Let's put this thing over with a bang!"

A commonplace phrase, but one that may nonetheless have strayed into Kaufman and Ryskind's consciousness by its celebrated use in Robert Benchley's *The Treasurer's Report,* first performed in the Algonquin revue *No Sirree!* (1922, in which Kaufman had also appeared) and perfunctorily filmed by Fox Movietone in 1929. What makes Benchley's address funny is in the disparity between his lecturer's ineffectual delivery and the stridency of his words. He stammers nervously, begins sentences that trail into nothing before completion, fails to tell jokes, manages to nervously undo his tie, dips his notes in his soup, and inflicts a string of meaningless financial statistics on his listeners. Finally, when he concludes by enjoining his audience to "help us to put this thing over with a bang!" he accompanies the injunction with a feeble arm gesture that entirely undermines its inspirational purpose.

7:03/7:21—Cyril Ring

A film trivia question. (Although not a terribly demanding one, as I've already given the answer.) What actor appears alongside The Marx Brothers, W.C. Fields, Laurel & Hardy *and* Abbott & Costello, as well as being featured in *Laura, Mr. Skeffington, The Seventh Victim, I Married a Witch, Holiday Inn, This Gun for Hire, Saboteur, Sullivan's Travels, Two-Faced Woman, Meet John Doe, The Lady Eve, North West Mounted Police, The Great Dictator, The Roaring Twenties* and a little something called *Citizen Kane?*

Yes, Cyril Ring. Poor Cyril Ring.

It seems to me he makes a perfectly good job of villainous Harvey Yates, but for some reason he got the most terrible reviews, and his career didn't so much decline as nosedive almost immediately afterwards. Okay; many stars don't make it, perhaps the majority of Hollywood careers are brief. Stars are rare, numerically speaking at least. But the sad thing about Cyril Ring is that he didn't disappear. He kept working in the movies until the early fifties, making many, many films a year throughout that time, for virtually all the major (and minor) studios. But always in the tiniest roles, demeaning walk-ons, a glorified extra, perhaps a line or two at most, always there, somewhere; turning up for the check, doing next to nothing. A face in the crowd, but a haunting one. Once you tune your eyes to spot his distinctive visage, with its pencil moustache and slicked-back hair—a look he never changed—you'll see him all the time; silent, reproachful, living testament to Hollywood's heartlessness. After *The Cocoanuts* he made over 350 films; he received screen credit in maybe three or four. One for which he didn't was *Monkey Business* (1931). What must it have felt like for him on that set? A major supporting actor in the first Marx Brothers movie and then, just two years later, a nobody in their third.

7:04/7:22—Kay Francis

Kay Francis plays Penelope, the vampish bad girl who inspires the jewel robbery. If you don't know the name, it may be surprising to discover that she was perhaps the biggest star of all Marx co-stars barring Marilyn, though, sadly, few others of her magnitude have been quite so thoroughly forgotten. An amazingly chic woman, and a celebrated clotheshorse who set rather than followed the styles, she thought herself of little account and did not greatly enjoy her stardom, though it lasted until the end of the thirties (despite a considerable speech impediment and a far-from-conventional beauty), and only slowly and respectfully tapered off thereafter in low-budget variations. She said that she couldn't wait to be forgotten and for reasons genuinely mysterious, more or less has been.

She had been part of the huge contingent of Broadway actors and actresses imported to Hollywood to cope with the new demands of talking cinema, and her slightly decadent, aloof style and air of European sophistication ensured that she ended up at Paramount, the most stylish of the major studios. Her appeal, I think, is that she was very much an icon of the "lost generation"; she would have made an excellent Brett Ashley. She often plays characters of great material attainment and deep existential dislocation; few actresses of her generation so ably conveyed ennui, fatalism and erotic gloom. Watch her in the opening scenes of *24 Hours* (1931), one of the forthcoming releases promoted alongside *Monkey Business* in *The House That Shadows Built* (see *Monkey Business* 9:00). She's at a small party, depressed, bored, sewn into a translucent white dress, clearly the most fascinating woman in the room, but crippled with dissatisfaction and a physical beauty she carries like a hernia. You have to go back to Louise Brooks in Germany for anything comparable. Like the Marxes, Kay left Paramount for another studio (in her case, Warners) and her work altered significantly in the transition. At Warner Bros., she made high society issues films and women's pictures. But her work in her early Paramount films still makes you sit up and take notice.

8:17/8:38—Mary Eaton

Mary Eaton, the somewhat wan and witless Polly Potter in *The Cocoanuts*, was, in truth, a lively and vibrant performer, as well as an exceptionally gifted dancer, whose talents, including her trademark pirouettes, eye-openingly but briefly indulged in *The Cocoanuts,* are far better displayed in *Glorifying the American Girl.*

With various brothers and sisters she had been one of "The Seven Little Eatons," but also found considerable solo success on Broadway, notably in several *Ziegfeld Follies* revues, and with Eddie Cantor in *Kid Boots* and *Sunny*. (She is introduced by Cantor, together with Oscar Shaw, in the cabaret audience of a Paramount short directed by Joseph Santley concurrently with *Cocoanuts* called *A Ziegfeld Midnight Frolic*.) Like her co-star Oscar Shaw, Mary was not in the original Broadway cast of *The Cocoanuts* but debuted in the film version, drafted in by Paramount to exploit the popularity of their latest contractee. Alas, her popularity faded quickly in the thirties. Her last stage appearance was in 1932, and her last film role (and her first after 1929) was, as a result of circumstances I have been unable to unravel, an uncredited bit in the British Flanagan & Allen comedy *We'll Smile Again* (1942). Sadly, it seems that Mary did not. Enduring three unhappy marriages to three unhappy alcoholics she almost inevitably fell victim to the bottle herself, dying of liver failure in 1948 at the age of forty-seven. (Of her fellow Little Eatons: two others succumbed to alcoholism, and sister Pearl was murdered in 1958; the crime remains unsolved. Sister Doris stopped being the last surviving Ziegfeld girl in 2010 at the age of 106. Broadway dimmed its lights in her honor.)

8:37/8:58—"John W. Berryman was here to see it last month. You know, Berryman practically built Palm Beach and Miami...."

This enterprising gentleman, also the "man with a black moustache" who arrives off-screen at the end to offer dopey Bob Adams a job and feed Groucho one of his most enduring gags, shares his name with the lead character of *Business is Business*, a 45 minute playlet written by George Kaufman and Dorothy Parker and commissioned to provide a special live accompaniment to the film version of *Beggar on Horseback* at the Criterion, New York. This John W. Berryman is a shoe tycoon and a pompous ass, lavish in his self-regard but stingy with his sycophantic employees, and, according to *Variety*, "a buncombe artist whose every mention of his own name is met with a resounding crash in the orchestra." The piece ends with Berryman unveiling a monument to himself as a bequest to the city. The *New York Times* review (by Mordaunt Hall) is quietly positive, but *Variety* more or less writes it off as a dud ("the unoriginality of caricaturing the big business men of the land as impossible fools just because they don't read James Joyce and enjoy the music of Schoenberg is so great, one wonders why Kaufman should have stooped to it once more"), while also noting that some of the material is too subtle for the motion picture audience as opposed to a more receptive Broadway crowd. Sadly, it would seem no copies of the script were preserved, so you won't have a chance to decide for yourself. Whether the re-use of the name was done arbitrarily, or in the manner of an in-joke, is not certain. But as we ponder the matter, don't forget to enjoy watching Oscar Shaw grapple with that wet architectural plan.

12:59/13:32—Margaret Dumont

Playing the wealthy Mrs. Potter, Dumont was carried over from the original Broadway cast into the movie. (Immediately prior to filming it she also appeared briefly in Donald Ogden Stuart's short *Humorous Flights,* another nice example of cross-pollination between the Marx company and the Algonquin set.) I need not add that from this beginning she went on to become Groucho's celebrated statuesque straightwoman, enduring his crude insults and even cruder sexual advances in an additional six films. So fine are their performances together that she is frequently referred to as "practically the fifth Marx Brother"—billing that would have come as news to Gummo and was fortunately never made official (thus sparing us the necessity of having to refer to her as Practicallyo). But so perfectly matched is she with the Brothers in general and Groucho in particular that seeing her with other comedians is almost like finding out your best friend's wife is having an affair. Nonetheless her indiscretions were many and shameless: with Wheeler and Woolsey in *Kentucky Kernels,* as the fearsome Mrs. Hemogloben opposite W.C. Fields in *Never Give a Sucker an Even Break,* waking in the night to find Laurel & Hardy hiding under her bed in *The Dancing Masters,* even getting a face full of soot from Lou Costello's vacuum cleaner in *Little Giant.*

Take with a barrel of salt, however, the frequently stated claim that she was in reality fully as remote from her surroundings as she appeared in the movies, to the extent that she did not understand any of Groucho's jokes and would often ask him why the audiences were laughing. This story has become orthodox and is still often heard, but was decisively blown out of the water by Simon Louvish in his book *Monkey Business.* There, he reveals that the former Daisy Baker had been a showgirl and "vocal comedienne" in vaudeville. Like many another young stage beauty, she was lured from the chorus in 1910 by a wealthy marriage, only to return to it—whether by choice or necessity is not known for sure, but Louvish speculates it could well have been the latter—when millionaire sugar heir John Moller, Jr. suddenly died in 1918. (She is frequently a widow in the films, and some of her banter with Groucho—"I was with him till the very end; I held him in my arms and kissed him." "I see, then it was murder!" and so on—must have echoed for her.) "Born in very ordinary circumstances, to a professional family, she had learned a role in the theatre and then become, by marriage, the creature of her fantasy for seven lucky years," notes Louvish. "She was, in fact, an accomplished comedienne, who found her character and then stuck to it for the next fifty-eight years."

In a 1935 interview she spoke fondly of her association with the Marxes: "Working with the Marx Brothers is an art. It requires a great deal of study and concentration to remain at perfect ease when they spring surprise lines. Groucho is the creative one. He is spontaneously creative. On the stage he seldom repeats dialogue, thinking up new lines and new gags on the spur of the moment. I never have been disconcerted by his unexpectedness and I believe, because of that, Groucho feels comfortable when he is working with me. It wasn't easy, at first, to keep a straight face at all times.... It has been amusing, as well as profitable, to be associated with the Marx Brothers. But please, don't refer to me as their stooge—it's a terrible word, isn't it?"

14:24/15:01—"This is the biggest development since Sophie Tucker."

Tucker (1894–1966), of course, was the Jewish singer and entertainer known as "the Last of the Red Hot Mamas," who popularized the song "My Yiddishe Momme." *Groucho,* with characteristic chivalry, is drawing our attention to the star's considerable girth, which she herself highlighted in numbers like "Nobody Loves a Fat Girl, But Oh How a Fat Girl Can Love."

14:39 / 15:16 — "...entertainment, sandwiches and the auction. If you don't like auction we can play contract."

The first of many references in the Marx scripts to the tabletop diversions with which they filled their idle hours, first when they should have been at school and then when traveling the country or killing time backstage with fellow vaudevillians. Pinochle seems to have been their particular specialty, but all card games were grist to their mill, and this reference to bridge presages the classic bridge sequence from their next production, *Animal Crackers,* and in particular Chico's line, "He thought it was contact bridge."

14:51 / 15:29 — "...glorifying the American sewer and the Florida sucker...."

"Glorifying" was a fashionable buzz-word at this time; in the same year as *The Cocoanuts* Paramount produced the film *Glorifying the American Girl* at their Long Island studios, also starring Mary Eaton, photographed by George Folsey and with musical contributions from Irving Berlin. It's a Ziegfeld Follies revue for the movies, offering a "singing and dancing chorus of 75 glorified beauties" in its opening credits (a slight decrease on the "hundreds of the tastiest babies on Broadway" promised by the *Milwaukee Sentinel*). It's as important as *The Cocoanuts* to the historical record, as well as being of specific value to Marx enthusiasts as an example of exactly the format that *The Cocoanuts* and *Animal Crackers* both (basically) adhered to and (gently) subverted and parodied. In addition to a vapid plot, delightfully typical of its time (shop girl Mary dances her way to stardom but loses the man she loves), the film makes frequent halts and digressions to accommodate revue sequences featuring some of the great Broadway names of the time, notably Eddie Cantor, Rudy Vallee and the magnetic Helen Morgan. (Morgan was the star of Rouben Mamoulian's masterpiece *Applause,* another Paramount Long Island classic photographed the same year by Folsey—clearly as tireless as he was innovative. Marx fans familiar with the Warner Bros. animated short *The CooCoo Nut Grove* [1936] will also recall her in animated form, sitting on the piano as here, being washed away on the river of tears resulting from her heartwrenching ballad singing.) Others appearing briefly as themselves include Berlin, Ziegfeld and Zukor. Marx fans will enjoy the scene in which Mary and her boyfriend, Buddy, take a punt in a little boat, the latter serenading his girl on a ukulele, a reminder of how so much of what we take for random invention in the Brothers' Paramount movies was, in fact, parody of well-established clichés and recurring situations; it's hard indeed not to imagine the stuffed duck following along behind. But best of all is Cantor's Jewish tailor sketch, which not only gives us references to blue serge suits, "Sweet Adeline" and the phrase "that's some joke," but also partners Cantor with none other than Louis Sorin—Roscoe W. Chandler to you—uncredited here as he often was in his mere nine film appearances. Interesting to see him playing not pompous straight man but co-comic; sly and very funny with Cantor in their mutual fleecing of an unfortunate customer.

15:10 / 15:48 — "Take the alligator pears...."

This is another name for the avocado, derived from its rough, vaguely reptilian skin. Groucho's bizarre use of the term to imply sexual union between pears and alligators may be informed by some residual awareness of the long-standing connection between avocados and sexual potency. Long believed to possess aphrodisiac qualities, within polite society their consumption by the virginal or chaste was often frowned upon. Interestingly, the name comes from the Nahuatl word for testicle, a reference, in this case, to its shape rather than its sphere of influence.

17:36/18:21—The Marx Brothers

Harpo's bulbhorn announces this transcendent moment where all four Marx Brothers encounter one another on screen for the first time, captured splendidly by Florey in a respectful medium shot that keeps each of the quartet in view and preserves the lovely physical interaction that was presumably choreographed originally for the stage. With Chico and Harpo showing up over 17 minutes in, however, this is the latest entrance of any of the Brothers in any of the films.

19:09/19:57—"Everything will be AK"

At one time my favored explanation of this seeming alternative to "OK" was that it was derived from "Ace-King," a card combination in poker. A much more satisfying suggestion, however, is that it references the Yiddish term *alter kocker* meaning literally "old shitter" and referring with comic disparagement to the elderly. In the 1931 stage musical *Of Thee I Sing,* Ira Gershwin has the Supreme Court sing "We're the AKs who give the OKs...." Though its use here would have no specific meaning in context, it may be that it is a simple bit of linguistic mischief. (Interestingly, while this moment is not to be found in Kaufman's original playscript, a separate example is to be found elsewhere: Groucho, while wooing Dumont, says, "But if there was a bungalow, and you and me, and maybe a couple of other fellows, what do you say? Does that strike you as being AK?") Lawrence J. Epstein, in *The Haunted Smile,* endorses both the explanation and that reading of its intent, seeing the many Jewish references in the film as a kind of secret code, essentially "prizes offered to Jewish audiences":

> In another scene, Groucho says: "All along the river, those are all levees." Chico says, "That's the Jewish neighborhood," and Groucho responds, "Well, we'll pass over that." Such an interplay was at least more obvious to urban audiences who had met Jews named Levy and understood that Passover was a Jewish holiday. Rural audiences, though, were probably much more confused by the talk. Chico is involved in other Jewish references. When leaving a detective, Chico mutters, "Ah, shalom." Chico is introduced as "Señor Pastrami" as he prepares to play the piano. Chico says to another character, "Bravo, Galitzianer." A Galitzianer is a Jew from Galicia, a province in Poland (later Austria) as opposed to a Litvak, or Lithuanian Jew. The two were often at odds.

19:22/20:11—"Would you like a suite on the third floor?" "No, I'll take a Polack in the basement."

A daft play on words: for "suite," hear "Swede." It's a typical vaudeville-style pun, where ethnic humor was all the rage. There were, in fact, as many funny Swedes in early 20th century American humor as there were funny Italians, though posterity has only really retained El Brendel as the high point of the former, as it has Chico, of the latter.

20:27/21:19—"Have one of these flowers, they're buckwheat."

I always assumed that buckwheat was a poisonous plant and Groucho is cheerfully offering it to Harpo on those grounds, as if he were to say, "Here, drink this, it's cyanide." Buckwheat, however, is widely eaten, so instead the joke seems to be that he is offering a presumably inedible plant on the spurious grounds that it is buckwheat. But with Harpo eating telephones and drinking ink with no ill-effect, it seems a curiously unrealistic gambit on Groucho's part either way. In *The Marx Brothers Scrapbook* director Robert Florey recalls the (chocolate) telephone and (Coca Cola) ink as his own inventions. So presumably in the original play, from which the buckwheat line is retained, Harpo's gustatory exuberance was a little more restrained and less magical, thus giving greater sense to the joke.

21:06/21:59—Chico and Harpo play the "Anvil Chorus," using a till and a bulbhorn

This is the first appearance in the Marx canon of this composition from *Il Trovatore*. *Animal Crackers* the following year sees a spirited rendition with Chico on piano, Harpo on horseshoes and Groucho on a woman's leg, while in *A Night at the Opera* they get the chance to disrupt a live stage performance of Verdi's undefending masterpiece.

25:20/26:24—Harpo's first Gookie

This grotesque facial contortion characterized by bulging eyes, inflated cheeks and visible tongue is assumed by Harpo at least once in every Marx Brothers movie. "The fact that it seldom failed to get a laugh is quite a tribute to the original possessor of the face," he notes in *Harpo Speaks*, the original possessor being a cigar seller who sat at his window rolling cigars, slowly taking on the same gargoyle-like visage as he concentrated on his task. Harpo would stand outside and imitate him, to his fury.

26:39/27:46—"You know you look like the Prince of Wales?"

This is the first of a few mentions for what may seem a surprising point of reference in a twenties American comedy. It is possible this is simply a phrase, a hypothetical Prince of Wales used as a byword for smartness of appearance. My feeling, however, is that it does indeed refer to the actual Prince of Wales at that time, the future King Edward VIII, later famous for abdicating so as to marry American divorcée Wallis Simpson. He undertook many foreign trips through the twenties, and his aristocratic good looks, eligible bachelor status and reputation as a ladies man made him among the most photographed men of his day. He was also a Marx Brothers fan, and slipped incognito into a theater where Harpo was performing when still officially in mourning for the death of his father. Later, Groucho's co-authored screenplay for *The King and the Chorus Girl* would raise eyebrows in Britain, with its obvious echoes of the abdication scandal.

27:10/28:18—Harpo plays the clarinet

A virtuoso on harp and piano, the former Adolph (later, Arthur) Marx was no mean clarinetist, as this charming rendition of "When My Dreams Come True" reveals. In his later career he also liked to get laughs with a prop clarinet on which he would play "I'm Forever Blowing Bubbles" while a cascade of soap bubbles streamed from the instrument. Nonetheless, this is the only time he played it on film, and it was always the harp that remained his first love and daily source of recreation, relaxation and contemplation (thus sparing us the necessity of having to refer to him as Clarinetto).

29:12/30:26—Groucho and Margaret enter, stage right

Often cited as one of the most amusingly hackneyed moments in the film, this sequence shows Groucho and Mags walking on-set in long shot before cutting to a medium shot as they begin their dialogue. The point, of course, is that the walk on is a purely theatrical convention quite unnecessary in a film, which might more zippily have cut straight to the dialogue. For exactly this reason, I find it absolutely delightful. What we can all agree on, however, is the excellence of the ensuing, our first Groucho-Dumont wooing scene. There is nothing tentative or embryonic about it; both are in top form.

29:53/31:08—"If we could find a little bungalow...."

This Groucho line anticipates one of Irving Berlin's songs from the original show excised, presumably for time, from the screenplay. Several other lines from "A Little Bungalow," for so it is called, find echo in Groucho's dialogue in this scene; in particular: "Away from all the crowds we'll watch the clouds go drifting by / And when the moon above presents a lovely view" evokes his memorable line, "When the moon is sneaking around the clouds, I'll be sneaking around you...." This was the song that Kaufman observed was not reprised in the second act because there was no way the actors could remember it that long.

31:06/32:24—"A 'yes' like that was once responsible for me jumping out of a window."

A Groucho line which, depending on your preference, is either gloriously meaningless or evocative of some unspecified but clearly disastrous sexual indiscretion. The many anecdotes concerning the brothers' erotic escapades tend more often to involve incorrigible Chico than bookish, less experienced Groucho. One exception, however, is recounted by Groucho in *Groucho and Me*. According to this anecdote, Groucho encountered a young woman pushing a baby carriage, and upon enquiry was informed it belonged to her sister, and she was looking after it for the day. Having ascertained that she herself was unmarried, Groucho "gave her the customary routine about loneliness and what a gasser she was," and they adjourned to her flat. Unfortunately for Groucho, the single baby-sitter routine was a regular act of subterfuge in which she indulged to pass the dull afternoons while her husband was at work. When he too arrived home unexpectedly Groucho was forced to hide in the closet until the coast was clear, then unceremoniously ushered out of the window, where a fifteen foot drop was broken by bushes. Then there is the story told by Dick Cavett of Groucho and Chico enjoying the afternoon attentions of the daughters of a prominent Jewish businessman who had invited them to dinner later that week. The parents unexpectedly returned, and another window exit followed. Groucho recalled: "Fortunately, we were on the ground floor. In any case, the penultimate thing the parents saw were our two buck-naked rear ends disappearing over the windowsill. The *ultimate* thing they saw was Chico's head reappearing momentarily, saying, 'I hope this doesn't affect Friday night.'"

The theme is extended in the original playscript of *Animal Crackers*, where Groucho, as Louis the 57th, makes certain that Madame Du Barry's husband is definitely out of town: "You're sure this time? You know it doesn't look right for a king to keep jumping out of the window at three o'clock in the morning. The last window I jumped out of, I forgot to open. I'd show you the scars but I know you don't smoke."

35:01/36:29—The Connecting Door Sketch

This beautifully played scene, with Dumont having to resist the attentions of Groucho and Harpo while retaining her customary battleship dignity, Kay Francis having to resist the attentions of Groucho, Harpo and Chico while looking great in a slinky gown, the first of a number of dumb Irish cops called Hennessey (or something very similar) rushing ineffectually from room to room, and Zeppo presumably downstairs manning the lobby, is notable partly for its excellence and also for its being revised by Kaufman to equally fine effect in *A Night at the Opera*. It is also very ably directed: though the staging looks simple to us now there is no denying its efficiency, with the cuts from the master view (the screen bisected by the wall between the two rooms) to the individual rooms always made to the best advantage of the scene's rhythm, pace and laughs.

What it also does is remind us how very probable it was that the first proper Marx Brothers movie might have been a silent. United Artists expressed an interest in filming it a whole year before Paramount stepped in. It feels impossible, but then so would a silent W.C. Fields, if it weren't for the fact that such an animal actually exists. A mute version of *The Cocoanuts,* its physical action emphasized and its verbiage shorn to the minimum, is quite a thing to contemplate: this is the only scene as we know it certain to survive the process almost entirely unharmed. As such, it would almost certainly be regarded today as the undisputed highlight of the movie.

Given that sound was in its infancy, Paramount was certainly taking a chance spending so much money on a film crammed with fast dialogue that, it was feared, couldn't be understood in London, let alone non–Anglophone nations. Dubbing had been tried and found unsatisfactory, and the studio was now experimenting with subtitles and, for musicals, the creation of what Scott Eyman in *The Speed of Sound* called "weird hybrids" in which the songs were retained but dialogue scenes cut and scored to music with title cards. Eyman quotes an amusing memo on *The Cocoanuts* from Paramount to perplexed foreign exhibitors: "If we had this picture to do over again we would have eliminated the dialogue entirely, taken out some of the purely American comedy scenes, and would have synchronized the entire picture, retaining the musical numbers. It's too late for us to attempt this work now." No question, we are *very* lucky to have this film.

40:26/42:08—"I'm not going to have that redheaded fella running around in the lobby."

As this line makes clear, in this film Harpo wears his dark red stage wig, which photographs very darkly, almost black. I really like it; it makes him look more interesting to me, less overtly cherubic than the later blonde one. The story goes that a blonde wig was substituted because this looked too dark—for what, or for whom, we are never told but presumed to understand. But he seems to have retained the red one for live appearances: he is clearly wearing it in the photographs of the pre-tour of *A Day at the Races* and in the 1957 color film *The Story of Mankind*. The confusing thing is that in future "blonde" movies, well into the MGM period, there is dialogue (and character names like "Rusty") that suggest the wig is *still* lightly red, perhaps a strawberry blonde. Yet there's no question that he did have ordinary blonde wigs, many of which still exist.

40:42/42:24—"I can let you have three lots watering the front, or I can let you have three lots fronting the water."

Is this a mis-delivered line, as sometimes claimed? Clearly the obvious way of phrasing it is the other way around. But is it funny this way? Yes, it is, though like so much else in this film, it's hard to put your finger on exactly why. Certainly the odd reverse structure of it smacks to me of Kaufman, who loved to subvert language and find ways of getting it to do things it hadn't done before. Another example is Groucho's assertion to Dumont: "Do you know that property values have increased 1924 since one thousand percent?" It may alternatively be an example of the admirable comic obsession Groucho shared with Spike Milligan: the desire to replace a joke line with one that makes no sense at all if he's said it too many times and become bored. "Thomas Lindbergh, mighty flier" (see *Monkey Business,* 19:26) and "This is a hope chest for a guinea pig" (see *Animal Crackers,* 52:08) are further examples.

41:10/42:53—"I come from Italy on the Atlantic auction"

Chico era un italiano vero, o stava solo facendo finta di essere un italiano?

Caution, now! What we may well be walking into here is what Gilbert Ryle termed a category mistake. To many, whether Chico is *really* Italian or not is one of the deepest, most profound questions thrown up by the entire Marx canon, similar to—but in its way even more vexing than—"Is Harpo a man who does not speak or a man who cannot speak?" Now, obviously, in one sense the answer to both questions is obvious. Harpo definitely could talk and often did (when communicating, for example). And Chico was born in New York to a German mother and an Alsatian father: as foolproof a recipe for not being Italian then as it remains today. But just as obviously, that is not what we really mean when we ask the question. We mean: is Chico playing a character who is a funny Italian or a character who is pretending to be a funny Italian? Allen Eyles tells us, "Chico sports a phony Italian accent and uses this as an excuse to misunderstand words." This view is taken on, as often as not unconsciously, by many other writers on the subject.

The first level of complication is this: does Chico play the same character in every film? They do, after all, have different character names. If you want to be literal about things then you have to say no, the eccentric musician Ravelli is a different character to the speakeasy employee Baravelli.

But this would be silly. Chico is an actor possessed of a definite persona, and it is that persona that reappears, regardless of whether he be called Ravelli, or Chicolini, or Faustino the Great, or even Tony. (Those MGM writers knew their stuff, eh?) Just as Groucho always plays Groucho, so Chico is always Chico. Note that he also used the accent (and costume) in interviews, when ostensibly "himself."

The line that causes the most mischief is in *Animal Crackers,* when Chandler says, "How did you get to be an Italian?" and Chico replies, "Never mind; whose confession is this?" This, writes Eyles, is "the only time Chico's dialect act is ever questioned." But it seems to me that this is not Chandler asking the question of Ravelli but Louis Sorin asking the question of Chico; it's an in-joke, perhaps a retained ad-lib like all that "you're Chandler, I'm Spaulding" nonsense. It's amusing to think of Chico pretending to be Italian so as to annoy people; it makes the character funnier, more original, more Marxian—but there's no real justification for believing it.

In truth, Chico's was by far the most stock-drawn of all Marx characterizations. Ethnic characters played by dialect comics, scores of Italians among them, were vaudeville staples. The original playscript of *The Cocoanuts* includes a little more of the kind of vaudeville ethnic humor that Chico was outgrowing than does the film: he is known in police circles as "Willy the Wop," and his first encounter with Groucho runs thus:

CHICO: Hello. We sent you a telegram. We make reservache.
GROUCHO: Oh, welcome to Cocoanut Manor. What do you boys want, garage and bath?
CHICO: We go together him.
GROUCHO: You go together him?
CHICO: Sure me.
GROUCHO: Would you mind coming in again and starting all over?

Chico seems to have wandered into the characterization for want of anything else to do, and then simply outlived it, so that by the end he was representative of no comic style other than his own. Even the costume, topped by the soft felt hat, is not original to him; as the *New York Times* reviewer noted in his appraisal of the *Animal Crackers* stage play, he is clad "in the ungainly attire of an immigrant." Almost everything we consider typical of him—the clothes, the accent, the pidgin English interspersed with Italian, the obtuseness, the wiliness—were all the stock features of the Italian ethnic comic. His greatness is that he doesn't settle for that: he is also a brilliant comedian. The absurdism and wordplay, hilarious flights of anti-logic, and all those features that are uniquely Marxian, do not really arise from the specifics of the character but merely use them as its medium. Whatever nominal "character" he had settled on, he would still have transcended it. But it would be mistaken, I think, to go further, and find any element of Marxian subversiveness with roots as deep as the essential characterization itself, and thus posit so suspiciously postmodern a notion as that which insists Chico's character, rather than merely Chico, is assuming a persona or enacting a role.

Ultimately, if we accept that Chico is always the same character from film to film, the clodhopping literalists of MGM must have the last word. And under Louis B. Mayer, sworn enemy of witty comedy, Chico becomes *explicitly* Italian, just as Harpo becomes explicitly mute and Groucho becomes explicitly less funny. There's a fascinating moment in *The Big Store* where he encounters Henry Armetta, another refugee from the Golden Age of funny Italians, by this time a reasonably busy small-part comic-relief character actor. Armetta's character accuses Chico of mocking his accent before they remember treading grapes together in Italy.

That neither Harpo nor Chico felt able to step outside of their self-set defining characteristics is shown by the fact that they both accepted TV roles in the fifties that cast them as unambiguously mute and Italian. Harpo, in a straight role, played a deaf-mute who witnesses a murder in the TV play *Silent Panic,* while in the charming comedy *Papa Romani* Chico is cast as the flustered head of a rumbustious Italian immigrant family.

I propose a middle-course out of this dilemma. Chico is a Chico, of which there is one. By that I mean not the actor Chico, whose real name is Leonard, but the comic persona Chico, who is variously known as Ravelli, Chicolini and the rest. These sub-individuals, these Ravellis and Chicolinis, they are not anything, not real Italians or fake Italians. They are fantasies of light and celluloid. We do not need to take the hammer of finality to such inconsequential questions. What are you, some kind of MGM scenario writer? Just ask yourself this: does Groucho have a real moustache or a greasepaint moustache? Of course, it's a greasepaint moustache. Of course it could never pass as a real one. But it's only there because it's absurd and funny: he's not playing characters who have a greasepaint moustache. He's playing characters with moustaches, but signals the unreality of the enterprise, and the concomitant perils of rational interpretation, with this overt visual gesture. Does Captain Spaulding wake up in the morning and apply a greasepaint moustache in the mirror? Of course not. Only Julius Marx does that. Spaulding does not get up in the morning at all. He only does what we see him do; he only exists as long as we are watching. Chico's nationality falls into the same category. He has an accent because it's funny. We need go no deeper. Try, and the laughing stops. Perhaps we should give the last word to the man himself, who reflected in a late interview that he used to be Italian, but when he saw what happened to Mussolini he became Greek.

41:52/43:37—"You know what a blueprint is?" "It's oysters."

Chico's error here is to confuse blueprint with bluepoint, a bluepoint oyster being a type of oyster named, pleasantly enough, after the Blue Point area of Long Island, incidentally where the film was shot.

42:24/44:11—"Come over here, Rand McNally."

Groucho mocks Chico's inability to get to grips with the details of his map of the locality by referring to him as America's most famous publisher of maps and atlases.

42:34/44:21—"Is there a remote possibility you know what 'radius' means?" "It's-a WJZ."

Chico compounds his blueprint/bluepoint error with a further confusion, this time between radius and radio. WJZ refers to a New York radio station based at that time in Newark, New Jersey, originally homed in a shack on the roof of the Westinghouse Electric Corporation meter factory, and accessible only by ladder. Owned by NBC, WJZ was the station from which the first and final episodes of the Groucho-Chico radio sitcom *Flywheel, Shyster and Flywheel* was broadcast in 1932 and 1933. (But you're on your own with Groucho's rejoinder, "that's a rodeo you're thinking of.")

43:12/45:00—The torn blueprint enigma

Observe at this moment the tear working its way through the limp map Groucho has been incautiously clutching since the beginning of the scene, as the brave little prop finally concedes to gravity and the essential nature of wet paper. It points out one of the oddest aspects of this whole "watering the paper" business: the fact that it's often unnecessary. Yes, when Zeppo arrives with the telegrams he has to hand them to Groucho, and Groucho has to read them. But why not just leave the damned blueprints on the table? The only reason for wetting them is so Groucho can wave them about distractingly at the beginning of the scene, something he doesn't need to do for any reason at all. Yet it would seem at no point, as they soaked them to a slimy pulp while the cast and crew waited, did it occur to them that if Groucho only left them on the table and pointed at them when necessary they could avoid the whole nasty business.

43:55/45:45—"I'm not playing *Ask Me Another*"

From *The Time of Laughter: A Sentimental Chronicle of the Twenties* by Corey Ford:

> So great was the parlor-game craze in the twenties that Viking Press brought out a question book called *Ask Me Another*. To arouse added interest, the editors tested the questions in advance on various celebrities.... George Kaufman [was tested] on geography, a subject which bored him thoroughly. When asked "What is the longest river in South America?" Kaufman pondered a moment, and then countered, "Are you sure it's in South America?"

44:10/46:01—"Look, Rook, look"

No, Groucho is not calling Chico "Rook," or anything similar. What is he actually doing? I suspect the answer lies in the fact that while shooting this by day, they were also performing in *Animal Crackers* by night. What we are surely hearing here is Groucho starting to call Chico "Ravelli," and stopping himself.

45:36/47:31—"Be alert—or papa don't go out at all."

A (presumably) meaningless reference to the song "Mama Goes Where Papa Goes," made famous by Sophie Tucker ("Mama Goes Where Papa Goes / Or Papa don't go out tonight"). First published in 1923, Tucker also recorded a Yiddish version the following year.

51:49/53:59—"Milk from contented cowcoanuts."

The first of a few references to advertising slogans in the team's work. The line "the milk from contented cows" was first used to advertise Carnation condensed milk in 1907, and stuck well enough to provide the title for the Carnation-sponsored radio show *The Contented Hour*. (Carnation also famously sponsored Burns & Allen's TV show.) A second reference pops up in another 1929 comedy, the Hal Roach short *A Pair of Tights*, in which Anita Garvin exclaims, "I'm so hungry I could eat a contented cow!"

Today, a comic reference to some advertisement or other seems déclassé, and about as easy a way to get a laugh from your audience as possible. To exonerate Kaufman, Ryskind and the Marxes from this charge of comic laziness you have to transport yourself back to the twenties, when saturation advertising and the idea that people might make a good living just thinking up the doggerel to go with the billboards was new and epoch-making. To cite these slogans in a secondary context seemed fresh and innovative and snappy.

Just how much a 1920s phenomenon it seemed is shown by a lovely Paramount film of 1931 set in the advertising world. In *It Pays to Advertise*, Skeets Gallagher is compelled to counter the cynicism of hero Norman Foster, who believes the advertising fad is already over!

"Nobody reads ads anymore," he opines. "I don't!"

"Oh you don't, don't ya?" says Skeets. "I guess you don't know what I mean when I say *four out of five have it? It satisfies? Good to the last drop?*"

Look at Listerine. Produced since the nineteenth century as a combined floor cleaner, surgical antiseptic and VD cure, it was transformed into a mouthwash by the bright minds of twenties advertising, bad breath being a far greater concern to Jazz Age sensibilities than post-operative infection. While they were at it, they also coined a totally spurious medical-sounding term—halitosis—that remains in use today, and a slogan—"Even your best friends won't tell you"—that helped double the company's profits in seven years. A contented cow joke in *this* context is right on the money.

It may be worth noting finally that while this, their first film, placed them in the vanguard of advertising's absorption into popular culture generally, so their last, *Love Happy*, made twenty years later, helped pioneer the even more insidious art of product placement.

53:39/55:54—"What's become of Peter Rabbit?"
54:32/56:49—"Keep Winnie the Pooh out of here!"

Why Groucho refers to Chico as a brace of children's characters is not immediately clear, though the second presumably refers to his muddled reasoning. Neither appears in the original playscript; instead Groucho there asks, "Where did Joseph P. Day go?" referring to New York's famous real estate magnate and auctioneer. A. A. Milne was, for some reason, something of a bête noire to the Algonquin fraternity: Dorothy Parker's snarky review ("And it is that word 'hummy,' my darlings, that marks the first place in *The House at Pooh Corner* at which Tonstant Weader fwowed up") remains legendary, and their revue *No Sirree!* featured a parody of *Mr. Pim Passes By* called *Mr. Whim Passes By*.

53:49/56:04—"What am I offered for Lot 25 and a year's subscription to Youth's Companion?"

This famous American children's magazine, that in its latter years widened its scope to aim at the family generally, ran for over a hundred years, beginning in 1827; coincidentally its last issue was published in 1929, boding ill for Mr. Hammer's college plans.

56:55/59:18—"This guy's letting on to be a dummy"

A line (present in the original play) that offers the most unequivocal evidence in the whole Marx canon that Harpo doesn't speak, rather than cannot speak.

60:36/63:08—Harpo offers sobbing Polly a lolly

This utterly disarming moment in which Harpo abandons all trace of lechery and mischief, and manages to be affectingly sweet without any hint of unwelcome pathos (the blank facial expression is the trick) is one of the most celebrated moments in the film. In the original play, this moment closes Act One, and the stage directions say that Harpo winks at the audience. What we have here is much subtler and more effective. In *Animal Crackers* he will again use a lolly—and the same licking gesture, as if anyone might be confused what to do with it without his helpful demonstration—to try to lure a blonde he had been chasing from the room into which she flees. Then, at the very other end of their film career, he produces a lolly during the "Who Stole That Jam?" number from *Love Happy,* leading to the song line: "I don't want that lollipop!"

60:59/63:32—Announcing the wedding of Polly to Yates to Polly

This is the much-noted prison breakout scene in which Chico struggles heroically with dialogue he can only vaguely remember, having probably left his script behind at the pinochle game he's just reluctantly rushed from in order to shoot it. (His unfamiliarity with the material may be partly explained by the fact that the whole prison break scene was written specifically for the film: in the play Adams is bailed, off-stage.) It is certainly amusing to listen to his garbled attempts to tell the incarcerated Bob that Polly and Yates have announced their engagement; it's going too far, however, to claim that he ultimately fails to do so, and that Oscar Shaw's exclamation, "Polly's gonna marry Yates!" shows him grasping the situation far more completely than is possible given the meager information he's obtained (specifically because Chico never mentions Yates by name). Though he mumbles and gropes for words, Chico does definitely tell him "Polly, she wants you" because "tonight she's gonna be engaged." Then, when Bob asks who to, he replies, "To Polly, Yates to Polly."

62:03/64:39—"Hey, Paisan!"

Chico's term to summon Harpo is an affectionate Italian (and Italian-American) greeting meaning "brother," colloquially or, in this case, literally. Chico's daughter, Maxine, writes in her memoir *Growing Up with Chico:* "Any Italian coming backstage to ask if he were really a fellow countryman would get an enormous grin, a hug, and a kiss, as Chico would warmly exclaim, 'Paisan!'" In the original play version of *Animal Crackers,* Chico uses the term again in the "Abe Kabibble" scene; Kaufman and Ryskind spell it "Byzon."

71:30/74:29—Harpo's big spliff

The most eye-openingly pre–Code moment in the entire Marx canon is when Harpo enters the fancy dress wedding party dressed as a Mexican gaucho puffing on an enormous joint. Though I had known of many who had not noticed this, and were therefore doubly amused to have it pointed out, I had assumed until recently it was beyond contention once spotted. Nonetheless, I have lately encountered a few who protest the notion most noisily, usually on the assumption that it is unlikely or even impossible for a film of this period: it is neither. Reference to marijuana use was not taboo in American popular culture at this time (look out for Cab Calloway's rendition of "Reefer Man" in the 1933 Paramount comedy *International House*), and, though frowned upon by respectable consensus, the practice was not yet even illegal. (Some states banned it in 1931, and it was 1937 before prohibition was nationwide.) Two things clinch it as a certainty for me (not counting Harpo's obviously exaggerated behavior, which others prefer to attribute to alcohol consumption). One is the size of the cigarette itself (and it *is* a cigarette, hand-rolled in white paper, not a Mexican cigarillo, as has been suggested). While big businessmen are often shown with comically large cigars, very large hand-rolled cigarettes exist both widely and typically as representations of marijuana cigarettes. If it were an ordinary cigarette, such as Harpo is seen smoking in *Animal Crackers*, it simply would not be this big. The other giveaway is his Mexican costume, to which the cigarette is adjunct. The rise of recreational marijuana use in America was generally attributed to the wave of Mexican immigrants that came to the country following the Mexican revolution of 1910, and anti-drug campaigners often blamed both it and they in tandem for various crimes: culturally, the people and the practice were linked inextricably. (*Variety* refers to joints as "Mexican cigarettes" in a 1929 piece noting their popularity among musicians.) Groucho's "breath of old Ireland" line and subsequent foolishness also seem less explicable if he had merely received a face full of ordinary cigarette smoke.

73:21/76:25—"I Want My Shirt!"

What happens here is unique. The detective's request that Harpo return his stolen shirt turns into a joke song, with the lyrics set amusingly to the music of Bizet's *Carmen,* in which the whole cast enthusiastically join. It's such a disarmingly silly and funny sequence ("It was given to me by my brother Bert / That's why I love this shirt!") that it is easy to forget that nothing like this ever happens in any other Marx Brothers film. Of course some characters continue to burst into song, in carefully segregated numbers, but never again will a "straight" character, let alone a detective, get a chance to be absurd, and, more importantly, to leave reality behind on a whim, as is the Brothers' sole right.

75:42/78:52—"Oft in the stilly night, the trembling of a leaf can be heard sighing through the trees, and the babbling brook...."

I think that rather than any one quote, this is a kind of generic, half-remembered conflation of several poems and poetic-sounding phrases, with "Oft in the stilly night" derived from Thomas Moore, and the babbling brook, possibly, from New York poet Elaine Goodale Eastman.

76:06/79:17—"Western cattle opened at fifteen and a quarter"

Groucho goes into stock market talk just as he would in *Animal Crackers* but with one big difference—the Crash came in between. So whereas there is a pointed, almost nightmarish quality to the stock market humor in the second film, here it's still throwaway and breezy.

79:18/82:37—"That's that good Gulf gas."

More advertising humor: Groucho's comment on Harpo's flatulence refers to the slogan used by Gulf gasoline, displayed on the side of pumps in service stations.

80:07/83:28—"'A Cup of Coffee, a Sandwich and You' from the opera Aida"

I must confess, I was a little disappointed to learn that Groucho's hilarious intro to Chico's first onscreen piano number refers to the title of a real song. It seemed such a wonderfully banal title. And, of course, one made doubly funny by Groucho's suggestion that it is from *Aida*. The latter element, at least, survives the revelation that it was genuine, and written in 1925 by Joseph Meyer, with lyrics by Al Dubin and Billy Rose. (Unless you believe that this is a pun on "I-eat-a": I refuse to until I see inarguable proof, not because I am certain it is not, but because I would never find the line funny again.)

The song was a favorite of Carl Stalling's when he was scoring the Looney Tunes cartoons, where it pops up repeatedly on the soundtracks. Fred Allen also had something of a penchant for mentioning it in jokes on his radio program. And it *is* an absolutely adorable song. So I invite you to seek out this section on *The Cocoanuts*—safe in the knowledge that things will work out from here on, Penelope and Harvey will be exposed as villains and Polly and Bob's skies will all be blue—by winding up the gramophone and giving it a spin.

2

Animal Crackers (1930)

You see, if we don't rehearse, we don't play. And if we don't play—that runs into money.—Signor Emanuel Ravelli (Chico Marx)

Robert Benchley called them "a frantically transitory comet formation which we can proudly tell our grandchildren of having seen one night in 1928." Oh, to have been there too! Oh, to have seen the Marx Brothers on Broadway! Next to that experience, I feel, none of these films would hold much more than a sputtering and stubby candle.

Animal Crackers is the second and last of their New York movies, based on the play they were performing simultaneously with the shooting of *The Cocoanuts*. Next time, in *Monkey Business* (their first written expressly for the screen), the difference will be obvious: the new writers are working to the beat of screen editing, in a series of short, punchy sequences that match the pace of the material itself. But the relentlessness of the Brothers' humor, when it's going at full sledgehammer force, is dissipated by slickness, by energy in the presentation, by creative direction ... in short, by the mentality with which movies were made, and by which they sought to distinguish themselves from theater. Visual comedy is liberated by cinematic translation. But when dealing with wordplay, it's more bludgeoning when you're just trapped there, watching it spill out before you, with nothing else to distract you and nowhere else to go.

That this is broadly speaking true is surely suggested by the fact that almost all of the Marx Brothers' most famous and cherished sequences—why a duck, the contract scene, the crowded stateroom, the ice cream scam—are revue-style sketches, the essence of the Broadway Marx Brothers. Those Hollywood Marx Brothers can do more, like get chased round ocean liners and wreck opera houses, and that's hilarious too, but it's not of the *essence*. The very fact that as late as *A Night in Casablanca* they were still benefiting from pre-filming live shows, put on to assess the effect of the material on audiences, shows how little they relied on the art of cinema to display their own. Though doubtless of equal value to them as a guide to audience response, it would simply not have been possible for Chaplin or Keaton to have done the same, because their work was cinematic by definition. The Marxes are theatrical. They're the whole show.

In adapting *Animal Crackers* for the screen, Morrie Ryskind is far more ruthless an editor than he'd been with *The Cocoanuts*. Whole characters have disappeared, scenes combined and excised, and pairs of characters turned into individuals. Arabella is now a mixture of herself and Mary, a journalist and John Parker's original love interest. Chandler is a com-

31

Animal Crackers: Groucho works the anvil; Margaret Dumont does not approve.

posite of himself and Monsieur Doucet, the character who exhibits the painting in the play. The play's Chandler is a wealthy patron of the arts but not the snobbish connoisseur he claims to be, in the absence of Doucet, in the movie. Indeed, he happily affirms his lack of discernment, thus making Parker's resentment of the need for his patronage, and his line "What does he know about art?" much less provocative.

Other, similar moments reveal that Ryskind has condensed the text sometimes to the verge of abstraction. The film is full of lines and notions that, while they don't *quite* play as confusing, nonetheless take on an unexpected clarity when one peruses the playscript. For instance, Arabella's odd little rejoinder to Mrs. Rittenhouse's request that she take her society parties more seriously—"What would you suggest, suicide?"—originally follows her being admonished for not having received a single proposal of marriage after two full months as a debutante. Likewise, it is made much plainer that the minxy Mrs. Whitehead and her sister Grace are not merely guests but rival society hostesses, peeved that Mrs. Rittenhouse has bagged both the great unveiling and the famous explorer, and, thus, looks set to be the social hit of the season. Their switching of the painting, then, is not idle devilment but a serious effort to ruin the weekend and make Mrs. Rittenhouse look ridiculous. Their copy of the painting is signed on the opposite side of the canvas to the original, revealing that the forger is left-handed, providing at least some sort of solid diving board for Chico's magnificent logical leap that left-handed moths may be responsible for the weekend's intrigue.

And Chico and Harpo's routine about finding the "flash" originally involved Harpo looking for the flashlight in various places around the set, including the sofa on which Spaulding and Rittenhouse later sit, thus giving some semblance of explanation for Groucho's glorious line, "Pardon me, Mrs. Rittenhouse, did you lose a fish?"

Though the basic plot follows the exact same lines of *The Cocoanuts,* Ryskind has opted not to retain a number of sly intertextual admissions of the fact: Mrs. Rittenhouse twice makes reference to a "Mrs. Potter," another society matron and her own character in the previous play; Mrs. Whitehead acknowledges Mary's first entrance with the line, "The love interest, and about time too," and the prospective arrest of John and Mary for the theft of the painting is successfully halted by Groucho's interjection, "Why, you can't arrest them. That's the hero and heroine."

But according to most reports it was director Victor Heerman rather than Ryskind who decreed that almost the entirety of the show's musical numbers be jettisoned, along with the play's entire grand finale. This had originally been a costume pageant, in which Groucho appeared as King Louis the 57th and all the Brothers performed a number called "We're Four of the Three Musketeers." One wonders how much this decision must have rankled with Zeppo, who sang in the scene, and with Margaret Irving, who does little enough as Mrs. Whitehead, but there got to do some very funny material opposite Groucho as Madame du Barry. It seems to have gone simply because it was the most "separate" and therefore easy to lose section, but without it the film just coasts along gloriously in no kind of a hurry and then suddenly ends with Harpo's arbitrary business with the narcotic Flit spray, originally the ending to Act Two, Scene One. (The "Musketeers" number, meanwhile, shows up unexpectedly in a 1938 Paramount movie called *Cocoanut Grove,* performed by a singing group called The Yacht Club Boys.)

Though generally felt to be a more confident film than the virginal *Cocoanuts, Animal Crackers* is surely still less cinematic, with long, talky scenes and few setups, played out on single sets from which the actors enter and exit while the camera sits there looking at them. (In his review in *The Nation* Alexander Bakshy was even irked by the retention of Groucho's greasepaint moustache, writing: "That a character supposed to be merely a freak should be stamped as a stage comedian is an incongruity to be explained only by the inability of the actors and director to shake off their memories of the stage.") Allen Eyles notes how every scene is shot front on with no reverse shots, how each of the Brothers makes a separate entrance, announced and then descending a staircase, explicitly cuing our applause, and how an obvious thunder sheet is wobbled to simulate the sound of bad weather.

At over ninety minutes it's not one of their shorter films either, and there is certainly a sense of exhaustion as it nears the last turn (albeit of a contented sort). I used the word "bludgeoning" earlier and that really is the effect: there is an intense and utterly unyielding quality to the Brothers' comedy in this film. It contains many of their most obscure, confusing jokes, bewildering logical connections and inspired flights of absurd invention, and little else is allowed to intrude. There are no stylistic flourishes to ventilate the claustrophobia, no guest turns to dilute the cumulative effect of their attack, and very few narrative diversions to parcel their contagious unreason into safer doses.

Did they ever have better entrances, or more individually generous first scenes? (Even Zeppo gets a solo song to start, albeit about Groucho, and Harpo and Chico are given individual chances to shine unlike in any of the later, narrative-led films, which all start off running, as it were.) Groucho's interjections and asides ring the bell time after time and there are *so many*: it seems like every time someone makes an innocuous comment he comes back with an irrelevant, hilarious response, whether he is the one being addressed or not. Indeed, such is the profusion that he can afford to treat them with cavalier disdain. Lines that *A Day at the Races* would kill for, scaling heights that *Go West* never reaches once, are tossed away nonchalantly, sometimes mumbled, or buried in overlapping dialogue, or delivered offscreen. So many laughs a minute! And beautiful, witty songs. Glorious art deco sets, too!

We are safe in the hands of the Marx dream team: Kaufman and Ryskind, Kalmar and Ruby. We have the African lecture. We have the bridge game. We have "Hello, I Must Be Going." We have Groucho taking off his jacket and threatening, "Come outside and say that!" after Chandler says, "And now, ladies and gentlemen...." And we have moments like these:

> SPAULDING: Tell me, Mr. Chandler, where are you planning on putting your new opera house?
> CHANDLER: I thought I should like to put it somewhere near Central Park.
> SPAULDING: I see. Why don't you put it right in Central Park?
> CHANDLER: Could we do that?
> SPAULDING: Sure, do it at night when no one is looking.
>
> (*Groucho simultaneously wooing Margaret Dumont and Margaret Irving:*)
> I don't think I've ever seen four more beautiful eyes in my life. Well three, anyway.
>
> RAVELLI: Now to find the painting, all you've got to do is go to everybody in the house and ask them if they took it.
> SPAULDING: You know, I could rent you out as a decoy for duck hunters. You say you're going to go to everybody in the house and ask them if they took the painting? Suppose nobody in the house took the painting?
> RAVELLI: Go to the house next door.
> SPAULDING: That's great. Suppose there isn't a house next door?
> RAVELLI: Well then of course we gotta build one.
> SPAULDING: Well now you're talking! What kind of a house do you think we ought to put up?
> JAMISON: "Honorable Charles H. Hungerdunger, care of Hungerdunger, Hungerdunger, Hungerdunger and McCormick...."
> SPAULDING: You've left out a Hungerdunger! You left out the main one, too. Thought you could slip one over on me, didn't you, eh? All right, leave it out and put in a windshield wiper instead. I tell you what to do, Jamison. Make it three windshield wipers and one Hungerdunger. They won't all be there when the letter arrives anyhow.

Nothing else comes remotely as close as *Animal Crackers* to my fondest imaginings of what it must have been like to see them live and on fire, and that's why it's my favorite of their films by a mile. Indeed I can only second the breathless puff piece issued by the studio and endorsed by circulation in countless newspapers:

> Nine yeows and a tiger for bigger and funnier laughs, laughs, laughs. The Groucho spiel, the Harpo pantomime, Chico and Zeppo multiplying the music and comedy flare; Lillian Roth, playing the very devil with hearts; other fascinating girls in a pageant of negligee-and-swimsuit blond and brunette "it." ... You've been looking for something—tra-la—something just like this—and there's no known substitute for the Marx Brothers—*Animal Crackers* goes their laughing limit. As Groucho would say to Miss Dumont—"And what a limit!"

Oh, to have seen the Marx Brothers on Broadway!

Roscoe W. Chandler in the process of not being unmasked as Abe Kabibble: (left to right) Harpo, Louis Sorin and Chico in *Animal Crackers*.

1:34 (NTSC)/1:38 (PAL)—The Butler's song

A misleading (if delightful) opening that leads us to assume that the film we are about to see is what the show upon which it is based was: a musical comedy. In fact, after the round of musical introductions that conclude these first scenes (culminating with the legendary "Hello, I Must Be Going") music will be almost entirely absent. ("*Animal Crackers* is slightly reminiscent of comic opera," noted the *Spokesman-Review*, "but after making an opera take-off, thinks better of itself and veers off into nothing but nut comedy.") In the original play, this number went on much longer, with sung contributions from the other butlers, the maids and the guests. It is likely, however, that these later portions were deleted as much for censorship reasons as for time, or would have been: the maids sing about how the married guests always seem to end up in variant combinations and different rooms, and make such scandalous observations as "the people that we work for are below us…. We have to swallow all the bull they throw us," and "We're looking down upon the upper classes, while they are looking down on us." The odd thing, given the savagery of the musical abbreviation, is that the second verse (beginning "Treat him as they do a king") appears to have been written for the film.

Playing Hives, the butler, is the wonderfully sepulchral Robert Greig, who may be best known as one of the unofficial repertory company with which Preston Sturges seasoned his great comedies of the 1940s, but who also deserves a special place in Marx lore for being one of the surprisingly few players to have taken speaking roles in more than one of their movies. He is also, of course, the luckless professor whose biology lesson is interrupted by Groucho and two empty dunces in *Horse Feathers*. The six footmen are played by The Music Masters: this is their only film credit, and I can find no other information on them.

2:51/2:59—"Mr. Roscoe W. Chandler...."

Louis Sorin, as Chandler, is the man that Joe Adamson rightly says "must be one of the best straight men a fellow ever had." He's surely the best pompous foil Groucho ever had—and with the likes of Sig Rumann also in the running for the title that is praise indeed. Sorin gets to do all sorts of things a Marx straight man is not normally allowed, including woo Dumont with a ferocity that goes past the calculated flattery of Rumann in *A Night at the Opera* or Louis Calhern in *Duck Soup,* and into authentic Groucho territory: "Please do not go, Mrs. Rittenhouse! I love you! Do not take away your hand, I love you!" He even gets to act a phony flub and ensuing ad-libs, further strengthening the sense of him as "one of the boys" (see below, 30:16). Sorin is good for the reason that all the best straight men are good: because they know how to play comedy. Comedy timing needs to be in a straight man's bones same as in a comic: the difference between those who have it and those who don't is as obvious as the difference between a great and a mediocre comedian. That Sorin *is* also a fine comedian can be seen in his double act with Eddie Cantor in the previous year's *Glorifying the American Girl* (see *The Cocoanuts*, 14:51) but his film appearances are incredibly few in number, and he is often uncredited. Groucho told Richard Anobile that Sorin had been a great friend of Harry Ruby's, so it is possible he joined the company via that association. Groucho also recalls Eddie Cantor joining the cast after hours during the run of the show, perhaps providing the other entrée.

3:51/4:01—Lillian Roth

Promising audiences "more pretty girls in lingerie and bathing suits than most revues boast," the *San Jose Evening News* review went on: "You'll understand what we mean by pretty, when we say Lillian Roth heads the feminine talent." As Margaret Dumont's daughter Arabella (so much feistier and more resourceful than Margaret Dumont's daughter Polly had been), Roth gives an effervescent performance and shares with Hal Thompson a delightful Kalmar and Ruby number, "Why Am I So Romantic?," which did not feature in the play but was added to the movie, with utmost perversity, after all the other songs had been pulled. (The *Spokesman-Review* thought her underused, but was philosophical about it: "Even a beautiful girl is unable to combat the idiotic capers of three idiotic nuts—but it doesn't matter, you don't go to see beautiful girls, you go to see a trio of nuts.")

As you probably know, it was supposedly Roth's *bad* fortune to have been cast in the role. As she has it in her autobiography *I'll Cry Tomorrow,* the casting was punishment for her alleged on-set temperament and difficulty (and this at a time, she claimed, when of all the Paramount stars, only Clara Bow was getting more fan mail). "We're sending you back to New York to be kicked in the rear by the Marx Brothers until you learn how to behave," is how she recalled the news being broken to her. Most writers interpret this to mean that specifically *being cast in a Marx film* was the punishment; it's more likely that being banished from Hollywood to New York was what they had in mind. (Though how that was a punishment either is beyond me.) From *I'll Cry Tomorrow*:

> It was one step removed from a circus. First, Zeppo, the youngest, sauntered into the studio, about 9:30 am. At ten, somebody remembered to telephone Chico and wake him. Harpo, meanwhile, popped in, saw that most of the cast was missing, and strolled off. Later they found him asleep in his dressing room. Chico arrived about this time. Groucho, who had been golfing, arrived somewhat later, his clubs slung over his shoulder. He came in with his knees-bent walk, pulled a cigar out of his mouth, and with a mad, sidewise glance, announced: "Anybody for lunch?"

Lillian was reunited with Groucho in 1962 when she appeared as a guest on *The Tonight Show*. Sadly no video copies survived, but in a privately-made audio recording the two can be heard reminiscing about the production of *Animal Crackers*, with the expected mix of fact and exaggeration. Groucho recalls that they used to be "pretty close friends" before qualifying: "Not as close as I wanted to, but as close as I could get at the time!" "I don't think you were interested in me," she says later; "I had a cute sister." "Was I interested in her?" asks Groucho, the Chico affair (see below, 4:16) seemingly now forgotten. She repeats the story that it was virtually impossible to get all four brothers together on set at the same time (something the screenplay very rarely demands, in truth) and claims that the film took sixteen weeks to shoot, instead of the intended four, chiefly for this reason. She also recalls (with some confidence) working with the Brothers in vaudeville at the age of eight: Groucho is unsure, but she seems certain even of the names of the venues. She then recites a short poem about Groucho that she claims to have written that morning, and the two end with a duet of "It's Been a Long, Long Time." (Groucho suggests they perform "I'm a Dreamer, Montreal" [see below, 48:08].)

If you want to see more of Lillian, you can't go far wrong with anything she made in the thirties, and her 1930 Paramount short *Meet the Boyfriend* is an essential. Her best performance of all may well be as gold-digging hoofer Trixie in DeMille's *Madam Satan* (1930). As well as handling cross-talk comedy and extremely physical farce with aplomb, she wears some incredible outfits, sings a great number in shorts and a top hat, and finishes off by leaping out of a zeppelin in a parachute and landing in a Turkish bath. (Some nice stories about this in her book, too: "'*Me, jump from up there?' I gasped. 'Into that net? In these high heels and feathers? Oh, Mr. De Mille, I couldn't possibly!*'")

4:16/4:27—The house guests

Jumping butterballs! Is that Donald MacBride? I'll say it is! The explosive character actor and later the fearsome Mr. Wagner, Groucho's nemesis in *Room Service*, can be seen doing that style of acting so beloved of screen extras—looking around for somebody to make eye contact with and then making a big expressive gesture to them—throughout the film, but our first clear shot of him is here, in sweater, jacket and tie behind and to the right of Lillian Roth. Oh, to be in a sweater, jacket and tie behind and to the right of Lillian Roth!

According to *Motion Picture News*, Lillian's younger sister Ann is also in the melee. The two look very similar, so I'm going to tentatively wager she's the girl in the middle of the group of three stood next to Lillian when the "Captain has arrived" song commences.

I'm strengthened in my conviction by my re-reading of a delightful gesture Lillian makes immediately after Dumont says, "I say, Captain Spaulding has arrived!" I always took this adorable display to be a slightly mocking show of excitement at the news. I now see, however, that it is preceded by a double-take: she looks at the other girls, looks away, then acts as if she has belatedly recognized one of them, looks back in surprise, and makes that "say, whaddayaknow!" gesture to one of them. I'm not saying it's genuine or unrehearsed, but I do think that is what she is doing, and that the middle girl, who strongly resembles her, is therefore Ann. Ann has a further connection with the Brothers: in the later thirties, at around the time of the move to MGM, Chico began a love affair with her and seriously contemplated divorce so as to make it official. According to his daughter Maxine in *Growing Up with Chico* he was persuaded not to by her entreaties and the fury of the other brothers.

5:55/6:10—Enter Captain Spaulding....

Depending on how old your copy of the film is, one of two things will happen at this point: either Groucho will take his pith helmet off, or he'll take his pith helmet off twice. The version I saw on television in the 1980s, and the first videotape I had of the film (on Betamax) retained the continuity error (the result, presumably, of a reel change being incautiously mastered). These days, it's been removed. But anyway, here is the captain: probably Groucho's most famous "character," yet possessor of one of his least eccentric character names. There are no real grounds for thinking the name refers to anyone in particular, but it is of course possible that inspiration could have been transferred in a semi-conscious way. The most likely means by which the name might have lodged is from vaudeville, where a fire-eater called Captain Spaulding was billed as "The Man Who Is Hotter Than Vesuvius!" A far less likely candidate, who has nonetheless made it to Wikipedia, was an army officer arrested not long before the film was made, after being exposed as a drug dealer to the Hollywood community. Various theories are doing the rounds as to who this shadowy Spaulding may have been and why he seemed to escape serious censure. But nobody seems too bothered about accounting for why Kaufman and Ryskind should have taken the smallest interest in him—or *any* Hollywood tittle-tattle, considering the lack of interest New York theater folk had in the film crowd generally, and remember that *Animal Crackers* was written, staged, filmed and set in a world far removed from Hollywood. (More recently Captain Spaulding has been used as the name of the killer clown in the horror film *House of 1000 Corpses,* which also has characters named Rufus Firefly, Otis Driftwood, Ravelli and The Professor, and is rubbish.)

One other thing: look at Groucho's lapel from the very first moments of this scene: the caterpillar that Chandler will eventually pluck from his jacket causing him to faint is already there. If you're ever lucky enough to see the film on the big screen you'll notice something else, too: it's real, and crawling the whole time as well. Pre-CGI movie magic!

Not at 8:04/8:25—"I think I'll try and make her!"

This line has been excised—rather carefully, it must be said—for the benefit of people who might be shocked by it, as well as those who prefer songs not to have rhythm and rhyming couplets. Simon Louvish reprints the various Hays Office edicts concerning the film, many of them revealing an amusing unfamiliarity with the individual Brothers. The offending line is attributed to "Harpo's song," while further exception is taken at "the business of Zeppo pulling an intimate undergarment out of the woman's bosom with his teeth" (what would you give to see that?) and, most mysteriously, to "the following scene on the couch with the girl throwing her legs in the air and exposing her crotch after he bites her." (A few more opportunities like that and maybe Zeppo wouldn't have left the act after all.) The song line, "The men must all be very old / The women hot, the champagne cold" was going too far, but the substituted "the women warm" was acceptable. Note also that Jamison mentions the absence of "any tramps here" as one of the conditions under which Spaulding "camps here": in the original play, he "comes here" on condition that "he won't have any bums here." Oddly, however, many other cuts demanded in these memos remain in the version we have (such as the Groucho-Chico badinage about the location and function of the maid's room in their imaginary house, and Groucho's lines about "'Somewhere My Love Lies Sleeping' with a male chorus" and "we took some pictures of the native girls but they weren't developed"). Also making it to release are Groucho's confusion over which magnificent chest should occupy his attention, and my personal favorite Marxian outrage: Chico's line "She can't take it there!" when Harpo is walloping Margaret Dumont repeatedly in the abdomen.

9:09/9:32—Groucho interrupts himself—well, somebody's got to do it....

One of those simple, very funny little moments you're only likely to find in a Kaufman–Ryskind script: the crowd that has so enthusiastically greeted Groucho in song repeatedly interrupt him when he starts to speak by enthusiastically greeting him in song again, for no reason at all. On the third occasion, Groucho leaps in and does it himself, topping the laugh with the splendid aside, "Well, somebody's got to do it!" The mystery here, though, is what he actually sings. They are saying, "Hooray for Captain Spaulding, the African explorer." But he does not, and it's proved impossible to find anyone even able to guess at what he does say. It sounds like "the Afrikent enqueero," and it may well be pure gibberish.

9:52/10:17—"I feel that the time has come, the walrus said...."

Groucho quotes Lewis Carroll's poem "The Walrus and the Carpenter" from *Alice Through the Looking Glass.*

12:28/13:00—"The Professor!"

Thinking up character names for Harpo is a mug's game, because he doesn't really play characters, and so the thought of them having names, and therefore having been given names, is ultimately as odd as the thought of them going to sleep at night and getting dressed in the morning. Harpo simply is, so giving him a name is like deciding God is called Gerald. At Paramount, they twice just call him Harpo, that is to say don't really give him a name at all (in *The Cocoanuts* and *Monkey Business*). At MGM they give him appalling names like

"Stuffy," "Punchy" and—worst of all, indeed bad beyond eclipsing—"Wacky." "The Professor" is the real odd one out: like so much else in this film, it's simple and clever and unusual. It's all he's ever known as through the film; presumably he is a professor of music, but it is so strangely inappropriate a name, especially in its lack of pizzazz, that it works just perfectly. The disjunction between Robert Greig's announcement (and why *would* he just say "the Professor" and not his full name?) and the figure that eventually emerges is a masterstroke. There's real tension as he slowly makes his way down the stairs, calm, contained, but brimming with repressed insanity, in a sequence fraught with comic menace. Soon the gentility will be swapped for underwear and a revolver—was there ever a more ideal introduction to the sheer uniqueness of Harpo's comic character? The music to which he enters is "Collegiate" by Moe Jaffe and Nat Bonx, which had been a big hit for Fred Waring's Pennsylvanians in 1925. It's the same piece Chico plays for his instrumental solo in *Horse Feathers,* though owing to the tempo change it is easy not to realize that, as I did not for many years.

12:48/13:21—"The gates swung open and a Fig Newton entered."

For years the only time I'd heard of Fig Newtons other than in this scene was, coincidentally, in *Harpo Speaks,* in the passage where he describes his relative anonymity offscreen by noting that he could have been "the fellow you let pass ahead of you in the check-out line at the market because he was only carrying two bananas and a box of Fig Newtons." For some reason I always assumed they were cigars. In fact, as you surely know, they are what we Brits call fig rolls: pastry rolls filled with fig jam. Quite why Harpo is being likened to one here remains slightly mysterious, though the meaning of the observation is clear enough. In 1920s slang a Fig Newton was a derogatory term for a white person who acts black; equivalent (but opposite) to the contemporary use of the term "Oreo" (i.e., someone who is white on the outside but black on the inside like a Fig Newton, as opposed to black on the outside but white on the inside, like an Oreo.) Why Harpo qualifies as a Fig Newton in this sense only Groucho knows.

20:23/21:14—"You're very fortunate the Theatre Guild isn't putting this on."
20:28/21:20—"Pardon me while I have a strange interlude...."

The Theatre Guild was the celebrated New York theatrical society that had been putting on highbrow stuff since its formation in 1919. One of its most celebrated successes had been Eugene O'Neill's groundbreaking five-hour monster *Strange Interlude* in 1928. (Future Marx savior Irving Thalberg produced it as an MGM movie in 1932 with Norma Shearer, Clark Gable and future Judy Standish Maureen O'Sullivan: O'Neill reportedly hated it. Such was his reputation in Britain that the film was deliciously retitled *Strange Interval.*)

"The reason that the play takes so long is that each character, in addition to speaking his lines, must also speak his thoughts," wrote Robert Benchley in his review on February 16, 1928. "This would not be so bad if their thoughts were worth speaking, but, for the most part, they could easily have been guessed by any alert child in the audience." Groucho is here parodying this device of having characters step forward and recite internal monologues, revealing their true feelings to the audience, while the rest of the cast freeze and, like Margarets Dumont and Irving here, stand around like berks. (If you can, take your eyes off Groucho during these sequences and observe the two women: while Dumont, ever the trouper, maintains perfect composure, Irving finds it increasingly difficult to avoid betraying her amusement, and capitulates delightfully at **22:10/23:06**.) Charles Marsden, one of the characters in the play, is the "poor old Marsden" to whom Groucho refers. You have to wonder if Kaufman or Ryskind had read and taken note of that Benchley review, especially this section: "There are few of these 'asides' of O'Neill's which any good actor or actress could not indicate without speaking a word or any good playwright get into his lines without resorting to tricks. Some day this method will be used by an author whose characters don't act as they think and who also has the gift of humour. That will be something different." How right he was!

20:46/21:38—"How happy I could be with either of these two if both of them just went away"

Groucho is here parodying a line by John Gay, from *The Beggar's Opera:* "How happy could I be with either / Were t'other dear charmer away!"

21:41/22:36—"Are you suggesting companionate marriage?"

A hot topic of the time, following the publication of the book *The Companionate Marriage* in 1927, in which authors Ben B. Lindsey and Wainright Evans advocated a new kind of marriage in which birth control was deployed to prevent parenthood until both parties could be certain the marriage was a goer, and easy divorce by mutual consent the solution if it were found otherwise. It remains to be seen if it catches on, but I wish it the best of luck.

21:47/22:42—"You could sell Fuller Brushes...."

The Fuller Brush company was founded in New York in 1906 when, according to their website, Alfred C. Fuller, perched precariously "on a bench between the furnace and the coal bin in his sister's New England home," suddenly had the idea to make and sell brushes. Groucho is referring to the company's innovative use of door-to-door sellers to promote their products, a practice which continues today. Famous former–Fuller Brush salesmen include Billy Graham, Jack Nicholson and Pee Wee Herman. You may also have encountered Red Skelton as *The Fuller Brush Man* (1948), or Lucille Ball as *The Fuller Brush Girl* (1950). Daffy Duck disguises himself as a Fuller Brush Man in a 1944 Looney Tunes cartoon called, of all things, *Duck Soup to Nuts.*

22:11/23:07—"Steel 186, Anaconda 74, American Can 138...."

Groucho's "strange figures, weird figures" refer obviously to the stock market, and carry the bitter tang of proximity to the Wall Street Crash of 1929. The reference to Anaconda (like Groucho's exclamation of "jumping anaconda!" in *Horse Feathers*) is not arbitrary in this context:

In late 1928 the National City Bank created a pool for Anaconda Copper (a Montana mine owned by investor Percy Rockefeller's father, William) and started pushing its stock, then priced at $40, even though underwriters knew that copper was fetching weak prices in Chile. The share price leapt to $128 in three months and at its peak in October 1929 was selling for $150. Anaconda Copper became one of the magic phrases of the boom years, whispered like a talisman from one gullible investor to the next.... In the trough of the Depression in 1932, Anaconda Copper was worth just $4.—Lucy Moore, *Anything Goes: A Biography of the Roaring Twenties*

The crash occurred during the stage run of *Animal Crackers*, and Groucho in particular was badly hit. "Everybody I knew was affected by the crash," Groucho recalls in *The Marx Brothers Scrapbook*. "They were either wiped out or became very poor." Harry Ruby remembered having to go backstage while Harpo and Chico improvised on stage to deal with Groucho, who was flatly refusing to go on, and only relented when Ruby threatened to take his place. ("No audience deserves to look at you for a whole evening!") According to his son, Arthur, Groucho never again had an uninterrupted night's sleep. He would refer to the crash again in *A Night in Casablanca* ("Remember what happened in 1929!"), elliptically in *A Day at the Races* ("I want to win, but I don't want the savings of a lifetime wiped out in the twinkling of an eye!"), and in *The Story of Mankind*, in which, as Peter Minuit, he advises an Indian chief suspecting he is getting a raw deal over the purchase of Manhattan Island: "You think you're being robbed, eh? Be glad it's not three hundred years later. You might have been wiped out in the stock market."

24:23/25:24—"You're not Abe Kabibble?"

Most reference sources insist that the answer to this question is "yes": Chico has correctly guessed the true identity of Roscoe W. Chandler, and Abe Kabibble is the full name of Abie the Fish Man.

> GLENN MITCHELL in *The Marx Brothers Encyclopedia*: "Elsewhere in the house, Chandler is recognized by Ravelli. He is difficult to place, never having spent time in any prisons, but a birthmark on his forearm pinpoints him as Abe Kabibble, a former fishpedlar from Czechoslovakia."
> SIMON LOUVISH in *Monkey Business*: "At one point he was 'Rabbi Cantor' but on screen he ended up as the ethnically neutral Abe Kabiddle."
> ALLEN EYLES in *The Complete Films of the Marx Brothers*: "The prominent art critic Roscoe W. Chandler hides the fact that he is a former fish peddler from Czechoslovakia called Abie Cabiddle."
> STEFAN KANFER in *Groucho*: "The Czech rabbi was now exposed as Abe Kabibble, a former fish peddler."

Okay, nobody seems sure if it's a *k* or a *c*, "biddle" or "bibble," but that this man and Chandler are one and the same no one doubts. But look at the scene again (stopping for just a second to notice how it all unfolds on perhaps the most strikingly beautiful set ever constructed for a comedy film). Chico apprehends Chandler at the end of the previous scene: "*Some place I met you before because your face is-a very familiar....*" Chandler is nonchalant: "*Well, after all I'm one of the most well-known men in America. The newspapers will keep on running my photograph.*"

It is at *this* point that Chico says without a second's deliberation: "*You're not Abe Kabib-*

ble?" Chandler's response is equally immediate and unflustered. "*Oh, nonsense!*" he says, and walks away, with irritation at being bothered, but not the smallest hint that he might be someone whose secret identity has been discovered. Here the scene cuts to another set, Chandler and Chico walk on, and it is at this point that the scene in question actually begins. Chico continues: "*If you're not Abe Kabibble, who are you?*" Chico resumes his struggle to identify him, and it is ridiculous to assume that a name he has already offered twice has suddenly eluded him: "*Some place I met you before because your face is-a very familiar. Now wait. Let me see. Were you ever in Sing-Sing?*" More deliberation and wrong guesses follow, before Chandler volunteers that he spends most of his time in Europe. This sets a train of thought moving in Chico's mind. "*Europe ... I got it now! I know—you come from Czechoslovakia!*" Even now, however, he can't quite place him. He even asks Harpo for help. "*You remember him. Who was he? He comes from Czechoslovakia.*" Then, finally, realization dawns: "*He comes from Czechoslovakia and I know who it is! It's Abie the fish peddler!*"

And this, with the revelation of a matching birthmark, Chandler eventually admits to be the case. Of Abe Kabibble, whoever he may be, there is no more mention.

It can't even be Chico the actor getting it wrong, introducing the name too early (along the lines of his famous confusion during the prison break in *The Cocoanuts*), because the name is *never* reintroduced—Abie the fish peddler is never given a second name. Plus there is practiced calm in Sorin's reaction to the suggestion; he brushes it off just as he has been doing all day in rehearsal. And Chico says it in two different scenes, anyway: at the end of one and the beginning of the other. There can be no doubt that Chico is supposed to say Abe Kabibble at this early stage, and that therefore it is not the secret identity of Roscoe W. Chandler, but a joke. Note that both Chico and Chandler seem to recognize the name, as if he were a famous person, and that Chico suggests the name specifically in response to Chandler's statement: "The newspapers will keep running my photograph."

The original play of *Animal Crackers* featured a character cut entirely from the film called Wally Winston, a journalist based obviously upon Walter Winchell. And Chandler himself, unmasked in the play not as a fish peddler but as Rabbi Cantor, was originally intended as a thinly veiled parody of Otto Kahn, the art mogul famous for his efforts to disguise his Jewish background. Chico's likening Chandler to Abe Kabibble is indeed another intertextual reference—but not to a real person. Abe Kabibble was the star of *Abie the Agent,* a syndicated comic strip popular in the first decades of the 20th century, created by cartoonist Harry Hershfield. Abie was a Jewish immigrant car salesman, created in response to a request from Hershfield's editor to write a strip revolving around Yiddish slang, Jewish humor and the immigrant experience in America. Though all but forgotten now, he would certainly have been a recognizable pop-culture figure to the original audiences of *Animal Crackers.* Such was the character's popularity he was featured in two theatrical cartoons in 1917, and was made the subject of a song ("Abie! Stop Saying Maybe" by Jo Swerling, author of the Marxes' first legit musical revue *The Cinderella Girl* (a.k.a. *The Street Cinderella*) and their first, instantly lost film, *Humor Risk* (a.k.a. *Humorisk*). And his resemblance to Chandler is definite and amusing.

25:50/26:55—"Piker! Five hundred dollars!"

Chico's reasoned and considered dismissal of Chandler's bribe employs a term commonly used to describe a gambler who makes only small bets.

30:16/31:32—"Tell me, Captain Chandler...."

Now this is strange. What we are watching here are two men pretending to make a mistake, and what we are expected to believe is that they used that take in the finished film because it's funny. Now my guess is that during one performance of the original show, Louis Sorin really did make this error: momentarily confusing his character name with Groucho's. And the resulting session of comic improvisation went so well that it was retained, that is to say feigned, in every subsequent performance. And it probably seemed less bizarre to them than it does to us (with nearly a century more experience of talking cinema conventions) to carry it over to the film. (They've even rewritten the dialogue so that it pertains to movies instead of theater: "I could be the *News Weekly* for all he knows," Groucho observes, "or 'Coming Next Week'" as opposed to the playscript's "I might be [the] intermission for all he knows.") In fact, in all the years subsequently I know of only one other film with a staged fluff in it: Spike Milligan's comparably untamed *The Great McGonagall,* and that was so convincingly done it was only when I saw the shooting script with my own eyes that I even accepted it *was* faked. The big surprise concerning *Animal Crackers,* though, is that this moment is also actually *written* in the playscript held in the Groucho archive at the Library of Congress, and presumably in the slightly earlier version at Princeton. Now, it must be recalled that neither is an original pre-performance text, and both feature interpolations developed in performance, almost certainly including this one. Alternatively we can go further, and get off at the depot (or at "Mt. Vernon" as the more New York–centric playscript has it), and acknowledge the possibility that as with the Milligan film the "mistake" was written in from the very first, as a means of getting an easy laugh or two at the actors' supposed mistakes and subsequent "ad-libs."

30:49/32:07—"You take Abyssinia and I'll take a hot butterscotch sundae on rye bread"

Before Chandler has a chance to respond, Groucho summarily rejects his own suggestion to discuss (presumably) the very early stages of the Abyssinian crisis that was unnerving the League of Nations countries within seconds of his first proposing the topic. But is his bizarre choice of alternative something more than mere nonsense? While the thought of a butterscotch sundae on bread is bizarre indeed, note the way it begins with a suggestion of hot buttered rum, and then offers a potentially double-meaning use of "rye" to finish. Is it possible therefore that this is a subversive suggestion of alcoholic libation, couched in a kind of prohibition code?

30:54/32:12—"Let's go and see what the boys in the backroom will have...."

For film buffs, the phrase instantly conjures images of Marlene Dietrich, standing on the bar of the Bottleneck Saloon in *Destry Rides Again* (1939), belting out the famous song of the same name. However, Groucho is not citing the song, which was written for the film and therefore post-dates Groucho's usage by almost a decade. While the phrase clearly has a life extending beyond these two references, its origins are somewhat obscure. The boys in the backroom themselves have nothing to do with "backroom boys" in the sense that became familiar in World War II: behind-the-scenes research scientists coming up with ever more elaborate inventions, plans or codes. The backroom in question here is of earlier vintage, and refers to the room at a tavern or fashionable party where men would retire to gamble. The phrase, therefore, is an injunction to penetrate their clandestine gathering in order to offer further refreshment. As to its earliest usage, however, the best guess was one nominated by S. J. Perelman in a 1978 issue of the *New York Times Magazine,* in which he recalls it as the caption of a 1929 cartoon by Tad Dorgan. It is not certain this was the original usage but it seems like a good fit: Dorgan has been hailed, along with Ring Lardner (see *Monkey Business,* 54:03) and George Ade (see *Horse Feathers,* 15:21), as one of America's most prolific coiners of new words and expressions. His many contributions to the vernacular include "dumbbell," "for crying out loud," "cat's meow," "drugstore cowboy" and "yes, we have no bananas." Of special interest to Groucho fans is his popularizing of the term "23 Skidoo." For his other bequest to our Marxian heritage, see *Duck Soup,* 0:00.

34:03/35:29—"You play bridge?"

As a non-bridge player, I've long suspected that this lengthy and hilarious sequence (one of the very best Groucho-less routines of their career) is even funnier to those who understand the extent to which the rules of the game are being perverted. And apparently that is indeed so. So here are some vague hints and intimations for anyone whose understanding of the scene, like mine, began and ended at the pun on "contract bridge" ...

Bids include a number and a suit (or "no trump"), and must always ascend; 1 club is the lowest bid. But Harpo bids 1 club after the bidding has already gone far beyond that level, prompting Dumont to throw down her cards and exclaim, "I don't understand this kind of bidding!" Whereupon Chico (who has already swapped his hand with Harpo after calling a misdeal, at which point the entire game should have been stopped and all hands re-dealt) swaps his entire hand, which had been Harpo's hand, with hers.

When they restart the bidding, Harpo begins with "one," refusing to name a suit, while Chico follows with "two," qualifying that on request as "two of the same he bids" before arbitrarily declaring the bidding over. The play of the hand after bidding is in 13 "tricks," requiring one card from each player, clockwise. Because Chico simply gets tired of the bidding before it's over, it's never established what suit is trump in the first place, nor how many tricks Harpo needs to take in order to win. For the first play of the first trick, Harpo goads Irving to lead an ace of spades, which he then "beats" with his last card, a heart (the trump suit which was never decided upon). Chico then declares that was a demonstration of "what you call a finesse." A "finesse" *is* a bridge term, but Chico's use of it here is about as far from its real meaning as one could get. (It's actually when you lead a card that you know one of your opponents can beat, hoping to get away with winning with the lower card, or at least flush out one of your opponent's high cards.) A classic Chico provocation, therefore, to tell people who must know *exactly* what a finesse really is that Harpo's ridiculous behavior qualifies as a textbook example. Through all of this, the two Margarets display only the mildest of frustration, and a commendable willingness to continue, even when Harpo decides to play several aces of spades in sequence, an anomaly Chico glibly brushes away with the explanation, "He's got thousands of them." It's even funnier when we remember that this is the very card they forced Margaret Irving to play, from her own hand, on the very first play of the very first trick.

Though I described the scene as one of the team's very best routines *not* to involve Groucho, in the 1928 version of the playscript preserved among Sam Harris's papers at the University of Princeton (as opposed to the 1929 version kept in the Groucho collection at the Library of Congress) there is a hilarious extension to the scene featuring both Spaulding and Jamison that is one of the most regrettable of all omissions from the original texts in the now-definitive film version.

There are several amusing real-life anecdotes concerning the Brothers and bridge. Two of my favorites: Gloria Stuart and Arthur Sheekman hiring a professional instructor to teach the finer points of the game to themselves and Groucho and his wife, Ruth, so that they could all play together, and Groucho making her flee, never to return, after telling her on a moment's whim that Stuart and Sheekman were not a married couple but an incestuous brother and sister. And Chico's wife, Betty, attempting a romantic reconciliation following a breakup by leaving a pack of cards around the house and leading up the stairs where she had left the jack of hearts outside her bedroom door and the king on his pillow; he went straight to his own room and when she angrily asked him for an explanation on the following morning he replied, "When I saw the jack in front of your door and the king on my pillow I knew I had to finesse."

An article in the *Evening Independent* (October 12, 1936) claims that the bridge craze is consuming Hollywood, and that Chico is "generally conceded" to be "the champion of all film bridge players." It continues: "Chico and Harpo have played with many of the world's best professionals and tournament champions.... Chico has written a book on bridge and has a system of his own." A strange but seemingly true story that turns up in a number of sources is that Harpo and Chico challenged bridge expert Ely Culbertson to a public game in 1933, after he claimed there were no serious players in Hollywood. He accepted the challenge, then backed out at the last minute, for reasons that were apparently uncertain, but which the Brothers inevitably interpreted as fear. One of Chico's most intriguing TV gigs was a 1960 personal appearance in a potentially deadly dull and yet oddly hypnotic program called *Championship Bridge,* in which four bozos play bridge for half an hour while an off-screen commentator spells out the action as if it were as dynamic as a prize fight. Chico, in a smart black hat, doesn't speak much, but when he does it is not in his Italian accent. As Simon Louvish drily adds: "He lost."

40:15/41:56—"Atsa Flitz!"

Note that in this brief shot, the brand name Flit on Harpo's pest-control spray, laboriously scribbled out frame by frame in its later appearances, is clearly visible. This crude censoring of the brand name is a bit of a mystery. The film's pressbook suggested tie-ins with local suppliers of the stuff, so the blacking out must date from a later reissue. It's hard to imagine why they'd bother, especially with the dialogue reference to Fuller brushes left intact.

40:48/42:30—The great Marx Brother doppelgänger mystery

From the time the lights go out to the time they come back on again in this scene (in which Chico and Harpo noisily steal the painting while Groucho and Margaret Dumont comment from a nearby sofa) all three Marxes are doubled by other men. Though we never see Chico's face clearly, the plainly inauthentic Harpo is briefly illuminated by a lightning flash (freeze-frame it), while "Groucho" is visible throughout: thin and wiry, and with close-cropped hair entirely different from the fluffy, sharply center-parted and v-shaped coiffure sported by the real man elsewhere, you could throw a brick from a moving bus and hit someone who looks more like Groucho than this guy.

Note also that they are plainly miming. Their physical gestures are forced and overt in order to match the dialogue, which they sometimes anticipate. When Groucho asks if anyone is there and Chico replies, "Groucho" turns to Dumont (who is the real Dumont, by the way) and nods slowly for ages while he waits for the soundtrack to catch up with his actions. Look at big, bulky, slow "Harpo" flapping his arms when he's hanging from the painting. "Chico," too, makes a bunch of strange, slow gestures completely unlike his normal self.

Also, note the transitions in and out of the darkness. As the sequence begins, the lights go out on Chico and Harpo, and for less than a second we get to see them in the dark, as clearly defined as they need to be and as "they" will be as the scene continues, moving with their usual pace and energy. Then, for no other reason than the one proposed, there's a cut—but to what is essentially the exact same angle: it's slightly off, but there's no deliberate change. Why? And note how the pair is now suddenly doing that slow pantomime style that reveals the body language of two entirely different people. Even more strikingly, when the lights come back on at the end of the scene, they do not simply switch back on. The scene goes from twilight to pitch black—for no logical reason at all—before then cutting to full illumination—with the camera in a totally different position.

So, why should this be? Over the years I've considered a few possibilities. First, recall that this is the film in which director Victor Heerman supposedly had cells built and brought on the set so as to ensure the Marxes could not escape between takes. This popular story, stated as fact by Zeppo in his interview with Barry Norman, may have a kernel of truth but has surely been much exaggerated, first for publicity purposes and thereafter for legend-endurance purposes. (Heerman himself pooh-poohed it: "These were adult men, and they didn't have to be locked in. There was a jail left over from another picture and we used it as a make-up room or for the actors to lie down in. It was never locked.") But the point of the yarn—that it was genuinely difficult to get all four Marx Brothers on set and doing what they were supposed to be doing at the same time—is backed up by the testimony of just about everybody who worked with them. So perhaps the scene was shot on a day when they were AWOL, on the grounds that it was dark and nobody would be able to see them properly anyway? Or maybe it was planned that way from the first, as a scene that didn't need the real Brothers on set, thus relieving anybody of the need to find them all? Or did an original shoot prove unsatisfactory—maybe the light levels were wrong, and when a reshoot was ordered, it was decided not to bother recalling the Brothers themselves on the grounds that the soundtrack didn't need re-recording, and it doesn't need to be them if the room is dark? Or could it be that the early sound recording techniques were still so cumbersome that no opportunity to get round them would be missed? So here we have a scene in the dark—why use live sound when you can't really see the lips move? Get the boys to record the dialogue, then they can mime to it without the sound department needing to get in on it at all. And from that realization, came the decision not to use them physically at all....

Another possibility is that it was shot while Harpo and Chico were ill. Both were indisposed during the filming, Chico with a kidney complaint that made physical business painful, and Harpo with an enlarged gland in his neck that required hospitalization and surgery. Reports state that the latter did delay reshoots on the film, and clearly Harpo would have welcomed any chance to avoid the strenuous physical elements of the sequence in such a condition, even after his doctor confirmed he was capable of going back to work, some two weeks after close of principal photography. It may well be that this scene made an obvious choice for one that could be reshot without the need to recall the stars.

The likely (and very interesting) answer as to why a reshoot was needed in the first place showed up in a few newspapers when the film began its run:

> Believe it or not—a real thunder-shower spoiled one of the "storm" scenes, while *Animal Crackers*, the new Marx Brothers comedy feature, at the Strand today and tomorrow, was being recorded at the Paramount New York studio. A sequence shows Chico and Harpo Marx removing a painting from its frame during a storm which has put out the lights at the country house where they are guests. Arc-lamps were being switched on and off to simulate lightning and a property man was producing artificial thunder when a sudden spring storm burst over the studio. "Cut," shouted director Victor Heerman, "we'll finish the storm scene when the storm scene's over." (...) The New York studio is as completely sound-proofed as possible. Street noises do not filter through its thick walls, but no way has been found to keep out electric discharges produced by lightning, and work has to be stopped whenever real thunder rolls over Long Island.

So if not the real Marxes, who are the people we see? A popular rumor among those who have only spotted the phony Groucho and not the phony Chico or Harpo, is that the Groucho stand-in is actually Zeppo! (One always has to be alert against the temptation to see whatever it is one wants to see. To test that hypothesis, I watched it again while pretending that I thought it was Claudette Colbert. Ironically, I remain convinced that it is.) Most likely, this is plain wishful thinking, plus a dash of confusion with the old story of Zeppo playing Groucho's role on stage and nobody noticing. (It's true that Zeppo stood in for Groucho when he had appendicitis, but not that nobody noticed: *Variety* called him "adept at the substitution" in a generally negative review.) But given that he's hardly in the film even when his brothers are, it's vanishingly unlikely that Zeppo would have been anywhere near the set if the other three were elsewhere. (Certainly the online chorus reveal something of the perils of magical thinking when they go on to speculate that Zeppo can be discerned impersonating Groucho's voice, when one of the most obvious giveaways that it is a double in the first place is the imprecise manner in which he is miming to a soundtrack—the voice is unquestionably Groucho's own.)

The most likely explanation, if not the most exciting, is that what we are seeing are their stand-ins. Like any other stars, the Marxes had reasonably similar stand-ins, never normally seen on screen, to take their place on set while the scene is being set-up. Given that it is intended to be impenetrably dark, it would have seemed entirely sensible to use them here, especially in a costly reshoot. We can be sure that stand-ins were used on the film generally, because *Film Daily* saw them and told us about them: "Anyone visiting the *Animal Crackers* set at the Paramount New York studios might be led to believe that the Marx Brothers are twins, since an extra set of stand-ins dressed exactly like the famous comedy quartette are always in evidence."

So if I am right, and the men we see on screen *are* the stand-ins, here—for the first time since 1930—are their names. As Harpo: Jack Cooper. According to *Film Daily*, Cooper "gave up songwriting to become an actor" and "looks so much like the real Harpo that visitors frequently rush up and shake his hand, thinking that he is the original." Is he the same Jack Cooper who appears in bit parts for Hal Roach and Mack Sennett? I don't know, but thanks for asking. As Chico: Packey O'Gatty. Packey drifted into films from the boxing ring; it's possible he wound up here via a personal acquaintance either with Chico or director Victor Heerman, apparently an obsessive fight fan. Unlike the man he was impersonating, Packey was a genuine Italian, having been born Pasquale Agati in Sicily, and that's almost certainly him stood directly behind Chico as he explains his rates for performing and rehearsing. And as Groucho: Henry Van Bousen (or sometimes Bausen). In a long career that took him from featured roles in D.W. Griffith silents to many years as a department store Santa, Van Bousen also served as stand-in to actor Milton Sills and appeared in scores of settings as a photographic model, most notably offering to walk a mile in some of the iconic Camel Cigarettes advertisements. He, too, is to be found somewhere among the assembled guests at Rittenhouse Manor, though I can't identify him with certainty.

42:46/44:33—Asthmatic roaches

Meanwhile, forget the doubles for a moment, and consider that weird, hacking, guttural laugh that Groucho attributes to roaches with asthma. What actually is it *meant* to be? The playscript makes plain that it is indeed Chico making this noise (and the cuckoos)—but why?

44:58/46:51—"The principal animals inhabiting the African jungle are moose, elk and Knights of Pythias."

The Knights of Pythias are one of America's oldest fraternal secret societies, founded in 1864, and today boasting over fifty thousand members in over two thousand lodges all over the world. That's roughly twenty-five members per lodge, so they're either fairly small lodges or very big Knights of Pythias. Groucho yokes them into his account of African fauna in recognition of the two meanings of "elk": an animal and a member of the Benevolent and Protective Order of Elks, a similar society founded in 1868. Hence: "The elks on the other hand live up in the hills, and in the spring they come down for their annual convention...." Think Masons if you're British, or Sons of the Desert if you're a Laurel & Hardy fan. Groucho also refers to them in the Broadway version of *The Cocoanuts,* when Hennessey appears without his shirt.

46:37/48:34—Chico's piano tune

The first appearance of what became Chico's unofficial theme tune, reappearing in different contexts in *Monkey Business, Horse Feathers* and elsewhere. But there's some confusion here. In common with several other published sources, I always thought it was the tune *Sugar in the Morning*. But it's not, though it's *incredibly* similar. It's Chico's "trademark song" "I'm Daffy Over You," written by Chico and Sol Violinsky. Over the years, this theme became the standard way to introduce him on radio and television, and he is heard playing it at the end of his very last recorded appearance, in the aborted *Deputy Seraph*. To make matters even more confusing, it exists in two different versions. "I'm Daffy Over You" is a song with lyrics, while an instrumental version, with very slight melodic changes, was published as "Lucky Little Penny" and credited to Chico, Violinsky and Benny Davis.

48:08/50:08—"I'm a dreamer, Montreal."

A pun on the song title "I'm a Dreamer, Aren't We All?" by Ray Henderson, Lew Brown and Buddy G. DeSylva, and featured prominently (sung by Janet Gaynor) in the 1929 Fox talkie *Sunny Side Up*. Recorded many times over the years, among its more notable recent incarnations is its appearance alongside "Hooray For Captain Spaulding" and numerous other Marx references, in Woody Allen's *Everyone Says I Love You,* sung (or mimed, rather) by Drew Barrymore, who always seemed to me an ideal Arabella Rittenhouse.

48:14/50:15—"...one of my own compositions by Victor Herbert"

I always thought this line referenced Victor Heerman (whose name was pronounced "Herman") and was just a meaningless citing of the film's director for want of any better name in a throwaway joke. The playscript confirms that it is Herbert, composer of *Babes in Toyland* and *Naughty Marietta*. Obviously this makes more sense, except that while Chico does play Herbert's "Gypsy Love Song" in *The Cocoanuts,* the piece he goes on to play here is "Silver Threads Among the Gold," which is by H. P. Danks and Eben E. Rexford. The explanation was that the line was (characteristically) retained even though its purpose was not: in the original play he went on to perform "Gypsy Love Song" here. He does so again in *Love Happy.*

50:26/52:33—"The old red team scored that time.... And that was the old blue one"
50:41/52:48—"That's one for old Purdue."

We seem to be looking ahead to *Horse Feathers* here, with a couple of references to college football. Groucho, Chico and Harpo have just decided to interrupt the musical soiree with a display of their football skills, using one of Mrs. Rittenhouse's cushions in place of the ball. Groucho hails the resultant "score" as one for "the red team," then tests a young lady's reflexes by tapping her below the knee so she involuntarily kicks Harpo in the rear, which he concedes as a point to "the old blue one." This is most likely a reference to the sporting colors of Yale and Harvard universities, who wore blue and red, respectively. When the "game" degenerates into one of Harpo and Chico's famous choreographed fights, Groucho decides one of Harpo's leg swings was "one for old Purdue," i.e., a point for

Purdue University. It may be that the slightly risqué nature of the attention Groucho was paying the girl, and the placement of her subsequent kick, is intended to add a secondary meaning to his designating that particular point a "blue one."

50:56/53:07—"Play the song about the Irish chiropodist ... 'My Fate Is In Your Hands.'"

As the great Randy Skretvedt put it when he learned of this book: "I've been hoping that someone would write a book like this! Now, when somebody doesn't get Groucho's joke about the Irish chiropodist, I don't have to explain that "My Fate Is In Your Hands" was a pop song written by Fats Waller and Andy Razaf, and a chiropodist was a foot doctor, and Irish folks pronounced "feet" as "fate." ... I can just point to this book!"

51:18/53:27—Anvil Chorus

Second of the Marxes' three encounters with *Il Trovatore* (see also *The Cocoanuts*, 21:06), with Chico playing the melody in response to Harpo arbitrarily banging two horseshoes together, at which point Groucho takes off his jacket, wraps it round his waist like a blacksmith's apron and mimes working a forge using the piano and the same girl's leg he and Harpo had been fooling with earlier.

52:04/54:15—"The whole thing was done with the white of an egg."

Groucho describes the "magnificent chest" which he offers to Mrs. Rittenhouse at a very low figure as "all hand-painted," before making this slightly obscure follow-up comment. It's slimly possible he's referring to the painting technique "egg tempera," involving an egg yolk (although some accounts claim egg white or whole egg) being used as a binding agent for the pigments. On the other hand (which is not necessarily to rule the first hand out of consideration) there is something about the way Groucho phrases the line that suggests the language of household hints, and there was certainly a vogue around this time for using eggs in all manner of usefully creative ways, from stain removal to stiffening the brims of hats, after a demonstration of any of which one can easily hear the breezy summation, "The whole thing was done with the white of an egg!"

52:08/54:19—"This is a hope chest for a guinea pig"

Groucho goes on to describe the item as "a hope chest for a guinea pig," a hope chest being a large box in which unmarried women collect the household items they will need when matrimony strikes (what we in Britain, with no specialized furniture for the task, would call "the bottom drawer"). In 1920s American slang the term was also used to mean a carton of cigarettes; presumably Groucho is using it in its original sense here, though the addition of "for a guinea pig" reflects nothing more comprehensible than Groucho's admirable tendency to rewrite and obscure lines that had begun to bore him. The original Kaufman-Ryskind joke had been a straightforward one: "It's a match-box for an elephant."

56:35/58:57—"Whoever took it was right in the room with us. Just like Raffles!"

Raffles, the gentleman thief, was a high society burglar who appeared in a series of stories by E.W. Hornung. Ronald Colman played the role in the 1930 film *Raffles,* one of many screen versions of the stories. Kay Francis, who knows a thing or three about jewel theft, played his love interest.

56:58/59:21—"I've been on the pan...."

Lillian Roth's litany of woes in the opening to "Why Am I So Romantic?" includes this slightly mysterious observation, which to seasoned Marx fans will instantly evoke the musical sentiments of Professor Wagstaff in *Horse Feathers:* "I soon dispose of all of those who put me on the pan." "On the pan" means to receive censure or criticism, and has the same root as "panning" in the extant sense of dismissing a piece of art or entertainment. *The Oxford English Dictionary* dates it to 1899, and notes its falling out of use in the mid–20th century. The phrase also served as the title of a 1933 animated short.

63:30/66:09—"Morning, Mrs. Rittenhouse."

Morning, Zeppo! Look, everybody—it's one of the Marx Brothers, justifying his fourth billing by breezing back into the film a mere hour after we last saw him in scene one. That Zeppo was little used and ill-used is commonplace, but in this film it's plain absurd. He didn't have much to do in *The Cocoanuts* but at least we saw him hanging about the place on the off-chance. Here's what he does in *Animal Crackers:*

4:48/5:00—He comes in and announces Groucho's arrival in song.

9:12/9:35—After standing around for a bit he disappears, long before the end of the scene; *before Chico and Harpo's entrances, even.* When Groucho says, "Well, somebody's got to do it!" you can actually *see* him slinking off. He is not present in any later long shot.

63:30/66:09—After many crowd scenes, the musical soiree and the unveiling of the painting, at none of which is he present, he returns for the letter-dictation scene.

69:07/72:00—Exits after a dozen or so lines and one genuine joke ("Do you want that *ahem* in the letter?")

84:43/88:15—Re-enters with his brothers singing "My Old Kentucky Home." But he has no lines, and melts back into the crowd the moment the song is done.

85:16/88:50—Again, we actually see him sneak away, and in several subsequent long shots of the whole room he is clearly not present.

88:11/91:52—Reappears at the very end of the scene just long enough to say, "Hey! What's the idea!"—his first line in twenty-five minutes—before instantly succumbing to Harpo's flitz.

And that's your lot: a bit of singing in scene one, a bit of "yes sir" and a semi-joke in one dialogue scene, and a face in the crowd at the end. His total onscreen time is something like ten minutes. That said, this dictation scene is his one chance to shine, and he takes what chances he gets. He even gets to display a Chico-like obtuseness, leaving out the entire contents of the letter he has been tasked to take down because they "didn't seem important." ("It takes a Marx Brother to pull something like that on a Marx Brother and get away with it," notes Joe Adamson.)

In the original play, "Charles H. Hungerdunger, care of Hungerdunger, Hungerdunger, Hungerdunger and McCormick" was "Charles D. Vasserschlogel, care of Vasserschlagel, Vasserschlegel, Vasserschlugel and McCormick." The current version of this scene contains two cuts, both removing references to an "Elsie," whom Groucho briefly elects as the letter's addressee. He begins the dictation with "Dear Elsie...." before withdrawing it: "No, never mind Elsie."

"Do you want me to scratch Elsie?" asks Zeppo.

"Well, if you enjoy that sort of thing it's quite all right with me," Groucho replies. "However, I'm not interested in your private affairs, Jamison."

The second, subsequent cut snips a further reference to Elsie, presumably in the interests of continuity. It would seem to imply that this only very mildly suggestive exchange was cut for a Code-era reissue, possibly at the same time as "I think I'll try and make her." That it was presumably present in first-run prints is suggested by one of the early posters for the film, in which the four brothers are each provided with speech bubbles. (There's only a stream of question marks in Harpo's.) Zeppo's says: "Scratch Elsie." Just Zeppo's luck to have what was once isolated as his most distinctive moment completely removed in the reruns.

64:43/67:25—"I'd like to see you crawl out of a rumble seat!"

Groucho is presumably mocking the butler Hives's girth and likely lack of agility in this reference to what in Britain was known as a "dickey seat"—an exterior seat on the back of pre-war cars for use by servants.

74:57/78:05—"Remember the Charlie Ross disappearance?"

A somewhat tasteless reference to the 1874 abduction of a four-year-old boy and his brother by two men who enticed them by saying they would buy them some firecrackers. They took them in a cart to a shop, where Walter, the older brother, was sent in to make the purchases. When he came out Charlie and the men were gone. Walter lived until 1943, and the family never gave up hope that they would hear from Charlie again, but neither his fate nor the whereabouts of his body has ever been discovered.

75:31/78:40—"It's a hair! A red hair!"

This is the first of many references, in several films, to Harpo having red hair *after* he's switched to a blonde wig. It's possible that this one has been carried over unconsciously from the stage script, where he would have still used his original red one. Nonetheless, the profusion of later moments lend weight to the suggestion that the "blonde" wig was, in fact, a light shade of red.

75:50/79:00—"Get that gang of flagpole-sitters of yours...."

This is one of those lovely lines that brings the era back to life. Among the myriad manifestations of the Roaring Twenties' thirst for idle novelty was the popularity of flagpole-sitters: folks who sat on the top of flagpoles as a display of endurance, often at great and daring altitudes. The fad dates from 1924, when stunt actor Alvin "Shipwreck" Kelly sat on a flagpole for thirteen hours and thirteen minutes on a dare. It soon caught on, with new records set and broken constantly, until Shipwreck stepped back into the fray in 1929 and sat on a flagpole in New Jersey for forty-nine days. It looked like history was made, but the following year, the year of *Animal Crackers,* the record was broken yet again by a man in Iowa whose fifty-one-day stint on the top of a flagpole was ended only when a thunderstorm brought him down. Meanwhile back in the movie, Groucho is referring to Hennessey's policeman thus, presumably to cast doubt on their practical use.

76:17/79:28—"Anything I retain now is velvet. Except the coat. That's Prince Albert."

"Velvet" in this context means profit, or an unanticipated sum of money, usually acquired through gambling. Groucho then evokes the fabric velvet with a reference to Prince Albert coats, more commonly known as frock coats. Well, all the jokes can't be good; you've got to expect that once in a while.

76:44/79:56—"Beaugard is dead? Then it's murder!"

Watch Lillian Roth smiling when Groucho delivers this joke. This is the famous line she recalls in *I'll Cry Tomorrow:*

> Groucho and I had a scene that had to be shot over at least ten times ... I burst into giggles every time he said that, ruining the take. The line itself wasn't so hilarious, but I knew Groucho was going to say it with the big cigar jutting from his clenched teeth, his eyebrows palpitating, and that he would be off afterwards in that runaway crouch of his; and the thought of what was coming was far too much for me.

You may generally disapprove, as I usually do, of the modern tendency to include "blooper reels" on DVDs, celebrating the self-indulgence of the cast. But on this one occasion.... What wouldn't you give?

77:32/80:46—"If we can find the left-handed person who painted this, we'll have The Trial of Mary Dugan with sound."

Ah, "with sound"! Once again 1930 opens up afresh before us! *The Trial of Mary Dugan* was a courtroom melodrama, originally a play, written in 1927 and adapted into an MGM movie in 1929 starring strange interluder Norma Shearer and produced by her husband, *A Night at the Opera*–boy genius Irving Thalberg. It was MGM's second all-talking picture.

79:42/83:02—"In that case I'll get in touch with Chic Sale."

Sale was a vaudevillian specializing in rural characters. Groucho's citing of him, in the context of the imaginary house he and Chico are constructing (and directly in response to Chico's line, "You just want a telephone booth"), is a reference to *The Specialist,* a 1929 play and book about an outhouse builder, written and performed by Sale. Apparently, an outhouse for a while became known as "a Chic Sale." Sale thought this was "a terrible thing to have happen."

80:29/83:51—"I may be wonderful but I think you're wrong, Ravelli!"

A reference to the song "I May Be Wrong," written by Henry Sullivan and Harry Ruskin and published in 1929, the real lyric, obviously, being "I may be wrong but I think you're wonderful." Hoagy Carmichael recorded a delicious version in 1946.

83:01/86:29—"Didn't you ever see a habeas corpus?" "No, but I see Habeas Irish Rose."

Abie's Irish Rose was a Broadway comedy popular throughout the twenties concerning the many problems encountered by an Irish Catholic girl who marries a Jew against objections from both families. (It was filmed by Paramount in 1928, with Charles "Buddy" Rogers, and, in a tiny part, Thelma Todd.) Despite its huge success, it received terrible reviews, most famously from Robert Benchley who in *Life* magazine declared it the worst play in town and then found himself in increasing difficulty finding new ways to make the same point week after week in his capsule reviews column. "People laugh at this every night, which explains why democracy can never be a success," was one such effort. On other occasions he appealed for information ("Where do people come from who keep this going? You don't see them out in the daytime"), and even tried optimism ("In another two or three years, we'll have this play driven out of town") and wishful thinking ("Closing soon [only fooling]"). But as it proceeded regardless on its inexorable path to setting a Broadway record of 2,327 performances he resorted to more ambiguous comments, such as "A-ha-ha-ha-ha! Oh, well, all right," "The Phoenicians were among the earliest settlers of Britain," and "There is no letter 'w' in the French language." The simplest was "See Hebrews 13:8" which, as those who bothered to look it up discovered, was the verse "Jesus Christ the same yesterday, and today, and for ever." In its fifth year he announced a prize competition for the best review: the winner was a certain Mr. Harpo Marx, with "No worse than a bad cold." (Oddly, one of the few dramatic critics to give the play a pass was Harpo's Algonquin mentor Alexander Woollcott, whose cynical demeanor concealed a sucker for sentimental corn: his first night rave became the subject of much derision as the general consensus formed.) Such was the play's popularity it was able to inspire and sustain an overt rip-off, *The Cohens and the Kellys,* the only concession to originality of which was the fact that this time it was a Jewish girl and an Irishman. Even this proved popular enough to spawn six sequels and retain sufficient pop cultural longevity to be echoed in the lyrics of *The Big Store*'s "Tenement Symphony" as late as 1941, which mentions "The Cohens' pianola, The Kellys and their victrola."

84:57/88:30—"This program is coming to you from the House of David."

One of several explicitly Jewish references in the early films. Groucho's statement co-opts and mocks the wording of a radio announcement, but the "House of David" is, of course, the Davidic line (*Malkhut Beit David* in Hebrew), referred to many times in the Bible. Though it was also the name of an entrepreneurial religious commune that was very active (and notorious) around this time, it seems unlikely that this is what is being referenced here. In the version of the playscript held in the Sam Harris collection at Princeton University, the program was coming to you from the Battle Creek Sanitarium.

85:10/88:43—"Einstein or no Einstein!"

Groucho confuses Einstein's theory of relativity—pretty hot stuff at the time—with the law of gravity, which was, of course, discovered much earlier by Sir Harpo Newton.

85:21/88:55—The strange shot of Chico

In the cut that occurs when the cop says, "But he's not innocent," Chico's appearance and demeanor bizarrely change. Instead of his usual smiling self, he is now suddenly adopting a surly expression, and his hat is pulled down so it almost obscures his eyes. When we see him again in the long shot at **85:32/89:06** he's back to normal. So odd is the change that some have speculated it may not be Chico at all, but I think it fairly obviously is, without even considering the unlikeliness that he might not have been around for that one shot. (Much less jarring for the viewer to leave him out entirely in a crowded medium shot than to bother briefly dressing someone else like him and have them pull their hat down!) Presumably when that shot was taken he was simply in that quixotic mood that occasionally came over him, like when he pulls that face singing "Freedonia, oh don'ya cry for me" in *Duck Soup*. Still, it's a strange little moment and worth looking out for.

85:33/89:07—"I did it with my little hatchet!"

"I cannot tell a lie: I did it with my little hatchet," were supposedly the young George Washington's words when asked if he chopped down a cherry tree. Groucho is gallantly claiming to have stolen a painting via the same method.

89:01/92:44—The mysterious, now missing last words

Like Groucho taking off his pith helmet twice, until well into the video age there was a snatch of speech after the end credit music, now excised from official editions of the film. I always fancied it sounded like Chico, but could never work out what was being said. It was, apparently, "NG!" meaning "no good" (i.e., that the music take was not acceptable, a presumably over-ridden decision). If you have an early video tape, you may still be able to hear it, if that's your idea of a good time.

3

Monkey Business (1931)

Quiet, everybody, quiet! A lady's diamond earring has been lost. It looks exactly like this. In fact, this is it.—Groucho

"The year's most assorted list of bit players for a film production was gathered today by the casting office at the Paramount studios in Hollywood," claimed a publicity piece that ran in the *Pittsburgh Post-Gazette* and elsewhere on May 23, 1931:

> The demands for extra talent, which were strange enough to stir comment in an industry where few things cause wonder, were listed on the call sheet for *Monkey Business,* starring the Four Marx Brothers:
> 1 good looking girl to wrestle with Harpo, 1 plump woman, 1 bald-headed man, 1 dignified society woman, 1 beautiful girl (must be tall), 1 woman wearing bustle, 1 timid man, 1 girl for jack-knife gang, 1 dowager, 1 opera singer, 1 man escort, 1 gentleman for dance gag, 3 butlers, 5 crooks, 2-piece orchestra, 1 Indian, 1 pretty girl, 1 good-looking girl, 1 girl who can run, 1 attractive matron, 1 ugly man, 50 extras (varied types).

In other words, the Marx Brothers had invaded Hollywood, and like all good conquerors were immediately setting about refashioning it to suit their whims. That, at least, is what publicity items like the above strove to imply. In reality, given an original script, with no stage tryout, and all to be shot in Hollywood, they must have felt some chill of uncertainty as the prospect of this fresh gamble loomed. Did they ever know for certain that their Broadway days were behind them? Had the success of *Animal Crackers* convinced them of a safe future on the sound stages, or was this the decisive moment?

They needn't have worried, of course. Robert E. Sherwood attended a sneak preview, and reported tumultuous applause at the revelation that the unknown subject was to be a new Marx epic: "This coatless California gathering provided conclusive proof of the fact that the Marxes had made good in the movies." And as the reviews showed when they came in, they were not merely accepted now as screen comedians, they had *become* screen comedians. *Monkey Business* is a masterpiece not merely of wit and invention, but also of pace, editing and cinematic structure: it's a great film comedy, not just a great filmed comedy. The change is total and instant: as obvious as it is that the first two films are based on plays, it is even more obvious that this one is *not*. Straight out of the gun, it moves like a film, to a filmic drumbeat. Sherwood noted "nowhere near as large a quota of quotable wisecracks" as the first two films, but felt the new emphasis on the physical ample compensation, and most critics agreed. Noted Dawn O'Dea in the *Milwaukee Sentinel:* "Smartcracks aren't as plentiful as in *Animal Crackers,* but that lack is more than made up for in action that is as speedy as it is dizzy. And that lack also makes *Monkey Business* better entertainment for the youngsters than previous Marx pictures."

The big decision has been to give them *movement.* An extraordinary thing about *The Cocoanuts* and *Animal Crackers* is how physically contained the Brothers are in them: Harpo chases a few blondes, Groucho does his Spaulding dance, and the four first meet in *The Cocoanuts* in that lovely choreographed encounter in the hotel lobby, but the rest of the time they stand in front of us, talking. Here, within a minute of their appearance they are being frantically chased along the decks of an extensive ocean liner set—and with a tracking camera keeping up with them yet! Whereas before they had occasionally interrupted stasis with frenzy, here they are bodies in flight, stopping just long enough to make it essential that they rush away again. And not only is it more quick-moving, it is quicker in the literal sense: while the two "Broadway" Paramounts run in excess of 90 minutes, the three Hollywood Paramounts come in around 75 minutes or less.

Now, I am in that minority that prefers the arrogant, intense style of the New York films,

Chico (left) and Groucho on the brink of devouring the captain's lunch in *Monkey Business*.

but not for one second would I argue that there is any indictable sense of loss here; not yet. The new circumstances have dictated revisions to the team's comic style, to a much greater degree than is often spotted or conceded, but what the hell: it all works. Groucho, in particular, has been revolutionized: he's now a dervish. And Harpo is like a dog that has been tethered in the yard for a week suddenly being unleashed in some wide open space. Run, Harpo, run!

Even Zeppo is given a couple of breaks. At last he has an actual part written for him: he's one of the gang in a way he hadn't been before, he's given dialogue, and he serves some sort of narrative function, since he's now the love interest, such as it is. This lucky streak continues into *Horse Feathers,* but is disappointingly reversed again in *Duck Soup,* his last hurrah with the team, and may in part be attributable to the influence of director Norman Z. McLeod as well as to the obviously greater advantages afforded by the two scripts. McLeod made careful efforts to balance the four, analyzing their strengths and functions, and striving to ensure that each was given their own chances. Of Zeppo he observed, "Zeppo, as in the case of most straight men, often is overlooked when one weighs the comedy of a production. However the foil always is important, and being a foil for three comedians is no easy task." Robert E. Sherwood at the preview spotted that one, too:

> The really big news concerning *Monkey Business* is that it imposes the burden of the love interest on the hitherto understressed shoulders of Zeppo Marx. It is a prodigious responsibility, for Zeppo has to be dashingly romantic and, at the same time, the brother of Groucho, Harpo and Chico—an impossible task, which he undertakes with his usual uncomplaining fortitude. Some day, someone should write a character analysis of this heroic soul, Zeppo, who is content to go down to posterity as "that other Marx." There is the famous story of how, during the rehearsal of *Animal Crackers,* Sam H. Harris approached him and asked, "Can't you get a little more variety into your performance?" Which provoked Zeppo to inquire, "Just how many ways are there of saying 'yes'?"

It is Chico alone who comes out of the process at best unchanged or even very slightly diminished. From here on he will have increasing trouble keeping up with his Brothers: since he is essentially indolent and opportunistic, wily where they are instinctive, he becomes increasingly peripheral in situations governed by the unmediated abandonment of his peers. He still gets his moments, here and throughout the Paramount sequence and finally in *Opera,* but mere moments they surely are. He is not the constant nagging, inescapable presence he had been; he's more of a specialty turn in discrete guest spots. As even Groucho discovers to his cost, Chico's comic magic flourishes best when you can't escape him. He is the eternal unwelcome guest, at hotels and house parties both; he is the man who came to dinner. Drop him into a narrative free to move between locations and adventures and he inevitably becomes sidelined, unthreatening, before long even *loveable.* Here, though, that process is instigated with negligible perceptibility: everything in *Monkey Business* is done too well to permit griping from any quarter.

The secret of success, as always, was assembling the right team. The loss of Kaufman and Ryskind seems a lesser worry in retrospect, now we all know how great the next three movies were, but at the time it must have seemed like preparing to cross the street blindfolded. Under new producer Herman Mankiewicz, and at Groucho's own instigation, the solution was as simple as it was shrewd: instead of studio scenario writers, employ a pool of bona fide humorists in part-collaborative, part-combative unison. Mankiewicz's approach was the exact opposite of the one pioneered by Irving Thalberg at MGM: all he cared about was that they should be funny. ("If Groucho and Chico stand against a wall for an hour and forty minutes and crack jokes, that's enough for me.") His haul of gag merchants included S.J. Perelman, Will B. Johnstone, J. Carver Pusey, Arthur Sheekman and Nat Perrin. They made for a combustible enough bunch as it was, and things were hardly calmed by Mankiewicz's tendency to jovially dismiss them all as hacks, and greet their new lines with exasperated cries of "For Christ's sake! Gene Bendini's *Chuckles,* 1928!" It's fun to think of them all shouting over each other to get their jokes in, in my mind irresistibly evoking images of the press room in *The Front Page:* overflowing ashtrays, rolled shirt-sleeves, and the stale late-afternoon smells of cigar smoke, discarded baloney sandwiches and the manly perspiration that comes of conjuring lines like "I've worked my way up from nothing to a state of extreme poverty" on nothing but the fumes of typewriter ink and spilled bourbon.

Of the above roster, it is surely Johnstone who provided the most useful and reassuring presence, even if it is Perelman who tends to get the spotlight. Johnstone had been the chief writer of *I'll Say She Is,* the Broadway revue that introduced them to the Algonquin set and gave them the smash hit on which the entirety of their subsequent career was built. In that sense, he could be called the most important writer they ever had, and his recall here after the loss of Kaufman seems only right and proper. While he brought the right kind of craziness to the project, Perelman added sophisticated barbs and devilishly torturous puns. The two did not get on personally at all, but on the page and screen their union clicks like George and Gracie.

The scripting process was marked by delay and indecision. When Paramount wanted to include an extract in a forthcoming attractions section of their twentieth anniversary promotional film *The House That Shadows Built,* the team had to admit they had nothing workable to use at all, so a scene from *I'll Say She Is* was shot and included (see below, 9:00). A further measure of how difficult a pot this was proving to boil is the information contained in one of the early posters. They had the shipboard beginning, but the rest, it seems, was still anybody's guess:

> It starts with the Marxes as stowaways on an ocean liner, with the whole ship's company in pursuit. Arrived in New York, they interview the ship reporters sent to interview them, then embark for Florida, by request. Having wrecked a millionaire's home family and nerves there, Groucho psycho-analyzes a horse in his well known style. From there on it gets louder and funnier. Frank Tuttle will direct the Big Four of Fun, which is good news too.

It sounds like one part *Cocoanuts* and one part *Animal Crackers* to two parts sheer frustrated guesswork as to how the thing might eventually pan out, though points must be awarded for the audacity of claiming that Groucho has a well-known style of psychoanalyzing horses.

Note, too, the film being assigned at this stage to director Frank Tuttle, a very lively film-maker, one of my favorites among the Paramount men, and a missed opportunity to be regretted, I think. Nonetheless Norman Z. McLeod was, for me, the most suitable director they were ever ascribed, and a man who always reminds me of Sherlock Holmes's barbed praise for Watson: "Some people, without possessing genius, have a remarkable power of stimulating." For a comedian's director like McLeod, praise rarely comes any higher. After all, there's something innately ludicrous about the notion of anybody actually *directing* the Marx Brothers (or W.C. Fields, for that matter, but McLeod also signs his name to *It's a*

Gift, a work of comparable perfection to his Marx assignments). Because of their reputation for unruliness, the Marxes were often assigned taskmasters with little comic sense (Victor Heerman, Sam Wood), leading to much anecdote-worthy friction, but a far bigger mistake was to give them directors with a strong comic personality of their own, such as Leo McCarey, who imposed various alien innovations on *Duck Soup.* McLeod was the best of both worlds—he obviously got the jokes, but he didn't think he was funnier or knew more about comedy than his stars.

It should be admitted without too much regret that one inevitable result of this all-hands approach is a degree of comic inconstancy. If it is decided that it is a good joke that a photographer's camera be revealed as Harpo hiding under a sheet then that is what it proves to be, and as in a Warners cartoon we are asked not to wonder just how he achieved such a masquerade without the photographer noticing, or where the original camera has disappeared to. But when a moment later they decide to impersonate Maurice Chevalier as a means of escaping the ship the joke becomes the inevitable *lack* of magical invention they bring to the deception, and, in Harpo's case, the sheer impracticality of the mechanics deployed. Who wouldn't sacrifice consistency for great jokes? Nonetheless, there is a skittishness here that seems to me less *cumulatively* satisfying than the sustained and leveled assaults they had unleashed twice previously. The film plays as a montage of quickie jokes and sketches on a connected theme; it never *builds,* and one needn't be dissatisfied with the result to detect inexperience more than intent behind the effect. *Horse Feathers* the following year is just as generous with its laughter but in the main a smoother assembly.

No amount of behind-the-camera expertise could give the Brothers the one thing they surely felt the absence of most: the certainty that comes of having delivered the jokes dozens of times already, and gauged the reaction, and altered and shaped them accordingly, until they knew exactly how each would go over, how to time them, and how to delay the response. Here, even though it must have been obvious the material was worthy of them, still just as obviously they must have felt as if at a first read-through. Given their nervousness, there may be an element of pure agitation, even fear, informing their physical vitality in this film, their desire to hurry from laugh to laugh, in case the previous one hadn't hit the way they expected. Anything to avoid long silences—the nightmare of every stage comic. It may have occurred to them that the screen comic need not fear audience apathy in the same way, since they will not personally endure it, only their projected shadows. But onstage, one bad night can be compensated for, next time. On film, every night is the first night, over and over. Worse, they were prone to Spike Milligan's disease of constantly rewriting in rehearsal (or demanding rewrites, rather: they lacked even his excuse of being brain and mouth both). Onstage, they got laughs time after time because it was a different crowd each night. When you're playing to the exact same workers and technicians, even the best jokes are going to lose impact eventually. But to the Marxes, silence meant ineffectuality, so off went the scribes to come up with something new. The gags-used to gags-written ratio must have been more wasteful here than on any other film in history. To think of what some of their later films could have done with the doubtless great lines so unsentimentally jettisoned!

And maybe something of their insolence is gone, too. They are rude and lacking in propriety still, but it is more impish because so much more frenetic; they plunge into confrontation and then out again as if on a dare. They are tameless spirits but their engagement with the world of conformity is ritualistic, as if both sides acknowledge the necessity of the other for their own existence; it's ordered disorder. They are made stowaways for their convenience and our consent: it is their lot to be chased around the deck, and their duty to retaliate with invective and bravado. What have they to lose? They have no status anyway. In *Animal Crackers* they were actually *invited,* which makes their provocations more malevolent and their motives more inexplicable. And they had roles in society that it might be naively assumed they would want to maintain. They have no real motives in *Animal Crackers,* but no choices either. Everything that happens is preordained from the second of their arrival, just as fire and gasoline will never make pleasantly warm gasoline no matter how many times you introduce the two: it's in the essential nature of neither to permit it. They are not truly *characters,* merely types let loose in a situation, living juxtapositions, thought experiments in the art of disjunction. There, they had been amusing us only incidentally: the game was to amuse themselves. Now, they are licensed to be outrageous because their existence seems predicated on the fact of us looking in and egging them on, and their affronts are tempered by a sense of knowing mischief in place of the earlier films' bloody-mindedness. With variation comes familiarity: they are making films, ergo they are making them for us. In *The Cocoanuts* and *Animal Crackers* they seemed not so much making films as *being* filmed. From here on they are film comedians, releasing our tensions as much as their own. Mrs. Rittenhouse invited them to *Animal Crackers,* but we are doing the inviting now.

Luckily, they reward our summons magnificently, as both audiences and critics happily recognized when the film was finally released. John Mosher in *The New Yorker* thought it "the best this family has given us," before concluding: "There is something a bit shoddy and casual about the sets ... which is regrettable." True enough, but let us not forget that, as the *Sydney Morning Herald* was moved to note, "There is a fine picture of the New York waterfront as the ship arrives at her destination."

0:00 (NTSC/PAL)—Opening Credits

In what could well be the archetypal Marx Brothers credits sequence we hear a lovely tinkly medley of tunes, beginning with Chico's theme song "I'm Daffy Over You," as a series of barrels roll out at the camera at high speed before stopping and revealing the information on their sides. I especially like the fact that this is not superimposition: the words and the pictures are plainly *stuck* on the sides of the barrels. They are presumably miniatures, and the effect is absolutely adorable. Given the incredibly abrupt manner in which they come to a halt, and the obvious difficulties inherent in getting them to roll forward and stop with the decorated side positioned exactly right, it is most likely this sequence was shot with the barrels rolling away from the camera, and then shown in reverse.

What do we think of the title? I'd cautiously suggest it's the least inspired of the "animal trilogy." Not that I have any strong feelings about it, which is more than I can say for Olsen and Johnson. The *Hellzapoppin'* funsters didn't like it one little bit, and mounted a legal challenge to Fox Coast West Theaters, Inc. to have it changed. But their claim that they had been using the title for a stage act for several years previously was dismissed by Judge Walter S. Gates in January 1932. It seems to have been a second choice for the Marxes: the film was

Four kippered herrings—but how many voices sing *"Sweet Adeline"*? (Left to right) Harpo, Zeppo, Chico and Groucho in the opening scene of *Monkey Business*.

extensively announced under the much more amusing title of *Pineapples*. In gangster slang a "Chicago pineapple" was a hand grenade (Chico asks Harpo if he has brought any when they are stealing the painting in *Animal Crackers*), though Groucho accounted for the unusual title to a reporter by explaining that it was chosen for the film "because there is nothing about pineapples in it." This, and possibly some measure of indecision or dispute as to which title they should plump for, explains Zeppo's otherwise mysterious line at the end of the adapted vaudeville sketch used to promote the film in *The House That Shadows Built* (see below, 9:00): "I'd like to read this manuscript for you. It's a wonderful play and these fellas would fit in it.... Now this is not *Monkey Business*, or is it *Pineapples*...."

1:31/1:35—"Sweet Adeline"

Beautifully setting the tone for the ensuing film, we open with all four Brothers popping out of kippered herring barrels simultaneously after a rendition of the above-mentioned song. It is a quartet—that's how the shipboard staff know there are four stowaways. Of course, with Harpo being mute the joke does not quite work. Or does it? Is Harpo singing? Several writers (Glenn Mitchell being the most notable) have thought so, since, they explain, there are clearly four voices, and the one that holds the longest note at the end is not a voice we have heard before. I've listened to this over and over again, but I can only hear three. Marx experts are adamant but conflicting as to which is which, however. The most common accounts have either Zeppo or Chico starting, either Chico or Groucho coming in second, and either Groucho or Zeppo doing the strangulated "funny" voice heard last. I had always instinctively heard the order of the voices as Chico-Groucho-Zeppo; on reflection (and after much bullying) I've lately leaned towards Zeppo-Chico-Groucho. "We'll have to agree to disagree," maintains Glenn Mitchell. "It's definitely Chico who starts and maintains the lead vocal. I know Zeppo's and Groucho's singing voices and that nasal one that comes in as harmony, then holds to the end, belongs to neither of them. I still think it was an in-joke, giving us Harpo's voice under conditions where it couldn't definitely be identified as his." (For still more on "Sweet Adeline," see *Room Service*, 57:31.)

6:31/6:48—"You can't do it with irons, it's a mashie shot."

This refers to a type of golf club. The word derives from the convention of naming clubs "mashies" or "niblicks," depending on whether they were short-irons or well lofted clubs. The clubs that are somewhere between the two were known, with logic if minimal invention, as mashie-niblicks. This terminology was used from 1903 until about the 1940s, whereupon it was rendered obsolete by the introduction of the standardized numbered iron set produced by ... the Spaulding Sporting Goods Company.

7:12/7:31—"I'm the Captain, you wanna choose up sides?"

The above is a sporting term, meaning to pick players: Groucho is therefore melding the concept of ship's captain with the captain of a baseball (or other sporting) team.

7:34/7:53—"I didn't eat yesterday, I didn't eat today, and I'm not gonna eat tomorrow: that makes-a three days."

A typically logic-mangling Chico joke which interestingly also turns up, delivered by Stan Laurel, in Laurel & Hardy's *One Good Turn* released the same year. The Marx film was released in September of '31, Laurel's was shot mid to late June. So it's most likely the joke is a classic howler long predating both, and their proximity here merely a coincidence.

8:10/8:31—"That's Columbus Circle."

Chico is here referring to the famous Manhattan landmark, a traffic circle dominated by a statue of Columbus, completed in 1905 and located at the intersection of Broadway, Central Park West, Central Park South and Eighth Avenue.

8:42/9:04—"Sure I can vessel!"

No I'm not going to bother to explain that this is a pun on whistle, but I will point out that what Chico chooses to whistle is, again, "I'm Daffy Over You." He hums it a third time later on, and Harpo plays it on the harp. It shows up again in *Horse Feathers*.

8:57/9:20—"Mutinies, Wednesdays and Saturdays."

Matinees, of course.

9:00/9:23—"There's my argument: restrict immigration!"

A Groucho line which a) gives the "Is Chico Italian?" obsessives plenty to ponder, and b) also turns up in the very funny theatrical agent sketch that the Brothers shot while the script for *Monkey Business* was still gestating.

Paramount was preparing a fifty-minute puff piece called *The House That Shadows Built,* designed to celebrate the studio's twentieth anniversary and to look ahead by plugging forthcoming productions. *Monkey Business* was a film they particularly wanted to feature, but with the script still in the air the infinitely more valuable decision to shoot an old sketch was born of necessity. So, through the sheerest fluke, we have the opening scene of *I'll Say She Is* on film. And given that this in itself was based on a scene from their vaudeville sketch "On the Mezzanine" its value needs no further stressing. (The choice was not as left-field as it may seem: its value as an entirely self-contained sketch had already been established in 1928 when, in the break between *The Cocoanuts* and *Animal Crackers,* they combined it with the final scene of the former to produce an instant vaudeville act, untitled but eventually known as either *Spanish Knights* or *Spanish Nights.*) Perhaps the nicest surprise of this window into a part of their careers we had no business ever expecting to peer through is that it's all so reassuringly hilarious, though unquestionably different from their work as we know it, in several interesting ways. (Most obviously notable is Zeppo's centrality to the antics, still not actually a comic presence, but in spirit very much part of the ensemble.)

Three things link it explicitly to *Monkey Business,* one being the immigration line, which doesn't appear to date from "Mezzanine" or *I'll Say* (it certainly isn't in Will Johnstone's *I'll Say* typescript) and so seems to have either crossed over from what little there was of the new script, or perhaps more likely, been a line of Groucho's own that he retained for the film. Another link is the fact that the agent is played by ship's captain Ben Taggart (while Glenn Mitchell speculates that the briefly seen secretary may be Ruth Hall). Most interesting by far, however, are the Chevalier imitations. Here the sketch deviates from its source but only incidentally: the impressions *were* originally there, but they were of the vaudevillian Joe Frisco. The choice of Chevalier for an update suggests original inspiration applied to this direct task, rather than the happy marriage of need with a coincidentally readymade solution: in other words, it would seem the traffic is again flowing from sketch to feature film, and this actually *inspired* the Chevalier scene in *Monkey Business.* Simon Louvish confirms that it is definitely not present in the earliest surviving treatment Johnstone and Perelman assembled for the film.

So if the opportunity to make this had not come about, or even if the script of *Monkey Business* had been completed in better time, we may not have had the sequence that has, for my dollar, as strong a claim as any to being their greatest moment in cinema. That means no "Are you Maurice Chevalio? Well, there you are!" or "You go in the back of the boat, it's just like me" from Chico; no "Well, look at *that* face!" or "the barber shop wasn't open this morning" from Groucho; no Harpo stalling for time by producing from about his person anything he can think of that vaguely rhymes with "passport," before attempting the masquerade with blithe confidence slowly giving way to sheepishness as the gramophone winds down. Above all, no chance to enjoy the cumulative comic effect of the same snatch of song being sung in different but equally ridiculous ways by men who could not look or sound less like Chevalier if they tried, yet somehow think complete confidence in themselves and a straw hat are all that's necessary. It's a thought to keep you awake at night if ever there was one.

9:46/10:11—"Don't forget, my fine fellow, that the stockholder of yesteryear is the stowaway of today!"

It sounds like a typically nonsensical Groucho joke, half-buried in a barrage of genuinely typical nonsensical Groucho jokes. But it's not hard to detect a certain satirical edge to this one, given how many businesses and life's savings had been wiped out by the crash, and how life had changed for so many in the Depression. That the Marxes might play stowaways on a ship was the first idea they approved of, securing Perelman and Johnstone their ticket on the movie, and the way it seems to have instantly ignited the imaginations of all involved hints at it being something more than just a funny idea. Images of rail cars full of people trying to travel undetected are among the most abiding of the era; the concept of stowing away on a ship seems frivolous to us now, but perhaps carried comparably meaningful connotations at the time. Certainly contemporary audiences might have been disposed to wonder—as most of us surely never do today—just *why* the Marxes are traveling in this way. Is it possible that we are not necessarily intended to assume that they are stowing away because they're free spirits and don't want to pay, but because they *can't* pay? Or even can't travel at all, given their lack of passports? Such a suggestion seems to be supported by the opening dialogue:

> GROUCHO: I was going to bring along the wife and kiddies but the grocer couldn't spare another barrel.
> CHICO: I was going to bring my grandfather but there's no room for his beard.

It seems odd to suggest they are emigrating, especially as there are good reasons for assuming the ship is traveling to America from *England,* but this does strongly convey that impression. It is therefore possible at least to infer that the Brothers are channeling something of their own family history, playing, however tacitly, European immigrants to America, and illegal ones at that. (Maybe the ship docked in England to pick up more passengers, en route from somewhere else.) Note also that Chico's reference to "my" rather than "our" grandfather suggests that they are seemingly not playing brothers; their fellowship might therefore be the brotherhood of immigrants. They are also bonded by ethnic sensibilities: Lawrence J. Epstein in *The Haunted Smile* observes that their common Jewishness is suggested by the choice of kippered herring barrels for their hiding places. (Or perhaps, notes Glenn Mitchell, given that they had recently made the journey from England to America after a not entirely successful live stint in London, they are playing themselves and "implying an ignominious return from their C.B. Cochran engagement!")

12:17/12:48—The enchanted Punch & Judy show

Another of the film's most famous scenes, and certainly among the most celebrated Harpo sequences in the canon. Like much else in the film it plays as a completely self-contained idea, reflecting the piecemeal and many-handed nature of the scripting. It also plays somewhat eerily—when you realize that there is no puppeteer in the booth. Some of the puppetry is being done by Harpo, some is not—and Punch's voice, heard from first to last, can only be coming from Punch himself. Note also Harpo's first use of a mask on the back of his head: the means by which he will introduce himself to us in *Duck Soup*. Originally this scene was followed by one in the ship's nursery, which got as far as production but was deleted pre-release. Stills, showing Harpo in a nurse's uniform with Billy Barty, survive.

15:31/16:10—"You got 'it.' And you can keep it."

Chico's take on one of the greatest pop-cultural obsessions of the times: what is "it" and who has "it," "it," of course, being that extra indefinable something some of us have and some of us don't, that is almost but not quite a synonym for sex appeal. Authoress Madame Elinor Glyn conceived of "it," Clara Bow had "it," Glyn proclaimed (as a result becoming "the It Girl" for all time) and so did Gary Cooper (who was less enduringly tagged "the It Boy" by the same decree). Paramount put Clara into a delightful but hastily put-together film called *It* in 1927. The number of times "you've got 'It'" was used as a pickup line around that time must be unimaginably vast, but only Chico has mastered the art of using it as compliment and insult simultaneously.

16:00/16:41—The barbershop

A variation on this scene can be seen in *Road to Rio* (1947). The moustache snooping is repeated, and, like Chico and Harpo, Bing and Bob are stowaways on an ocean liner, pretending to be barbers to avoid their pursuers. The common denominator between the two films? Director Norman Z. McLeod.

17:57/18:43—Thelma Todd

The introduction of one of the foremost comediennes of thirties Hollywood to the Marxian menagerie was noted in approved style by the *Spokesman-Review*: "beauty (is) added to the cast by the addition of Thelma Todd and some other lookers." Rare was the great comedian of the thirties who did not call on her services at least once, and they were always enlivened by the association. Long employed at Hal Roach (he admired how she combined elegance and sexiness with a willingness to fall on her ass and take a pie in the face), she can often be seen to great effect opposite Charley Chase and Laurel & Hardy, though this author most heartily recommends her series of starring shorts, teamed first with ZaSu Pitts, then Patsy Kelly.

Because she is genuinely sexy there is an edge to Groucho's pursuit of her that contrasts markedly with his essentially mocking wooing of Dumont, and this desirability also creates a different dynamic when time comes for her to get thrown in the lake, or jumped and sat on by all the Marx Brothers at once. (In *The Marx Brothers Scrapbook* the 82-year-old Groucho recalls how keen he had been to get to know Todd rather better than he did. If you take my meaning.) There are almost no recorded instances of her discussing her work with the Brothers, but one exception appears in a rarely seen 1932 interview:

> The Marxes often insert comedy we haven't rehearsed, which is one of the reasons for their success. I've had to train myself not to see anything funny in these spontaneous bits, but I have spoiled many a scene by failing to suppress my sense of humour. The Marxes, moreover, know my weakness, and on the set make it a rule to do everything possible to make me laugh in the wrong places. I've almost bitten off my tongue on numerous occasions in order to keep a straight face.

Thelma died tragically in 1935 of carbon monoxide poisoning in her locked garage. It's *de rigueur* at this point to quote Groucho's line from *Monkey Business*: "You're a woman who's been getting nothing but dirty breaks; well, we can clean and tighten your brakes but you'll have to stay in the garage all night"—a line that was for years habitually misquoted as "Now you be a good girlie, or I'll lock you in the garage." (How that got started I don't know, but you can find it thus quoted in upwards of a dozen sources, including Andy Edmonds's untrustworthy but compulsive biography *Hot Toddy*.)

19:26/20:15—"That's what they said to Thomas Edison, mighty inventor, Thomas Lindbergh, mighty flier, and Thomashefsky, mighty lak' a rose."

A knotty one, this. We'll begin with another anecdote from Corey Ford's lovely book of twenties reminiscences, *The Time of Laughter:*

> An even more popular indoor sport in those days was charades, and we spent long hours acting out political slogans and book titles and well-known songs. The longest of the hours was spent by Heywood Broun, who described in his slow, deliberate drawl a very large yak in a zoo which, after several thousand words of description, got up to its feet. When nobody could guess what song title it was, Broun told us triumphantly, "Mighty yak arose."

Is that really how you play charades? No matter, since the thing we learn from this story is that "Mighty Lak' a Rose" is a hugely popular song of the time. (It was written in 1901 by Frank Lebby Stanton and Ethelbert Nevin in then fashionable "negro dialect" form, and has been performed by scores of singers on record and film, including Paul Robeson, Frank Sinatra, Deanna Durbin and Nina Simone.) So far, so straightforward. Now we run into difficulties over the three Thomases.

First, you don't need me to tell you that mighty flier Lindbergh, perhaps the most celebrated American of all around this time, was called not Thomas but Charles. I can find no reference anywhere to a flier called Thomas Lindbergh, or any other kind of Thomas Lindbergh. The best I can come up with is a Lindbergh Bay, in St. Thomas, which is not a mighty flier but one of the Virgin Islands. (It was originally Mosquito Bay, but was given an upgrade in nomenclature when Lindy landed in a nearby field on a 1928 flight from Paris to the United States, supplying the islanders with the excuse they had been dreaming of to give the place a more attractive name to tourists than Mosquito Bay. According to the island's tourist board, the bay is "great for swimming and also a popular gathering place for locals who use the area for political rallies.") True, the location is sometimes hyphenated to "St. Thomas-Lindbergh" but I think you'll agree with me that the odds of any of this having anything to do with Groucho's comment are still slim enough to call into serious question the wisdom of my bothering to mention it at all. I just wanted you to see how committed I am to this thing.

Of course it's possible that Lindbergh was *so* popular, that simply giving him the wrong name was itself a kind of joke back then. On the other hand it's important to remember the extent to which the Brothers tinkered with the script before filming. What seems at first glance to be a vastly more comprehensible misquote—"Thomas Jefferson, mighty President, Thomas Edison, mighty inventor, and Thomashefsky, mighty lak' a rose"—often turns up in published sources: I suspect this may have been the originally scripted version, which Groucho rendered more meaningless for his own amusement in rehearsal. (Morrie Ryskind recalls in *The Marx Brothers Scrapbook* that Groucho "would get sick of saying the same lines. After he said a line three times he would try something [different] and if it turned out that it was OK we'd keep it in.")

Now then, to Thomashefsy, or as other sources would have it, Thomashevsky. There are almost as many Thomashevskys famous enough and contemporary with the remark as there are Hungerdungers. Oddly, there are three who are called not only Thomashevsky but Boris Thomashevsky. Two of them are Russian writers. The third is a former Ukrainian who came to America and became a pioneer of Yiddish theater, changing his name from Thomashevsky to Thomashefsky so it would sound more American. (The effect is uncanny, I'm sure you agree.) This, I suspect, is the man we are looking for. Further evidence is supplied in *The Groucho Letters,* where our hero discourses with T.S. Eliot on the subject of the latter's first name: "The name Tom fits many things. There was once a famous Jewish actor named Thomashevsky." (He is also mentioned, incidentally, in Mel Brooks's *The Twelve Chairs.*) Ah, but why partner his name with the song "Mighty Lak' a Rose"?

I thought you'd ask that. Perhaps he performed it sometimes? Or maybe it's more sheer Groucho nonsense along the lines of "'A Cup of Coffee, a Sandwich and You' from the opera *Aida.*" Either way, it's one or the other of the two, and my money's on both, though I'm not sure which.

19:52/20:42—"Your honor, I rest my case."

Old Hollywood trailers were very often compiled not from the master negative but from out-takes. Often, therefore, if you know a film really well, you can detect subtle differences in intonation and delivery in the trailers. With the Marx Brothers, this is especially apparent in the trailers for *Animal Crackers* and *Monkey Business.* (Most fascinatingly, the trailers for *Go West* and *The Big Store* feature Groucho lines not used in the film at all: "It's just like a movie!" and "I used to do this in vaudeville!" respectively.) This moment marks one of the more obvious differences between film and trailer: in the latter Groucho delivers the line quite differently and adds "right here!" after "I rest my case."

22:57/23:55—"How many Frenchmen can't be wrong?"

What sounds like a typically absurd Groucho riddle is actually a reference to a popular phrase, and the answer is fifty million. "Fifty million Frenchmen can't be wrong!" turns up all over, sometimes slightly rephrased: in advertising, in Mae West, in publicity for Chevalier, in the title of a smash hit Broadway revue by Cole Porter and starring Olsen and Johnson (filmed in 1931 with a script by Marx writer Al Boasberg). So far as I am aware it is as a song title, the song written in 1927 and directly inspiring the show, that it was first used, though perhaps the song title itself refers to an already extant phrase.

27:42/28:52—Joe Helton reads the paper

On board ship, the reformed gangster Joe Helton reads about himself and his daughter in the "late London edition" of the *Daily Sketch,* presumably suggesting that the voyage takes place between London and New York. ("The Marxes obviously knew the *Sketch* was considered a somewhat downmarket paper for its times, which is precisely why a rich-but-lowbrow gangster would be reading it," notes Glenn Mitchell.) The article on Helton is headed "MILLIONAIRE RACKETEER RETURNS TO AMERICA" and tells us that his daughter is a "recent graduate of continental finishing school." It's one of the more upbeat stories in this particular edition of the *Sketch,* much of the rest of which is given over to accounts of peculiar road accidents written as a string of odd, semi-incomprehensible headlines. On the left of the Helton story we find:

YOUNG GIRL TIED IN A WOOD
Her Story of Motor Ride After Road Smash
"HIT FROM BICYCLE"
Struggle to Loose Herself from Her Bonds

And on the right:

SAFELY SWINGS IN 700 FEET FALL
Amazing Escape When Car Hurtled Over Cliff
LANDED ON LEDGE
Somersault in Mid-Air Saves Motorist's Life

33:53/35:18—"A man who has licked his weight in wild caterpillars"

A joke that is funny in itself, that is to say in the inadequacy of the boast, but rendered additionally amusing by the addition of the word "wild," as if there was any other sort of caterpillar, by the general grotesqueness of the image conjured, and of course by the evocation of Captain Spaulding in *Animal Crackers* fainting at the sight of the caterpillar on his lapel.

34:32/35:59—"Keep out of my business!"

An unusual though subtle example of a retained flub, where Groucho forgets that Briggs says "Keep out of my business!" twice, and comes in too early with his line, "Your turn."

40:17/41:58—"You know who's on this boat? Maurice Chevalier, the movie actor!"

As well as the perfect choice of a well-known figure the Marxes could never by any reasonable estimation expect to get away with claiming to be—especially en masse—this is also, of course, a bit of extra publicity for a fellow Paramount contractee (not that he needed it:

his status at the studio is clearly shown in the previous year's *Paramount on Parade,* also known as "The Maurice Chevalier Show"). Paramount certainly get their publicity dollar's worth out of *Monkey Business:* as well as the reference to *It* (and, by implication, Clara Bow) we also have Groucho's line, "You're wrong girls, you're wrong; in the first place, Gary Cooper is much taller than I am." Something else I like about this is that it is *Zeppo* who swipes the passport, and therefore thinks that all four of them can avoid detection by pretending to be a world-famous Frenchman. ("You've got to sing one of Chevalier's song to get off this boat!") Anyone who thinks he wasn't really a proper Marx Brother might usefully consider the logic of that.

44:46/46:38—"Sure I'm a doctor. Where's the horse?"

One of those lines that coincidentally underlines the difference between the Paramount and MGM incarnations of the team. Here, Groucho leaps at the chance to impersonate a doctor as a possible aid to getting himself off the ship undetected (and with little concern for the patient, who has collapsed, while the crowd can be heard speculating that it might be heart failure) and still has time to slip in this self-incriminating joke. Contrast that with *A Day at the Races*, in which he really is a horse doctor pretending to be a physician, and spends most of the film cringing and creeping about in panic trying to keep his secret hidden. It is not a small difference: the two approaches to the situation are polar opposites. I'll take this Groucho, who recommends an ocean voyage to his stricken patient, then exits with the request that the crowd get close so he doesn't recover.

45:40/47:35—The fifth cast member named Marx

In this memorable sequence, the dapper, somewhat Roscoe W. Chandler–like gentleman we first see in long-shot waving his handkerchief at the approaching ship, and then in medium-shot, smiling broadly with his hand on some foxy dame's shoulder, is Sam Marx, a.k.a. Frenchie, the Brothers' father. It is often claimed, including by Groucho, that he is also to be glimpsed on board ship, though the evidence of the film itself would seem to contradict this. Nonetheless, this remains the only time that four Marx Brothers and one Marx Father appeared together.

46:25/48:22—The party

My guess is that this sequence was originally intended as a much more sizeable part of the film but was squeezed ever tighter as the shipboard portion swelled. The film is structured as three chunks: the ship, the party and the barn. The barn provides the finale, but the ship eats up the lion's share of the running time and almost all the best material. As a result the party scene seems a little redundant, and very rushed. The Marxes don't interact with each other at all, and hardly with the other guests. Chico does his piano routine; Harpo plays the harp, chases women and is repeatedly thrown out, while Groucho incessantly wanders into shot, says something funny and then wanders out again. There are some good laughs but no momentum at all because nothing ever connects: it's just a string of jokes and then, abruptly, the abduction that leads to Act 3. I can't imagine such an elaborate second act was conceived and staged—posh sets, plenty of music, dozens and dozens of extras—just because they needed somewhere for the girl to be kidnapped. It's reasonable to suppose that the original idea was to have them first fleeing and goading authority on the boat and then have them returned to their more accustomed milieu: tweaking the noses of high society at some swanky do. Unfortunately, by the time they get there there's simply no time for them to go to work in anything like the intended way, so what may well have been intended as *Animal Crackers Part Deux* ends up as a swift medley of quickie jokes, with scant opportunity for them to make any kind of sustained impact.

51:19/53:28—"Come, Kappellmeister, let the violas throb. My regiment leaves at dawn!"

According to Perelman, this now-stranded line originally segued into a parody of *The Merry Widow* (the enduringly popular 1905 operetta by Franz Lehár, Viktor Léon and Leo Stein). The ensuing sequence was vetoed by Groucho, however, on the grounds that it wouldn't mean anything to "the barber in Peru" (as in Peru, Indiana). Perelman appears to want us to read the story as an illustration of Groucho's philistinism (they seem to have had an oddly antagonistic relationship, founded in mutual respect) but, in fairness, it doesn't sound all that funny to me. Odd, too, to imagine Groucho of all people declining anything on the grounds that the reference point was too highbrow: perhaps he was just being polite and he didn't think it was all that funny either. "I hated the son of a bitch and he had a head as big as my desk" is Groucho's recollection in *The Marx Brothers Scrapbook,* but in an earlier time, their puckish mistrust of each other had more productive results. It was to an early Perelman volume that Groucho contributed the immortal publicity blurb: "From the moment I picked up your book until I laid it down I was convulsed with laughter. Some day I intend reading it." (Even better, perhaps, was George S. Kaufman's response to a later request to provide an appreciation of Perelman for a dust-jacket: "I appreciate S. J. Perelman— George S. Kaufman.") The exact nature, extent and value of Perelman's contribution to the film has been debated almost from the start: no question he was a witty man, but Groucho in particular rarely missed an opportunity to minimize his importance to the finished product. (It should be noted, however, that the structure of the film notably resembles that of the Brothers' old vaudeville sketch "Home Again," which had likewise begun on an ocean liner and ended at a swanky party. And as Louvish reminds us, of the assembled writers it was Perelman who had actually seen and reviewed it, back in 1915.)

53:03/55:16—"Oh, Emily!"

Oh, Emily indeed! Is there any chance at all this small speaking role was ever intended as a brief reappearance for Margaret Dumont? The actress we see, Charlotte Mineau, both looks and reacts like her, and sports a near-identical hairdo. Neither is she a nobody, indicating that (though unbilled, as most poor souls were in these films) the part was conceived as a small featured role. Mineau was a veteran of teens and twenties slapstick, and chalked up several appearances alongside Chaplin and Laurel & Hardy. She retired from the screen after an appearance in a Thelma Todd and ZaSu Pitts short in 1932, but lived until the age of ninety-three in 1979.

54:03/56:19—"You must have been married in rompers. Mighty pretty country around there."

A line with a definite echo—perhaps intended, perhaps not, but definite all the same— of Ring Lardner's celebrated theatrical parody *I Gaspiri—The Upholsterers:*

> FIRST STRANGER: Where was you born?
> SECOND STRANGER: Out of wedlock.
> FIRST STRANGER: That's a mighty pretty country around there.
> (*The curtain is lowered for seven days to denote the lapse of a week.*)

In a late sixties Dick Cavett interview, Groucho nominated Lardner as one of the most important writers of his century, while in a 1933 article for *Collier's* he called him "one of the wittiest men in America; certainly he is the most humorous." Sadly, Lardner died before the article was published. In *The Marx Brothers Scrapbook* Groucho claims that he once gave Lardner two bottles of whisky at the end of a prohibition era party, and woke the next morning to find him still there and completely unconscious, having drunk both during the night.

54:38/56:55—Weird lighter shot

From the unfathomable directorial decisions department: this lengthy scene, which has until now been played entirely in long- and medium-shot, suddenly plunges into a close-up of Groucho lighting his cigar so extreme that all we can see is his hand, the lighter and the tip of his cigar, with the composition so sharp we can clearly see the hair on his fingers. Then, a second later, we're back to normal. The best explanation I've been offered is that we need to see the lighter in close-up to get the joke that, once used, he then tosses it away as if it were a match. (I must confess, I missed this joke entirely.) But it's clearly identifiable as a lighter in the long shot as he brings it up to his face, even on the small TV screen for which it was never intended, and we hear it loudly land afterwards. If that *was* the purpose of the close-up, it's certainly overkill.

54:45/57:02—Harpo chases a blonde girl across the lawn on a bicycle with an enormous flower sticking out of the front of it

A strange and delightful bit, but one which comes absolutely from nowhere. It's filmed in the dusk, whereas the scene had begun in darkness. Harpo and Chico had arrived at the house by car: this is our first and only glimpse of the bicycle. The fleeing girl, though distinctively dressed in striped culottes, doesn't seem to be around elsewhere in the film either. Most intriguing of all, however, is the fact that, with the exception of stock-shots of the ship (and the Frenchie shot, presumably taken on the lot just outside a studio building), these five seconds of film represent the only location photography in the entire movie.

57:07/59:30—The disgruntled dancing partner

This is my very cautious nomination for Cyril Ring's walk-on role (see *The Cocoanuts,* 7:03). There's something about his map that's usually unmistakable, but I've never been able to identify him with certainty in this one. While the film abounds with potential candidates, none strikes me as *unquestionably* our man. He is supposedly in the party scene, but there are so many briefly glimpsed men here with his distinctive look it's almost as if they've been invited to a dress-as-Cyril Ring party.

58:27/60:46—"No, you're wrong, girls, you're wrong. In the first place, Gary Cooper is much taller than I am."

This popular Groucho line is actually carried over from the Broadway version of *The Cocoanuts,* which—given that it was written in 1925—has Groucho supposedly mistaken for Valentino rather than Cooper.

61:00/63:33—Harpo begins to play

Look at the genuinely happy faces of the orchestra as Harpo launches into yet another rendition of "I'm Daffy Over You." Clearly, they find him every bit as enchanting as we do.

63:38/66:18—The old barn

By common consent, this is one of their weaker finales. Truth is there *are* enough good laughs here to save the day: Groucho's inane commentary (a joke repeated in *At the Circus*), "The only game in the stable," "125th Street, 125th Street and 125th Street" ... but clearly, this is a film that has run its course and the only thing now is to wrap it all up as quickly as possible, which it does. And for the first and last time, Zeppo gets the girl, having scratched Elsie in the previous movie.

4

Horse Feathers (1932)

"As I look out over your eager faces, I can readily understand why this college is flat on its back. The last college I presided over, things were slightly different. I was flat on my back. Things kept going from bad to worse, but we all put our shoulders to the wheel, and it wasn't long before I was flat on my back again."
—Professor Quincy Adams Wagstaff (Groucho Marx)

One point easily overlooked about the three Hollywood Paramount films is that they are all to a greater or lesser extent parodies. *Monkey Business* distracts us with the wildness of its shipboard scenes from the fact that it is first a pastiche of the argot and iconography of modish gangster movies. *Duck Soup* is a double parody: of Ruritanian fantasies and the Depression-era "dictator craze" (of which more when we get there.) And *Horse Feathers* spoofs the popular college pictures that Paramount in particular produced in the most extraordinary profusion at the time—especially extraordinary given how almost completely they have been forgotten.

Imagine if the western genre had disappeared. Nobody paid it the least interest anymore, they stopped making any in, say, 1940, and it thereafter slowly passed into the slough of film pre-history. *But* because people still revived the Marx Brothers, *Go West* still existed. Suddenly that film would appear to have no relation to cinema as such, and would just seem like the result of someone having the strange, potentially interesting idea of putting them in a different time period. All the things in it that are mere variations on generic conventions would seem like ideas specific to that production. We might even start thinking it was taking satirical swipes at that era and its mores.... Well, that's sort of what's happened to *Horse Feathers*, now that college films no longer operate as a sub-genre all their own, with all that status implies in terms of standardised ingredients and the supposition of recognition.

These college pictures might make a stab at being anything from serious drama to murder mystery, but the majority were pure froth, using the campus setting as a kind of readymade backdrop for various star attractions to do their thing within a simple, formulaic plot. That they were knowingly formulaic is hinted by the titles: *College Humor, College Rhythm, College Swing, College Scandal*, and so on. You don't need to have seen any of these movies to enjoy *Horse Feathers*—clearly—but watch a few of them and you'll see element after element of the Marx movie being played out: the new students trying to fit in, the lecture scene, the tension between tradition and modernity, the rival college, the vital football game, skilled football players being enrolled as fake students, the duplicitous, sexually mature woman on campus diverting a promising student into irresponsibility, even the arrival of a new, seemingly inappropriate president (a woman, of all things, in 1929's *Sweetie*), who has to win over the fuddy duddy staff and mistrustful student body. Horse Feathers is a sarcastic take-off of all these conventions. Further, this strikes me not just as an inspired decision that happens to pay off, but the calculated solution to a clear problem: *what to do with the team from now on*.

The difficulty lies in locating them as characters in a Hollywood narrative. There was no background of realism in *Cocoanuts* or *Animal Crackers*; they were just revues with comic agitators inserted without the need for verisimilitude on any level at all, as if monkeys were loosed in a wedding service with no better explanation than that the results might be worth seeing. Hollywood movies lacked Broadway's license to evoke without cause, and it was long-established that Hollywood comedians worked their magic against a background of realism (often keenly so, against a background of observed social-realism). Chaplin or Keaton or Laurel and Hardy may be enigmas, outsiders or incompetents, but they can still pass as normal in a world of others. The Marxes didn't have this option and so represented a challenge to scenario writers.

Monkey Business had to some degree carefully dodged the whole issue, making them unknown quantities who come and go like spirits, utilising the idea of their being literally on the run as the means to facilitate a series of staccato entrances and exits. First emerging from barrels and finally disappearing in straw, they are visitations from a world of folklore. Tellingly, these "characters" all have their own names—Groucho, Harpo, Chico and Zeppo— as if to underline that narrative integration has been consciously fudged. But this would not be an option forever: soon enough, some sort of new cinematic convention would have to be established to integrate them meaningfully into settings and plots, and avoid making the very presence of the star turns impossible in their own films. The idea hit on was to explore the comic potential of *using* that impossibility as the premise, inserting them into extant generic situations as absurd replacements for the various stock functionaries we should be expecting to find there.

All we knew for sure about Spaulding was that he was a house guest: he may not have really been an explorer: he might have been just the fraud he seemed to be. But this man Wagstaff really is the new President of the college, and so it *should* be perfectly reasonable for us to wonder why. How come we don't, then, other than with tongue in cheek? Our present day answers to that question—because there's no rhyme or reason in a Marx Brothers film; because he can be anything he wants because he's Groucho—are fair enough but, I'm suggesting, not quite what's really going on here. I suspect the decision taken was not so much *"he can be anything"* as the rather subtler and more considered *"wouldn't it be funny specifically if he was the new President..."* And funny not just because it is an intrinsically funny idea, but because it would be instantly understandable as a parody of American popular culture. A specific point of reference seems to have been the 1927 film *The College Widow* (of which more in the guide at 15:21), and that the student led astray should be Zeppo— cast to our eyes beyond reason as Groucho's son—might be to deliberately spoof the often plainly overage juvenile leads of the other college pictures. (He's in his twelfth year as a freshman, a joke that was made central in early ads and publicity.)

The gradual fading from memory of these cross-cultural reference points is a process

Harpo contemplates mortality on the set of *Horse Feathers*.

from which myths and legends can emerge, precarious but cocksure, on illusory supports. Thus the whole notion of the Marx Brothers as social critics. *Animal Crackers* was a comic assault on society, in the strictly limited sense of "high society," but there is nothing truly iconoclastic in this film's take on American education: its mockery is aimed not at the institutional but, once removed, at the cultural. Folks who proclaim this a satire on the American college system are like those who think *Duck Soup* is an anti-war satire (among other things:

ubiquitous). The irony here is that it was just such a reading that inspired and fuelled the campus revival of the late sixties and early seventies that, if nothing else (and I *am* struggling to qualify that "if" with any other benefit), helped keep the team in the public consciousness right at the time when it seemed possible they might be about to slip away into the cinematic night. I'll thank it here for *that*.

When realism does intrude here, it is at the margins. *Monkey Business* hinted at the Depression but held on by its fingernails to the social strata in which the first two pictures were set, albeit with *illicit* wealth now providing the canapés and paying the band at the big society function. Here, for the first time, the times intrude, not pointedly, but simply because how could they not, now? A forgotten man tells Harpo he wants a cup of coffee: ever obliging, Harpo produces a steaming cup, with saucer, from his pocket. But there's two layers to this: part of the joke is that the guy's asking Harpo in the first place. There's plenty of people in this street set, any one of which would surely seem a safer bet. This is not the silk-hatted "Professor," present legitimately at Rittenhouse Manor. This is a Harpo that has come substantially down in the world: a dog catcher, with clothes so tattered and shredded they seem only a stitch away from complete disintegration. But such hints aside, what we have here is still basically fantasy—sharp indeed as parody, but with no real desire to mean anything outside the movie house, even by extrapolation. (Actually, the Marxes and the Depression collided most overtly not onscreen but in the advertising. Ads for *Monkey Business* hailed it "a depression-chaser," promising it would "banish your cares, even if there's a regiment of bailiffs around the corner." Typical of the *Horse Feathers* reviews is one in the *Evening Independent* that calls it "a temporary cure for depression blues," adding: "No one could remember such a thing as hard times... Antics of the four Marx brothers drive away all thoughts of business worries.")

The film's greatest heresy is reserved for the cinematic institution of the vital, nail-biting football match finale. Where Harold Lloyd in *The Freshman* had the tact to make sure his climax remained authentically nail-biting, the Marxes mock audience engagement with an ending in which Harpo dumps ball after ball out of a horse-drawn garbage truck. All of this would have had obvious resonance to movie audiences at the time, and of a more misleading sort to would-be undergraduate anarchists in 1970.

They'd have had even more fun with it had it still come with its original intended ending, in which the college is burned down while the brothers play cards. It got as far as being shot, and a few stills survive, as does one in which Groucho appears to be ironing Zeppo, for reasons I imagine it would be futile to guess. But the *Horse Feathers* available to us now is lacking far more than these intended omissions. The scene that now begins with the cup of coffee gag originally had several preceding bits involving Harpo luring dogs with fake lampposts. And the later scene in which all four brothers, *and* David Landau, converge on Thelma's room to make love to her at the same time originally went on longer, with more business between Thelma and Harpo. Not only is it not certain why these moments have been excised, it is not even certain when. For a long time it was thought they were cut for TV, but this apparently now seems not to have been the case. Allen Eyles has noted the odd coincidence that the missing parts all seem to involve Harpo, and speculated they may have been removed for some specific compilation or tribute. (They are also the two moments singled out as the film's best in more than one contemporary review: an odd coincidence, but *presumably* no more than one?) That there were people who chopped bits out and threw them away merely to make the film shorter is to suggest simple barbarism, but may yet be the most likely solution (and I wish they were in it). Censorship hardly seems plausible, and despite frequent claims to the contrary, censorship cannot *possibly* account for the spliced and jump-cut jigsaw that remains of what we *do* still have of Thelma's boudoir scene. The one really censorable line ("I'm the plumber, I'm just hanging round in case something goes wrong with her pipes") is ironically intact: the damage and decomposition that has blighted the rest is the result not of opprobrium but callous indifference. There may be no other major movie officially released on DVD in such inadequate condition, simply because so far as anyone knows, there is no other option. This is what posterity has left us, of a film so touchably recent that my grandfather could have seen it on release, but which we may never see again in anything but a mutilated form. (Needless to say, until such a miracle occurs, the timecoding in the guide below refers to the currently circulating edition.)

The confidence of the film reflects that of its stars and writers both. *Monkey Business* had done very nicely, so all Paramount demanded was more of the same: they recalled Mankiewicz, they recalled McLeod, and they recalled Johnstone and Perelman. The real new *masterstroke* was the return of Bert Kalmar and Harry Ruby, whose songs had done so much for *Animal Crackers*, not merely as songwriters this time but as screenwriters too.

Apportioning individual responsibility for the various elements of these films is always, ultimately, a guessing game, especially as Sheekman and the usual cartload of anonymous gag men were also brought back to add seasoning. Adamson establishes a definite group genesis for the basics, with Kalmar, Ruby, Perelman, Johnstone, Mankiewicz and the Marxes all banging their heads against the furniture and each other in New York, before taking off for Hollywood—significantly without Perelman—where they split into parallel outfits. While Johnstone did work with Harpo on visual gags, it appears that the studio considered his contributions to be of the Sheekman variety, and originally intended to withhold screen credit. Mitchell mentions a piece from *Hollywood Reporter* claiming Johnstone sued for onscreen recognition, citing the fact that his work had been further augmented with lines from *I'll Say She Is* (one such being "the Lord alps those that alp themselves").

It's always unwise to rely too much on the order in which the writers are listed in the credits, or even which of the known writers do or do not get credited at all. It wasn't until 1933 that the Screen Writers' Guild was formed, specifically to address such anomalies and potential abuses. (As Philip Dunne told Barry Norman in his book *Talking Pictures*, "the big issue was control of screen credits more than anything else. The credits were then allocated by the studios and, of course, they went to studio favourites ... that was the most important of all the issues.") Nonetheless, most accounts agree on Kalmar and Ruby doing the really important work on the film. Adamson quotes Ruby taking responsibility for the basic ideas of Groucho as a college professor who "goes against all the rules" and Harpo as a dog catcher, as well as the cup of coffee joke and "I'd horsewhip you if I had a horse", a line that seems to many Perelman's by default. And that makes Bert and Harry into proper heroes, because don't forget—they wrote all those songs, too.

Funny writers are funny writers: if they were funny once, chances are they'll be funny again. But songwriting genius is a fickler maid: all too often coy with her favors, especially if she went all the way on the first date. Difficult to imagine being in the position of the guys

The president gets his priorities in order as Huxley burns: Zeppo (third from right) Groucho (second from right) and Thelma Todd (far right) in a moment from the abandoned original climax to *Horse Feathers*.

who wrote "Hooray for Captain Spaulding" and "Hello, I Must Be Going," to say nothing of "Why Am I So Romantic?," being given the instruction: "hey, let's have a couple more like that!" and not only bothering to return the call in the first place, but actually turning in "Whatever It Is, I'm Against It" and "I Always Get My Man," to say nothing of "Ev'ryone Says I Love You." But that's merely to say it's difficult to imagine being Kalmar and Ruby, because that's exactly what they did. This is what separates me and you from Bert Kalmar and Harry Ruby. (That and at least eighty rotten years.)

The net result was a film that does the seemingly impossible: takes *Monkey Business* as its template, and very slightly improves on perfection. It is a joyous thing from the first second, when that cartoon horse comes whinnying out of the title in perfect synchronisation with the theme, until the finale, when the film gives up and exits without warning, simply because its allotted running time is up and people need to get the last tram home. It could have gone on three times as long, and the abiding message it leaves us with is: "and don't you forget that!" *Horse Feathers* does not *end*, as such, the way normal films do; it *stops* merely, as if the janitor has turned up and started putting the lights out. And if you've stopped laughing for a minute or two during the whole 70 or so minutes it takes to happen, that was probably only to bathe in the beauty of Harpo's harp playing, or damn to hell the fates that denied Thelma Todd a happy old age of gin and reminiscing. The rest of the time, I trust, you were watching comic genius pass by as relentlessly as one city becomes another from the window of a long-distance train.

So let us away to Huxley College. It's time to cut the watermelon open.

2:27 (NTSC)/2:34 (PAL)—"That's the spirit—1776!"

No American will need this joke explained, but to Europeans it may be worth pointing out that the "spirit of '76" is the spirit of American pride relating to the signing of the Declaration of Independence. The same joke turns up in the original Broadway version of *The Cocoanuts*, wherein Groucho responds to Margaret Dumont's request for a pre-war vintage champagne with: "What war? Civil? Revolutionary? Oh, you want the spirits of seventy-six." Variations on the joke occur elsewhere; one is in the 1936 Three Stooges short *Disorder in the Court*, in which, believe it or not, it is done rather more subtly than here.

2:48/2:56—"Hello, old-timer!"

This sweet introduction for Zeppo has for some reason been messed about with in the editing, so that this moment, obviously intended to follow the line "Where is my son?" has been moved to follow the later "would you mind getting up so that I can see the son rise?" Thus Zeppo appears to ignore a greeting, get up, be instantaneously sitting down again, then acknowledge the father he has already acknowledged as if for the first time by responding to the initial greeting as if it had just been made. I can only imagine that they briefly let Harpo into the editing room.

4:50/5:03—The Professors dance

According to the *Brooklyn Daily Eagle* of March 31, 1932, this sequence was choreographed by "Harold Hecht, young Broadway ballet master" and was "one of the strangest assignments ever given a dance director." The *Schenectady Gazette* picks up the story and gallops with it on August 17, noting that the combined age of the twenty actors playing the professors is 1,257 years: "This averages approximately 63 years to the actor, yet all of them execute dance steps in the comedy. The oldest of the lot is 77." Hecht, incidentally, never returned to the world of ballet. After a few years of dance direction he became a producer, later notable for a number of films he made as an independent in collaboration with their star, Burt Lancaster.

4:59/5:12—"No matter if he's in Peru, Paducah or Japan...."

I quote this line not because it needs explanation, but merely on the off-chance that, like me, you first heard it at the age of ten and took it to be "no matter if he's imferoofadoofer or Japan," and still, despite a further thirteen years of education, retain a pair of ears that stubbornly insist on hearing it that way. If so, I'm afraid I've got some bad news for you.

5:05/5:18—Huh?

Two completely indecipherable lines of the song, delivered by the student chorus. No attempt is made to reconstruct them on the (generally appalling) DVD subtitles, and—to these ears at least—not one word could be discerned, until an online search among the similarly troubled yielded this highly satisfactory guess: "Oh what a wiz this fellow is, a will like his is rare / For he's a very square American."

5:11/5:24—"I soon dispose of all of those who put me on the pan / Like Shakespeare said to Nathan Hale, I always get my man"

To be "on the pan" is to receive censure: for more, see *Animal Crackers* (56:58). The rest is a nice bit of historical mangling; Shakespeare obviously said nothing to Nathan Hale, who was born two centuries later.

7:30/7:49—"But a college needs something else besides education"

Notice how, as Zeppo is delivering this line, Groucho removes his mortar board and puts it behind his back. Whereupon he presumably drops it on the floor, as it is never seen again and in a moment we will see that his hand is now empty.

8:45/9:07—Mullen and McCarthy

The two footballers Groucho intends to recruit to the Huxley team, snapped up instead by dear old Darwin, were both played by professional athletes turned actors. James Pierce (Mullen) had been a star player for Indiana University and later a coach. He played Tarzan on film and radio, and lots of cops. He is one of many Marx names colliding in the 1937 Ritz Brothers film *Life Begins in College* in which he plays, of all things, a football coach. Also showing up on this campus are director William A. Seiter (the year before *Room Service*); future *Big Store* crooner Tony Martin; Arthur Sheekman's wife, Gloria Stuart; and none other than McCarthy himself, Nat Pendleton. Pendleton was a former Olympic wrestler turned Hollywood tough guy, who also plays Goliath, the villainous strong man in a spare Harpo wig, in *At the Circus,* making him another member of the highly select "two speaking roles club" in the extended Marx film family. He also appeared in a few other college pictures, had a recurring role in the *Dr. Kildare* series, and essayed one of Hollywood comedy's definitive bullying sergeants in Abbott and Costello's *Buck Privates,* a role he pleasingly reprised in the wistful post-war sequel *Buck Privates Come Home.* He died in 1967, from too many muscles.

9:01/9:24—"Here's to dear old Darwin"

My own personal toast of preference whenever called upon to raise a glass in company: it works whether its source is known or, just as well, if taken to be a reference to the man rather than the college. I spent my youth assuming that the real-life Darwin and Huxley were rivals, simply because the colleges were. Quite the surprise to eventually learn that, on the contrary, they were colleagues, indeed Huxley (Thomas Henry Huxley, nicknamed "Darwin's bulldog") was the principal proponent and public face of Darwin's work. I kept expecting a last-minute twist as I read their biographies, where the once-devoted acolyte turns on his old master. Such is the power of the Marx Brothers.

9:13/9:37—Baravelli, the bootlegger

Chico's character is introduced to the delightful accompaniment of a speakeasy pianola version of his theme song, "I'm Daffy Over You." This and later pianola tunes heard in the film's speakeasy scenes reappear in a number of contemporaneous Paramount movies with bar-room or speakeasy settings. The tune heard at **14:04/14:40** is "You're the One I Crave," sung by Miriam Hopkins in a really sexy nightclub sequence in the previous year's Paramount film *24 Hours,* also starring *The Cocoanuts'* femme fatale Kay Francis, and previewed alongside *Monkey Business* in *The House That Shadows Built* (1931, see *Monkey Business,* 9:00).

Speakeasies were concealed drinking establishments, sometimes large clubs with live music, where alcoholic beverages could be illicitly sold and consumed in defiance of the Prohibition laws in force between 1920 and 1933. The film is surprisingly frivolous about bootlegging: given that the law was still in force when the film was made, the scenes of Chico pouring the same liquid into different bottles and Groucho's clear familiarity with speakeasy etiquette establish both as cheerful lawbreakers in a manner that would have been problematic in the Production Code era. Ironically, by the time the Code was enforced and the film came up for reissue, Prohibition itself was history. Had it not been, the film would probably have been deemed unreleasable. The film's levity over the matter here is therefore an often-missed but very significant aspect of the film's status as pre–Code.

The other odd thing, though, is how little is made of the bootlegging issue once introduced: as soon as Chico and Harpo are recruited for the team it is entirely forgotten. Given that bootlegging and speakeasy scenes were elements of the controversial gangster films of the era, it's possible that these moments are remnants of a very different, now-forgotten first idea. The studio publicity material released to newspapers included the claim, widely printed in reviews, that Chico "takes cakes of ice, bores holes in them, and then conceals bottles of rye, scotch and gin in the holes." Presumably cut from the script at a relatively late stage, this would make his function as iceman an overt front for his bootlegging, something that is no longer made at all clear in the film. According to Groucho's grandson Andy Marx, Paramount had been so encouraged by the success of *Monkey Business* that they initially considered a direct sequel, but the Lindbergh baby kidnapping of 1932 soured them on the idea of trivializing gangsters. It's possible that the bootlegging scenes that now seem so peripheral here are but the ghost of something that was originally much more substantial. This is hinted at—albeit very vaguely—by Nat Perrin in *The Marx Brothers Scrapbook,* who remembered the first, completely unused draft of *Monkey Business* being "about prohibition and bootleggers." Though the supporting characters of the film are obviously gangsters, no mention is made explicitly of bootlegging or prohibition, so it is possible this material served as the initial impetus for *Horse Feathers.* (Also in the *Scrapbook,* Groucho claims that he used to smuggle bottles of alcohol into America from Canada in the clothes of his then-baby son, Arthur.)

10:04/10:30—"'Swordfish' is the password"

Entrance to a speakeasy was dependent upon knowing the password, which must be delivered to the person standing guard at the door. "Swordfish," the password here (which Harpo elaborately mimes with unlikely props), has since been used in many dozens of other films, TV shows, books and computer games, including *Scooby Doo, Mad Men, The Muppets,* and *Star Trek.* It also directly inspired the title of the movie *Swordfish* (2001), some sort of thriller or something.

10:50/11:18—"I'd walk a mile for a calomel."

Triple confusion here between calomel (another name for mercurous chloride, used as a laxative, disinfectant and treatment for syphilis until the early 20th century, and what Baravelli takes for a haddock), caramel ("you mean chocolate calomel"), and a Camel—the brand of cigarette whose advertising slogan Groucho is paraphrasing.

11:37/12:07—"I'd like to get a cup of coffee."

A celebrated joke, as well as tacit acknowledgment that the times they have a-changed: Mrs. Rittenhouse's parties seem a world away now. As Harpo wrote in his autobiography: "Life would never be, ever again, all fun and games." The joke is so funny it's easy not to notice that it can't have been all that easy to engineer. The steam is presumably dry ice, and the cup not really hot, but still, note how Harpo carefully holds his coat over it as he walks into shot (either to keep it in position or to prevent any steam escaping prematurely), and also the hard horizontal support that remains in his pocket when he takes it out. There may also have been some technical assistance with the breeze to emphasize the steam: note how once the guy is holding the cup the steam suddenly blows out straight to the left as if unnaturally compelled.

15:07/15:45—Theresa Harris

The very and variedly talented Harris appeared in nearly ninety films, predominantly as a maid and often in uncredited blink or miss them roles like this one. In one of her more substantial appearances, alongside Barbara Stanwyck in 1933's *Baby Face,* she plays a character called Chico.

15:21/16:00—The College Widow

For years I wondered what a college widow was, and nobody seemed to know. (Louvish freely admits that he doesn't.) It's actually quite simple: she's a heartbreaker, a man-eater, a sub-species of black widow. The girl who toys with the affections of men, especially the year's new intake of freshmen, then discards them when a better prospect appears. Every college has one, it seems. There is also a sexual connotation, of course. A college widow in this sense is desirable enough to be hugely sought after but capable only of short-term, frivolous relationships; she puts it about for her own gain, and she's not into commitment. Notwithstanding its present-day obscurity, in America in the twenties and early thirties the term was used widely in books, plays and films. (A college widow stood for something in those days.) The term seems to date from the long-running 1904 stage comedy of that name by George Ade: it appears Ade coined the term himself. It was filmed in 1915, 1927, as *Maybe It's Love* in 1930 and as *Freshman Love* in 1936. (The college widow of *Maybe It's Love* was played by Joan Bennett, who at the time of production was living next door to Chico and his family in Malibu.) The 1927 version (directed by Archie Mayo, future director of *A Night in Casablanca*) seems to have been a direct source of inspiration to *Horse Feathers*. The plot features two rival colleges, Atwater and Stanley, about to play each other in a vital football match. The heroine is the daughter of Atwater's president, and on his instruction she seduces the star players of the Stanley team so as to recruit them for Atwater! The film not only has the big game climax in common with *Horse Feathers* but also, less expectedly, a scene in which the college widow deliberately falls out of a canoe to secure the attentions of one of her targets.

15:50/16:30—Herbert Marx says I love you

One of the most charming aspects of the film is the way in which all four Brothers are given their own interpretation of Kalmar and Ruby's splendid song "Ev'ryone Says I Love You." Zeppo gets the first crack at it, and it's no surprise that his is the straightest version. But it's a delightful number, and he performs it most endearingly, while buttering toast and feeding it to Thelma.

The song proved a popular hit in 1932, with a version recorded by Isham Jones & His Orchestra, featuring vocals by Eddie Stone, rising to #10 on the charts in America that year. Another version with a different lyric ("How Do You Do?") turns up in the Fleischer/Paramount Betty Boop cartoon *Betty in Blunderland* (1934). It also appears as incidental music in a Paramount *Hollywood on Parade* short also from 1932, danced to by puppets manipulated by Bob Bromley's Famous Olivera Puppeteers. (Bromley is often credited with being the first man to introduce "cabaret puppetry," in which the puppeteer is visible to the audience, was the first puppeteer to appear on BBC television, and created the first puppet stripper, which he presented at the Folies Bergère among other venues.) More recently it has served the title of Woody Allen's Marx-reference–suffused musical. Incidentally, the line "the tiger in the jungle and the monk in the zoo" does not refer to some now forgotten practice of caging monks in zoological gardens, but rather to the equally forgotten popular currency of "monk" as a synonym for a "monkey," as in the famous "Sherlocko the Monk" cartoon strip that originally inspired the Brothers' professional names, and the song "Aba Daba Honeymoon" ("Aba daba daba daba daba daba dab, said the chimpie to the monk"). Lastly, treat with extreme caution any claims you may encounter that the singing voice we hear is not Zeppo's own; suffice to say there is no evidence for this and no good reason to suppose it.

16:47/17:29—Arthur Marx says I love you

Or whistles it, rather. Alone among the four, Harpo gets two shots at the number. This first, whistling version, is dedicated not to Thelma but to a horse, recalling Margaret Irving's line in *Animal Crackers:* "You love a *horse*?" He later plays it on the harp (at **38:15/39:51**), while Thelma, the college widow, watches from an upstairs window. Arthur is lost in music, Thelma smiles, is beautiful, and all is right with the world.

17:42/18:27—Ben Taggart

The bulky actor, who played dozens of usually uncredited thugs and dumb cops, seen here harassing Harpo in the street, is also the rather more refined ship's captain in *Monkey Business* and Mr. Lee, the theatrical agent, in that film's accompanying *I'll Say She Is*–derived promo. If the latter counts as a Marx Brothers film, this propels him into the very select company of Margaret Dumont and Sig Rumann, with three or more speaking roles in a Marx movie.

19:26/20:15—Cooling heels and waxing wroth

The poor actress tasked with delivering these two utterly thankless feedlines to Groucho deserves special mention here for her heroic, unbilled devotion to the cause of groanworthy puns. (In shameful fact, the entire cast, with the exception of the Brothers, Thelma and villain David Landau, are uncredited.) Her name is Sheila Bromley, and she kept busy in the industry in walk-ons and bits well into the TV era. She died in 2003. Is she any relation to Bob Bromley, of stripping puppet fame, I wonder?

As for the term "waxing wroth," it is an old English expression; "waxing" meaning "growing" or "becoming"—as in "waxing poetic"—and "wroth" meaning "wrathful" or "majorly bummed out." The phrase turns up in Edmund Spenser's *Mutabilitie* ("Thereat Jove wexed wroth") and reappears in Joyce's *Ulysses,* among other works. Its appearance in *Horse Feathers,* however, is the only time it ever got a laugh.

21:05/21:58—"looks like a tongue war!"

A pun on "tong war," the popular journalistic term for eruptions of sometimes-murderous gang rivalry between competing factions of Chinese immigrants in late–19th and early–20th-century America. Tong wars and talk of tong wars featured frequently in American films of the twenties and thirties.

21:38/22:33—"There's your coat...."

I always thought the garment that Groucho hands Chico here—a large, shapeless fur coat—was meant to be silly, the moment a mere gesture of Marxian eccentricity. In fact, it is another element of the film instantly recognizable to any fans of the college pictures, or for that matter to any student of a real college at or around this time: in the manner of John

Held's iconic illustrations, "Galoshes and raccoon coats were indispensable to every male undergraduate wardrobe," writes Corey Feld in *The Time of Laughter*. Hence Chico's coat, and hence the galoshes Groucho keeps taking off and putting back on again. The fad was immortalized in song in 1928 by George Olsen and His Music, under the title "Doin' the Raccoon" ("Buy a coat and try it, I'll bet you'll be a riot").

22:32/23:29—Robert Greig

The biology professor with the bushy stuck-on beard (later stolen from him and worn, in the manner of Roscoe Chandler's birthmark, by Harpo) is this delightful Australian actor, who also plays Hives, Mrs. Rittenhouse's butler in *Animal Crackers*. But here's a trivia question for you: what is this character's name? He doesn't have one, you scream. Well according to the credits, which don't even bother to acknowledge Greig at all, you're right. But according to the studio's press releases, used as the basis for many contemporary reviews and based presumably on early scripts, he's called Professor Hornswoggle. (To "hornswoggle" is a 19th-century American slang term meaning "to deceive.") *Photoplay* spells it "Hornsvogel." One such review (embedded firmly in the *Tuscaloosa News* of September 11, 1932) also cites a line not to be found in the film we now have—Groucho to Greig: "You were crazy to break up a mattress for a thing like that!" Greig expressed high praise for the brothers—and made some decidedly tall claims on their behalf—in a curious interview published during the shooting of *Animal Crackers*:

> Each has a well-disciplined and active mind. Of course everyone knows that all are talented musicians. Groucho is rated one of the best guitar players in America and he also performs on piano, mandolin and harp. Harpo gets his name from playing the harp, but he is good on piano, flute and trombone. The distinguished pianist Arthur Shattuck heard Harpo play the piano and declared he was potentially a master of first rank. Chico on the stage plays the piano with the technique of a caricaturist. But he can play it like an artist too, and he is the master of cornet, zither and violin. Zeppo performs on the saxophone, piano, cello and flute. Each also is a voluminous reader and has a passion for serious drama. The latter taste is most pronounced in Chico, who, since his return to New York a few weeks ago after the road tour of *Animal Crackers* has seen every important show on Broadway. Strangely enough, he has avoided the musical comedies, explaining that he does not want to hear the gags for fear he might unconsciously plagiarize them. I have been on the stage in every country where the English language is spoken, among them India, China, Java, Burma, South Africa, England, America and my native Australia. But nowhere had I had a more enjoyable time than when working in a Marx Brothers show.

22:51/23:49—"Ten cents a dunce"

A straightforward pun on the popular song "Ten Cents a Dance," which details with unsentimental realism the lot of the Depression-era taxi dancer. (Taxi-dancing figures frequently in early thirties movies, a nice example being the Thelma Todd–ZaSu Pitts short *Asleep in the Feet*.) The song was sung most popularly by the magnificent Ruth Etting, and the year before *Horse Feathers* had inspired a movie of the same name, directed by Lionel Barrymore, starring Barbara Stanwyck and co-written by occasional Marx scribe Jo Swerling.

**23:16/24:15—"What do you think of that slide?"
"Well I think he was safe at second but it was very close."**

A sporting reference, and probably a transparently clear one to any American readers. Europeans be advised, however, that we are now in the mysterious world of baseball. The reference to the slide (delivered in meaningless response to the Professor's inquiry about his microscope slide) evokes the baseball tactic whereby a player drops to the ground and slides to the base he is approaching. "Safe at second," of course, refers to second base (the position What plays).

25:06/26:09—"The Alps are a very simple people, living on a diet of rice and old shoes."

I love this joke because it is such a throwaway bit of pure Groucho nonsense. It cannot possibly be scripted, and it means nothing to the audience, because it is only later that we get a good close-up of what he's talking about, by which time the joke is forgotten. It surely just occurred to him on set, when confronted with the anatomical chart to which he is referring. The "rice" is an illustration of coiled intestines; the "old shoes" are two internal organs which look—very, very vaguely—like a pair of extremely battered old shoes. A great comedian amusing himself is a wonder to behold.

26:37/27:44—"According to Von Steinmetz, the eminent physiologist, there is ever-present a group of white phagocytes...."

A sentence which means nothing at all the way Groucho delivers it, devoid of all context (ever-present where?), suggesting that it may have been plucked at random from a genuine text book that therefore remains to be discovered by dedicated Marx fans with access to a good university library. Greig's own lecture also consists of largely unlinked statements, further suggesting that both men might be randomly reading from genuine books: there is a shot of the cover of the one Greig refers to at **23:30/24:29**, but it looks to me like a mock-up. Phagocytes are cells that ingest harmful foreign particles and are vital to the immune system. They were first identified by Russian zoologist Ilya Ilyich Mechinov, and named by his colleague Carl Friedrich Claus, neither of whom, sadly, lived to see their work immortalized in this film. The eminent Von Steinmetz, to whom Groucho refers, is a bit of a mystery, however: the only eminent Von Steinmetz I have been able to track down was not a physiologist but a German general in the Napoleonic wars. So this is likely to remain a mystery until that textbook turns up!

30:29/31:46—"Be a lamp in the window for my wandering boy."

A confusing reference. I found a cartoon in the *Montreal Gazette* from 1939 showing a woman with "Liberal Party" written on her apron, holding a lamp at her window, which is emitting a light labeled "peace efforts." On the wall is a portrait labeled "Mitch," which must be Mitchell Hepburn, then premier of Ontario. The cartoon is captioned, "A Lamp in the Window for Her Wandering Boy." So this *must* be a well-known phrase, but it seems to have passed from use and taken its origins with it. Most likely it's a recollection of a popular hymn called "Place a Lamp in the Window," which features the following lines:

> Place a lamp in the window
> Some poor boy may discover,
> Far away from his mother,
> Light that a safeguard will be.

No "wandering" there, but the second verse begins, "Oh, how many that wander down where the tempter is leading," so it is possible that these various pieces became conflated into the spoken expression.

32:53/34:16—Leonard Marx says I love you

Chico's version of the song is the most upbeat, with room found for his own particular brand of verbal confusion. (The rooster "when he hollers" says not "cock-a-doodle-doo" but "cock-a-doodly-doodly-doo.") Especially worthy of note is another variation on the historical flexibility that enabled Shakespeare to say, "I always get my man" to Nathan Hale, this time a hypothetical encounter between Christopher Columbus (or *Columbo*, as Chico would have it) and Pocahontas.

41:33/43:19—Julius Marx says I love you

Groucho's rendition of the number is the only one to offer a sour, cynical and ironic take on the sentiments of its title. It's in keeping with his screen image as the arch-debunker, but may also be read as a slightly poignant reflection on the man's own real-life sentiments. The documentary *The Marx Brothers in a Nutshell* uses it as counterpoint to one interviewee's claim that his third wife, Eden Hartford, said she would never have left Groucho if he had even once told her he loved her.

On a lighter note, this is one of the few occasions on film where we get a chance to see Groucho playing his beloved guitar. Other examples are to be found in his solo film *A Girl in Every Port*, while ridin' the range in *Go West* and, briefly and manically, in *Monkey Business*. Notice how it changes just before he throws it in the lake, suggesting that a prop, or at least a much cheaper model, actually hits the water.

43:03/44:51—"You know this is the first time I've been out in a canoe since I saw the American Tragedy?"

Groucho is here referring to the 1931 Paramount film *An American Tragedy* directed by Josef von Sternberg, based on the 1925 novel by Theodore Dreiser. Inspired by real events, the book pivots on a sequence in which the main character takes his pregnant mistress for a canoe ride in upstate New York, strikes her on the head with a camera, knocking her overboard, and leaves her to drown while he swims ashore. Professor Wagstaff evidently fears something similar happening to him.

44:50/46:43—"Throw me a life-saver!"

As seen in helpful close-up, Lifesavers are hard candies with holes in the middle, creating a resemblance to a life-saving ring and therefore inspiring their name. Available in mint and mixed fruit flavors, they seem to be more or less the same thing as the British Polo mints and fruits. Needless to say, Thelma was after a real life-saver, not a hard candy with a hole in the middle, as she has just fallen in the lake. In *The Marx Brothers Scrapbook* Groucho claims that Thelma, in fact, could not swim—a fact ascertained by no one prior to the scene being shot—and had to be saved by crew members. This can't be true, of course, if not for the obvious fact that she would not have begun the scene in ignorance of how it transpires then surely for the equally obvious one that there's quite a bit of dialogue after she falls in—game of her to keep going like that. However, that there may have been more to the scene originally than in the version we now have is perhaps suggested by the two shots of Groucho at **44:52/46:45** and **44:56/46:49**, where he appears to have unnaturally flat and slicked-down hair, suggesting a dunking of his own, or at least a far more thorough drenching than he receives in the final cut.

45:00/46:53—Harpo's hat

Note that it now reads "Kidnapper" rather than "Dog Catcher." The switch from one to the other happened in a now-missing scene where Harpo tries to net a girl.

50:43/52:50—Arthur Sheekman

I had briefly entertained the fantasy that I might have been the first person to notice that the fellow with enormous ears sitting next to the radio announcer was screenwriter, friend of Groucho and Gloria Stuart-marrying lucky swine Sheekman, but the IMDb reveals that others have got there first. It is still not widely known, however.

52:46/54:58—"Hey, which way a-you going?"

Note Chico's limp as he makes for the stretcher, and the heavy-duty kneepads he wears throughout the football scene. This is because of a real traffic accident in which he had shattered part of his leg. Sad to say, but it is probably only his inability to do physical stuff in these sequences that accounts for Zeppo's pleasingly central presence in them (and may, at a push, account for the deletion of the inexplicable "Zeppo being ironed" shot that turns up all the time and was even used as the cover illustration on recent DVD issues—was he originally to have been invalided out of the game?) On the very rare occasions when Chico is needed for physical action, an especially poor, obviously eleventh-hour stand-in is substituted, seen most clearly at **59:55/62:25**. The hat doesn't even fit!

56:37/58:59—"How do you like the game, Doc?"

According to Scott Meredith in *George S. Kaufman and the Algonquin Round Table*, this line originated as a Groucho ad-lib to the audience during the Broadway run of *The*

Cocoanuts. It made it to film at least once in between times, however: in the Thelma Todd/ZaSu Pitts short *Catch as Catch Can* (1931). "Is there a doctor in the house?" asks a drunk in the audience at a wrestling match. "I am ze doctor!" answers a bearded Germanic gentleman, close cousin, it would seem, to the professors of Huxley University. "Hi, Doc!" replies the drunk.

60:15/62:46—Harpo wins the game
60:28/63:00—Thelma marries the Marx Brothers

These two scenes show exactly what the Marx Brothers had in their earliest films and lost thereafter. The fact that Harpo's ridiculous behavior with the garbage cart and the multiple balls actually *wins the match for Huxley to the satisfaction of the judges* reflects the complete disinterest on the part of the writers, director and the Marxes themselves in having the movie conform in even the most cursory way to the rules of cinematic storytelling. What the Marx Brothers were offering was a different kind of comedy—totally new—in which a sixty-nine-minute feature can end by pretty much flipping the bird at anyone who expected silly things like plot and internal logic. This anarchistic abandon is part of that Broadway irreverence they brought to the movies, and it would be one of the key aspects of their work that Thalberg targeted and dismantled. He thought it made them unpopular. Who knows, he could have been right. But look at what he made them do instead. Look at the boring, unpleasant and depressingly straight horserace finale of *A Day at the Races*. Now let us turn to the last scene in the film, in which Thelma marries all three brothers at once, who then jump on her during the ceremony. (I say all three, because the fourth figure, standing almost unnoticeably behind Thelma and summarily pushed out of shot by Harpo when the fun begins, is presumably not Zeppo, sadly.) Now, in its own brief, silly, not all that inspired way, this could be the most subversive of *all* Marx endings, especially coming as it does straight after the debacle of the climactic football game. This is a collective Marxian goose to all the rules of cinematic comedy. It is sheer comic insurrection, and it was not to last.

5

Duck Soup (1933)

> Monday we watch Firefly's house, but he no come out. He wasn't home. Tuesday
> we go to the ball game but he fool us: he no show up. Wednesday he go to the
> ball game and we fool *him*. *We* no show up. Thursday was a double-header:
> nobody show up. Friday it rained all day. There was no ball game, so we stayed
> home and we listened to it over the radio.
>
> —Chicolini (Chico Marx)

Once upon a time, there was a Marx Brothers film called *Duck Soup*.

Irving Thalberg thought it defined everything that was wrong with the Marx Brothers, and for decades they agreed with him. Legend insists that the film flopped at the box office on original release and lost the team their Paramount contract.

Then, in the late 1960s, the Marx Brothers were rediscovered by a new generation, who—with the boundless confidence of youth—fancied they saw something of their own impulsive iconoclasm in the team's cultivated comic artistry. *Duck Soup* became a favorite because, as well as anti-establishment, it appeared explicitly anti-war. They also liked the fact that it did away with various other un-hip elements, like subplots and musical solos. From here, it began its swift mutation into the greatest Marx Brothers film of all, an opinion Groucho lived to endorse just as heartily. Now it's one of those untouchable artifacts, where anything less than adoration is taken as an insult. It is the only Marx Brothers film to have been the subject of an entire book, all on its own. So unquestioned and elevated is its reputation that merely to say one *likes* it is taken to mean that one doesn't much care for it at all.

Well, I *do* like *Duck Soup*. I like it *a lot*. In the first place, it's a Marx Brothers film, putting it automatically ahead of almost any other type of film, real or imaginary, in my affection and esteem. Second, it is, numerically at least, one of my favorite Marx Brothers films: my sixth favorite, I'd say, of fourteen. And yet, I do have a couple of bees in my bonnet about it that I would like to get out as quickly as possible. (It's bad enough that I'm still wearing a bonnet at my age, surely I can do without bees in it as well.) *First bee:* I do not think it is the best film the Marx Brothers ever made, and I think that it is the weakest rather than the best of their five Paramount films. *Second bee:* I do not think it is an anti-war satire.

Let us begin with the first bee.

A friend of mine who hadn't seen *Duck Soup* for a while once reported back to me from a screening of it: "You know how it was supposedly MGM that first started enforcing rules on the Marx Brothers and messing with their comic style: well it starts here!"

And this is pretty much how I feel about the movie. Regardless of what one's personal

The Brothers feign merriment at the prospect of a film they didn't want to make: (Left to right) Groucho, Zeppo, Chico and Harpo in a publicity photograph for *Duck Soup*.

opinion of it may be, it is surprising to me that it is not more commonly seen as *an attempted reinvention* of the team, a film that is for large stretches very atypical of their established style, and that Leo McCarey deserves almost as much credit, or flak (again, delete according to preference), for setting out to make something more to his own personal taste of them as does Thalberg in the next round.

"McCarey added a lot to the film," Groucho recalled in *The Marx Brothers Scrapbook*. "He had an important influence on the picture." McCarey, who made no bones about his lack of appreciation of the team and his disinterest in the assignment, was a professional comedy director, a graduate of the Hal Roach studios and the man who teamed Laurel & Hardy. The first sign that he's in charge and there's nothing we can do about it is the title, which had already seen service for a 1927 Laurel & Hardy short, and constantly thereafter we sense his hand, or more accurately his boot, leaving its prints all over the ideas and the material.

There is too much visual humor, and too much of it is silly. Too much is insufficiently tailored to the Brothers' own idiosyncratic talents.

For instance, consider the famous running joke where the call goes out for "His Excellency's car." Harpo pulls up in a motorbike and sidecar; Groucho gets into the sidecar and Harpo's bike pulls away leaving Groucho behind, going nowhere. A little later it happens again. Then, a little later still Groucho gets on the bike instead, instructing Harpo to get into the car, whereupon.... Well, you don't need me to tell you. You've seen the movie.

But here's the thing: you wouldn't need me to tell you even if you hadn't. Now, I'm not saying these bits aren't funny. I like them; I laugh at them. But this is not what makes the Marx Brothers great; it's not what they *do*. It's an old gag, an easy gag, and it would be every bit as funny if it were Wheeler and Woolsey doing it, or Olsen and Johnson, or Hope and Crosby. Can you even be sure you haven't seen one or other of those teams doing it somewhere, or doing some other gag so similar in construction that it makes no difference? But try to imagine Hope and Crosby doing the contract scene from *A Night at the Opera*. It would be impossible: the characters and delivery of Groucho and Chico are an integral part of the material.

Then consider the scene with Chico, Harpo and Edgar Kennedy. In the first place, the Brothers play best against *straight* straight-men: McCarey makes the elementary mistake of thinking that they'll be even funnier pitted against a supporting *comic*. Kennedy is a talented and likable presence in movies, and a wonderful foil to Laurel & Hardy, but this whole scene is misconceived. It comes from nowhere, and the escalating aggression comes from nowhere, and it forces Chico and Harpo to behave in ways their characters are not normally required to behave. What it is, all too clearly, is a Laurel & Hardy tit for tat routine, with the Marx Brothers grafted on. Harpo does his best to work in some original and characteristic business but it's still uphill, uninventive stuff. The climactic image of him paddling in the vat of lemonade is a wonderful one but the scene as written and developed has not earned the right to it. It's not just the strangely motiveless aggression displayed by all parties, nor the deliberate pace, both obvious carry-overs from Laurel & Hardy. Like too much else in the film it's simply not as clever as the material of their previous films. It's not as witty; not as sharp.

This is the first Marx Brothers film that *feels* directed, *obtrusively* directed, where the direction is as important as the script. Their other directors either pointed the camera and just let them go off, or else took the written material, watched the performances and worked out the best way to get as much as possible of both effectively on the screen. That's certainly what McLeod did, and that's why he's my favorite of their directors. McCarey may have been more talented, but he gets in the way.

It certainly took a lot of effort to get him. The trade journals are full of reports of negotiations, and scheduling alterations, and always with McLeod condescendingly named as "standing by" lest the great McCarey proves unavailable after all. One week the job would be announced as definitely McLeod's; the next, the studio is back around the table with McCarey.

Did the best man win? To make room for his innovations McCarey extensively pruned the original script, turning sequences that should have been carefully paced exercises in mounting insanity into virtual blackout quickies, as well as taking out entire scenes, the Harpo and Chico solos, and a lively Kalmar and Ruby song, intended for Zeppo. (It was called "Keep On Doin' What You're Doin'" and can still be enjoyed, fortunately, as it eventually found its way into Wheeler and Woolsey's *Hips Hips Hooray,* with no less than Thelma Todd helping out.)

The quintessential McCarey addition is the mirror scene, one of those sequences often placed alongside the stateroom scene from *A Night at the Opera* and the ice-cream scam in *A Day at the Races* as among the best suited to the task of introducing the team to unfamiliar audiences. I don't know. They may prove the most attractive to *unwilling* audiences, because they combine a superficial gloss of Marxian absurdity with a solid, mainstream comedy idea such as would appeal to almost anybody. But their *best*? Their most representative? Yes, there are distinctive touches in the mirror sequence: the impossibility of Harpo's correctly guessing Groucho's every innovation designed to catch him out, his cheating on the 360-degree turn, their swapping positions yet still continuing the game, and best of all, the sublime moment when Chico appears. But the idea was as old as the hills, strongly associated with Max Linder but also predating him, and it is a purely technical exercise; it is mechanical comedy, an idea waiting for the afterthought of a comedian.

Give me the Chevalier impressions in *Monkey Business* any day. Give me the auction scene in *The Cocoanuts,* the soiree scene in *Animal Crackers.* Their best material, for me, is, by definition, to be found not in those moments that convey most to unsympathetic audiences but in those which most perplex and infuriate them. I've always thought they got the keenest pleasure—visibly so: watch their faces—when delivering material with the potential to annoy some audiences as thoroughly as Spaulding annoys his hosts, and Ravelli annoys Spaulding. The confusion of those unwilling to enter their world is as much a source of pleasure to them as the delight of those who feel at home there, and the first contributes to the second.

The pre-production was chaotic, long drawn out and interspersed with periods of shutdown as the Marxes attempted to leave Paramount and mount a production of Kaufman and Ryskind's *Of Thee I Sing* as an independent concern. For a time it was announced as *Oo La La!* with Lubitsch, no less, in the frame to direct. (According to *Variety,* when asked what the film would be about, "the Marxes replied that the title explained it.") Troupes of additional writers passed through its front doors and out the back, as the title changed from *Firecrackers* (very nice) to *Cracked Ice* (my favorite) to *Grasshoppers* (very nice too) to *Duck Soup* (an old Laurel & Hardy title). Their father, Sam "Frenchie" Marx, passed away during this period also. And all the while, the Brothers were suing Paramount in the Supreme Court for $205,000 still owing from the profits of *Monkey Business.*

The *Hollywood Reporter*, of March 8, 1933, states that they have "packed up all their belongings and walked off the lot," claiming that their contract is invalid so long as Paramount withholds the sums owed on previous pictures. On March 11 it reports them forming their own company, which they intend calling "International Amalgamated Consolidated Affiliated World Wide Film Productions Company Incorporated of North Dakota."

On April 3 it notes that "Marx Bros. Inc." (the new name for the former International Amalgamated Consolidated Affiliated World Wide Film Productions Company Incorporated of North Dakota) will function as a subsidiary of a new concern called Producing Artists Inc. The latter's founders included two names the Marxes knew very well: Max Gordon (a long-term theatrical friend and advisor who helped negotiate their Hollywood contract) and Sam Harris (Broadway producer of *The Cocoanuts* and *Of Thee I Sing*). The others were Mark Hyman and Sam Katz, and Katz announced the company's plans to the trade journals:

> This new venture is formed for the purpose of benefiting the creator of motion pictures. This includes the artist, writer and director. They will be permitted to make pictures under conditions that heretofore have never existed in this business, in that there will be an entire elimination of all the evils of overhead, carrying charges and the bugaboos that generally lift production costs to unreasonable proportions. In Producing Artists Inc. the creators of pictures will reap the full benefit of their creations. If their efforts are successful, their returns will be greater under our plan than has ever been possible under the old arrangement.... Our organization will do all the financing as our part of the contribution.

The only one of their plans to have been released at the same time was the suggestion that *Of Thee I Sing* might be their first collaboration with the Marx Brothers, whom they had signed to a five-year contract.

On April 4, the *Reporter* reports that Producing Artists and the Marx Brothers are attempting to buy the script of *Grasshoppers* from Paramount as a possible alternative project to *Of Thee*. On May 3 we learn that Paramount has nixed that idea, and are instead having the script revised as a vehicle for Jack Oakie, W.C. Fields and Ken Murray. And *this*, mind you, was the cast in place on May 9, when Paramount confirmed that McCarey had officially signed as director.

Then, on May 17, the game is up:

> The Four Marx Brothers signed a deal yesterday with Paramount to do *Grasshoppers* at a reported flat salary of $300,000 for the picture. No percentage in this one. To avoid legal complications on both sides, arising out of disagreements between the company and the Marxes over percentages due them on pictures already made, Sam Katz, who has the Marx Brothers under contract, urged them to accept the deal and complete their contract. The making of this picture will have no bearing on the Marxes' first for Katz, *Of Thee I Sing*, which goes into production in November. *Grasshoppers* will start July 1.

And that's how McCarey, a director who could afford to choose his own projects, ended up with a comedy team he did not want to work with and a film he did not want to make. Even then, Paramount remained intent on maintaining the upper hand by fair means or foul, even to the extent of feeding this little tidbit to the gossip column of the *New Movie Magazine*:

> Ted Healy, who has been appearing at a Hollywood night hangout with his three stooges, tells me that there is a good chance that the four of them may go into Paramount features as a sort of Irish replacement for the Four Marx Brothers....

(Good luck with that one, Moses, Jerome and Louis!) McCarey meanwhile so enjoyed himself that as late as 1967 he was still telling *Cahiers du Cinéma* that "I don't like it so much, you know."

Kalmar and Ruby again take the principal screenplay credit, with Arthur Sheekman and Nat Perrin getting an upgrade this time round to secondary credited writers. Among the many others passing through were Norman Krasna, Edward Kaufman, Grover Jones, Lou Breslow and Richy Craig, Jr. (The trade papers played up the fact that the latter, a Broadway revue comedian and sketch writer of whom much was expected, was only thirty years old, but within a few months he was dead, his heart fatally weakened by illness and overwork.) Still another was Hal Roach stalwart James Parrott, making that lemonade stall scene even more of a foregone conclusion.

Perrin and Sheekman joined the project hotfoot from the radio series *Flywheel, Shyster and Flywheel*, and obligingly brought a bulging sack of some of that show's best one-liners along with them. As a result, the film at times seems to play, as Andrew Smith puts it in *Marx and Re-Marx*, like "an edited highlights reel of the best of *Flywheel, Shyster and Flywheel*." The celebrated "run out and get me a four-year-old child" line, Chico's puns on elephants, Dallas and lemonade, and Groucho's superb ripostes to characters who tell him he tries their patience ("I don't mind if I do, you must try mine some time") and that they intend washing their hands of him ("you can wash your neck, too") all originate in the radio scripts. Indeed it is no coincidence that the three scenes I had independently isolated as the film's best, and most authentically Marxian—Chico's trial, Groucho in the Chamber of Deputies and Chico and Harpo's progress report to Ambassador Trentino—turn out to be those where the *Flywheel* leftovers have been most liberally scattered.

Thanks especially to Perrin and Sheekman, then, that much of *Duck Soup* is as fine as anything the Marx Brothers ever did. But thanks, I fear, to McCarey, too much of it—think also of the inane "help is on the way" scene, or that nonsense with Harpo on his horse— does not play to their strengths and makes it all too easy—for them and for us.

The only thing more likely to annoy the average Marx devotee than saying that you think *Duck Soup* is generally the weakest of their Paramount films is saying that you don't think it is an anti-war satire—so I am a pariah twice over. (I am, however, in agreement with the large number of key creative personnel that Adamson quotes disavowing any suggestion of editorial intent.)

Louvish has persuasively suggested that something of its attitude may be attributable to the influence of *Of Thee I Sing,* a.k.a.: What George and Morrie Did Next. But it's not like anybody had to look far for political ferment in popular culture. In 1933, the movie trade journals were all abuzz about what they called the "dictator craze" in American movies.

At a time of widespread despondency, the obvious dynamism of Fascism was seen as stimulating and inspiring in many quarters of the West, including Hollywood (and Washington). In recognition of what to some degree Hitler, to a larger degree Stalin and to a massive degree Mussolini were all doing in the countries they ruled, a rash of films were produced about the vision, grit and resilience of one individual taking charge of failing institutions and revolutionizing them. There was Walter Huston as the dictatorial cop taking on organized crime in *Beast of the City* (1932), Spencer Tracy as the strike-breaking railroad tycoon in *The Power and the Glory* (1933), and Huston again as the weak president who, after a visitation from the Angel Gabriel, declares martial law, establishes himself as a dictator and saves America in *Gabriel Over the White House* (1933 again). These ideas, drawn largely from the example of Mussolini, were presented as both viable and stimulating solutions to world, domestic and economic crises. A film from Columbia, *Mussolini Speaks* (1933 yet again!), was an unabashed paean to the virtues and achievements of Il Duce, dedicated "to a man of the people whose deeds for his people will ever be an inspiration to all mankind."

Duck Soup, too, emerged in this year of the dictators: 1933. It is a comedy about the Fascist moment in Western culture, but it uses its subject without thought or true purpose. Freedonia, as the film begins, is in exactly the position of these institutions dynamized by dictators in the other movies: weakly governed by exhausted rulers, mismanaged and in economic dire straits. Mrs. Teasdale, the main donor of the party, will continue to inject life-saving funds, but only if the present leaders are replaced by what she tellingly terms "a progressive, fearless fighter." ("Progressive" was the big buzz-word of Fascism; oddly, it seems to have escaped its legacy.) So it is accepted that Freedonia will hand over all its powers to one man, on the grounds that he is progressive and fearless. This is the narrative of the dictator movies to a tee. The writers are not taking on Hitler and Mussolini: they're taking on Walter Huston and Spencer Tracy. (Interestingly, an article in the *Milwaukee Sentinel* of March 25, 1932, entitled, "Long Series of Political Pictures Due" and predicting the "dictator craze," shows that the forthcoming *Phantom President* was originally to have been directed by Norman McLeod, who "is now working with the Marx Brothers ... from the ridiculous to the sublime, or maybe it's the reverse." But most intriguing is some talk of a forthcoming Will Rogers film called *If I Was President,* and, whaddayaknow, "Leo McCarey conceived the idea and suggested it to Fox ... and has also been signed to direct.")

But there is another reason the film should not be read as condemnatory of Fascism.

Fascism simply was not an unequivocally dirty word in 1933. Many people were openly admiring of much of its ideology and effects, and many of them were to be found in the Roosevelt administration. Let us not forget that Freedonia's is not the first proudly waving banner we see in the film—before it even begins we see the imposing eagle of the NRA, the film colony's acknowledgment of support for the New Deal. All the major studios, including Paramount, pledged their support, and made pro–Roosevelt movies. Universal's *The Fighting President* (I'll let you guess the year) was promoted with the tagline, "America cries out to its fighting President: Show us the way and we will follow!" At Warners, Dick Powell plays a songwriter charged with composing an anthem to the NRA. The film is called *The Road Is Open Again*; I forget the year for a moment. I'm sure it'll come back to me.

Roosevelt's New Deal was explicitly centralist and widely compared to Fascism in its mechanics and dynamics—and with approval, what's more. Mussolini was a fan: he praised the New Deal publicly on several occasions. Roosevelt, in turn, explained that "what we were doing in this country were some of the things that were being done in Russia and even some of the things that were being done under Hitler in Germany. But we were doing them in an orderly way." The National Recovery Act was presided over by an ardent and self-described Fascist called Hugh "Iron Pants" Johnson, who ensured that the eagle symbol of the NRA was widely likened to the Nazi swastika, and was every bit as ubiquitous in its home country. The Blue Eagle symbol adorned the premises of stores and businesses, rallies and marches were staged for the mass pledging of allegiance, and Boy Scouts swore an oath to "do my part for the NRA" and "only buy where the Blue Eagle flies." "When every American housewife understands that the Blue Eagle on everything that she permits to come into her home is a symbol of its restoration to security," Johnson's rhetoric explained, "may God have mercy on the man or group of men who attempt to trifle with this bird." (Such as Jacob Maged, the immigrant dry cleaner sentenced to three months in jail in 1934 for not charging enough to press a pair of trousers.)

If anything is being *satirized* in *Duck Soup* it is generic clichés; in so doing, themes such as war, dictatorship and Fascism are likewise subjected to Marxian irreverence, but they are not—*surely*—being scrutinized as such. They're just tossed into the pot along with everything else. "They left Clair and Chaplin to make the films about Fascism and mass-production" (wrote Roger Manvell in *Film*) and to, as it were, "take the Reichstag to pieces and peel the moustache from Hitler's face."

Duck Soup is surprisingly frivolous about war, given its proximity to World War I; in no way can it be called impassioned. World War II was still in the unimagined and unimaginable future, and Fascism was not at this time linked in the public mind with war other than metaphorically. (Mussolini had successfully waged war against his country's problems and FDR vowed to follow his lead, assuming "unhesitatingly the leadership of this great army of our people dedicated to a disciplined attack upon our common problems.")

The plotline of the war between the two states more likely evolved via the interpolation not of the "dictator craze" formula so much as that of the film's other major thematic component: Ruritanian fantasies. Typically concerned with political intrigue in imaginary kingdoms, these stories had been inspired by Anthony Hope's 1894 novel *The Prisoner of Zenda*, but had by this time grown into a burgeoning subgenre of popular literature and cinema. Without this safeguard of fantasy, of unreality, I doubt they'd have been permitted (or, for that matter, inclined) to make so cynical a comedy about war anyway: the film's *divorcement* from reality is its most important feature.

The other thing we all know for sure about *Duck Soup* is that it flopped, costing the Brothers their Paramount contract and, for a time, endangering their whole future as film stars. Just glance, if you can, at this stinging review from the *Sydney Morning Herald*:

> Too often, it depends for laughter on episodes that transgress against good taste, rather than on genuinely clever material such as Harold Lloyd used in *Movie Crazy.* The effects of the "gag-man" are everywhere too apparent. One has a vision of huge staffs of employees busily thinking of things that it will be amusing for the Marx Brothers to do and say: and then pouring the result of their pondering into a seething, chaotic mass.... Harpo, who plays the harp with such extraordinary skill, looks more lunatic than ever with his shock of fair hair, his vacant smile, his ragged attire and his habit of darting to and fro.... At times, he is definitely repulsive. Judging from the reports of the film that have come from overseas, the Commonwealth censor has taken some of the incidents from it: but there remain one or two others which the Sydney public might well have been spared. Everything, of course, is very American.

Ouch! But hold on a minute—that's not a *Duck Soup* review: it's a review of *Horse Feathers,* which everyone knows was a much-loved smash hit! The point being that there was nothing new about what bad press *Duck Soup* did receive. There were always plenty of people (the spiritual brethren of Groucho's "barbers from Peru") who resented the team's wiseass style and seeming disregard for propriety, just as there always were (and presumably always will be) people everywhere who simply don't get absurdist humor. And such people are never unwilling to make their feelings felt in exhibitor and audience feedback reports. But to go further and imply that the nation had tired of them suddenly and completely, and turned their back on the film as one (often, it is explained, because their irreverence no longer seemed appealing in much straitened times), is to go too far. The film was generously budgeted (there are some senselessly lavish sets, and hordes of extras doing nothing), and it certainly did not make the expected profit, as many films did not in 1933. But even without living up to Chico's enthusiastic prediction of audience response to Bert Kalmar ("They'll piss!") it still ended up among the studio's six biggest grossing films of the year. Critics generally felt it to be not up to their highest standard, but they still enjoyed it, and recommended it, as usual, as antidote to Depression blues. (Harold W. Cohen, for instance: "Perhaps *Duck Soup* isn't as consistently funny as some of the previous Marx vehicles; perhaps it lacks the spontaneous tomfoolery of *The Cocoanuts* and *Animal Crackers,* and perhaps it does lose its comedy focus every so often. But all this is of little consequence, because the fact remains that the Marx Brothers, even in a slightly inferior vehicle, are better than anybody or anything else Hollywood has to offer in a similar vein." This review is not only typical of the majority, for my money it sums up the film sensibly and accurately.) As late as April 1933, *Film Daily* could print an article titled "New Vogue in Comedians Set by Marx Brothers." ("Since the success of the Marx Brothers' type of comedy," it begins, "directors at practically all studios are engaged in a search for a new type of comedian who can deliver the 'mad Marxian humour.'")

Everyone had their troubles in '33, not excluding Paramount, which was about to go into receivership, and who with Mae West and W.C. Fields also on their books probably felt they could lose a comic iconoclast or four if push came to shove, especially uppity ones with old-fashioned ideas about the right to be paid as promised. So when the time came for them

Sylvania's master spies report on their progress: (Left to right) Chico, Harpo and Louis Calhern in *Duck Soup*.

to renew their contracts, Paramount most definitely did make an offer, but when the two outfits could not come to satisfactory terms, they parted by mutual consent.

But then, *Duck Soup* has long been one of those films around which myths cluster like barnacles on a busted boat. Rarely has so much symbolic importance been piled on such frail shoulders. So with that in mind, one last thought to ponder before we pay a detailed visit: Trentino really *is* plotting the overthrow and invasion of Freedonia.

Which means Firefly is right to go to war, isn't he?

0:00 (NTSC/PAL)—Duck Soup

As we know, the title *Duck Soup* did not originate with the Marx Brothers, having already been used for a Laurel & Hardy short, re-appropriated here by the film's ex–Hal Roach director, Leo McCarey. It also turned up in the title of the 1941 animated cartoon *Duck Soup to Nuts* (coincidentally mingled with the title of another Laurel & Hardy film) and a 1942 short starring Edgar Kennedy (who also appears here). But what does it actually mean?

The phrase itself is an idiom for an easy task, as would have been commonly understood at the time (the *Spokesman-Review* observed that "it's duck soup to wear a grin while watching it"), but its origins are not known for certain. The earliest known usage of it is in a 1902 cartoon (showing a man juggling a plate, a bottle and condiments) by the prolific coiner of strange terms and phrases Tad Dorgan, who has already intruded once on our story (see *Animal Crackers,* 30:54). Possible explanations for why an easily accomplished feat is duck soup have included the easiness of duck soup to prepare (apparently specifically disputed by chefs), or perhaps as a variation of "sitting ducks," given the symbolic resemblance between ducks sitting on a lake and the bowl of soup they will become. On the other hand, apparently more or less meaningless food references are often used in this context, such as "easy as pie" and "a piece of cake." Groucho preferred a simpler explanation: "Take two turkeys, one goose, four cabbages, but no duck, and mix them together. After one taste, you'll duck soup for the rest of your life."

1:08 / 1:11—Mrs. Teasdale

Duck Soup marks the pivotal return of Margaret Dumont to the Marx family, no longer incidentally, as part of the bag and baggage of their Broadway team, but as a full-fledged cinematic adjunct. Note how from here on, her relationship to the plot will shift somewhat: instead of someone merely responding to the unlikely overtures of Groucho, she will play a slightly more cartoonish figure, who actively seeks out Groucho in a variety of unlikely capacities, and remains for the most part absurdly blind to, or absurdly forgiving of, his deliberate unsuitability in whatever function she employs him. Here she refuses to give more money to the Freedonian treasury (she considers previous donations to have been senselessly squandered) unless control of the country is given over to a man—for reasons of past association or favorable impression to which we are never made privy—who is not only certain to be even more wasteful but cheerfully announces the fact on arrival, denting her enthusiasm not a bit. Likewise unaccounted for is her already-cemented faith in him, before the film begins, as her business manager in *Opera* and her personal physician in *Races* (though *Opera* is the film in which she makes her exasperation plainest and the only time she consents to having him fired). In *Races* she is again insisting on his employment as a condition of her giving financial support, and this time the film makes clear that her high regard is definitely rooted in a previous acquaintance, seemingly of a professional *and* personal nature. Her faith in his skills despite obvious evidence of disproof, and in the sincerity of his romantic proclamations, despite the barrage of insults and plain references to her wealth in which they are couched, is funny but ultimately makes her as unrealistic a character as they are. We never feel sorry for her, for instance, which technically we most certainly should. The fact that her characterization is slightly beefed up, and her mastery over Groucho's fate slightly emphasized, in *Opera* hints to me that Thalberg had been having some of the same thoughts. After his death, though, it's unthinking business as usual. Groucho's storming of her house in *At the Circus* is seemingly the first occasion on which they meet, yet within seconds she is ludicrously lost to his charms, and in *The Big Store* she seeks him out at random as a private detective and, without him even feigning romantic inclinations, is somehow instantly made certain of his suitability. In all of this, we are irresistibly reminded of her own uneasy relationship with the team in real life. In a delightful, rare interview in *Modern Screen* magazine to accompany the release of *Duck Soup,* she recalled their earliest Broadway appearances ("I knew my lines all right, but I might as well have been quoting 'The Face on the Barroom Floor' for all the attention those lunatics paid to the script"), Groucho's new habit between takes of *Duck Soup* of imploring her to scratch his leg ("If I had refused, Groucho would simply have shouted: 'What's the idea? You've scratched it before. Don't be coy, Tootsie!' So, I scratched it."), and her warm feelings for them in general ("I can't get angry with them.... They're just like a bunch of schoolboys. Not in the least malicious. Everything they do is in the spirit of fun and I always try to be a good sport, even though I generally get the worst of it. Honestly, I enjoy every minute of it!")

2:51/2:59—"This is Miss Vera Marcal"

I'll say it is. The harp and piano solos are not the only casualties of this pared-to-the-bone screenplay. With the return of Margaret Dumont to the Marx family, there is also precious little room for this character, cut from the Thelma Todd cloth but played by Mexican spitfire Raquel Torres. A short-burning Hollywood flame (after debuting in 1928 she made ten of her remaining eleven films between '29 and '33), Torres rode the wave of Hollywood's first Latin-American craze. An unmistakably pre–Code presence on screen, Raquel specialized in uninhibitedly sexual characters, and performed with a candor contrived to drive the Breen Office to distraction; *Soup* was one of four she slinked through in '33. Excluding an uncredited bit in Mae West's *Go West, Young Man* in 1936, it proved to be her final year in Hollywood. The same year, she also appeared as the leader of a tribe of Amazonians alongside Wheeler & Woolsey (and future Marx associates Esther Muir and Henry Armetta) in *So This Is Africa,* written by Norman Krasna. Other films include 1931's *Aloha* (also starring Thelma Todd), 1930s *Estrellados* (the Spanish-language version of Buster Keaton's *Free and Easy,* also starring Carlos Villarías, Hollywood's Spanish Dracula) and 1930s *The Sea Bat* ("the *Jaws* of its day" according to Halliwell, and according to the posters: "THE MOST STIRRING ROMANCE ADVENTURE YOU'VE EVER GASPED AT!") She's particularly good as an extremely annoying character in *The Woman I Stole,* as Fay Wray's rival for the affections of stolid Jack Holt. Splendid she may be as the duplicitous Vera, but she might as well be Zeppo for all the use the film seems to have for her. It looks at one point as though we're in for some good hi-jinx when she joins Harpo and Chico in their efforts to rob Mrs. Teasdale's house but the script, as ever, gives her virtually nothing to do and soon excuses her from the fun. Perhaps without that mirror scene we'd have had the musical solos *and* some more of Raquel.

3:34/3:43—"I want you to meet His Excellency's secretary, Bob Roland...."

Just one more time, Zep....

I understand you've had it with the outfit and you don't want to make movies anymore. Well okay then. Just come on once more, introduce your big brother in song and then let him completely take over. Tell you what, we won't even make you hang around while he's doing it: it'll be just like in *Animal Crackers....* You can disappear completely once you've done your bit, then stay out of the film for as long as you like, just pop up here and there when you're needed to take a letter or something....

What's that? You were a fully-fledged member of the team and a passable romantic hero in *Monkey Business?* We know you were; we know you were. And what? You sang a solo number and joined in at the climax of *Horse Feathers?* I hear you, Herbie, I hear you. Yeah, I did hear that you're said to be the funniest brother offscreen, too. Whattaya know, eh Herb? But this script has no room for you to do anything other than introduce your brother. Them's the breaks, I guess. Better luck next time, maybe. Huh? Oh sorry; yeah, I forgot. Well, it's like I say. Them's the breaks, kid. Them's the breaks...

Zeppo Marx's Film Career (1929–1933).

3:49/3:59—The clock on the wall

Whatever you feel ultimately about how *Duck Soup* shapes up, let us at least agree that this has been a pretty dull opening so far, and that this curious musical sequence is an unexpected and ill-advised attempt to restage the opening of *Animal Crackers*. With so much of the film's finest wordplay directly traceable to Perrin and Sheekman, it might not be too unfair to speculate that Kalmar and Ruby rather coasted with their contributions this time. Where the previous two movies had been so fluently cinematic we could almost be back on stage again here, with another long introductory song to announce Groucho. But this one is a bit of a dud compared to its inspiration. It's not funny. It doesn't try to be funny. It just wastes time. Then we have "Hail, Hail Freedonia" repeated several times as Groucho fails to show up. This is presumably inspired by the bit in *Animal Crackers* where the guests keep interrupting Groucho to sing "Hooray for Captain Spaulding" over and over again when he tries to speak. But in that film they are being irrational, so it's funny. Here they're doing it for a reason. And it doesn't even pay off comedically. Dumont simply spots Groucho in the line and the film proceeds. Compare all this to the economy and hilarity of the opening scene from *Horse Feathers*! Incidentally, we now see Dumont's return here—and quite rightly, of course—as the exciting harbinger of a further four collaborations, and the sealing of her status as honorary Marx Brother for posterity. At the time, though, it might well have seemed like—and been—just another curious, obvious attempt to recall *Animal Crackers*.

Incidentally, somewhere in this scene is a guest played without credit by the English actress Florence Wix, notable for also playing an uncredited party guest in *A Day at the Races*. In fact, Wix seemed to specialize in playing uncredited party guests, appearing in exactly that capacity in a mind-boggling 45 films between 1926's *For Alimony Only* and *High Society*, thirty years later.

6:08/6:24—The mismatched insert

A surprisingly un-remarked upon continuity massacre. Groucho makes his first appearance in a black tailcoat. It's visible in the long shot of him walking towards Dumont as she says, "I extend the good wishes of every man woman and child of Freedonia." This then cuts to a medium shot of the two, lasting for over a minute without a cut, barring one brief close-up of Groucho as he makes an aside to the audience. This was plainly shot separately from the rest of the scene. Throughout this section Groucho is wearing a grey coat with black braid on the cuffs and lapels, and with what looks like a flower, but is actually the fingers of his gloves, sticking out of the breast pocket. Then, when the scene cuts back to the original wide shot (at **7:36/7:56**, after one of my favorite exchanges: "Oh, your excellency!" "You're not so bad yourself....") he is again wearing the black tailcoat, with nothing in the pocket. It would be neat if it could be suggested that this portion was reshot at the same time as the later sequence where war is declared, thus explaining the presence of the gloves (which are used to strike Trentino in the face). Sadly, this will not do, as Groucho is again wearing the tailcoat for that sequence, this time with the gloves as well. A mystery.

6:28/6:45—"You better beat it: I hear they're gonna tear you down and put up an office building where you're standing!"

A joke that had appeared in episode six of *Flywheel, Shyster and Flywheel*, broadcast in early January of 1933, and which sounds like it could only have been written for Groucho to deliver. Nonetheless, it was earlier featured in the 1932 Paramount comedy *This Is the Night* (starring Thelma Todd, and directed by Frank Tuttle, who had originally been assigned *Monkey Business*). Oddly, then, if it came to *Duck Soup* via *Flywheel*, it is presumably coincidental that the film in which it originally appears was also a Paramount production with slight Marxian connections: Sheekman or Perrin might just as easily have heard it anywhere and filed it away. Or perhaps Sheekman and Perrin made uncredited contributions to *This Is the Night*'s screenplay. As a Groucho line, I always thought that the idea of Dumont being torn down and replaced by an office block was a cruel jibe at her proportions. (It's preceded by the line "Say, you cover a lot of ground yourself," and in the radio show was delivered to a comparably statuesque character called "Mrs. Van Regal.") But in *This Is the Night*, delivered by Roland Young to willowy Charlie Ruggles, it's just a meaningless gag, and phrased as a threat: "I shall tear you down and put up an office building where you now stand." It sounds to all the world as if Young is cribbing a Groucho line, but no.

8:41/9:03—"Take a letter!"

This recollection of the great Hungerdunger scene just about seals the contention that *Animal Crackers* was Kalmar and Ruby's principal point of reference here. It also has the unfortunate side-effect of reversing the considerable strides that had been taken in the previous two movies in terms of lengthening and strengthening Zeppo's involvement. Now he's Groucho's secretary again (see above, 3:34). But this moment also underlines something else that will become increasingly noticeable: like much else that's classically Marxian in this film, it is rushed through at a self-defeating pace, the better to make room for all the new visual stuff McCarey has in store for us. In *Animal Crackers* the letter dictation was a hysterical self-contained sketch. This is pointlessly rushed through in a few lines, as if the first and last lines of the scene had been retained and everything in between abandoned. It lasts for just eleven seconds.

9:07/9:30—The laws of his administration

This encompasses what is easily the best of the new songs, not just in terms of wit but also in its effectiveness in context. Though equally founded in earlier models, this time both "Hooray for Captain Spaulding" and "Whatever It Is, I'm Against It," it has a genuine cutting edge. While Professor Wagstaff's nihilism in the earlier song had seemed merely mischievous, Firefly's innovations are as tyrannical as they are cheerfully proposed, and his promise, "If you think this country's bad off now, just wait till I get through with it," has an undercurrent of genuine threat. "From all reports the new leader will execute his duties with an iron hand," claims the newspaper we see announcing Firefly's appointment, and that he does, immediately making arbitrary and unjust decisions, and exempting himself from their influence. The death penalty will be extended not to those caught taking graft but only those who do not cut him into the deal. He forbids both whistling and chewing, conspicuously doing both himself even as he lays down the injunction. The previous government had requested Teasdale's money so as to head off revolt by lowering taxes, but Firefly has a more radical approach: "If you think you're paying too much now, just wait till I get through with it!" Few comic songs have been so genuinely sinister as well as funny; it rather resembles Ko-Ko's song ("I've got a little list....") from *The Mikado,* much beloved (and performed) by Groucho in later years.

9:35/9:59—"...and in the hoosegow hidden"

A hoosegow is a prison, a term of probably 19th-century origin, but not known in print until the early 20th. It's derived from "juzgao," the Mexican-Spanish word for jail. *The Hoose-Gow* was also the title of a 1929 Laurel & Hardy short, another of the doubtless coincidental but no less numerous hints of Stan and Ollie's work in which this film abounds.

11:30/11:59—"If you run out of gas get Ethyl, if Ethel runs out get Mabel"

Ethyl is Ethyl fluid, which any dunce can tell you is our old pal Tetraethyl lead, blended gaily, not to say impishly, with 1,2-dibromethane and 1,2-dichlorethane, and patented with characteristic devil-may-care abandon by the Ethyl Corporation of Virginia. Ethel, on the other hand, is a girl's name, hence Groucho's joke. I spell this out not because I doubt your ability to unravel puns, but merely as a precaution, because the DVD subtitlers spell it "Ethel" throughout, thus taking a simple gag and burying it alive.

Lou Costello experiences similar confusion in *Hold That Ghost* (1941):

BUD: If a car drove up here and asked you for ethyl, what would you do?
LOU: I'd say that she don't work here anymore.
BUD: No, no, no, you'd put ethyl in the car!
LOU: Why would I do that? I don't even know the girl.

11:43/12:13—Spy stuff

Off to Sylvania, where after some amusing business with the great Leonid Kinskey (at this time Paramount's in-house wild-eyed revolutionary loon, just used to great effect—"*Phooey, phooey, phooey!*"—in Lubitsch's *Trouble in Paradise*), the villainous Trentino welcomes his two latest recruits. It's Chico at last! And in a glorious sequence, kicking off with Chico and Harpo entering backwards with masks on the back of their heads (duplicated, somewhat more elaborately but still with deerstalker hats, in the Three Stooges short *We Want Our Mummy* [1939], in which the Stooges make their first entrance not only with reverse masks but reverse jackets and shoes as well). The discovery here that Harpo is spying for Trentino makes relevant the odd touch of his taking Groucho's photograph in the earlier "His Excellency's car" sequence. The ensuing dialogue with Louis Calhern is a reminder of how funny, and how *uniquely* funny, Chico can be when given the right material, and how wrong it is to write him off as "the third one," or even—as Anobile and others claim—Groucho's straight man. *At'sa some joke.*

16:18 / 16:59—Groucho in the Chamber of Deputies

Nice how this fast-paced scene has such a slow, deliberate opening, with Groucho bouncing a ball on his desk while the other notables wait impotently for his attention. We first hear the ball, over a shot of a "Do Not Disturb" sign outside the room, then cut to a medium shot of Groucho bouncing it, then to a long shot, which slowly pans back in over the heads of the plainly frustrated cabinet. He's actually playing a game called "jacks," very popular when I was a boy, which involves throwing a number of irregular shaped objects on to the ground and picking up first one, then two, then three and ultimately as many as possible, in the time it takes the ball to bounce, keeping the ball bouncing at all times. (The game has many names and variations, is apparently ancient in origin and exists in just about every nation and culture.) The jokes here, many derived from the *Flywheel* scripts, are top-drawer stuff, and ably maintain the energy of the previous scene, but as usual (see 8:41 above and 22:20 below) it's all over incredibly quickly. The whole scene, including the jacks game, lasts just over a minute and a half, and isn't allowed to build sufficiently to make the most of its excellent lines. And Zeppo's back for his quarter-time pit-stop, albeit sitting there like a lemon not saying anything.

22:10 / 23:06—"You know he went with Admiral Byrd to the pole?"

He being Chico's dog, whose name is hard to make out: "Pastano" according to the DVD subtitles; "Pastrom" according to the published script. For my money, I hear only two syllables, but I don't hear an "r" in the middle. (Note how crudely overdubbed the previous line "Believe me, he's some smart dog" is: obviously Chico's voice didn't record properly when his head was turned.) This is one of the very few times a Marx Brother is seen with a pet, but Chico was certainly a dog man in real life. Nat Perrin recalls him bringing one along to script conferences for *Monkey Business*, which proceeded to annoy all present; according to another story he once gave Groucho a dog as a present, which Groucho promptly named Chico. And in our very last authentic sighting of Chico, in *Love Happy*, he is playing cards with a dog, and losing. The *New York Times* (January 5, 1932) reports him judging a dog contest at Bloomingdale's: he saw over five hundred dogs in order to determine the "nicest" and "funniest." ("While pictures were being snapped, Mr Marx insisted that a vote be taken as to which end of the leash a dog belonged on. 'There's no sense in it, but I like the question,' he added.") In *Growing Up with Chico*, Maxine suggested a less benevolent reason for his fondness: he kept them as a source of protection against the gangsters to whom he invariably owed money.

But to get back to the reference: it may be that Byrd (Rear Admiral Richard Evelyn Byrd Jr, 1888–1957) might *not* have flown to the North Pole in 1926 as he claimed, with or without his dog (Igloo, 1924–31). There is apparently a strong case for believing that instead he merely got pretty near (maybe three feet?) before turning back and falsifying his log-book.

22:20/23:16—Chico vs. Groucho

If I had to choose one regular feature of the Marx Brothers formula I love the most, it would have to be the Chico-Groucho duologues. I love the way they spiral off from prosaic beginnings to the wildest flights of absurdity; I love the way each man keeps topping the other in comic invention; and I love the fact that Chico usually wins. Only Chico can beat Groucho at his own game, and reduce him to shivering frustration with the simultaneous impenetrability and confidence of his logic. Once again, this one's rushed, way shorter than their classic encounters in *The Cocoanuts* and *Animal Crackers,* but fully as inventive in the word play. The ending is magnificent: Chico suggests the deployment of a standing army on the grounds that they will save money on chairs, whereupon Groucho grabs him in a stranglehold and kicks him out of the room.

25:03/26:06—The dog in Harpo's chest

A very effective process shot, and the moment—used in a trailer to advertise a season of Marx Brothers films in the Christmas of 1983—that first attracted me to the team. A strange little joke, probably McCarey's, but very funny, partly because it is so unexpected and partly because it is done so well. The tattoo was originally to have been of an outhouse, the door of which would swing open and be closed again by an emerging hand, but was changed to a kennel for reasons of taste.

25:24/26:28—Zeppo enters wearing half a hat

A bit late in the day to start getting laughs, son. Take a letter!

33:13/34:37—"I'm letting you off easy: I was going to ask for the whole wig"

Groucho's typically gallant codicil to his request for a lock of Mrs. Teasdale's hair is a pretty straightforward insult gag—until one remembers that it is generally believed that Dumont was genuinely bald and always wore a wig for real. True, legends cling to this woman like moss to a log, but I've never read of this claim being challenged. So which is it: another Dumont myth or an incredibly insensitive joke?

34:14/35:40—"The Headstrongs married the Armstrongs, and that's why darkies were born"

Like laughter when Kitty Carlisle begins to sing, we must now accustom ourselves to the sharp intake of breath that invariably accompanies this line whenever the film is shown to contemporary viewers. But in the first place, Firefly is not using the word "darkies" himself: he's citing the title of a then-popular song, and for no contextually relevant reason whatever, merely for the hell of it. "That's Why Darkies Were Born," by Ray Henderson and Lew Brown, was first featured in the 1931 *George White's Scandals,* and has been performed by Kate Smith, Paul Robeson and many others. And second, the song is plainly ironic, and intended to satirize complacent attitudes, with only the use of the word "darkie" itself lending itself to any other possible reading. Andrew Smith has noted an earlier reference in an episode of *Flywheel, Shyster and Flywheel*, where it is used as a proper pun: Chico describes a woman who only plays the dark keys of the piano. Cue Groucho's inevitable reply: "That's why dark keys were born." It presumably made its way to *Duck Soup* from here.

Not at 37:35/39:09—The harp and piano solos that never were

There may be still some small uncertainty as to whether they were shot and edited out or never shot at all; certainly they were not cut from the finished film itself, though it is possible that they may have been shot and the surrounding footage later re-shot without them, perhaps at the same time as the "Big Bad Wolf" footage (see immediately below). Obviously it is at this point that they were intended, or at least suggested for inclusion. It is generally accepted that they were excised on McCarey's orders, more than possibly to make room for his mirror wheeze. Photographs exist of Chico playing the piano on this set, but then, he would.

39:17—"Who's Afraid of the Big Bad Wolf?"

The tune that plays when Harpo picks up the beer mug, and which he then accompanies on his improvised piano-harp, is the huge song hit from Disney's *Three Little Pigs*. *Film Daily* announced that Paramount had acquired the rights to the song from Disney in October of 1933, a week after principal photography had wrapped. According to the *New York Times* of October 29 the Brothers had been recalled to the studio to shoot "a post-script scene which will make appropriately antic use of the *Three Little Pigs* song. Groucho, it seems, will portray the big bad wolf in the sequence." The *Milwaukee Journal* of the same day also claims that "although the picture was finished a week ago the Marxmen will come back for one more scene, in order the use the 'new national anthem.'" (The report goes on to claim that the song's composer, Ann Ronell, was also hired to write a title song for the studio's forthcoming production of *Alice in Wonderland*, directed by Norman McLeod. Ronell would go on to marry Lester Cowan, and write the score for *Love Happy*.) Hard to imagine what this bizarre suggestion could mean, or where and how it could possibly have slotted in the film, and luckily the studio must have rapidly reached the same conclusion—leaving them with an expensive piece of music and nothing to do with it. Presumably, then, it was in the interests of making the best of a bad lot that it was decided to use it here, for no particular reason and getting at best a chuckle of recognition from the audience—a far cry from the showstopper they must have originally intended. An open question—given that the decision to use it does seem to have been taken after completion of principal photography—is whether it was added via reshooting the scene or, perhaps, just overdubbing it. (Dubbing is epidemic in this movie, and Harpo's body and hand movements are too few and too vague for certainty either way.) Despite its brief and arbitrary use in the final film, many contemporary reviews —primed from studio press releases rather than actual viewings—continued to absurdly play up the presence of the piece, as if it was a major part of the movie. To add insult to absurdity, the following year (when the song's bubble had perhaps burst a little) Hal Roach was able to acquire it gratis for use in *Babes in Toyland*. He and Disney had a cosily reciprocal relationship; Disney had used Laurel and Hardy caricatures, perhaps on the same generous terms, in *Mickey's Gala Premiere* (1933) and would do so again in *Mickey's Polo Team* (1936) and *Mother Goose Goes Hollywood* (1938).

39:09/40:47—Chico applies a greasepaint moustache!

It takes a moment or two of reflection for the funniness of this to strike. In order to imitate Groucho, Chico does what he would do if he was improvising the facial appearance of any mustached man: he draws it on with greasepaint. But he's sitting at Groucho's own dressing table, and the greasepaint is on the table ... so this must be the greasepaint that Firefly himself applies every morning.

42:32/44:19—The Mirror Scene

A corny old routine, performed very well, which Groucho confirms in *The Marx Brothers Scrapbook* was entirely McCarey's doing. There is no ambient noise at all on the soundtrack, just a few dubbed on, hollow footsteps. A moment's thought should reveal the reason why: McCarey is obviously shouting instructions to Groucho and Harpo, enabling them to achieve perfect synchronicity of action. As soon as you realize it, you can almost hear him, and the scene becomes less magical. According to an on-set report in the November 1933 issue of *Silver Screen* the nightshirts the Brothers are wearing are not white but pink. Harpo also appears disguised as Groucho in *The Incredible Jewel Robbery*.

45:15/47:09—Chico on Trial

The trial receives front-page coverage in *The Freedonia Gazette,* a newspaper which, almost imperceptibly, is subtitled "an independent newspaper published in the interests of the people." Also making news in Freedonia that week: "Foreign Radio Artists Arrive," "Mayor and Aid in Train Wreck," and, my favorite, "Woman Driver Gets Jail Term." (Later, of course, the *Freedonia Gazette* became the name of a long-running, well-beloved and now much-lamented Marx Brothers fanzine.) Interestingly, the paper claims that Firefly is to prosecute. In the event, so far as he does anything, he seems to be defending, with the prosecution left in the capably menacing hands of Charles Middleton, another draftee from Roach.

47:41/49:41—"I suggest we give him ten years in Leavenworth or eleven years in Twelveworth"

At the time, this was the largest maximum security federal prison in the United States, located in Leavenworth, Kansas. Bugs Moran and Machine Gun Kelly are among its more famous guests. There is an additional layer of absurdity in Groucho's line, of course, in that the film is not set in America.

49:26/51:30—"Why, the cheap four-flushing swine!"

This is a poker term. A four flush is a hand one card short of a full flush: four-flushing therefore means bluffing or empty boasting; the term can be used more generally to describe a braggart or a welcher. It turns up in Harold Lloyd's *Dr. Jack* (1922) and the title of a 1919 MGM movie; it also punningly inspired the 1954 Popeye cartoon *Floor Flusher. Variety* announced on March 18, 1925, that Margaret Dumont had been added to the cast of a forthcoming play called *The Four-Flusher* by Caesar Dunn.

49:42/51:47—Freedonia's Going to War / All God's Chillun Got Guns

Surely the oddest song number in any Marx film: parts of it good, parts of it bad, but all of it strange. It's so strange it certainly holds your attention, and makes you feel like you're watching good stuff, but I don't know. That bit where they do a parody of "Oh! Susannah" in silly voices with Chico pulling a silly face ... and the extras all kicking their legs up and holding contorted poses ... is it good? I just don't know. Harpo at least has a bit of visual fun, and there's the nice bit where they all play a tune on the soldiers' helmets; this, of course, is what cheers up Woody Allen's character when he thinks he's going to die in *Hannah and Her Sisters*. (Notice that an alternate, closer take of Harpo snipping the helmet plumes is used in the film's trailer.) "All God's Chillun Got Guns" parodies the "negro spiritual" "All God's Chillun Got Wings," which had also served as the title of a 1924 play by Eugene *"Why, you couple of baboons"* O'Neill. Rather charmingly in the present context, one verse begins, "I got a harp, you got a harp / All o' God's chillun got a harp." The song later served as inspiration for "All God's Chillun Got Rhythm" performed famously by Judy Garland and, of course, by Harpo and friends in *A Day at the Races*. Incidentally, this whole sequence, and the above-mentioned song parody in particular, is probably the film's most generous bequest to those who would read satiric anti-war intent into the film. Slim pickings, say I. Of course, the song's main point of interest—and ultimate justification—is that it is the only song number in the entire Marx canon to be performed by all four brothers.

52:52/55:05—Harpo on the horse

The point at which the film goes clean off the rails and strays into strikingly atypical, crude and witless new territory, pegged out and furrowed by McCarey in the belief—let us never forget—that the team he's been landed with need all the help he can give them. So here's some of his help. We open on a static tableau showing Zeppo, Chico and Groucho in military attire in front of a pedestal on which Harpo is sat astride a horse. (Damned if I know.) Harpo then gallops off into a long sequence (I'm tempted to say *insultingly* long, given the ruthless brevity of the Chico-Groucho duologue and the Groucho-Dumont wooing scene) which non–American readers may need reminding references Paul Revere's midnight ride. He soon becomes distracted by the sight of a woman undressing by her window to the accompaniment of "Ain't She Sweet." (Just as Charlotte Mineau in *Monkey Business* [see *MB*, 53:03] seemed a conscious echo of the absent Margaret Dumont, so this ice-cream blonde seems almost intended to remind us of the loss of Thelma Todd.) He sneaks in as she is beginning to take a bath and advances towards her—it has to be said—menacingly. Suddenly we see that her husband is returning home, and it's none other than Edgar Kennedy from the lemonade stand. Cut back to inside and we discover that the woman is now senselessly intent on hiding Harpo. This is all so inappropriate for a Marx Brothers film, it practically beggars belief. Anyway, Kennedy takes a bath but keeps hearing Harpo's bulb horn; it turns out that Harpo is lying under him in the bath (best not to even think about that one). And *still* it goes on. Now Harpo gallops to *another* woman's house, this time accompanied by "One Hour with You." We've no idea who she is but she coquettishly invites him upstairs. (Eyles accounts for this by presuming the house is Harpo's own, but I suspect the explanation is of an altogether simpler and more pre–Code variety.) This time he takes his horse with him, and in an infantile payoff we see the three of them in bed, Harpo and his horse together, and the horse's shoes next to Harpo's on the floor. At last, as the sound of neighing and obnoxious "funny" music fills the soundtrack, the scene mercifully fades. It's hard to imagine any of this being regarded as quality material if it were in one of the later MGM films.

55:13/57:32—The battle scene

The grand finale still has too many dud McCarey ideas (the library film of animals and athletes racing to Freedonia's aid, especially) but Groucho's constantly changing uniform (Union soldier, Confederate soldier, Revolutionary War British soldier, Davey Crockett and a Boy Scout) is an agreeably carefree touch. There are some good jokes, lots of bad ones, and some strikingly cynical and black ones in both categories. The scene's (and perhaps the film's) most famous line, **"You're fighting for this woman's honor, which is probably more than she ever did,"** like most of Groucho's dialogue in the sequence by the window between **58:24/60:50** and **58:48/61:15**, is overdubbed. Note how the background noise disappears, and compare its clarity with the obvious echo on Zeppo's and Margaret Dumont's lines. **Chico's rhyme** at **59:34/62:03** is one of many similar children's counting rhymes; this precise variant may well be Chico's own. Moe Howard uses another in *Boobs in Arms* (1940). (That *Duck Soup* may have been a reference point for *Boobs* is further suggested by the scene at the end in which a shell passes through a window, across the room and out the other side, and by Curly conking the enemy soldiers on their helmets one at a time.) An often overlooked moment is at **61:46/64:21**, when **Harpo grabs Margaret Dumont's backside** as his contribution to helping prevent the door from being battered in by the Sylvanian soldiers outside. Needless to say, she's having none of it ("get away from me!") but notice how he leaves a dusty handprint on her derriere, to which he then points with amusement. When **Groucho uses curtain rings to count the unconscious soldiers** at **61:55/64:30** he revives Chico's "only game in the stable" from *Monkey Business*. The line **"Goodbye, Mont Blanc, goodbye"** at **60:00/62:31** is mysterious. I have two tentative suggestions. One relates to the Napoleonic wars (and therefore possibly ties in with Harpo's uniform). Mont-Blanc was a department of the French empire that was restored to its former rulers after Napoleon's defeat at Waterloo, possibly accounting for the tone of wistful farewell in the phrase. The other is that it might refer to the Halifax disaster of 1917, in which a French munitions ship called Mont Blanc, packed with live explosives and chemicals, was struck by another vessel while harbored in Canada. The sparks ignited the cargo, and the crew rushed for the lifeboats as the burning ship drifted towards the harbor. There, the telegraph operator tapped out the message, "Munitions ship on fire in the harbor. Heading for Pier Six. Goodbye." At which point the ship exploded, killing at least a thousand in two seconds. The "goodbye" sounds like it might refer to this, but given the awfulness of the disaster and its comparatively recent date, it seems unlikely that even a comedy this dark would be treating the subject so trivially. For that reason alone, I'm plumping for a grumpy Napoleon's surrendering of his former territories.

Victory is ours.

6

A Night at the Opera (1935)

Signor Lassparri comes from a very famous family. His mother was a well-known bass singer. And his father was the first man to stuff spaghetti with bicarbonate of soda, thus causing and curing indigestion at the same time.
— Otis B. Driftwood (Groucho Marx)

The Marx Brothers had some big news to reveal in September of 1934. Here's Louella Parsons spilling it for them:

Bag, baggage, false mustaches and wigs, the four Marx brothers will soon bring their comedy to Metro-Goldwyn-Mayer. Irving Thalberg, who continues to have one idea after another, has signed the Marx brothers four—Groucho, Chico, Harpo and Zeppo—to make one of their inimitable comedies. I say Irving's ideas are as prolific as the flowers in May because this very first Marx comedy is his own story. Groucho plays an operatic impresario and Chico, Harpo and Zeppo are members of the company.

A Night at the Opera is a kind of optical illusion, a trick of the light. It's a film that seemed to announce the rebirth of the Marx Brothers as a permanent fixture in the Hollywood firmament yet it contains all the seeds of the precipitous descent that was just around the corner. Moving to MGM in 1935 redefined what a Marx Brothers film was, and who the Marx Brothers were (and not just because Zeppo opted to jump ship before the team's maiden voyage had even begun).

Thalberg's patronage came at a price: he isolated what he considered major flaws in their Paramount films, and determined to set them straight. ("I think it would have astonished him had he lived to see that Groucho and Harpo Marx would be regarded as confreres by such men of genius as Stravinsky and Picasso," Anita Loos said of Thalberg.) The problems he thought he identified were (a) a lack of sympathy in their characterizations verging on nihilism, and (b) no serious attention to narrative structure. The result of these supposed defects, he opined, was that the films were simply assemblies of jokes, joined by meaningless plots that hung between them like frayed string, and because there were no plot arcs or emotional crescendos women did not warm to them. (Those dames sure do love a plot arc.) But with his guidance they could make a film with fewer laughs but more audience appeal. The trick is to have a plot the audience becomes emotionally involved with (which they sort of had in *The Cocoanuts,* but bothered with less and less in each subsequent film), something that the characters are striving for, cute young lovers, production numbers and plenty of MGM wallop. Within this more solid structure, in strictly measured doses, the Brothers

The Marx Brothers wallow in victory, while Margaret Dumont (far left), and Kitty Carlisle (second from left) and Allan Jones (with his arm around Kitty) and Robert Emmett O'Connor (flanked by Groucho and Harpo) stand by, in the deleted finale of *A Night at the Opera*.

would then be free to carry on as usual, only slightly tamed and constrained by narrative realities and MGM's no-absurdity policy. And that's what happened, the story goes, and Thalberg was proved right, commercially and critically.

Still today, debate rages among Marx fans as to the value of the "Thalberg effect." Did he save them and propel them to new heights, as Groucho tended to feel? (Even as late as 1974's *Playboy* interview Groucho still quixotically dismissed their entire Paramount oeuvre as "those five turkeys.") Or did he remove and alter too much of their uniqueness merely to secure greater financial success?

Or even, do we give his interventions far too much credit? After all, we have no "other" 1935 Marx Brothers film, made under the familiar rules, with which to compare the box-office receipts. Now that we know the myth of *Duck Soup*'s commercial failure was just that, can we be sure that their return to the screen after a year away would not have been warmly received whether decked out with Thalberg frosting or not? Surely we can all agree that *A Night at the Opera* is indeed a beauty, but is it a beauty *because of* Thalberg's tampering, or in spite of it?

Me, I like them the way they were before. (I like very much a phrase by E.V. Lucas who, in his review of *Animal Crackers* in the British humor magazine *Punch*, wrote, "Their incon-sequence is radiant.") I'm not sure many of Thalberg's ideas were good ones *per se,* certainly not artistically, and maybe not even commercially, at least to the extent habitually assumed. If the romantic subplot, production gloss and sympathetic elements of *Opera* work, and I agree they do, isn't that just because they happen to have been done extremely well? The success of *Opera* might be just as easily attributed to a dozen other factors, chief among them the popularity of the comedy team starring in it. The promise of seeing them in an expensive MGM production might well have added to the enticement, but perhaps not to any extent that made the difference between success and failure.

Part of the pleasure, too, must have been in the anticipation of the Marx Brothers *taking on* the world of MGM, and—far from being submerged in it—being let destructively loose there. The unlikeliness of the collision is deliberately played upon. The very title carries this frisson, a brilliant juxtaposition: The Marx Brothers, promising wildness and chaos, and the deliberately classy, sober-sounding *A Night at the Opera.* Put the two together, and the result should be combustibility. We are so familiar with this title now—so that it instantly evokes images of the Marx Brothers and the Marx Brothers alone—that we forget how clever and exciting it must have sounded, what a masterstroke it is, just how *funny* a title it is. Audi-ences would have seen that title and *laughed at it,* and it carries a palpable tingle of antici-pation. (For that reason the title has rightly become iconic, and its power, like so much else that is great about the movie, was misunderstood when the formula was repeated. *A Day at the Races* and *At the Circus,* planned as *A Day at the Circus,* are similar titles, but they carry no frisson. The Marx Brothers at a race track: so what?)

Most flattering was the money Thalberg was willing to chance on them. ("With genius and a lot of luck you can get tragedy fairly cheaply," Groucho told the British historian Paul Johnson in the 1950s. "But comedy is always expensive.") Thanks to Thalberg's largesse, a pre-filming road tour allowed the Brothers to hone the material before a live audience. "I can't understand why it hasn't been done before," Harpo told the *New York Times*:

> We gave four shows a day for 25 days.... When a line didn't get the laugh we expected, we changed it or threw it out. Kept experimenting that way all the time. It was tough work. We were rehearsing all the time. When we got back to the studio we had everything lined up. We didn't have to rehearse, just go on to the set and let the cameras roll. In a day we'd shoot a scene that ordinarily would have taken 3 or 4 days. And that means something when your production cost is 10000 dollars a day. We shot the picture in 40 days and only needed one day for retakes. The best part of it from the producer's point of view is that this try-out on the road didn't cost him anything. We didn't make any money out of the show, but it paid for the costumes, scenery and time. That includes four weeks of rehearsals, too.

And Chico felt the same way:

> From our viewpoint the gag-testing nature of the tour was particularly great stuff. We are old-timers of the stage, of course, but we have been in pictures for a long time and we had almost forgotten what a wallop, what a build-up for our comedy, actual audience reactions had always given us. I think we've discovered a sure-fire way of testing screen comedy material that will be used in the future by every thoughtful comedian.

The tour certainly helped to *refine* some of the material (the stateroom scene being the most famous beneficiary of the process) and doubtless also helped restore the Brothers' faith in themselves as a viable option. But the main reason why the film is *funny* is because it has a funny script. And that's the *really* great thing Thalberg did: *he brought back George Kaufman and Morrie Ryskind to write it*. This could be the single most important reason why *A Night at the Opera* is the last film of the Marx Brothers' untouchable period, and not the first film in their decline. Accidentally, the Brothers were back at their Broadway best again. (By Kaufman's own account he did not reply to the first telegram he received from Thalberg requesting his participation, and likewise ignored a ticket to Hollywood that arrived in the mail shortly after. He changed his mind when he received a wire from the Marxes themselves, saying "We're coming to get you." "I took the next train to Hollywood," he says in an interview published in the *Philadelphia Inquirer*, "because I knew if I didn't, they would be here. I can control Groucho, Chico and Harpo when they are concentrating on a show or a picture, but not when they concentrate on me, as they have on several occasions. Shall I show you the scars?")

The originator of the script was a staff writer called James Kevin McGuinness, who came up with an idea that, while containing little that was actually worth using, did nonetheless get things started and gave others a starting point and a direction, which was presumably the idea. (He tellingly gets a credit for original story, the only writing presence other than Kaufman and Ryskind whose name appears on screen.) It was McGuinness's draft that famously had the nice idea of Harpo playing the world's greatest tenor, the joke being that, for no essential reason beyond the obvious, we the audience never get to hear him. Needless to say, this set the imaginations of the publicists down predictable and well-trodden roads, albeit with interesting variations. "Harpo Marx, who looked goofy and stayed speechless in all past film extravaganzas made by the comedy brothers," announced the *Chicago Tribune* on October 30, 1934, "will talk in his next one, *A Night at the Opera* for MGM. But his speech, like that in *Strange Interlude*, will be unusual in that it will seem a representation of unspoken thoughts, and a weird manner of speaking it was yesterday, when they screen-tested Harpo on the soundtrack." While the *Scranton Republican* (November 29, 1934) tells us: "Harpo Marx is slated to take a singing test for the next Marx Brothers comedy." But then, it goes on to tell us that the forthcoming film will be called *Ballet Laughs*, so form your own conclusions.

Next up, Kalmar and Ruby had a go, though according to Groucho their work "wasn't any good." Adamson quotes quite a bit of their treatment, and it sounds like an excellent Paramount script—just not what Thalberg was after. I especially like Groucho's pre-performance pep talk to the orchestra, as if he were a football coach and they his team:

> Boys, this is the beginning of a new season. Last year they said we were yellow, that we couldn't take it. But that was last year. This is the beginning of a new season, which I said before. Mind you, I'm not blaming it all on you boys. We had a little tough luck. The trombone player lost his tonsils. Six months later we found them in the trombone.

On the other hand, plenty of their draft does survive, not least the imperishable character names Mrs Claypool and Otis B. Driftwood. They also contributed the parody MGM logo intro with the Marxes roaring in place of Leo, the line "On account of you I nearly heard the opera!" and an embryonic version of the contract scene. Unsurprisingly, the notion of Groucho accidentally but cheerfully signing the wrong tenor, akin to his recruiting the wrong football players in *Horse Feathers*, proves to be their inspiration too.

Their draft was then handed to George Seaton and Robert Pirosh—principal contributors to *A Day at the Races*—for a little spit and polish (or speat and pilosh, in their case), and finally at Groucho's urging, to Kaufman and Ryskind, whereupon the saints smiled in the heavens and the three greatest aviators in the world began to tremble in their beards. (According to Mitchell, Kalmar & Ruby and Seaton & Pirosh continued to add ideas and make amendments, and more importantly, there were also the contributions of Al Boasberg to be factored in. A brilliant gagman, Boasberg came into his own as a shaper and polisher during the pre-filming tour.)

An essential component of the Thalberg masterplan not contributing overmuch to the funnies was director Sam Wood. He was hired on account of his being a disciplined taskmaster as well as for his proven track record in popular hits, but his humourless style and penchant for multiple retakes soon alienated his stars, whose antics, for his part, he found boring and undignified. "Even his daughter hated him" is Groucho's measured summing-up in *The Marx Brothers Scrapbook*. Gloria Swanson, who worked with him on many silent films, summed him up as "a real estate agent at heart," but good professional craftsmanship is hardly undeserving of praise, and Wood was a professional to his fingertips.

He was also a company man, happy to play the Thalberg line straight down the middle for any journalists curious enough to enquire. He explained that hitherto "the Marxes were

"Get your fresh-roasted peanuts..." Groucho and the comic sublime in *A Night at the Opera*.

doing tricks to the other characters in the films which the audience resented." This time it would be different: "In our picture we took care to have the Marxes on the side of the audience and against the heavies. Our recipe was to have them help the boy and girl and outwit the villain. That made all their games against the heavies acceptable."

So did the Thalberg touch save the Marx Brothers? The box office speaks for itself, Thalberg would surely have interjected here, and there would be no shortage of critics to affirm likewise. That the films had "too many jokes" had been a recurring refrain of critics since *The Cocoanuts;* countless reviews carried the injunction to see the film at least three times to catch them all. It takes a peculiar perspective, perhaps, to interpret this as the need for fewer, but justification by testimonial was nonetheless amply there. Likewise his emphasis on comedy relief—not comedy *as* relief, but rather relief *from* the comedy. The writer of the *Evening Independent*'s "Theater Notes" section, suggested after seeing *Duck Soup* in November of 1933 that "the Marx brothers, in my opinion, again make the mistake of putting too much of themselves into their films."

> I have said the same thing before, and it is just as sound a criticism now as it was some months ago. The audience grows weary of the Marx brothers after seeing nothing else for seven reels. In their first picture they had Mary Eaton and some lovely music to furnish variety, and the Marx brothers were in evidence only about half the time.... I must say that the subsequent films have been getting duller and duller. The last one is the poorest of all. The Marx brothers need, in my opinion, somebody like Mary Eaton or Marilyn Miller, with some good songs and a couple of attractive chorus numbers, to furnish relief from too much slapstick comedy.

Substitute Allan Jones and Kitty Carlisle for Mary Eaton and Marilyn Miller and you have pretty much Thalberg's blueprint for *A Night at the Opera*. But while he could equally have pointed to dozens more like this to endorse his prescription, the vital point is that such observations tended not to come from huge Marx Brothers fans. Those who really liked them liked them just fine. Such concessions made to the indifferent may have had short-term benefits, but they surely carried long-term costs: if you're only going on account of the incidentals, by definition your loyalty to the main course is conditional, and probably short-lived. And before long it also helped alienate those who never needed bribery, the loyal followers who now came increasingly to the films, as the *Montreal Gazette* put it in their review of *Go West,* with "an attitude perhaps a little more analytical, as of one who sits by the death bed of a dear friend." Kaspar Monahan called the film "howling, uproarious entertainment," but rushed to qualify that by that he means "howling and uproarious, of course, if you like the Marxes. I do. Some don't."

So nothing *really* changed, except the films.

0:00 (NTSC/PAL)—The MGM logo

All change—the Paramount mountain, with its promise of wit and sophistication, has given way to the MGM lion's imperious roar of self-approval. Possibly some audiences will be surprised to see Leo, half-remembering that MGM specially reshot this sequence to feature the Marxes themselves roaring (or, in Harpo's case, honking his horn while he mimes the roar) and with the slogan "Ars Gratia Artis" replaced by "Marx Gratia Marxes." So they did, with the original intention of starting the film with it, which would have been very impressive. But in the end propriety won out (oh, well) and this splendid sequence was used only in the trailer.

0:09/0:10—Groucho—Chico—Harpo

One of the truly great mysteries of the Marx Brothers' career—not because it is important, but simply because the answer is so hard to guess—is why their respective billing changes at this point. Throughout the Paramount years, they had always been listed in movie credits collectively before the title (as simply "The Marx Brothers" or "The Four Marx Brothers") and then, in the cast list, as Groucho first, then Harpo, then Chico. This ordering (though unfair to my way of thinking) *is* the one you would probably expect them to come in. But when they move to MGM, right when Chico's involvement begins its diminishment to almost Zeppo-like irrelevance, he suddenly leaps up one place. In the MGM films they are billed before the title as "Groucho—Chico—Harpo—Marx Bros," and this ordering is retained in the cast list. It's enormously tempting to think of it as accidental, or irrelevant, because the thought of them giving a damn is a tough one to imagine. But the fact is that billing in Hollywood is *never* accidental. It's *always* carefully worked out. So if this has happened, it's happened for a reason. Now, the fact is that it was through the machinations of Chico that they got their MGM contract. Could the billing be a gesture of thanks for that? Unlikely, since he is still behind Groucho, so that would mean Harpo was being expected to carry the full burden of their gratitude, which is hardly fair. So what does that leave? Could it possibly be something Chico himself specified when the new contracts were being drawn? My own feeling is that the only fair way to list them is alphabetically, and I wish they always had been. The fact that Chico would come first would in no way diminish Groucho's importance—indeed, it would simply draw attention to the fact that the listing *is* alphabetical, since there's obviously no other reason why Chico *would* be first. And Zeppo would still be last.

1:20/1:24—"...gentleman has not arrived yet?"

Not many movies begin partway through a sentence. And *A Night at the Opera* is no exception—or wasn't, at least. But the version of the film available to us today has been somewhat over-zealously shorn of all reference to the fact that it is set in Italy. (I suppose we should be lucky that Chico's still in it.) Among the many pointless cuts was an opening establishing sequence shot like the beginning of a Lubitsch musical, with various passers-by singing part of a song before "passing it on" to the next person, the last of whom is the waiter, who begins the first half of his sentence as the song ends. All of this was lost, apparently for no better reason than that it makes clear that it is set in Milan.

The suggestion that this may have been done for a war-era reissue (to minimize its uncritical treatment of an axis power) has come to be widely accepted and may indeed be the case, though I can't help thinking it a somewhat costly, complicated and above all unnecessary gesture. Partly for that reason I lean towards a different view: that the cuts were made shortly after the original release, and not as a gesture of hostility towards Italy but rather of appeasement. What is certain is that, with tensions in Europe increasing all the time, Hollywood had already instituted a policy of making as little trouble as possible with its increasingly fractious export markets, and Italy seems to have been an especially sensitive case, not least because of the large Italian-American audience. Louvish notes that to conform with the Hays directive that no foreign leader should be subjected to ridicule, the line "You can't Mussolini all of us!" was cut from the original script before shooting, and it may be that the characterization of the world's three greatest aviators was similarly amended at this early stage (see below, 36:09; also below, 2:25). But even with these alterations effected, it seems hackles were still raised. Louvish states that the film's release in Italy was "held up by the objection of the Italian government that it made fun of the Italian people," and that "cuts were made to remove any inference that the characters were Italian." In an article listing a number of current releases to have offended Italian sensibilities, *Variety* noted (July 1, 1936) that Italian censors have "k.o.'d *A Night at the Opera* for native consumption as n.g. for the Italian temperament." (And how's this for delicate relations: the same paper on July 28th reports Mussolini in talks with MGM to get Clarence Brown to make a movie in Rome "under auspices of the Italian government"!) I have a feeling that it may have been around this point that the film was further cut, not in the realistic hope of softening any negative treatment of its Italian elements (an impossible task, since the film is in reality completely innocuous) but rather to sidestep the problem entirely, simply by removing every reference to Italy that it was possible to remove (see below, 13:53). So while Chico's usual characterization and all the Italian character names of course survive, sundry dialogue references to Italy and the song opening, which establishes the setting beyond question as Milan, all got the chop. (Glenn Mitchell persuasively notes that there is "but scant possibility of the meticulous Irving Thalberg allowing such a choppy film into release," but in the immediate aftermath of his death in September of 1936 it may have been a different story.) Eventually, in 1938, Italy passed anti–Semitic laws and Mussolini embarked upon his complete and fatal capitulation to Nazism; the same year the Alfieri Law, designed to protect and encourage native film production, all but "pushed American producers out of the Italian marketplace," and "resulted in the temporary withdrawal of MGM, 20th Century Fox, Paramount and Warner Brothers from Italy." *Opera* was officially withdrawn from circulation in Italy in October, and Italian patriots were advised to shun all such non–Aryan entertainments. *The Milwaukee Journal* on October 19th, frivolously referring to Mussolini as "the irrepressible Italian," noted that he "last Friday started a war against Jewish comedians":

> The ultra-Fascist newspaper, *Tevere*, which is published in Rome, is now urging all citizens to boycott movies starring Jewish actors, on the ground that such players are lacking in the subtlety and delicacy that are such a delight to Italian audiences. "The Marx Brothers," Mussolini's paper has declared, "are only a big bluff. Their clowning may succeed in drawing smiles from maids, but Italians do not need to take delight in their stupidity."

The paper also reminds us of another easy-to-overlook point of contention for Italian censors: the film's seemingly disrespectful attitude towards their noblest art: "they lampoon that most sacred of all subjects, Italian opera." So if the cuts were made in a generous spirit, it could only have been before 1938: why bother making rational concessions for a film that was now being objected to on grounds that could never be sanely addressed? In any event, it seems that Louis B. Mayer was already wary of too much positive association with the Italian government by October of 1937, when he had been widely deemed complicit by association in the proposed production union between Mussolini's son Vittorio and Hal Roach, with whom MGM had a releasing agreement.

Given, therefore, this long and complex history of the film irritating Italians, I'm not immediately sure why the Italian references would then be cut during the war on the grounds that they were too favourable, when all the evidence suggested that official Italian sensibilities viewed them as entirely the contrary. Why should a film that had been effectively banned in Italy be expensively altered by a country with which it was at war? There is of course the fact that the characters, including the hero and heroine, are seen to actually come from Italy, a tough sell to audiences now primed to boo the very sight of an Italian, but that, as already noted, is encoded in their surnames and could never be realistically expunged. I could far more easily see the studio inserting a new title card at the beginning, saying something like "Before the war—when Italy was still the land of sunshine and song...." This would be easier, cheaper and surely as effective, if not more so. A wartime trim remains possible, of course, but all things considered I shall cautiously suggest the cuts were made in 1936 or early 1937, and that the explanation of why it was that version that was preserved, while the uncut one was lost, is exactly the same explanation that would have applied if the cuts had been made at any other time—namely that Hollywood is, was always, and always will be nuts.

Excitedly, an alternative version of the film was found in a Hungarian film archive, containing several lost moments present and correct, along with a couple of other odd differences from the version with which we are most familiar. Despite years having now passed since the discovery, however, frustratingly little has been done. The original discoverer only got as far as watching the first reel, because of prohibitive viewing charges, and the copyright holders presumably consider the commercial potential of the find such that rather than release a deluxe restored double-disc special edition DVD they opted for Plan B: pretending they've never heard of the film and whistling and looking the other way when you try to get their attention about it. So as nothing ever escapes from Hungary, it's unlikely you'll be seeing it any time soon. For the purposes of this section, however, it must be stressed that even this version is still lacking the introductory sequence, and begins just as ours does: with a nasty clicking noise, followed by a waiter saying "...gentleman has not arrived yet."

2:25/2:32—"Have you got any milk-fed chicken?"

Then squeeze the milk out of one and bring me a glass.
Not the greatest Groucho quip, perhaps, but a fortunate substitution for the one in an extant original draft script:

GROUCHO: Steward, do you have any French pastry?
STEWARD: But this is an Italian boat.
GROUCHO: Well then, what's the rate of exchange?

Perhaps the new version was improvised by Groucho during the pre-filming live tour and found to get a bigger laugh. Whatever, we're lucky it was changed, otherwise it would now be missing entirely, thanks to its reference to an Italian boat.

4:14/4:25—"Mrs. Claypool, Mr. Gottlieb, Mr. Gottlieb, Mrs. Claypool...."

Note Groucho's original dining companion over Dumont's left shoulder. Obviously recovered from her anger at Groucho landing her with the bill, she is now spontaneously and charmingly amused by his foolish behavior. A brief mention also for the line, **"I just wanted to see if your rings were still there"** at **4:24/4:36**, almost certainly implying that Gottlieb might have cleverly stolen them. As a child, however, I interpreted it to mean that the very toxicity of his kiss had somehow corroded and disintegrated them. I think I still prefer my version.

5:01/5:14—"He's the greatest tenor since Caruso."

Enrico Caruso (1873–1921) was the most famous Italian tenor of the early 20th century, hugely popular in America thanks to his pioneering commercial recordings (nearly three hundred of them) and performances at the New York Metropolitan Opera (nearly nine hundred of those). He also appeared in a few early Hollywood movies, including the Paramount release *My Cousin* (1918), which features him on stage performing "Vesti la giubba" from *I Pagliacci*. This is the opera in which we see Lassparri performing at the beginning of the film, and the aria which Groucho sings part of later on. In 1906, as well as surviving the San Francisco earthquake, Caruso was charged with goosing a married woman in the monkey house of New York's Central Park Zoo. Despite his ingenious defense—he blamed one of the monkeys—Caruso was found guilty and fined ten dollars.

5:35/5:49—The all-new Harpo takes a beating

Thalberg reinvention at its most transfiguring. The aim: make the team more sympathetic to women. The method: make Harpo a figure of pathos, and kill stone dead what could have been a delightfully funny sequence (in which he is seen to be wearing several costumes at the same time) by showing him getting the feathers kicked out of him by nasty Lasspari. (Boo! Hiss!) This is even lousy in the context of the scene itself, since it ends with Harpo returning to the room to take another going-over, the sound of which always elicits nervous and confused laughter from audiences. But as late as *The Marx Brothers Scrapbook* Groucho is still defending the scene on the grounds that it establishes sympathy for Harpo— the one thing Harpo didn't need from any audience hitherto. If there is one quality above all others that Thalberg removed from the team it is *self-sufficiency*. ("They don't need us but they treat us as equals and invite us to side with them," notes Allen Eyles. From now on they are going to need us, at least once a film.) At Paramount Harpo was half angel, half demon; totally sealed in his own universe, occasionally visiting ours entirely on his own terms, with no attempt at accommodation and a plain relish in every moment of confusion and incompatibility. Now he is a sweet clown, who feels pain and seeks consolation, and whose lack of engagement with reality seems to derive from some deficiency rather than indifference. Even his silence, once a simultaneous affront and provocation, is now just one more stick with which to beat him. "You dumb idiot!" exclaims Lasspari, in perhaps the single most disastrous line of dialogue in the entire film.

11:34/12:03—"You can get a phonograph record of "Minnie the Moocher" for seventy-five cents!"

This joke is reminiscent in its structure of one included in Moss Hart and Irving Berlin's play *Face the Music* (1932). Looking at the bill of major acts (including the Marx Brothers) performing at a vaudeville house, a character opines: "They've got an awful nerve, charging a dime for that show in these times. Why, at the Roxy you can get four feature pictures and a room and a bath for a nickel." Though Kaufman is not credited for any input into the book, it is established that he did contribute some lines, this surely being one of them.

"Minnie the Moocher" is a classic jazz song (first recorded in 1931) by Cab Calloway and His Orchestra. Like many jazz numbers of the time, it features several unabashed references to drug use: "he showed her how to kick the gong around," "he was cokey," etc. The song, and live action footage of Cab performing it (apparently his earliest-known film appearance), was featured in a fantastic Fleischer Studios "Talkartoon," also called *Minnie the Moocher* (1932), and starring Betty Boop, the most sexually desirable woman in film history. Like so much of Fleischer's product, it has a weird, otherworldly quality, and a visual and comedic imagination entirely distinct from that of other animation studios.

13:53/14:28—The contract scene

The last classic Chico-Groucho duologue—oh, *welcome back Kaufman and Ryskind!* This is the moment when you realize that the film really is going to be taking you right back, to the beautiful, theatrical material of *The Cocoanuts* and *Animal Crackers*. There's only one thing about this scene that fails to delight me, and that's the mass hysteria that the line, "You can't fool me, there ain't no Sanity Clause" seems to provoke whenever the film is shown today. It's a nice enough little joke and I have no real problem with it, but I've never understood why this odd consensus has sprung up that it's the funniest line in the piece, and must be greeted with a unanimous fake roar. It's not like you don't know it's coming, and there are so many other great lines:

> "We had an argument and he pulled a knife on me so I shot him."
> "Of course he won't be able to eat but he can live like a prince."
> "You haven't got a baboon in your pocket have you?"
> "I was blind for three days."
> "Why can't the first part of the second party be the second part of the first party? Then you've got something."
> "Well, that takes out two more clauses."
> "That's all right, there's no ink in the pen anyway."

Logically, the *best-known* lines should get the *smallest* laughs, *because* they're the best-known lines. Shouldn't they?

The joke where Groucho's cry of "Two beers, bartender!" is followed by Chico's "I'll take two beers too" is derived from *Socratic Dialogue*, a piece Kaufman and Ryskind wrote for *The Nation* in 1933. The piece, purporting to be a transcribed conversation between the authors, has Ryskind call out, "Waiter! Two beers," and Kaufman reply, "Make mine the same!"

Unless a major coincidence has occurred here, the sanity clause gag is inspired by a line in Groucho and Chico's radio show *Flywheel, Shyster and Flywheel,* but while Kalmar and Ruby were present at the very early stages of the film's planning, there is no evidence Perrin and Sheekman were. Of course, both men were friends who may have been asked to look over the script and add a line or two here and there: Gloria Stuart writes of Sheekman that "although he didn't always earn a writing credit, Arthur was on each and every movie as Groucho's consultant and pal." The other alternative is that the line may have been remembered and added by Groucho or Chico themselves.

Meanwhile, the influence of this scene is clearly apparent in Chico and Groucho's subsequent aborted 1937 radio project, in which they were to play Hollywood agents (perhaps inspired by Zeppo's real-life recent career change). The series never went beyond the pilot stage, but (as well as featuring instrumental versions of "Cosi Cosa" and "Alone") it includes this blunted but still unmistakable exchange:

> GROUCHO: Wait, there's no pen-point on the pen.
> CLIENT: That doesn't matter, I can't write.
> GROUCHO: Then we're even; we can't read.

The newly found Hungarian version of the film (see 1:20, above) confirms that the jump-cuts in this sequence do, as predicted, correspond with excised references to Italy:

> CHICO: I'm a stranger here myself.
> GROUCHO: Aren't you an Italian?
> CHICO: No, only my mama and papa is Italian.
> GROUCHO: What's his [the tenor he wants to sign] name?
> CHICO: It's an Italian name. What do you care? I can't pronounce it.

15:58/16:38—"Don't you know what duplicates are?" "Sure, those five kids up in Canada."

By "duplicates" Chico means the Dionne quintuplets, born in Ontario in 1934, and the first quintuplets known to survive their infancy. Everybody would have got the joke: the quintuplets achieved a degree of celebrity that was virtually unprecedented in their day. Their likenesses were featured on plates, cutlery, dolls, postcards and candy bars, while their mother ran a shop hawking stones from their farm as an aid to fertility. (Fifty cents each.) They were also used to advertise Quaker Oats and other products nationally. Six thousand people a day, including many top Hollywood stars, came to see them, via a special observation room at their nursery; the midwives who delivered them cashed in with a souvenir and dining stand of their own, and it was claimed in 1934 that they had brought $51,000,000 of tourist revenue to Ontario. As well as appearing in four Hollywood films, they are referred to in two Stooges shorts, *My Man Godfrey* (also written by Ryskind), *Miracle of Morgan's Creek, The Women, Dumbo* and an Agatha Christie novel. In the Warners cartoon *The Coo-Coo Nut Grove* (1936), they appear in animated form, alongside the Marxes. All of the quints were girls and two are still alive at the time of this writing.

21:45/22:40—"Alone"

Surely this is the best non-comic song in any Marx movie, superbly performed by Allan Jones and the luminous Kitty Carlisle. The Marxes never again, and never before, had a heroine quite as classy as Kitty Carlisle's Rosa. She is beautiful, quietly amused by the Brothers' destructive wit and horseplay without ever quite endorsing it or joining in, and her dignity is such that even they dare not attempt puncturing it. Groucho is clearly besotted with her, Harpo rests his head on her bosom for comfort after a beating. Even Chico is courteous in her presence (whatever he may be thinking)...

How I look forward to this moment whenever I watch the movie at home. How I dread it (and the bit where Allan Jones joins in at **23:08/24:06** still more) whenever I watch it in a theater, knowing that it will get a big, oafish laugh from people who should know better. It's an odd gesture, one that fancies itself iconoclastic and individualistic but is really all the things it feels itself least to be: unspontaneous, ritualistic, conformist and pompous. The Marxes themselves would doubtless have been appalled at such a show of rudeness to fellow show business professionals: Groucho's verdict on the phenomenon would have been worth hearing, and doubtless useful. This is the negative legacy of the Marx revival of the sixties and seventies. But it is not just the usual philistinism that rankles in this special case: it is that this performance of this song is *so very* beautiful.

31:42/33:02—The crowded stateroom

Aside from the climax, this is probably the most famous scene in the film, and one of the most famous of all scenes in the Marx repertoire. It's very funny, and very basic, with little that makes it distinctively Marxian except the repetition of the hard boiled eggs. Like the entire scene, this running gag (the means, according to Harpo, by which "a dud became a classic") was worked out during the pre-filming road tours. Its chief architect, according to most reliable testimony, was Al Boasberg, a gagman who (unlike Kaufman) accompanied Ryskind on the tour to develop the material. According to Groucho, the original Kaufman and Ryskind scene had him undressing in the corridor because of the lack of room inside, shocking a passing woman. It was Boasberg and the Brothers who worked out the idea of piling as many people as possible into the crammed room during the stage tryouts.

Many official sources, including the British Film Institute and Allen Eyles's *Complete Films of the Marx Brothers,* claim that blustery comic support actor Billy Gilbert plays two roles in the film, including the engineer's assistant, here. This is contradicted by the evidence of the face of the actual actor, which resembles Gilbert's to the extent that it is male but little further. Hard to know how these rumors get started, but you'd be surprised how many otherwise reliable sources still doggedly insist that the engineer's assistant and Gilbert are one and the same. Gilbert does appear, of course, in the steerage banquet scene; he talks at **39:26/41:05**.

36:09/37:40—The three greatest aviators in the world

It's odd the way these characters are never referred to by name by any character in the film; even when they are announced at the official function it is simply as "the three greatest aviators in the world." But if you freeze the newspaper that reports subsequently on the Marxian debacle that ensues, you'll see that they are called the Santopoulos Brothers.

Since Lindy's big landing, aviators had figured highly among America's greatest celebrity heroes, and it is a distinctively Kaufman and Ryskind touch to have the Marx Brothers let the air out of some. Such a pity, though, that Zeppo wasn't around to put one of those beards on—while Ricardo is not exactly a comedy part, he gets a far bigger share of the fun than Zeppo ever did. Of course, Zeppo could just about warble a song, but he couldn't have done the opera stuff. I suspect, however, that some of the ambiguity surrounding these eminent gentlemen may be attributed to pre-production caution regarding the potential offence the film might cause to Italian audiences (see above, 1:20). As Allen Eyles has noted, the primary inspiration for the bearded airmen was likely Italian Air-Marshal and Fascist hero Italo Balbo, who had received a rapturous official welcome in New York in 1933, after flying from Rome to Chicago. But unlike the ugly jump cuts that announce Italian references in the dialogue elsewhere in the film, the blurring of the aviators' identity is plainly a subtler job of work, carried out either from the first or some time before the cameras rolled: if it was ever noted outright that they are Italians, cautious hands have been at work subsequently. There is work to be done here: if changes *were* made, what exactly were they changed *from*, and when were they implemented? If the decision not to name the aviators in the dialogue was taken pre-production, why not have characters refer to them by an unambiguously non–Italian name rather than no name at all? Are we therefore looking at an attempt on the makers' part to both have their cake and eat it, and was the Greek-sounding "Santopoulos" seen in the newspaper an implication that they had not distanced themselves enough, and inserted as an *additional* safeguard after principal photography? If so, why is it presented in such a blink-and-miss-it fashion?

That Balbo *was* the primary inspiration seems overwhelmingly likely: as Allen Eyles has noted, there even exists "a newspaper picture of the bearded and uniformed Balbo taking a drink of water at the official greeting." If he saw the film, and perhaps influenced the negative reception it received from the Italian censors, I have found no reference to it. For the record, though a buffoon and a fascist agitator of long-standing, Balbo was among the vanishingly few openly opposed to the anti–Semitic racial laws Mussolini began implementing in 1938, and in a meeting of Italy's Grand Council in 1939 he condemned the policy of "licking Hitler's boots" and argued that Italy should fight on the side of Britain. He was killed in 1942 when an Italian anti-aircraft battery shelled his plane, mistakenly thinking it British.

42:33/44:20—Chico plays piano to an audience of cute kids

This is the first time there hasn't been something vaguely challenging or inappropriate in Chico's piano sequence. Normally his piano playing, though sure to win his audience over with sheer virtuosity, has a solipsistic, confrontational quality. Here it's just a musical interlude, and he's mooning over a bunch of adorable moppets and they're mooning right back. It's not exactly harmful as the film's innovations go, but it's not an improvement either, and the switch is telling. It certainly lays the groundwork for the infantilization and emasculation of Chico's character, which will proceed at high speed from here. The other thing you notice about this solo is that it's very short, to make room for Harpo being given a comedy piano spot as well as his harp solo. Considering that it was largely through Chico's industry that the Brothers got the MGM gig in the first place, there's something rather disgraceful about the way in which he is slowly allowed to become the new Zeppo as the films progress.

48:48/50:40—The rocking cabin/Harpo's escape

This, I think, is one of the most interesting and at the same time most misjudged sections of the film. In the previous scene, Gottlieb had alerted the ship's authorities to the presence of the three stowaways, and a chase ensued. So far, so *Monkey Business.* But as in *Monkey Business,* the Marxes can be chased, but they should never be caught. The fact that they are, and end up incarcerated, is regrettable in itself, but it also has a knock-on effect on the comic potential of the film's following scene, in which Harpo gets the idea to effect their escape by stealing the beards of the three greatest aviators in the world. In the film, we see Harpo escape through his porthole, and enter the nearest open one, which happens to be that of the sleeping aviators. So the idea presents itself to him through circumstance. Far better if they were still on the run but nominally at liberty, and the ridiculous scheme occurs to them not out of necessity but, like the Chevalier impersonations, because that's just the way their minds work.

The brig where Chico, Harpo and Allan Jones are incarcerated appears to be filmed through a tilted camera when we first see it, to suggest the fact that it is at sea. Later, however, when the water sloshes through the porthole and Harpo attempts his escape, it is obvious from the motion of the water on the cabin floor that the set really is rocking and tilting, and must have been specially built to achieve that effect. But if so, why is the effect deployed so sparingly, and so unnecessarily? It is never used for comic effect. Even Thalberg's mania for logic and authenticity can scarcely account for so elaborate a means of simply enabling water to briefly move in a shot lasting a couple of seconds, when the audience isn't even looking at it. So here's my guess. The rocking cabin appears to be a fairly well-known comedy device: you can see a variation on it in *Funny Bones,* Peter Chelsom's 1995 paean to British music hall comedy. (In that sequence, the rocking is giving the comic seasickness, and the water rushes in when he opens the porthole to be sick.) I think this is essentially a stage device: whereas a rocking ship can be easily evoked on film, on stage part of the fun for the audience would be their awareness of how the effect is being achieved. Possibly, therefore, this may have been another scene that was built up during the pre-filming stage tours. Back in Hollywood, however, though retained for its necessary plot function, its essential corniness and general lack of effectiveness onscreen as opposed to stage resulted in its being rightly whittled down to the almost nothing that now remains. I'm guessing that onstage the scene was more elaborate and much more happened in it, albeit of a presumably very basic slapstick nature. (Stills exist showing the three actors pulling the rope through the porthole in which Chico's wig is soaking wet.)

The bit with Harpo on the ropes, swinging on the outside of the ship and ending up in the bedroom of the aviators, is supposedly one of those that most earned Sam Wood his reputation as a retake-ordering tyrant, to the extent that Harpo was left with rope burns and cuts. Three things to look out for (or four if you count Harpo looking utterly deranged in a wet wig): the cartoon butterfly that emerges from one of the aviators' beards (often remarked upon with praise, but a strange and untypical joke that I've never been much keen on), the delightful moment when Groucho, looking out of his porthole, sees Harpo and warmly greets him, and the fact that when the scene opens Harpo is playing comb and paper: an instrument that demands a voice, rather than merely breath, in order to work.

52:07/54:18—The aviators' speeches

Make the most of this: Kaufman and Ryskind have provided Chico with a gloriously absurd, brilliantly funny monologue—his first since the last time they wrote for him, and pretty much the last great solo comic moment, of any kind, in his entire career. It's unmistakably the work of the men who wrote Spaulding's African monologue, and cut more or less from the same cloth. Compare how they begin:

> GROUCHO: My friends, I am going to tell you of that great, mysterious, wonderful continent known as Africa. Africa is God's country—and He can have it.
> CHICO: Friends, how we happen to come to America is a great story. But I no tell that. When a-we first started out we got-a no idea you give us this-a grand reception. We don't-a deserve it. And when I say we don't-a deserve it, believe me I know what I'm-a talking about.

And compare its sublime nonsense with this variant section of Spaulding's speech from the 1928 playscript held at Princeton University among the Sam Harris papers:

> GROUCHO: We landed on the coast of Africa. On February fourth, having lost an entire day crossing the Fifty-ninth Street Bridge, we at once proceeded four-hundred miles into the interior, where we were met by Grover Whalen. Well, of course, we turned right around, and went out five hundred miles in the opposite direction, and were again met by Grover Whalen. Well anyhow, there we were in the middle of Africa, by this time it was beginning to get dark and the jungle closes at two, with the customary matinees on Wednesday and Saturday.
> CHICO: So now I tell you how we fly to America. The first time we started, we get-a halfway across when we run out of gasoline and we gotta go back. Then I take-a twice as much gasoline. This time we were just about to land. Maybe three feet. When whaddya think? We run out of gasoline again. And a-back we go again to get-a more gas. This time I take-a plenty gas. Well, we get-a halfway over when what-a you think-a happened? We forgot-a the aeroplane. So we gotta sit down and we talk it over. Then I get-a the great idea. We no take-a gasoline. We no take-a the aeroplane. We take a steamship! And that, friends, is how we fly across the ocean.

Never again, through an additional seven movies and beyond, would Chico be funny all on his own. Never again would anybody even try to write great absurdist material of this sort for him. From hereon it's a bit of expository dialogue, some silly behavior, a lot of dunce humor and some piano playing.

53:45/56:00—"I would suggest you make your speech a little more direct than your brother's"

When Harpo is set to give his address, he drinks from a trick glass with sloping insides, so that it holds far less water than it appears to. It's only really noticeable on the big screen, but with a bit of zooming you should see the difference in glass texture, both when he is pouring and when he is drinking. For the final shot at **54:48/57:06** when he is no longer obliged to realistically drink and is simply letting the water gush out over his beard, it looks as though a normal glass has been substituted.

54:58/57:16—Groucho and the aviators converse in their own language

This must have sounded wonderfully weird at the time; today our technically sophisticated ears will instantly identify the sound of tape running backwards. The real dialogue when the film is reversed proves pretty straightforward: anyone hoping for hidden jokes, even mildly outrageous ones impudently slipped past the Breen Office, is going to be disappointed. Groucho says, "Did you hear what he said? He said you're frauds and impostors and you absolutely don't belong here at all." Chico and Allan Jones then bluster in unison; Chico can be discerned saying, "He said that about us?" while Jones exclaims, "Why that's ridiculous!" Then after the attempt at appeasement, Groucho returns to explain: "He says he didn't mean it and he wants to know if you'll stay here." Chico and Jones still remain indignant, however, and Chico can be heard saying, "I wouldn't stand for a thing like this!"

This is a strange in-joke. Presumably, audiences at the time would have assumed the three are merely speaking gibberish. But Chico, of course, goes on to speak in English. Thanks to Mr. Bob Gassel for making the astute point that it would have been much funnier if Groucho, as their interpreter, likewise spoke to them in plain English. Groucho's parting line—"Of course, you know this means war!"—feels like a deliberate echo of *Duck Soup,* but presumably isn't, even if it got into the script via Kalmar and Ruby's brief period of participation.

56:19/58:40—Harpo enters for breakfast

Note his somewhat pallid complexion here. My guess is that this is another of Sam Wood's famous retakes, and the powdered sugar make-up he applies at **57:03/59:26** has been on at least once already that morning. A minor mystery is the origin of Chico and Harpo's heretofore unseen clothing. Harpo is wearing a stylish coat and Chico a smart fedora. Presumably they have swiped them from Driftwood's trunk; nonetheless it is a slightly strange decision to have Chico in particular come to breakfast in a hat that looks completely unusual on him, without being in any way comic.

57:50/60:15—The adjoining rooms

Excellent extended farce, and, for Kaufman and Ryskind, a blatant revision of the jewel theft scene in *The Cocoanuts,* right down to the split screen between two rooms. Again, such a shame Zeppo's not in on all this fun—though he wasn't around the first time either, come to think of it.

65:15/67:59—Groucho falls down the stairs

Or rather, Driftwood does. Slow this sequence down to get a good look at the double's face. This is another of Thalberg's more dangerous ideas: to elicit audience sympathy by having the Brothers demeaned, as if the liberating destruction they wreak in the climax needs to be thus justified before we will laugh at it. It's also the first indicator that the new Marxes would not be above basic slapstick for its own sake. From here to Mrs. Dukesbury stuck in a cannon is but a blink.

66:34/69:21—"I can't feel cheerful about being such a hoodoo to you."

A line stems from the scene in which all the Brothers and Jones are shown on a park bench, humiliated and without ideas. Note that Chico and Harpo are still wearing their breakfast coat and hat (see above, **56:19/58:40**) and Chico is even still wearing the tie that Harpo cut in half in the same scene. "You goddamn hoodoo!" is a familiar line from Hecht and MacArthur's *The Front Page,* which would certainly have been familiar to Messrs. Kaufman and Ryskind (Kaufman directed the original production, and was doing so when the pair began writing *Animal Crackers*), but I haven't heard the insult much used elsewhere. It's a variant of voodoo, and so means a hex: Ricardo means that he brings Rosa bad luck.

67:13/70:02—The Brothers camp out in Gottlieb's office

Can this scene be the inspiration for all those surely apocryphal anecdotes about the boys invading Thalberg's office, roasting potatoes in the nude and creating artificial fires and the like? Or do we think any of that *really* happened?

68:23/71:14—"Take Me Out to the Ball Game"

The sheet music Harpo inserts into *Il Trovatore,* and that yields such comic dividends shortly after, is this popular 1908 number by Jack Norworth and Albert Von Tilzer. Part of the joke is not just the incongruity of the tune but also its familiarity to the audience, which (for American audiences at least) it still retains. A stroke of luck: there can't be many 1908 songs popular with 1935 audiences that are also just as well-known today. If you attend a Major League Baseball game today—and you'd be amazed how many people do—you'll still hear it during the seventh-inning stretch.

The pay-off at **72:04/75:05**, when the orchestra begins performing it, strikes me as one of the most perfect moments of comedy construction in film history. We saw Harpo put the sheet music in the folder four minutes earlier, and we know what's coming, so the moment carries a real weight of comic expectation. Will it be as funny as it promises to be? Of course it is: we laugh from the moment the music changes, and then we have the bits with Harpo and Chico playing ball with the instruments, and the laugh becomes a roar.... All this time we have no idea what Groucho's up to, but we have no reason to think he was in on this part of the jeopardizing operation. Then suddenly, with the audience already laughing as much as they think they can, there comes the impossibly perfect topper: without any anticipation at all on our part, Groucho enters down the central aisle, selling peanuts. It's masterly, sublime stuff.

68:38/71:30—"Hey, Shorty—will you toss up that kelly?"

"Take Me Out to the Ball Game" was also used as the title of a 1949 MGM musical starring Frank Sinatra and Gene Kelly, but this is an altogether different kelly. Just as you'd expect, it's a slang term for a man's hat. Though it usually refers to a derby/bowler, of the sort Groucho had been wearing in the previous scene, here he uses it to refer to the smart topper he has worn to the opening night. The origin is not known for sure; one possibility is that it is an early twentieth century reference to the tendency of stage Irishmen to wear derby hats. His grateful donation of a coin to "Shorty" in thanks for the favor is accompanied with the suggestion, "Get yourself a stogie!" A stogie (or stogy) is, of course, a cigar; specifically, however, the term is generally used to denote a thin, cheap, inferior one.

70:11/73:11—"Play, Don!"

Groucho's indication to the conductor that it is time to begin is a Jack Benny reference: Jack used the line on his show to introduce bandleader Don Bestor and, for no obvious reason, but as these things so often do, it became a nationally-quoted catchphrase. By the time most audiences heard Groucho use it, however, it was already a thing of the past: Bestor left the show in 1935. He retained fond memories of Benny, recalling later: "Jack made me. He put me in the public eye with his 'Play, Don' utterances."

71:07/74:05—"It's just the Tarzan in me!"

It's a funny thing, this popular-culture reference lottery. The fact is that nobody reading this, probably nobody in the Western world, needs me to explain who Tarzan is, nor why Groucho likens himself to him at this point in the film, nor why he then makes that guttural cry. But at the time, Tarzan was just one seemingly ephemeral pop-culture hero among legions of others: a character from a creaky old novel recently brought to the screen (by MGM, naturally) with Judy Standish as the ape man's foxy English squeeze, Jane. No reason in the world to have thought that audiences seventy-five years later would know instantly what Groucho means, any more than most would know why Patsy Kelly solemnly intones "Chan*du!*" when she hears a gong sound in one of her short films with Thelma Todd. That's the way it goes: Chandu endures among specialists only, but I'll bet most of you reading this gave out with that cry before leaping something or swinging on a rope when you were kids.

73:45/76:50—Is this the longest delayed gookie in Marx Brothers history?

The film's nearly over! It's a good one, though.

76:38/79:50—Harpo's acrobatics

Now, this is interesting, because it's the Brothers' first true stunt-slapstick climax. It's tempting to imagine it was something decided upon by the head office with which Kaufman and Ryskind were not at liberty to tamper, other than to make the individual jokes as brilliantly funny as they so surely are. But look at it in context. It's not a *mindless* slapstick climax, like the finales of *At the Circus* or *The Big Store*: it's totally in keeping with the Paramount Harpo, validated by the narrative (keeping Thalberg happy), that just happens to be made with the creative freedom of MGM resources. It was the later MGM movies, taking *Opera* slavishly as their models, which misread the scene and just assumed that if Harpo could run up and down theatrical backdrops then Groucho and Chico can unicycle about in a department store. This scene, like this film, is in so many ways a glorious last hurrah, as well as the portent of an altogether less interesting new beginning. In fact, however, all this glorious destruction was a late substitution for an original ending in which the Brothers burned down the theater. Due to fears that audiences would be made uncomfortable by it, it was abandoned just as the original fiery climax of *Horse Feathers* had been in 1932.

The only snag with this finale is that it helps to bolster the claim, often made, that the film is anti-opera in its attitudes, and that the Brothers are attacking the rarefied, highbrow, non-populist form of art it represents. The fact that they are all for it once Allan Jones is doing the singing is then either conveniently overlooked, or worse, taken to be a flaw in the structure. Not at all: the film dates from a time when opera was still widely popular, and the idea of a higher culture, into which it may prove edifying and pleasurable to dip one's digit occasionally, was not deemed oppressive. If there was such a thing as a *forbidding* high culture, it certainly wouldn't have been represented by Verdi. As with the sniggering that accompanies the Allan Jones and Kitty Carlisle solos today, we should resist the temptation to recast the Marx Brothers as cheerleaders for cultural philistinism: they are sophisticates at heart. Gottlieb is a fraud, and draws the Marxian ire not because he appreciates opera but because he doesn't: he is concerned only with reputations, status, and the superficial trappings of the opera world. And Lasspari is worse: a snob and an ass who despises his audience, beats his manservant and thinks his leading lady is obliged to worship him offstage and on. The Marxes destroy *Il Trovatore* in order to save it, because Gottlieb and Lasspari are *not worthy of it*. When the right singers are on stage they stand aside and enjoy the show.

7

A Day at the Races (1937)

No, we're not mad. We're just terribly hurt, that's all.—Dr. Hugo Z. Hackenbush
(Groucho Marx)

The first glimpse of *A Day at the Races* that many among its original audience would have seen was the trailer. In it, an actor, immaculate and serious, steps out from behind a curtain and calls for silence. He gets a custard pie flung in his face.

"I talked to several persons who declared that while they did not usually enjoy a Marx brothers picture they liked *A Day at the Races,*" noted the film correspondent of the *Evening Independent* in June of 1937. "One woman said that she went to see the picture only because her husband thoroughly enjoys the Marx brothers. She said she had usually been much bored by the comedy trio and went to the last one with great reluctance. But, she said, she enjoyed it very much and found it very amusing."

This is Thalberg's dreams for the Marx Brothers vindicated in full. At last! We've watered the Marx Brothers down so much that even if you couldn't stand them before, there's a chance you'll survive this one! Several such pieces even cite *A Night at the Opera* as an example of the older, roughhouse kind of Marx picture this marvel of ordinariness has transcended.

For much-needed relief from all this, let us turn to a lemon-sucker called Connery Chappell in *The Sunday Dispatch:*

> Metro [has], as it were, translated the Marx Brothers. They are now slapstick comedians of rare ability, doing their work better than almost any other screen team. But they are not those irresponsible maniacs who spun around like tops in a world where Freud came in at the window as Harpo went out eating the door.... To the real Marx admirers the film will be a landmark denoting the position beyond which it was no longer commercially possible for them to make films for a small minority.

True, *A Day at the Races* is not a *terrible* Marx Brothers movie, far from it. But it could well be their most over-rated. (And not just artistically: despite being their second big MGM smasheroo, it was so bloated and costly it actually lost $543,000.) It's also the longest, for reasons not to be justified onscreen. (And it's also my wife's favorite, for reasons that *are* to be found on the screen, but which don't make an awful lot of sense to me. Suffice to say that when Thalberg patronizingly suggested that the emasculation of the Marxes would make them more popular with women, he could have had my beloved in mind. Now back to the boys' stuff.)

Groucho (center) trying to escape from Margaret Dumont and Leonard Ceeley in *A Day at the Races*.

It's the film wherein the Thalberg deviations from formula, which *A Night at the Opera* was inspired enough and hilarious enough to withstand, or circumnavigate, or even turn into advantages, finally come home to roost. All those corny ideas—it's funnier with fewer jokes and a better plot, and audiences need something to root for, and Groucho would be more appealing if he had a limp and worked in an orphanage—all that nonsense Kaufman saw coming and more or less sent packing in *A Night at the Opera,* is lying in wait for *A Day at the Races* and this time Thalberg wins. And this despite the fact that the film is the most transparent imitation of *Opera* imaginable, with everything that was felt to have been successful in the first film repeated, only in almost every case just that little bit less effectively, because misunderstood.

The characterization is the first and most obvious casualty. *Opera* had the boys helping out the hero and heroine, but it wasn't like they were helping her save up for an eye operation: it was all about opera singers being nasty to other opera singers, and the villains, so to speak, were just pompous arty types. These were exactly the kind of people the Marx Brothers had always enjoyed annoying, and for no more benevolent a reason than that they deserve it. And so the fact that the Brothers had been turned into helping hands didn't show up as strongly, or destructively, as it might have done in another context ... a context like this, for instance. Here the villains really *are* villains, and the task in hand is to help Maureen O'Sullivan, as pretty Judy Standish, save her struggling business from nasty Douglass Dumbrille.

Groucho is his usual con man, except this time he doesn't want to be found out, and he keeps trying to flee when things get difficult. When he does let the inner Groucho free, with predictably chaotic results, we fade to the next day and find him writhing with remorse at having let Judy down. He's pretending to be a doctor, but not in the way that he has pretended to be a head of state or a college professor or an explorer—that is to say, *magically*—he's a *real* veterinarian, and a down at the heel veterinarian at that, posing as a doctor so as to deceive Margaret Dumont into thinking she is ill when she is not. (Why? We need a reason if we're going to take these people seriously, Mr. Thalberg! To extort money from her? Some hero!)

There's no point in playing it semi-straight because it just ends up making even less sense: the man that Judy thinks might be the one to turn around the fortunes of her ailing sanitarium may not be the Groucho of *Duck Soup,* but neither is he anyone's idea of a real doctor, and if she looks carefully she might notice that his moustache is painted on. Yet we are expected to believe not just that potty old Margaret Dumont is a soft touch for his evasions but that the sensible and intelligent Judy can take one look at him and say, "I am satisfied with Mrs. Upjohn's recommendation." (Curious, too, that the villains then spend so much of the rest of the film trying to expose this obvious fraud, when what they should really want is to leave him alone and let him run the sanitarium into the ground.) Otis B. Driftwood was an opportunist and a con man, but he had no "real" life; we knew nothing whatever about him, and most important of all *he was having a good time.* Hugo Z. Hackenbush is an unsuccessful vet, who can't afford his rent, and however hard he finds it to restrain his anarchic impulses, he plainly *wants* to. It's as if what we had always taken to be Groucho's conscious assault on propriety was, in fact, a kind of nervous compulsion, a sort of Tourette's syndrome. Pity poor Groucho: he's his own worst enemy.

Harpo does okay, but there are more vulgar efforts to make him pathetic—than to be which the Paramount Harpo can think of no worse fate—and *A Day at the Races* is the second film in a row that introduces us to him by showing him being beaten by a hiss and boo bully. But it is Chico who is most ruinously reinvented. Chico, whose logic was once so obtuse, whose motivation so mysterious, whose instinct for disruption so unyielding that he was even capable of reducing Groucho to frustration, is now working contentedly, and presumably efficiently, for the Standish Sanitarium, and so devoted to Judy that he's willing to do so without pay. Once he was unwilling to work, even, perhaps especially, *for* pay. And he's resourceful. Getting Mrs. Upjohn to bankroll the sanitarium? His idea. Sending for Dr. Hackenbush to sweeten her up? His idea. Ravelli the musician, who charges more the less he plays, and most of all for not rehearsing, this plainly is not. And he's not even given anything funny to do.

When it comes to this sticky issue of altruism, it seems to me that the very particular magic of the pure Marx Brothers lay in the fact that they were forces for good *inadvertently,* because they were first and solely forces of *honesty.* They act with both complete freedom *and* complete incorruptibility, and their very irreverence casts them as guardians of integrity.

When they attack pomposity, dishonesty and selfishness, the rightness of their attitudes has the *incidental* side effect of making life's journey just that little bit easier for the honest, good-natured, unpretentious people who would otherwise be entirely at the mercy of the world's Morgans and Lassparris. All the Paramount films, to varying extents, end with a wrong righted, but the Brothers themselves, though instrumental in bringing that end about, only serve the interests of rightness in the abstract. It's never explicitly their mission that Polly marries Bob or that John Parker is recognized as a great artist. That sort of thing just *happens,* when you have Groucho, Chico, Harpo and sometimes Zeppo about the place. This is a vital point: these films are saying that the world would be a better place with a few more Marx Brothers loose in it. And that simply isn't true of *these* Marx Brothers, of Hugo and Tony and Stuffy. They're just like the people they're trying to help: life's losers, not well off, not distinguished, always looking over their shoulders, up against it ... they're just a bit zanier than the straight heroes, that's all.

A Day at the Races, despite its length, contains remarkably little comedy. I don't necessarily mean that what *is* there isn't very funny. I just mean there's not much of it. There are, by my count seven comedy scenes in the film. The arrival of Dr. Hackenbush comes first (it's okay), and then—a quarter of an hour in!—comes the second, and everybody's favorite, the Tootsie Fruitsie scene. (Yes, I *do* think this scene is funny, in a straightforward kind of way, but it's a sketch that you could give to any comic and straight man and they'd get just as much fun out of it.) Next, twenty-five minutes in, comes the call to the Florida Medical Board. (This is much more like it, because Groucho has stopped sneaking about and is having fun again.) Then we have the scene where Hackenbush examines Harpo. (Not bad. And it's got that line you all love, something about his watch stopping. Can't quite think of it for a minute.) Then the Esther Muir scene, ending with the wallpaper free for all. (Yes, it's exuberant and funny, and I'll bet it was a riot on the road-show. But it's a bit basic; it's slapstick.) Then we have the Harpo-Chico whistling translation scene, of which opinion varies considerably. Finally, there is the Margaret Dumont examination: for my money, the film's one and only classic, fully sustained and imaginatively developed comedy sequence. The big finale doesn't count because, apart from a few half-hearted bits at the start where the Brothers try to delay the race, it doesn't even want to be funny.

Of course, we can argue into the night about how all these scenes stack up in terms of quality, but let's at least agree on this: in terms of *quantity* this is not an especially generous tally for a film that runs nearly two hours. As with *Opera,* the most self-contained scenes were toured live to gauge reaction and fine-tune performance, and it's almost as if the studio decided that these nuggets contained all the necessary comedy, and the rest of the film could be built around them with scarcely an effort to make it amusing. (If so, they were not in agreement with Groucho who, ever the torment of studio publicity departments, happily told reporters as the tour began that "the trouble is none of this stuff seems funny.") A report carried in *The Lewiston Daily Sun* and elsewhere in July of 1936 offers an interesting account of the touring process:

> This time the story they are whipping into shape is called *A Day at the Races.* The route has been extended to bring the comedians as far East as Cleveland. They will cover about 6000 miles in all, in contrast to a mere 3500 traversed last year. They hope to land at least a hundred healthy, full-grown, tasteful gags in each new community they visit. Most of them will be subsequently

thrown away.... On the present tour an innovation is being tried. Thirty-thousand ballot-cards have been taken along and are being passed out to audiences at every performance asking for comment on the funny lines, the unfunny ones and the general caliber of the performance. A clinical conference is held after each show and the old carnival axiom "every performance new and different" for once becomes an actual fact. The four gagsmen who accompany the Marxes often sit up all night formulating fresh lines and bits of action; after a brief rehearsal the next morning the additional material is incorporated into the show. It's the sort of thing that would send a traveling prima donna into tirades of invective, but the Marx brothers seem to dote on learning and unlearning new "sides." Some gags are born in Kansas City and perish in Omaha; others possess a longevity that carries them from the Corn Belt way back to the Golden Gate.

That last line reminds us how often we've read that the Marxes became experts at establishing why jokes get laughs in some locations and not others, and guessing what will play best in which territories. But Groucho took pains to dismiss the whole idea in an interview published in the *Evening Independent* of July 1, 1937, in which he reflects on the experience of the *Races* tour:

When I went into vaudeville years ago—and it's only my business how many more years that was—I used to hear comedians say they had to revamp their acts in different towns due to a difference in senses of humor. Maybe they only thought they did.... Never—at least never from the time we began having first rate vaudeville acts and hit musical comedies—have the Marx Brothers ever found that when something was a roar in one city, it might not be in another. A big laugh in a show is a big laugh wherever you play it, no matter if it is Burlingame, Kansas or Chicago, Illinois. And, by the same token, a joke that falls flat in Duluth is certainly going to fall just as flat—but no flatter—in Louisville.

Oddly, the *Lewiston Daily Sun* report above names George Kaufman as present with Boasberg, Seaton and Pirosh on the tour, something he didn't even bother with on *Opera*. It seems a certain error (albeit a hard one to account for given the knowledgeable nature of the rest of the piece) but it does remind us that the extent to which Kaufman was involved with the film *is* somewhat mysterious. While it was once thought that he excused himself immediately when approached after *Opera* to write more of the same, it is now generally accepted that he made some kind of a start on it, but officially withdrew when he decided he was unable—for reasons either of temperament or time—to devote himself to it. (What contributions he did make he deemed insufficient to warrant any sort of a credit, which with Kaufman—pretty much uniquely for a writer—does *not* mean such was automatically the case.) Biographer Malcolm Goldstein casts him in a more advisory role, script-doctoring the submissions of Seaton and Pirosh at Thalberg's request, and with the same daunting seriousness as his own had been received on *Opera*. Still more intriguingly, he states with certainty that Kaufman wanted to direct the movie, and specifically petitioned Thalberg to that effect, but without success.

The latter claim, admittedly an unfamiliar one in the standard Marx literature, is not to be dismissed lightly: though Kaufman directed only one film personally (and not until 1947) the idea had been mooted earlier and often, and Thalberg was certainly alert to it around this time. (He wanted him to direct *First Lady* for Norma Shearer, which of course provides reason enough for him to not want him working in that capacity on *Races*. The film ultimately emerged from Warner Bros. in 1937, with Kay Francis starring and Stanley Logan in the canvas chair.)

One other possibility, however, is that it was not the job of film director that Kaufman may have been angling for on the project, but rather overseer of a now largely forgotten plan to out-do the success of the *Opera* road tour by testing the emergent *Races* material in the form of a full-fledged Broadway show. *Variety* first got wind of that one in August of 1935, while *Opera* was still in production following its successful tour earlier in the year:

> Following the Broadway run, after the material has been sufficiently tried for the screen, Thalberg will have it scripted as the Marxes' second picture. Max Gordon and Sam Harris will be associated with the Metro exec in the experiment. Story will be written George S. Kaufman with possibly a Metro contract writer assigned to aid him on the screen angle... Until the Marx trio went on the road, idea has mainly been conversation. Numerous times major studios have backed plays on Broadway, for their screen possibilities, but this will be the first time a screen play has been written for the stage with the latter serving as the try-out for subsequent film production.

It's a fascinating idea, but one that sounds like a logistical nightmare, as presumably it proved, since by October *Variety* was noting that the plans "have been tossed overboard, with the trio deciding the experiment would be too costly... Instead a roadshow of the picture will be produced on the coast." And that (notwithstanding *Variety*'s announcement in November that "the Marx Bros' New York legit break in for a film play is on again... Metro is sending studio writers east to cook up a yarn with George S. Kaufman, who remains east") was the end of what could have been an all-new Marx Brothers musical show on Broadway.

If you look at the names under the screenplay credit, you'll get an even stronger sense that this is the work of a second team. Not that Robert Pirosh, George Seaton and George Oppenheimer are nobodies, of course. And they should have been joined onscreen by another: pivotal *A Night at the Opera* gagman Al Boasberg. (Boasberg was originally top-billed, but he sued for an entirely separate credit, lost, ended up bottom-billed, and peevishly took his name off entirely.) These were all good writers, but the sort of people customarily brought in to do the nuts and bolts work on a piece where the broad strokes have been painted by more maverick imaginations: Kaufman and Ryskind, or Kalmar and Ruby, or Perelman and Johnstone. Seaton and Pirosh were happy to confirm how loyally they adhered to the Thalberg formula. Responding to a journalist's assertion that "there must be rhyme and reason behind the Marxian escapades, else their pictures run the danger of becoming a mad jumble of unrelated incidents, too confusing for popular consumption." Seaton agreed: "That was their trouble two or three years ago.... MGM realized that when they were signed. The accuracy of that analysis was proven by the success of their first [MGM] picture." (But Pirosh does go on to offer a diverting portrait of their writing process: "Ordinarily, when we are working out their scenes, I impersonate Groucho and Seaton impersonates Chico. But it takes the two of us to impersonate Harpo. I wear the wig, Seaton chases the blondes.")

So, ultimately, this is a film that is what it is, which is to say that it is exactly what it set out to be. Adamson describes several earlier outlines and discarded scenes: they even *read* funnier than this film plays. Perhaps it was the sudden death of Thalberg early in the production that cast a pall over the movie. He was just thirty-seven years old, and Groucho in particular viewed his passing as the end of the road.

The real mystery is how something this derivative could have taken so much effort. It went through six screenplays, with fourteen incorporated outlines and treatments and the fruits of five touring vaudeville scripts, not to mention—if writing duo Henry Barsha and Dave Weissman and the terms of their $150,000 lawsuit were to be believed (and they were, by the court)—a few unacknowledged dollops of an entirely unrelated and supposedly rejected screenplay called *High Fever* ... only to end up as a paint-by-numbers copy of a previous success.

Yes, this is devil's advocacy, from a man who loves *The Cocoanuts,* defends *Room Service,* tires of hearing that *Duck Soup* is their best film, and sometimes just gets a bit grumpy for no good reason at all. I have nothing against this film, truly. It's pleasant viewing, it's impressively well made, and the Brothers are for the most part in hearty, healthy form. But I just don't get its reputation as among the very finest. Where are all the funny bits? Where are all the laughs? When you think how many laughs *Horse Feathers* crams into sixty-seven minutes, surely there should be a few more in the 105 minutes we get of this?

1:36 (NTSC)/1:40 (PAL)—"This way to the sanitarium! Free bus to the sanitarium!"

Chico's desperate efforts to tempt the new arrivals to come to Judy's health resort are harshly rebuffed in every instance, and back at the van, a wistful Judy predicts the business's collapse. But despite its unpopularity and financial precariousness, a look at the large hoard-

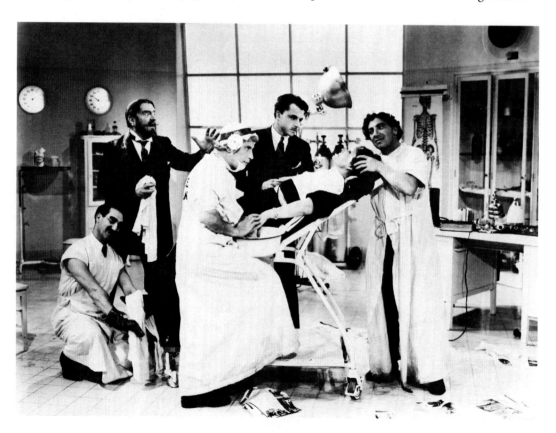

How to conduct a medical examination: (Left to right) Groucho, Sig Rumann, Harpo, Leonard Ceeley, Margaret Dumont and Chico in *A Day at the Races.*

ing welcoming visitors to Sparkling Springs Lake will reveal that the Standish Sanitarium *is* considered one of the four primary attractions in the town, and is even included on the advertised sightseeing tour.

2:10/2:17—Miss Judy

While Alan Jones has been retained as the singing Zeppo, our heroine this time is Maureen O'Sullivan, an interesting substitute for Kitty Carlisle in that she is solely an actress, and not a singer. This means that despite the huge success of "Alone" in the previous film there will be no duet number for Jones and his girl this time out. This runs so contrary to the film's general scheme of "if it happened in *A Night at the Opera*, copy it" that I wonder if it wasn't a contractual request of Jones himself. O'Sullivan was an MGM contract player familiar from supporting roles, the occasional second feature lead, and most of all as Jane in the Tarzan pictures (whose costume, before the Hays Code insisted on replacing it with a one piece, is one of the supreme eyefuls of early talking cinema). The year before making this film she had appeared along with Chico in an MGM short called *Hollywood—The Second Step*.

In an interview to coincide with the film's release she recalled the experience of sharing the screen with the Marxes: "They are quick with wisecracks and impromptu lines and I have found that one of my hardest jobs is keeping from laughing in the middle of a scene. I learned that danger the first day. It was a scene with Groucho Marx, Margaret Dumont and Leonard Ceeley, one of the villains. Groucho hands a pill to Miss Dumont. It is a huge thing, and Ceeley steps across and asks to see it. 'Isn't that awfully large for a pill?' he asks. 'Well,' said Groucho, 'it was too small for a basketball, so I didn't know what to do with it.' That was the end of his line, but he suddenly looked squarely at Ceeley and added, 'Aren't you awfully large for a pill yourself?' Right out of the blue sky that came, and I laughed. We did the scene over again, and I knew what was coming and kept a straight face. Margaret Dumont smiled at me, helpfully, after the scene and drew up a chair to give me advice. 'You'll soon learn to expect anything to happen in a scene with a Marx brother and that they never grow angry when you make a mistake,' she said. 'It's rather a proud moment to them when a player laughs during a scene. Then they know the audience will do likewise.'" Dumont goes on to point out that if she thinks they are incorrigible improvisers on a movie set, she should try working with them on stage!

3:37/3:47—Allan Jones

A unique return engagement for the romantic lead in a Marx picture, partly accountable to the *a priori* desire to recreate *A Night at the Opera* in every way possible, but doubtless also due to his very certain effectiveness and charm—and rarest of all, rapport with the brothers—in the earlier picture. His first scene here originally came complete with a lovely song called "A Message from the Man in the Moon," which was unfortunately cut, preferable though it seems to me to "Blue Venetian Waters." An instrumental rendition is heard over the opening credits and in the water carnival scene, while at the end Groucho delivers a short vocal reprise of a song audiences are, in fact, hearing for the very first time!

8:00/8:20—Mr. Morgan

The principal villain of the piece, owner of the race track and the successful Morgan Hotel, and instigator of the plot to get Judy to relinquish control of her sanitarium, is played by Douglass Dumbrille, one of the great specialists in the noble Hollywood art of playing villain to comedians and second-feature detectives. Over the years he shifted and schemed in the background behind Abbott and Costello, Bing and Bob, The Bowery Boys, Charlie Chan, Mr. Moto, the Lone Wolf and Michael Shayne, and appeared in over 150 films. He returned to the Marxes as the even nastier Mr. Grover in *The Big Store,* still scheming to take the hero's business away, but this time happy to resort even to murder to get what he wants.

Dumbrille made the headlines when, in 1960, two years after the death of his first wife and at the age of seventy, he married twenty-eight-year-old Patricia Mowbray. The marriage lasted happily until his death fourteen years later, thus justifying the statement he issued at the time of their engagement: "Age doesn't mean a blasted thing.... We don't give a continental damn what other people think."

Morgan's partner in crime, the inside man Mr. Whitmore, is played very well by the British actor Leonard Ceeley. He seems to have been around on Broadway since the twenties, but for some reason made only three films, one of which was unbilled, between 1936 and 1937. He lived until 1977.

9:08/9:31—Dr. Hackenbush arrives

Notwithstanding its considerable running time, it has been much lamented that no room was found in the film for Dr. Hackenbush's song, written by Kalmar and Ruby and originally to have been featured here. (Although usually deemed a crass studio decision, Groucho's son, Arthur, in his book *Groucho* [a.k.a. *Life with Groucho*] posits an intriguing alternative: "Since Groucho is essentially a lazy fellow, and was not particularly anxious to go through the agony of shooting a musical number, anyway, he saw to it that 'Dr. Hackenbush' got the axe.")

I don't mourn its absence as much as many fans do. It would doubtless be preferable to any three minutes of just about any later scene, but it doesn't strike me as any kind of lost classic, and Kalmar and Ruby's obvious reliance on "Hello, I Must Be Going" seems to stifle any of their customary lyrical inspiration. For the most part, the lyrics are artless and clunky:

> *So this is Dr. Hackenbush, the famous medico.*
> *You're welcome, Dr. Hackenbush ...*
> If that's the case I'll go.
> *Oh no you mustn't go!*
> Who said I mustn't go?
> The only reason that I came is so that I can go.

It seems likely that this (and "Message from the Man in the Moon") made it as far as the shooting script, and were cut (without being shot) during or immediately before the production, given that several reviews (working from studio materials) give away their lack of acquaintance with the film itself by claiming they are both present. ("Man in the Moon," at least, definitely got as far as being pre-recorded.)

The song became a favorite with Groucho, who subsequently performed it several times in surviving radio and television broadcasts. However, there is one performance which would be especially worth seeing but is, sadly, presumed lost. In one of Columbia's *Screen Snapshots* shorts from 1942 (Series 21, No. 8), Allan Jones introduces Groucho, who then performs the song. But what makes finding a copy so very desirable (besides the academic points that it is the only known example of Groucho performing the song for a movie camera and that it re-unites him on film with Jones) is that, according to two contemporary reviews I have seen, what he actually sings is not "I'm Dr. Hackenbush" but "I'm Dr. Quackenbush"—and there are *no* known recordings in existence *at all* of Groucho singing it with the original name intact. (See directly below, 9:30, for more on how and why the doctor changed his name.) Before we get too excited, let us remember not only that the film is lost, so far as we know, but also, first, that these films were only ten minutes long. So given that Groucho shares the bill with a half-dozen other star acts (including Harry Ruby and Jerome Kern), it is unlikely that the song will be featured in its entirety. And second, as noted above with regard to reviewers mentioning songs that are no longer in the film, contemporary reports are never to be entirely trusted. It could be that these, for example, are working from a list of songs supplied by the studio, and this one is still referred to under its originally copyrighted name, but nonetheless performed, as usual, as "Hackenbush" in the actual movie. But until it's found, the alternative remains a definite possibility, so go look in your attic *now*.

9:30/9:54—"This is Dr. Hugo Z. Hackenbush...."

Indeed it is, and I'm sure you don't need me to tell you that it very nearly wasn't. Until a very late stage, Groucho's character was given the more overtly comical (and fitting) surname of "Quackenbush," until fears were voiced that real-life Dr. Quackenbushes might object. So he became Dr. Hackenbush, presumably on the grounds that any real-life Dr. Hackenbushes would be made of sterner stuff, or perhaps just have more important things to worry about.

I was always surprised that so plainly jokey a name as Quackenbush could have existed in reality, but, in fact, Quackenbushes are legion in America. Lovely Monogram starlet Wanda McKay, for instance, was in reality Miss Dorothy Quackenbush, and a Google search on the name will bring up a whole bunch more, as well as a gun company of long standing.

All the same, I don't get why having the same name as a Groucho character is grounds to make the studio change it. Presumably there were hotel managers, perhaps even Florida hotel managers, called Mr. Hammer, and I doubt it did their business any harm when *The Cocoanuts* came out. It's not like seriously ill people in the vicinity are going to suddenly stop going to the doctor from fear that he might really be an interloping horse doctor with painted eyebrows. Universal somehow managed to call Lou Costello's character "Oliver Quackenbush" in *Here Come the Co-Eds*, without, it would appear, being besieged by indignant college caretakers.

The Quackenbush Affair differed from the earlier Beagle Debacle (in which the title of Chico and Groucho's radio series *Beagle, Shyster and Beagle* had to be changed mid-run to *Flywheel, Shyster and Flywheel* after a real-life Attorney Beagle spotted the coincidence and smelled $300,000) in that it was pre-emptive. There never was an actual complaint from an actual Quackenbush, but the safer path was taken, presumably, on the principle of once bitten, twice shy. On one occasion, Groucho himself took credit for the idea: "I had a hunch about that one so I consulted the telephone book. No Quackenbush. I tried the city directory. Still none. But that premonition persisted, so I looked in a medical catalog—there it was. We changed it to Dr. Hackenbush." So seriously did Hollywood take the threat of such opportunistic lawsuits that they began at this time to adopt the now standard onscreen disclaimer stating that any resemblance between the characters portrayed and real persons is purely coincidental. (The decision is generally thought to have been signaled by the costly proceedings following MGM's genuinely defamatory *Rasputin and the Empress* [1932], settled in 1934, but *Variety*, at least, notes that it is being implemented in July of 1936 "to sidestep nuisance suits" of a more general sort, and specifically cites the studio's cautious renaming of Quackenbush in this connection.)

9:58/10:24—"I knew your mother very well...." "But that's my father!"

It's a typically over-cautious MGM touch that the painting referred to could be taken as a person of either sex by anybody, and so Groucho's mistake is not an unreasonable (or funny) one. The Paramount Groucho would have made the same comment regardless of any actual ambiguity in the portrait.

10:16/10:42—"Dodge Brothers, late '29"

Groucho's response to the three doctors citing their prestigious medical backgrounds is this reference to the automobile manufacturing company, founded in 1900 and sold to the Chrysler Corporation in 1928. If there is any specific significance to the addition of "late '29," other than as an arbitrary mimicking of the doctors announcing their graduating years, it may be to suggest the considerable age of Groucho's car, in that he hasn't been able to afford a new model since the Crash. It is of some slight interest to record that following the merger with Chrysler, the Dodge vehicles became part of the same production line that made the Plymouth and DeSoto, the most famous sponsors of *You Bet Your Life*.

12:01/12:32—"Ixnay on the illpay!"

Groucho's admonition to Mrs. Upjohn is spoken in "pig latin," a schoolyard code hugely popular in the thirties that even today will probably need no explanation for American readers, though it is less familiar in Britain. The technique is simply to move the first letter of each word to the end and add the suffix "ay." The result, especially if delivered with sufficient pace, will sound baffling to those not in on the secret. It crops up in countless Hollywood movies, three of my favorites being Thelma Todd in *Pajama Party,* at a swanky party where the maid has been instructed by her snooty mistress to speak to the guests in French, responding with the pig latin translation of "I don't know what you're talking about but it's all the same to me"; the Stooges short *Tassels in the Air,* in which Moe and Larry attempt to explain the rudiments of the code to an uncomprehending Curly ("Curlicue!"); and the fabulous section of *Gold Diggers of 1933*, during which Ginger Rogers sings an entire chorus of "We're In The Money" in translated form.

12:58/13:31—"So it's war!"

Now the third film in a row where Groucho has made an exclamation along these lines.

16:18/17:00—Tootsie-Fruitsie Ice Cream

We're now a quarter of the way through the running time of *Monkey Business* or *Horse Feathers,* and apart from a few gags in Hackenbush's arrival scene the film hasn't really even tried to be funny yet. The sudden appearance of this full-fledged comedy skit, which can and often has been excised in its entirety to create a free-standing sequence that makes exactly as much sense out of context as in, shows all too clearly how the film has been conceived: as a series of chunks (plot, song, comedy sketch, etc.) each with its own allotted span and order, like a variety bill. According to columnist Hubbard Keavy the scene almost didn't make the cut: watching them rehearse it before the live tour, he observed that it would make more sense to gamblers than it would to those who had never indulged in a flutter. "That's what I've been afraid of all along," Groucho replied. "It's too technical. Many people won't understand—and won't care—what we're talking about. We'll have to dig up some other scene to substitute if it doesn't go over the first night. And, of course, if it isn't funny it won't go into the picture."

Though very highly regarded, and for many the highlight of the movie, for me the scene is a pale shadow of earlier Groucho and Chico encounters. Chico can sometimes get the better of Groucho in anti-logical argument, but this is a simple bit of sucker-fleecing, with Groucho cast uncomfortably as the dope and Chico as the wily huckster. In other words, Chico is behaving rationally and logically and cleverly, and Groucho's being taken for a ride. Funny as this may be, it's not the Marx Brothers, at least not the Marx Brothers I love best. It doesn't really build to much of anything, and crucially it doesn't rise to any pitch of self-defeating madness, the way these things used to do at Paramount. The obvious model for this is the contract scene from *Opera*, but while Kaufman and Ryskind's routine had that beautiful contempt for logic that characterizes their Groucho-Chico dialogues in *Cocoanuts* and *Animal Crackers,* with virtually every line contradicting the one preceding and setting off on some new comic direction, what we have in the *Races* script is *jokes.* They're not *bad* jokes, they're just *ordinary* jokes. Give the script to any other comedians and, while they may not do it as well, *it wouldn't need rewriting first.* Whereas the "why a duck?" or "left-handed moth" routines might as well be written in a different language.

No, they *are* written in a different language.

18:28/19:15—"I want to win, but I don't want the savings of a lifetime wiped out in the twinkling of an eye!"

This line must have resonated with Groucho, whose losses in the great crash of 1929 preyed on his mind ever after.

24:05/25:07—"I want to turn this place into a gambling casino before the season ends"

If he does, Morgan will have to fight off the rivalry of the one that already exists, and is advertised alongside the sanitarium and his race track and hotel on the huge hoarding at the railway station. Odd that he has gone to so much effort to snatch the sanitarium from Judy's hands, only to expensively turn it into something that already exists in the town. Why not just try to take over the one that's already there? Or turn the sanitarium into something else?

24:60/26:04—"Look, Miss Standish, suppose I were to tell you I'm not the doctor you think I am...."

An especially nonsensical and disastrous example of how Groucho's comic persona has been tinkered with, this is perhaps the most cringeworthy Groucho moment until those two immortal pinnacles of horror: the line "and yours truly who could certainly use the money for Jeff" in *At The Circus,* and the bit in *The Big Store* where he coquettishly fishes for compliments from Tony Martin as if one or the other of them were a girl. Even by those standards, the spectacle of a coy, sheepish and guilt-panged Groucho here is a demeaning one for all concerned. It ends with Miss Standish calling him "silly," while he stands there beaming at her like a simpleton.

25:15/26:20—The call to the Florida Medical Board

And then, suddenly, we're in a totally different movie. Look at the lead-in. Typical Thalberg scene-setting: Whitmore is overheard putting a call in to the FMB; Groucho realizes it's in an effort to discover the truth about his medical standing and rushes, panicked, into his office to avert disaster. The Hugo Hackenbush that rushes to that door is the one we've just seen cozying up to Judy; the same one that tries to stop Whitmore seeing that he's giving Mrs. Upjohn a horse pill; the one who says, "They can throw a horse doctor in jail for not paying his rent, too!"; the one who goes to run away when it looks like he's going to be exposed. Then we cut to the door opening from inside the office, and in comes the Groucho we've been praying for since his first scene.

All he needs to do is tell Whitmore that Dr. Hackenbush is the man he claims to be. Were he to simply do that, his problems would be, in large degree, over. Instead of that, he deliberately infuriates him, without allaying his suspicions in the smallest degree. The cost of his actions is to make Whitmore even more belligerent and probably even more suspicious, but he doesn't care. Baiting Whitmore is a pleasure, and a public service. Suddenly, Groucho's back.

29:20/30:35—Dr. Hackenbush in his consulting room

This scene reminds me of the bit in Wagstaff's office in *Horse Feathers;* the doctors are like the professors, the nurses like Wagstaff's secretary. Harpo and Chico arrive, looking to be accepted as patients rather than students.

30:60/32:19—"Goodbye forever, goodbye forever...."

The song of which Groucho sings just that snatch is "Good-bye!" by the Italian composer Paolo Tosti, with lyrics by Scottish novelist-poet George Whyte-Melville. The song was written in 1908 and became a popular standard; Deanna Durbin gave voice to it in a strange sequence in the 1946 film *Because of Him*, while Bert Williams enjoyed a 1920 hit with "I Want to Know Where Tosti Went (When He Said Goodbye)."

34:03/35:30—"I think he's a Ubangi"

Chico is here referring to the popular name for African women wearing lip plates, widely exhibited in sideshows and circuses in the early–20th and late–19th centuries.

The name is, in fact, something of a misnomer, apparently chosen at random from a map, for want of an authentic sounding name, by Ringling Brothers and Barnum & Bailey. Chico speculates that Harpo might be a Ubangi because of his habit of producing and inflating a balloon from his mouth whenever Hackenbush presses his stomach. Easy mistake to make. And I must say I do rather like Groucho's follow-up line: "I'll get a hammer and ubangi that right off." Note that in this scene Harpo is no longer wearing his hat from the previous scene. Several photographs exist showing this scene being tried out in the pre-filming tours; in them Harpo is shown to be wearing the much darker red wig familiar from *The Cocoanuts*. (Strangely, these appear to be the only known photographs of any of the team's four pre-filming live shows, for *Opera, Races, Go West* and *A Night in Casablanca*.)

34:29/35:57—"I can't do anything for him: that's a case for Frank Buck!"

Buck (1884–1950) was a flamboyant American big-game hunter and collector of wild animals for zoos and circuses. The title of his life story, *Bring 'em Back Alive,* passed into the language and became the title of a 1980s TV series. In later life he traded on his reputation by appearing as a featured attraction at Ringling Brothers circus shows, and in a series of movie roles, sometimes recreating his exploits straight and sometimes gently spoofing his popular image (as in Abbott and Costello's *Africa Screams* in 1949).

37:28/39:04—The Water Carnival

Mr. Thalberg would be gratified to learn that my wife loves this scene, the result of a curious decision to concentrate most of the film's musical interest in one self-contained sequence rather than dotted about the whole movie. The result is that it plays almost like a separate mini-movie, an effect heightened by the opening, which shows a close-up of the program being perused, showing the performers named therein (one of whom, Vivien Fay, is, of course, appearing under her real name), so that it looks as though the scene has its own individual credit sequence. Needless to say, this whole scene is the object of much derision, but viewed strictly on its own merits it's good stuff. Allan Jones puts in another sterling performance, singing in an enormous banana sundae dish floating in a lake in front of a massive ornamental fountain while a selection of cuties from the MGM casting couch smile fixedly at the camera, and at Jones, but never at one another, while pretending to play ukuleles. Was there *ever* a time when the waters of Venice were blue? Vivien Fay, next up, is even better, twirling on her axis at terrifying length and speed, ending on a perfectly composed freeze and smile, when all she must have wanted to do in reality was fall to the floor, groaning, while the world around her ebbed and flowed like she'd just followed two double vodkas with a whiskey chaser.

Chico and Harpo's swanky outfits in this scene suggest to viewers of the finished film that they, too, are officially on the bill. (What a lineup: internationally famous dancer Vivien Fay, up-and-coming singer Gil whatever he's called, and from right here in Sparkling Springs, the Italian weirdo who helps out at the sanitarium and his eccentric friend, the speechless hobo jockey.) In fact, a deleted scene had shown them sneaking into the event disguised as waiters, hence the plainly fugitive fashion in which they commence and conclude their performance.

43:51/45:43—"Change your partners!"

Some lovely dancing from Groucho here, and our introduction to the mysterious and much abused Flo, played by Esther Muir in a sprayed-on satin gown. Broadway dancer, friend of Edward and Mrs. Simpson and one-time wife of Busby Berkeley, Muir is very funny in this film and also appeared with the Brothers in their pre-production live tour, getting covered in talcum powder and wallpaper paste and having her derriere slapped with a wallpaper brush every night and twice on Saturdays. She also worked with Wheeler and Woolsey in *So This Is Africa*, and the film she made directly before *Races* was, intriguingly enough, called *High Hat*. She made her last film appearance in 1941, moved successfully into real estate development, and died in 1995 at the age of 92. In a 1937 interview she expressed her surprise at discovering how serious the Marxes were offscreen: "They are unassuming and courteous and listen to new ideas from any one." She recalls them laboring for days and weeks over the effect of certain scenes, and notes, for the record, that Harpo is an expert on world politics.

49:52/52:00—Chico's piano solo

As in *Opera,* Chico's specialty spot has been cut insultingly short—rushed through in less than two minutes—so as to allow Harpo to hog some piano time on top of his harp solo. He plays a bit of Rachmaninov and then smashes the piano to bits: Chico may have edged ahead in billing, but Harpo is clearly the preferred screen presence. The really amusing part is watching the orchestra in the background, who have obviously been told to react in comic fear to Harpo's antics, and who thus appear to flee, return and flee again, and again, every time he does something destructive. Look out for the lovely shot of the sheriff and two other men at **51:20/53:32**—they resemble a non-existent comedy team.

54:27/56:47—The Harpo whistling scene

This basic routine would prove a reliable standby, when inspiration ran dry, in both *A Night in Casablanca* and *Love Happy*. Many critics have noted that it is more ground lost to MGM literalism: instead of a Harpo just choosing not to speak, possibly because it amuses him to annoy people, here we have one who cannot speak, possibly because of laryngeal disease or some form of mental abnormality. If the scene is funny, and I have to say I do think it is, it's more because of the hopelessness of Chico's guesses, especially the immortal "Buffalo Bill goes ice-skating."

64:11/66:55—"It's the old, old story. Boy meets girl! Romeo and Juliet! Minneapolis and St. Paul!"

American readers will not need to be told that Minneapolis-St. Paul, also known as the Twin Cities, is a binary metropolitan area comprising Minnesota's two largest cities—Minneapolis (with the highest population) and St. Paul (the state capital).

64:35/67:20—Sig Rumann returns

Yet another transplant from *Opera,* and with Groucho given nothing new to do but make yet more jokes about the fact that he has a beard. But it's always good to see Rumann on the bill, and his third appearance, in *A Night in Casablanca,* makes him a fully fledged uncle in the Marx screen family. He has less to do here than in his other two appearances, however, and he comes in late, as a specialist brought in by Whitmore to expose the inadequacy of Hackenbush's diagnosis of Mrs. Upjohn. Coincidentally, but most bizarrely, he was to perform the same function in the same year's *Nothing Sacred,* again in 1954 in its remake *Living It Up,* and then *again* in 1966 in Billy Wilder's *The Fortune Cookie,* thus making him the only actor to have played an eminent doctor called in to expose a medical fraud on four separate occasions, smashing Bjorn Borg's previous record of three.

66:52/69:43—Mrs. Upjohn's examination

Insults, absurdity, anarchy ... the beautiful repetition of the hand-washing ... the three Dr. Steinbergs being introduced to each other ... Harpo and Chico lathering Dumont for a shave ... Chico yelling, "X-ray! X-ray! All about the operation!" ... Groucho asking, "How is it that a dame like that never gets sick?" ... oh, we've been *waiting* for this! The trick is in first establishing a premise, then tweaking it, then undermining it, and then, and only then, going bananas with it. The result should be the kind of laughter that builds too aggressively, so that you end up choking and sweating, half-hoping that there will be a break for you to breathe and swallow before the next majestic assault upon reason, and half-hoping that there won't. This is what the Marx Brothers do, and in this film, I suggest, they only do it here.

It has been suggested that for some of the more vigorous and/or demeaning parts of this scene, a stand-in for Dumont is used, and a male one at that. I must say I'm not convinced, not least because the contested shots are not from the most outrageous moments, in many of which it is plainly Dumont. The commonly cited evidence of the obviously unraveling wig is a certain dead end, given that Dumont is likely wearing a wig anyway. And the supposed giveaway shot as Harpo mimes handing out newspapers at **72:00/75:05** still looks like Mags to me, and is unquestionably a woman. Further, Dumont accompanied the Bros. on the try-out tour and this was one of the scenes they performed, presumably not in all that different a form, given the point of the exercise.

68:39/71:35—"I told you guys to stay down in that room with those pigeons!"

One of the film's great mystery moments! It would be lovely to think that this line is pure nonsense, put in for no reason at all other than because it is intrinsically funny, and to (just as meaninglessly) set up the appearance of the two pigeons that come in with the horse at the end. But that's not the MGM way, is it? Consensus leans toward the line referring to an excised earlier moment, the exact nature of which we can now only guess at. In the original screenplay, Groucho does tell Chico, with Harpo and Hi-Hat, to "stay here" before commencing the examination; still no mention of pigeons, though. Another strange little line in this scene is Groucho's "No, we're not mad. We're just terribly hurt, that's all" at **70:46/73:47**. This one had me foxed until quite recently, but as Glenn Mitchell points out, Groucho is simply indulging his occasional habit of lapsing into feminine clichés: "I'm not mad, just terribly hurt" is a stock woman's line in arguments with their other halves. For Groucho to use it in this context (deliberately confusing the literal meaning of mad with its American colloquial form) is thus a splendidly dismissive riposte to Sig's claims of serious malpractice.

70:03/73:02—"Down by the old mill stream, where I first met you...."

The song the boys sing when washing their hands was one of the most widely sung songs of the first half of the twentieth century, and a special favorite of barbershop quartets. It was written by Tell Taylor in 1908, published in 1910 and first performed by vaudeville quartet The Orpheus Comedy Four. The Marxes would doubtless have been familiar with it from their own touring days on the vaudeville circuit.

71:06/74:08—"This is absolutely insane!" "That's what they said about Pasteur!"

A reference to Louis Pasteur (1822–95), the French microbiologist, pioneer in immunization and the germ theory of disease, and inventor of pasteurization and the rabies and anthrax vaccines. Groucho is therefore likening to these achievements his efforts to convince a wealthy widow that she has high blood pressure on one side and low blood pressure on the other, and that the correct procedure for establishing this is to get her to wave her arms in the air until she flies away, on the grounds that both met with skepticism from reactionary authority. A nice touch of absurd arrogance—something he could have done with a bit more of in the film's first half.

74:12/77:22—"Hee hoo! Where did that come from?"

This moment always makes me laugh a lot. It's hard to explain what's funny about it: Groucho, enjoined to laugh, does so half-heartedly but producing a sound that is unexpectedly bizarre, and comments on it. It feels very spontaneous, and very modern somehow, almost like a line from *Friends* or something. (I appreciate the fact that *Friends* won't seem all that modern anymore to our younger readers, but you get the point.)

76:44/80:01—Harpo charms the ghetto

Harpo joins most of the black talent on MGM's books in this lavish musical number, incorporating "All God's Chillun Got Rhythm" (their second variation on the traditional "All God's Chillun Got Wings," following *Duck Soup*'s more acidic parody "All God's Chillun Got Guns"). So what is left to be said of this scene? Perhaps nothing, save to emphasize that it couldn't be less derogatory or mean-spirited: its purity of motive—or rather lack of motive—is too transparent to permit any other account of it. None of which is to insist upon its being a worthy or delightful sequence, and it certainly doesn't do much for me. But its crimes begin and end at taking the status quo as a given—and is that really such a faux pas in this context, especially when it showcases so much excellent talent in the process, not least the superb Whitey's Lindy Hoppers? This much is certain: not only are the Brothers not trying to give offense, they would have been horrified to think that they had. "All God's Chillun Got Rhythm" became a major hit and popular standard, memorably performed by Judy Garland among others, and original audiences seemed to have loved the sequence, to the extent that a repeat serving was ordered for *At the Circus*. One final irony: For his work on this scene, dance director Dave Gould secured the only Oscar nomination ever attained by a Marx Brothers film.

85:44/89:24—The grand finale

Again modeled closely on *Opera*, there is some fairly funny business here with the Brothers attempting to disrupt and delay the race, which recalls, but to less effect, the similar tactics they used to sabotage the opera. The big race climax to which it all leads, however, is played dead straight, and what Halliwell calls a "spectacularly well integrated racecourse climax" is for my dollar an almost total dead loss. Not Marx Brothers comedy; not any kind of comedy, and soured beyond salvation by some horrendous horse falls.

At the start of the sequence an instrumental version of **"Cosi Cosa"** from *A Night at the Opera* can be heard. Groucho's line, **"Ride 'em, cowboy, or we're heading for the last lock-up!"** at **87:50/90:48** adapts the title of Billy Hill's country standard "I'm Heading for the Last Round-up," a somewhat maudlin piece about a dying cowboy. (Groucho also sings a line from this number in *Room Service* [see *RS,* **54:30/56:50**].) Look out for **Groucho's stunt double taking a nasty tumble** in a long shot at **90:37/94:29**, as he attempts to walk tightrope-style along the perimeter fence, losing his footing and landing heavily on his portfolio of investments. Like an anonymous trouper he scrambles on to an adjacent car and carries on, without a camera cut. The shot at **90:46/94:39** appears to be the exact same one shown from a different camera and the opposite angle, but it can't be, because in the first he leaps onto the roof of another car but in the second he slides down over the hood. Which means Sam Wood, king of the retakes, had him take that nasty tumble at least twice, and we don't even know his name. (Let's call him Stunto.)

The big fade-out shot has virtually the whole cast (barring the villains) walking towards the camera, laughing and singing. It's cutesy for sure, but convincingly joyous. As earlier mentioned, Groucho gets to do a brief reprise of "A Message From the Man in the Moon," the Allan Jones number that was cut from the film. Chico, who, of course, does not sing in the film proper, makes a half-hearted stab at "Blue Venetian Waters" before exclaiming, "Hi-de-hi-de-Hi Hat!" and rounding it off by yelling, "Get-a your Tootsie-Fruitsie ice cream!"

A Night at the Opera had ended rather abruptly: here, at last, the film builds upon its prototype. But getting here has been a long, far from unpleasant, but all too often mildly frustrating journey.

8

Room Service (1938)

"I still think it's a terrible play, but it makes a wonderful rehearsal."
—Harry Binelli (Chico Marx)

During a visit by the *New York Post* to RKO studios the Marx Brothers reportedly declared ("over the luncheon table"): "If *Room Service* doesn't wreck our careers, we're set for life. And if it does all right, we're going to use proven properties from now on—no more anguish, no more laugh try-outs."

What they were making, and gambling on, therefore, was not a typical Marx Brothers movie, but a film in which the Marxes play characters already written, in material that was not created expressly for them. *Room Service* was an experiment, and one that a lot of interested parties had a lot of expectations for, almost all of them in one way or another confounded by the time the film was released.

Whether it stands up today as a successful or an unsuccessful experiment is of course a matter for the individual viewer, but from the outraged tone of most critiques, you'd think it was some kind of con trick, a bad case of selling goods under false pretences. At the time, however, many critics could only be described as fulsome in their praise, like the *Coquille Valley Sentinel*, who judged it "the funniest and fastest laugh vehicle of their careers."

I wouldn't go that far, but I am happy to declare myself among its defenders. Once you know what you're going to get, or rather what you're not going to get, the film is full of pleasures—and packed with interest.

Of course, I do *understand* those who resent seeing what are to all intents the established Marxes being forced into unnatural shapes. I accept, for instance, that Groucho shouldn't be called "Gordon Miller." (They could at least have given him a middle initial, or swapped his character's name with that of the name of the play's would-be financier, Zachary Fiske.) I agree that it was an error of judgement to leave in the references to his sister, which are only useful in plot terms for explaining the hold he has over the hotel manager (he's married to her). It would have been easy enough to have come up with a less mind-boggling reason (though there is talk of a wife in *Horse Feathers*, and a wife and kiddies in *Monkey Business*).

I'll even join in the speculation about how different it *could* have been, thus: Wouldn't it have been better if the Brothers' attempts to escape Wagner's goons at the end led to them gatecrashing the play itself, *Night at the Opera*–style, and reducing it to a shambles, and it is in that form that it brings down the house and proves the smash hit of the season? No offence to Leo Davis, but from the little we see it looks pretty awful, and surely the last thing

Room Service: a smash on Broadway, a curate's egg on screen.

likely to revive the theatre's fortunes. But I suppose the fact that this would leave no possible happy resolution for Davis rules that out (unless he too declares he no longer cares about the theatre, now that he has fallen in love?) Okay, it needs work. However, the idea is there.

The first surprise in coming to the original play (by John Murray and Allen Boretz) after seeing the film is just how similar they are. Consider, for instance, Harpo's being cast as Miller's assistant Faker Englund (a bizarre name that is no more accounted for in the play than in the film: my best guess is that it is a school nickname referring to winning deceptiveness on the sports field). This means, as has been noted elsewhere, that all of his important lines have gone to Chico; however, the play reveals that he talks like Chico anyway, with lots of "okey-doke" and "hello, Boss!" Director Harry Binion becomes Binelli for Chico's benefit; nonetheless most of the actual dialogue, from both characters, remains intact.

In many cases, as others have noted, Ryskind has taken existing lines from the play and simply added an extra line to give them a vaguely Marxian twist. ("Most actors would be tickled to death to get as close to a lamb chop as you" is present, but not "And I do mean you!"; likewise "You can't shake backers out of your sleeve," but not "Anyhow I can't!" and "We have no fireside," but not "How do you listen to the President's speeches?") But many other lines that I'd have guessed were especially written for the Brothers are to be found in the source exactly as is: "I can't get it out of the wall", "If you see one with onions save it for me," "He said the tapeworm will have to register," "You must come up and take a nap sometime," "He likes to hear the little bell ring," "Second straitjacket to the left," "You haven't got three chemistry professors out there."

More surprising are the many original lines that seem perfect for the Marxes but which *don't* make it into the screenplay. Miller tries to buck up Gribble's sense of optimism by declaring, "I can hear the seven fat cows mooing in the distance!" Binion nostalgically recalls a former love, a lady doctor from Baltimore: "She still sends me pills once in a while." "There must be somebody in New York with a hundred dollars," muses Miller. "If there is, you've borrowed it," reflects Binion. "What you have to do is wait for a new generation to grow up." Best of all is a very funny moment where Miller tries to account for the presence of a half-naked Binion in the bathroom: "Mr Binion is an eccentric director. When he gets an idea he can't stand clothes on his body. He rips them off and rushes into the bathroom to concentrate." Wagner is not convinced: "Does Ernst Lubitsch take his pants off?" The idea Binion then claims to have had sounds like quintessential Chico: "I caught a glimpse of a new art form. A stage without actors! A theatre without an audience! Just scenery and critics."

In terms of plot and incidental details, Ryskind follows the play almost exactly. Occasionally he takes an idea a little further than in the source (Faker is said to be bringing a turkey, but nothing more is made of it), but the furious eating scene, the moose's head and the iodine measles, for example, were all there waiting for him.

The biggest changes come at the very end: though the idea of sneaking the corpse (always Davis, never Faker) out of the room and dumping him in alley or leaving him in his seat in the theatre ("instead of a suicide it would be a mystery!") is mooted in the play, it's not acted upon as in the movie. Instead, Wagner sees the corpse sit up, realizes he has again been duped and is intent yet again on stopping the play and having them arrested, but at the last moment the owner of the hotel arrives to congratulate him on having the good idea of using the vacant theatre to put on a play that he is convinced will be a long-running critical triumph.

On the whole, what we seem to take from the film is that Ryskind has left the Marxes stranded halfway between their normal characters and the characters in the play. But then, when you look at Ryskind's actual final draft screenplay you find, to your surprise, that he *has* put effort into making it a viable, typical Marx Brothers project, considerable effort in fact, but most of his changes have been promptly cut out again! Look at the first scene with Groucho and Sacha the waiter. In the film, it's more or less the same as the play. But the script has twice as much dialogue for Groucho, all in his customary logic-defying, fast-talking style, none making it to the final cut. This pattern continues all the way through. In the film, Miller suggests having his entire cast re-register on the grounds that "instead of one big bill you'll have twenty two little ones." But in the script he continues: "Wagner can't kick at a little bill, can he? Even if he does, wouldn't you rather have twenty two little kicks instead of one big one? After the tenth kick you won't even notice it." For the opening night of the show, Chico hires "a huge man with terrific hands" to applaud for money, identified in the script as "Professor Zeno." When Harpo is painting measles spots on Davis to help him fake his illness, he also takes the opportunity to paint a battleship on his chest, which he signs "Faker Englund, 1938." "If I thought that was an original I'd buy it," Groucho observes.

So what are we looking at here? Too much effort or not enough? Too many changes or too few? Too much certainty or too much indecision? They check in, they check out. They skip, they don't skip.... What we are looking at here is *confusion*. The approved account of how *Room Service* came to be and how it ended up the way it is has this much over the truth: it's clear, and it makes sense. But getting to the heart of what *really* happened is not easy. In fact it's impossible. So here goes.

Most important to stress is that the film's half-hearted attempt to reconcile the style of the original play with that of a more typical Marx Brothers movie (the thing that supposedly places it beyond endurance for so many fans of the team today) reflects neither RKO's nor the Marxes' original intentions for the project, but was instead a late, unhappy and basically unresolved compromise, concluding an extensive period of debate, doubt and trial and error.

First, let's re-examine the processes that led them to make it, beginning with their departure from MGM. According to most accounts, the *Room Service* deal was simply a one-off offer that came their way (via Zeppo, now in the agency business) after completion of one MGM contract and before the signing of the next. But there are reasons for supposing the move may have been somewhat less harmonious, and intended rather more decisively.

If the *New York Times* is to be believed, rather than merely in a gap between MGM stints, the Marxes had in fact been "dropped last year by the studio in a disagreement over money matters". And the RKO deal was no one-off arrangement but a three-picture contract, of which *Room Service* was to be the first, and a revived *Of Thee I Sing* a likely second. Before taking that offer they had reportedly turned down $1,500,000 for three pictures at Republic; Chico was also actively courting Twentieth Century–Fox as a potential employer through 1936 and 1937. The latter connection is to be presumed from this, perhaps the most unimaginable of all their officially announced ideas (*New York Times*, January 2, 1938):

> The Marx Brothers, with the consent of RKO, are going to make a burlesque version of *The Three Musketeers* after they wind up *Room Service*. That will probably be in the late spring or early summer. This will mark the first time that Hollywood intentionally turned such an imposing literary property into a farce.

Now, that phrase "with the consent of RKO" *might* simply mean that the studio has authorised the stars' suggestion of the project for their third venture. On the other hand, it sounds more like a contract holder agreeing to a loan out. Given that we know Chico was in talks with Fox, and it was indeed from TCF that a burlesque version of *The Three Musketeers* emerged in 1939, it seems probable that this was the exact project Chico had initiated, albeit with the Ritz Brothers drafted in instead.

Right at that moment, however, it was all change again. Despite this talk of RKO projects *and* loan-outs stretching into the summer, the Brothers suddenly re-signed with MGM in early March, while Room Service was still only in its earliest stages of preparation, and by April *A Day at the Circus*, for producer Mervyn LeRoy, had been officially announced. What had happened to prompt this abrupt volte-face? And was it only coincidence that it was at this exact point that things began going wrong for *Room Service*?

The play (originally titled *Sing Before Breakfast*) had been a Broadway smash and a film seemed inevitable, but Warner Brothers, who had helped finance it, naturally assumed they had first refusal. As a result, their bid of $200,000 was presumed to be the lucky one: the deal "is expected to be closed in a day or two," opined the *Film Daily* on June 10, 1937. (The terms of Warners' original arrangement entitled them to half of the purchase price for screen rights; their bid, in effect, was therefore half what it appeared to be.) However, agents Bill Liebling and Audrey Wood, representing the interests of the playwrights and Broadway cast, successfully argued that rights negotiations had to be handled at open auction. This left the field open for RKO to swoop, reportedly adding another fifty thousand to the Warner bid. A grumpy Warners spokesman was quoted on the 14th as saying that the negotiations were "still in progress, but that no such price as $250,000 is contemplated." They were right, according to *Film Daily*: RKO had offered a mere $225,000, still enough to top Columbia's recent bagging of *You Can't Take It with You* for $200,000, and make it the year's biggest handover for film rights to a play. (Half of which, though, still went to Warners, which is why Louella Parsons noted on June 12th that "naturally they are not crying over losing the film rights..." Indeed, we might even entertain an image of them cynically encouraging RKO to bid up, like Groucho and Chico at the *Cocoanuts* auction!)

Early reports put Jack Oakie, Joe Penner and Burgess Meredith in the frame to star, and it wasn't until July that mention began to be made of the Marxes. On the 21st the Schenectady Gazette announced that "all indications" were that a period of huddled negotiation had ended with the Brothers being signed to the project. Director William A. Seiter was a later addition still. The *New York Times* (on October 2nd, 1937) had Gregory La Cava in the frame, though the director most persistently associated with it in its early stages was George Stevens. Stevens earned his ticket off the project circuitously: when *Bringing Up Baby* opened to disappointing business he was hurriedly moved to *Gunga Din*, deemed no longer safe in the hands of the originally-assigned Howard Hawks. This then created a vacancy at *Room Service* hurriedly filled by the (as is so often the way) much better-suited Seiter.

As with the later *Love Happy*, what looks to be an unusually starry supporting cast is

Organized chaos in confined spaces: (Left to right) Harpo, Frank Albertson, Groucho, Chico and Lucille Ball in *Room Service*.

merely the happy collision of minor celestial bodies in nascent stages of formation. Lucille Ball was only just starting out as an RKO contractee when she landed the role of Christine (who is, incidentally, Miller's girlfriend: a fact made clear in the play but understandably skirted in the movie). Likewise Ann Miller as Hilda, just fourteen when she started work on the production. But the earliest news reports claimed "the leading feminine role" in the film had been given to Mitzi Green, the former Paramount star and rather eerily sophisticated child sensation of early talkies, now eighteen and momentarily hot again after a massive Broadway success in *Babes in Arms* in 1937. It's unclear whether the "leading feminine role" means Christine or Hilda: Lucille Ball ends up higher-billed, but Hilda gets more screen time, *and* is the nominal love interest. (To further confuse matters, a report in the *Miami News* has the role as "third on Miss Green's schedule; it will be preceded by *Fiddlesticks* and *Carefree*", and suggests all three as having been awarded "on the eve of her arrival at RKO". But she'd been at RKO since 1932, though she hadn't made a movie since 1934. Not only did she not appear with the Marxes, or in *Carefree*, *Fiddlesticks* appears not to have been made at all.)

Yet stranger was the suggestion, made frequently in press reports, that a featured role was to be found for Milton Berle (presumably written especially for him, since there is nothing much to suit in the material itself). This lingered until at least early February of 1938, when the *Ottawa Citizen* quoted Groucho's response to being asked if he was worried about Berle stealing any scenes: "Not a bit, all we're worried about are the towels."

But such quixotic notions were as nothing to the plans being laid for the Marxes themselves. As Robbin Coons revealed in his "Hollywood Sights and Sounds" column in early February, 1938:

Groucho Marx is going to wear a mustache—a real one—in the Marx trio's next picture, *Room Service*. And Harpo and Chico will appear in more conservative attire, although Harpo will retain his red wig and his wild-eyed insanity. All of which portends a Big Step for the brothers. For the first time they will attempt characters that have been previously created on the stage by others, for the first time they will appear in a ready-made play that was not fashioned for their own exclusive zany uses.

"If we succeed," says Groucho, the sad-eyed, the soft-voiced, "we'll be opening up an entirely new field for ourselves. If we don't...."

Groucho seriously has his doubts about the piece as a Marxian vehicle, but thinks it is worth the gamble for the reward it will bring if happily received. "We make only one picture a year, to keep the public from catching on to us," he explains (...) "*Room Service* will be something new for us, and we hope will serve to defer the evil day when the public does catch on." In preparation, Groucho has already begun growing his real mustache. His usual grease-paint lip-ornament he deems out of place for the character he is to play: "In a real play we can't appear as caricatures or cartoons."

According to the *Harrisburg Telegraph* (November 23, 1937), the decision received some pretty heavyweight support:

Groucho, incidentally, was telling Charlie Chaplin yesterday that he thought he'd discard the painted black mustache in *Room Service*. Chaplin advised him to do so, pointing out that the Chaplin mustache so typed him that it's impossible for him to make a talking picture. His speaking voice couldn't possibly live up to the character he created.

Even more exciting, the *Spokane Weekly Chronicle*, as well as informing its readers of the real moustache, tells us that "Harpo, the red-thatched mute who has never spoken before, will talk."

It sounds like a typical (and not even all that original) publicity fantasy, but taken with the general commitment to stepping out of their usual characterisations and playing fair by the original play, it carries the ring of authenticity.

It's also borne out by later news reports, which, following the signing of the new MGM contract in March, suddenly take on an entirely different tone. Where once all was excitement at new ideas and opportunities, suddenly a pall of gloom seems to descend, as if the only things now worth reporting about the production are the problems it seems to be constantly running into. Sniffy, snarky little squibs start appearing, like this one from Walter Winchell:

> Although the Marx Brothers are hilarious comics, it was very poor judgement to cast them in *Room Service*. (You'd think RKO would have learned their lesson from *Having Wonderful Time*.)

Which seems to tally quite unremarkably with conventional wisdom ... until you realize that it was published some three months before the film even began shooting: a pretty mean-spirited case of letting the horse bolt while the stable door is still shut. (*Having Wonderful Time*, incidentally, was a stage comedy about Jewish holidaymakers in the Catskills reimagined as an entirely Gentile vehicle for Ginger Rogers—and it, too, had not yet been released!)

With their own interests to worry about, were MGM's publicity scoundrels enjoining the columnists to take shots at this now thoroughly inconvenient production? And did the team's faith in the production—perhaps already tentative, given their understandable nervousness about the changes to their characters and style—take a serious knock as a result? Or had something else occurred to unsettle the team and dampen their hopes for the production? Possibly, with MGM now back in the game—meaning that even if the film were a hit, it wouldn't lead to any permanent redirection for them anyway—the whole idea simply began to feel futile. Whatever the answer, what would seem to be a period of emergency rethinking now began. Shooting, originally announced for mid–May, was put off until June 27th, and in the newspapers, just about every big innovation that had so excited the columnists was publicly withdrawn and abandoned.

That included the provincial stage tour to test and refine the material, which they had found so useful on their two MGM films. This time, though, it would have been even more important, as it wouldn't just be the jokes they were trying out but a whole new approach; in effect a whole new Marx Brothers. In February, the Robbin Coons column had announced: "As is their custom, the Marxes will take their version of *Room Service* on the road, in tabloid form, to get audience reaction before they start filming." But the *Evening Independent* of May 28 had a sad new story to tell:

> In a change of plans, the Marx Brothers will not go on the road with *Room Service* before making it a picture. Instead, they'll give three performances at the little theater on the RKO lot. Attendance will be on invitation and the audiences will be selected to give a cross section of public opinion. For instance one group will be selected from rural communities.

In so sterile a setting it's difficult to imagine the performances being received any better than politely, and that too would have fed into the unease now besetting the production. Since April, the columns had been alive with stories of changed minds and ruffled feathers. "The three Marxes and RKO Radio are carrying on a heated argument," claimed the *Maitland Daily Mercury*, in what reads like a fait accompli being played up as an ongoing saga: "The studio wants Harpo to shed his famous silence for his role in *Room Service*. The Brothers are violently against it, but unless Harpo talks thousands of pounds will have to be spent for re-writing the script." Whereas the way the *Winnipeg Tribune* has it: "Most of the RKO executives, supported by Groucho and Chico Marx, wanted Harpo to talk ... but writer Ryskind and Harpo himself held out for straight pantomime."

The real moustache didn't survive, either, Groucho is quoted as confirming in the *Salt Lake Telegram*: "It would have been a beard by the time the picture started." (He tries to put a comparably larky spin on the other reversals in the same interview: "We were going to change our usual characters for the film. Harpo was going to talk for the first time—but it was too risky. Besides, if Harpo talks, there'll be less for me.")

The atmosphere on set when shooting finally commenced was characterised by a sense of resignation, to say nothing of an unprecedented secrecy that—regardless of whatever spin the publicity accounts attempted to place on it—speaks of a pronounced lack of faith in the material, and a continued uncertainty as to the right direction to take it in.

"The Marx brothers locked themselves in a room to rehearse a special scene for *Room Service*," noted the *Adelaide Mail*. "They wouldn't even let director William Seiter see it." If you smell paranoia already, prepare yourself for Harrison Carroll in the *Salt Lake Telegram*:

> Gag stealers will have to stay up late to pilfer any material from the new Marx Brothers picture. The comedians trust Hollywood so little that they will do the key scenes from *Room Service* on a closed set and in the middle of the night. This is no publicity blurb. The shooting schedule on the film calls for eight all night sessions.... Groucho, Chico and Harpo claim that in earlier pictures many of their laughs were tipped off in advance.

It's the bit about how little they "trust Hollywood" that most leaps from that one. And it's not just the filming that's being kept under wraps, according to the *Adelaide Mail*:

> Even in the final shooting script's descriptions of these scenes, all the best rib-tickling situations are omitted, in case some outsider might steal their comedy touches. The big comedy scenes in Room Service, which they have just begun, are being filmed at night, when there are fewer people around to see what they do.

Shooting was further delayed by a bout of flu for Groucho, and the death of Chico's mother-in-law, which combined to suspend production for two days. Sheilah Graham caught the mirthless mood in an on-set report just before the shutdown, with a laid low Groucho going through the motions:

> "The speech is too long," he complains. So the speech is cut in half. But this doesn't help very much. "I was terrible," Groucho tells director William Seiter... (It) is the quickest picture they have yet made. "We'll be finished within five weeks—the time we used to take over one scene at MGM—but don't quote me," says Groucho—"I have to go back there!"

And back they obligingly went, to join the circus and to go west, to take their medicine and take their orders, chastened and safely "cured" of their desire for experimentation (to borrow the word curiously yet revealingly used by the *Philadelphia Enquirer* in an early report on *At the Circus*).

Looking at it now, I suspect the biggest mistake *Room Service* makes is to go back on the seemingly superficial idea of giving Groucho a real moustache. Just that one tiny variation on formula might have been all that was needed to make clear to audiences that this is to be a slightly different Marx Brothers movie, but not a radically different one. Instead, confusion reigned, and reigns still. In an uncharacteristically forthright interview with the *New York Sun* in 1939, Chico spoke for posterity:

It was the first time we tried doing a play we hadn't created ourselves. And we were no good. We can't do that. We've got to originate the characters and the situations ourselves. Then we can do them. Then they're us. If we get a gag that suits our characters we can work it out and make it ours. But we can't do gags or play characters that aren't ours. We tried it, and we'll never do it again.

0:14 (NTSC)/0:15 (PAL)—Opening titles

I hope we're all on the same side thus far at least: these animated titles are lovely—surely the best credits sequence of any of their post-Paramount films, and a nice and jaunty theme tune too. And it's good to see them as caricatures again, though it has to be asked: just what is it about Chico that compels caricaturists to make him come out sinister?

6:04/6:20—Harpo drinks the cologne

Because the character Harpo plays is, by necessity, the most radically altered from the original play, and Harpo's character the hardest to assimilate into this alien context, it is generally and rightly agreed that it is he who comes off as most authentic (in general parlance: "best") in the film. I'd actually go further. Because he was more or less left to his own devices to create new bits of business, this is a return to the purest Harpo, the Paramount Harpo, the one whose wilder contours Thalberg so carefully sanded away. He's back to doing the impossible again, and there are several occasions when the Harpo of *The Cocoanuts* and *Animal Crackers* is overtly recalled, whether it be drinking perfume here, doing the old **hat swap routine with Groucho at 8:52/9:15, kissing a picture and then punching it out of the frame at 9:40/10:05, deciding he prefers the taste of his sandwich with the polythene wrap still attached at 36:15/37:48,** or **drinking the ipecac** (see below, **61:54**). This is, needless to say, an ironic side effect of a production that was designed to make them more realistic even than in their revised Thalbergian guises.

6:52/7:10—Frank Albertson

One of Hollywood's most unjustly undersung supporting faces, Albertson tends to get it in the neck from strict orthodox Marxians for his whiny performance as playwright Leo Davis, but he's always welcome at my house, in this or anything. And is he ever versatile! I especially like him here because he seems to so epitomize the gauche, corn-fed young man, just off the train and wide open for a Marxian fleecing, that I assumed this was his shtick generally. It was only later that I realized that if he specialized in anything it was in brash, loud characters, over-confident to the point of crass, the most famous example I suppose being the guy who says "hee-haw!" a lot in *It's a Wonderful Life.* And it was years later again that I realized he's the *totally* different guy that Janet Leigh steals from at the start of *Psycho.*

8:00/8:21—"You have no fireside? How do you listen to the President's speeches?"

A reference to President Roosevelt's "fireside chats," a series of innovative radio broadcasts delivered between 1933 and 1944. Roosevelt had shrewdly spotted the potential of radio (90 percent of American homes owned a set by this time) as a means of reaching a far wider and more diverse audience than the traditional methods of political speech-making, and the folksy, confidential style of his addresses added to their appeal. Needless to say he was not really sitting by his fireside but at a microphoned desk: the term was coined by CBS reporter Harry Butcher in 1933.

9:46/10:11—"Now I know how Gypsy Rose Lee feels"

Chico is referring to the regularity with which he has to don and jettison items of clothing by likening himself to the famous burlesque entertainer, striptease artist and writer. Sister of actress June Havoc, she was played by Natalie Wood in *Gypsy,* the 1962 film of the 1959 musical of her 1957 memoir. Her superbly titled 1941 novel *The G-String Murders* (a whodunit set backstage at a burlesque house where the performers are being found strangled with their nether-garments) was filmed as *Lady of Burlesque* (1943), one of the most full-bloodedly kinky movies of the Code era, with lead Barbara Stanwyck entering wholeheartedly into the spirit of the thing. The same year the real Gypsy appeared in the all-star *Stage Door Canteen,* along with Harpo, Kenny Baker and Virginia Grey.

16:04/16:45—"Are you from the We Never Sleep Collection Agency?"

"We Never Sleep" should ring recognition bells for keen-eyed Marx fans: it was also seen as the name of a taxi service on one of the stage flats used in *A Night at the Opera* (seen clearly at 77:03/80:20 in that film). The phrase originated as the logo of Pinkerton's detective agency. It served as the title of a 1956 RKO documentary short on Pinkerton's, as well as of the last of Harold Lloyd's Lonesome Luke comedies in 1917, in which Luke tries his hand as a detective.

24:58/26:02—"How about a two-handed game of pinochle while we're waiting?"

Another reference to the Marx family's card game of choice, frequently cited in their earlier work, much less often by this time. I also like the shot of Groucho playing solo and sneakily cheating himself.

28:47/30:01—"Gregory Ratoff! Nazimova! Ginger Rogovich!"

They being Groucho's list of Russians who have made it big in the west. Actor-producer-director Ratoff is probably best known these days for *All About Eve* but was an interesting man with an interesting life story worth finding out more about; equally worthy of re-examination to anyone unfamiliar with her life and career is the amazing Alla Nazimova. The third is obviously an amusing corruption of fellow RKO star Ginger Rogers, referring to her role as a phony Russian (with Russian accent) in *Roberta* (1935). In the original play the names that Miller offers are Ratoff and Akim Tamiroff.

32:14/33:37—Groucho squeezes the waiter in an intimate spot

An easily overlooked bit of business, not least, I imagine, by the Breen Office. When the much-anticipated meal has been brought in, and the other Marxes descend like locusts upon it, Groucho finds his path to the feast impeded by the waiter laying out the dishes. So he thrusts his hand between his legs, and Sasha yelps and jumps out of the way!

32:30/33:53—The eating scene

Often cited as the best bit of the film. Fair enough, say I: it's a splendid scene, reminiscent of the similar sequence in *A Night at the Opera* but also very funny in its own right, a blur of frenzied activity, excellently directed and edited to an almost musical rhythm, finally closing on Harpo robotically spearing and eating small pieces of food without ever seeming to swallow. Incidentally, what is he eating here? Lots of small, light-colored cubes.... No clear answer, but an interesting bit of insight on the scene, comes from the *Evening Independent* of July 8, 1938: "One of the big scenes will be where the hungry outfit promise a waiter a part in the play in return for a square meal. The scene will take two days to film and, during this time, Groucho, Chico and Harpo are supposed to eat endless fried eggs and French fried potatoes. No stomach, agrees RKO, would be equal to that amount of greasy food. So the prop department will resort to a little subterfuge. The fried eggs will be blobs of custard with a half apricot in the center, and the French fried potatoes will be slivers of raw apple." Philip Loeb, who had taken the lead on Broadway and here appears in the minor role of the man from the collection agency, was also employed as assistant to the director on the film, on account of his familiarity with the show. Oddly, it is stated in the shooting script that he will supervise the shooting of this scene, even though it differs significantly from the version in the play, and is a purely visual job of cutting and editing of a sort with which William Seiter would surely have needed no assistance at all. Yet it is the only scene thus identified in the script.

37:39/39:16—"But his hair wasn't red yesterday!"

Yet further evidence for speculating that the "blonde wig" with which Harpo replaced his supposedly unphotogenic red one after *The Cocoanuts* was, in fact, not blonde but merely a lighter shade of red that photographed blonde. For more on this vexed non-issue, see *The Cocoanuts,* 40:26.

44:55/46:50—Harpo and the turkey

Notable for having inspired this glorious piece of English understatement from the contemporary reviewer of the *Monthly Film Bulletin*: "...there is a scene in which a turkey is chased around a room. Not everybody will care for this." And indeed, few do, though at least the real turkey that briefly features is swapped for an obvious puppet after the first few seconds. For that, it seems, we should be grateful. According to the *Evening Independent* (July 25, 1938): "It is all right for the Marx Brothers to chase blondes in a movie scene but they can't chase turkeys. This is the ruling of the humane society (the part about the turkey, anyway) and it puts RKO to a lot of trouble this week during the filming of *Room Service*.... Due to the humane society, it is a prop turkey, strung on wires and supplied with a motor inside the body to make the wings flap. 'We wanted to put a real turkey on the wires,' Groucho says, 'but I guess they figured it's crueller to make a turkey watch the Marx Brothers act than it is to kill and eat it.'" Even if untrue, a pleasant surprise that such concerns might be voiced in the thirties. Harder to believe is this, from the same paper, two days later: "The film will never get out of the RKO cutting room, but Harpo Marx did talk in a scene for *Room Service*. It was a chase shot where the Marxes and Frankie Albertson are in a wild scramble to catch a turkey. In the excitement—rushes proved it conclusively—Harpo forgot himself and yelled, 'Stop that bird!'" Was there ever a Marx picture in which it was not claimed Harpo spoke, either secretly or accidentally?

50:40/52:50—The Whiteway Theatre and *Hail and Farewell*

As well as pulling a nasty surprise upon agoraphobics (who had presumably relaxed delightedly into a film they were by this time certain would be shot entirely in a couple of cramped rooms and a corridor), this sudden establishing shot of the outside of the theater always surprises me. First, because the theater they've been talking about all this time—that's part of the hotel and has been standing empty for an indefinite period until shoestring producer Gordon Miller turns up—is so big, glamorous and easy to fill with huge numbers of sophisticated patrons. And second, because part of what seems to have brought them there is Miller's name. So far from the fly-by-night he seemed, it looks as though he is respected enough to fill a theater with a marquee on which his name is as big as, and precedes, and possesses, the play's title.

54:30/56:50—"I'm headin' for the last round-up...."

The song Groucho sings off-screen is a popular, much-recorded western dirge by Billy Hill, famously voiced by Gene Autry in 1933 and serving as the title of an Autry movie in 1947. (Though Miller is described as singing it in the original play, Groucho also makes a vague reference to it in *A Day at the Races* [at 87:50, see *ADatR*, 85:44], while one of the suggested advertising catchlines in the *Go West* press book is "They're headin' for the Fast Clown-Up!," a bit of verbal wizardry for which, presumably, someone was paid actual money.) Billy Hill also wrote such similarly plaintive yeehaw laments as "Empty Saddles" and "They Cut Down the Old Pine Tree," such standards as "The Glory of Love" and "In the Chapel in the Moonlight," and such frankly head-scratching titles as "There's No Light in the Lighthouse" and "Was I a Rooster?" He'd also been a genuine Death Valley cowboy, so when he talks of little dawgies gittin' along and such like, he really does know whereof he speaks.

57:31/59:58—"What'll we do now, sing 'Sweet Adeline'?"

Given the nostalgic mood of the film, this seeming recollection of *Monkey Business*, not present in the original play, is especially charming. (Likewise, an earlier reference to the actors in the play rehearsing "on the mezzanine" has also been noted, though this *is* to be found in the play: the phrase "in the mezzanine" pops up three times. Nonetheless, it is always "in"; only Ryskind has it as "on," so there may be conscious in-joking to that extent.) First published in 1903, the song is, in fact, more correctly known as "You're the Flower of My Heart, Sweet Adeline," and was originally written as "You're the Flower of My Heart, Sweet Rosalie" but only became a hit after the name switch (a tough break on Rosalie, who must surely have taken it personally). Somewhat fabulously, the Sweet Adelines International is the name of a worldwide organization of women barbershop singers, founded in 1945 and still going strong. "Sweet Adeline" also served as the title of a 1929 Broadway musical adapted into a 1934 Irene Dunne movie, and the name of a popular brand of sweet potatoes.

61:54/64:33—"Here's some ipecac...."

Ipecac was, for decades, your first port of call if you wanted to remove toxic substances from the stomach at high speed and maximum visibility. Though no longer recommended by the top quacks, it remains the best use yet found for the dried rhizone and roots of the ipecacuanha, a plant which owes its celebrity almost entirely to its ability to make people vomit. This is one of two references to ipecac beloved by fans of classic comedy, the other concerns deciding whether to choose between ipecac or syrup of squill and features in W.C. Fields's immortal *It's a Gift* (1934), directed by Norman Z. McLeod. Incidentally, this scene features my favorite Harpo moment from the whole film. Wagner is preparing the ipecac and handing it to Harpo to give to Davis. But instead of administering it, Harpo is rushing to the bed and drinking it himself, in best Harpo fashion, not to be helpful but for his own inhuman pleasure. For the first two trips he does it secretively, but then, on the third, he openly chinks glasses with Wagner. Vintage Harpo.

66:15/69:05—"E pluribus unum"

Said by Chico, for sound rather than meaning, over Davis's supposedly dead body, this is, of course, the famous phrase on the seal of the United States of America. My guess is it's Latin, but this has never been proven.

66:19/69:09—Chariot or Cheerio?

One of two things will happen as you're watching at this point. Either they will sing "Swing Low, Sweet Chariot," or they will sing a totally different, specially written requiem that begins: "One last sweet cheerio, to my friend they're calling back home...." The version I knew, shown on British television and first released on British video, was the second one. When I saw the "Sweet Chariot" print on the Universal DVD I assumed it was a rare alternate print. Subsequent investigation, however, revealed that while very few of the Marx enthusiasts I consulted were aware of there being two versions, the majority were familiar not with the one I took to be standard, but with "Swing Low." It was "Sweet Cheerio" that was the anomaly.

The first interesting thing to note when comparing the two is that they are not two different sequences, merely two different soundtracks. The "Sweet Cheerio" version uses the same footage of the Brothers singing "Sweet Chariot," with the new song overdubbed. That's why it's written the way it is. It's funny, because I've always been familiar with the song "Swing Low, Sweet Chariot," but in all my years of unquestioned acquaintance with "One Last Sweet Cheerio" it never occurred to me what an obvious and deliberate pastiche it is of the other number. It has to be this way because it has to match the original sequence and, as much as possible, the lip movements. So full marks, then, to whoever wrote it, for managing to come up with a lyric that sensibly (indeed entirely effectively) conveys the genuine purpose and meaning of such a song, while making it as different from "Sweet Chariot" as possible, yet at the same time retaining many of the original song's vowel formations. Looked at with an informed and clinical eye, it *is* obvious that "One Last Sweet Cheerio" is an overdub, but by no means that it is dubbing an entirely different song. Here are the two lyrics side by side, with a little guesswork from me for one of the less-decipherable "Sweet Cheerio" lines:

Swing low, sweet chariot, / One last sweet cheerio,
Comin' for to carry me home. / To my friend they're calling back home
If you get there before I do, / A vow and then a fond adieu [or] Now and then, be fonder do (?)
Comin' for to carry me home. / To my friend they're calling back home.
Tell all my friends I'm comin' too / To all my vows I'm keeping true
Comin' for to carry me home. / To my friend they're calling back home.

The song features twice in the film, and in both cases is meticulously re-recorded, unquestionably utilizing the Marxes' own services, and a full orchestra for the finale.

So the question becomes: *why was the second version so carefully written, recorded and felt to be needed?* I've put this question to all the Marx fans and scholars I know, and between us we've come up with three possible explanations, none of which strikes me as entirely likely, but one of which, in the absence of anything better, seems the *most* likely, and for which I will therefore plump.

First, there is the explanation I automatically assumed to be the only and obvious one when I first saw the "Swing Low" print. At this point I still thought "Sweet Cheerio" was the standard (and "Swing Low" a rare, previously unreleased pre-dub), so assumed that RKO had been obliged to change it in post-production after discovering they were unable to use "Swing Low," presumably because of a copyright issue. There remains one strong piece of evidence in support of this notion, which remains unexplained if we accept any other explanation. This is that, in addition to changing the lyrics, the redubbed version also very subtly changes the melody, so that while it still fits exactly into the running time of the sequence and the length and scansion of each line, the actual melodic structure of the song is different. This would be as essential as changing the words if there was a copyright violation to be circumnavigated, but a completely unnecessary job of considerable work if the change was instituted for any other reason.

But the stubborn fact remains that while this is ostensibly the most satisfying explanation, it is also the one we can most certainly discount, for two insurmountable reasons. First, because I soon discovered that I was wrong about the two dubs (the "Swing Low" version was not rare and unreleased but the most widely available version) and second, because there just *couldn't* have been a copyright problem with "Swing Low, Sweet Chariot." It's a traditional number, dating from sometime before 1862.

Another possibility suggested to me was that it may have been altered to appease racialist sentiments in the American South, given that the song is inextricably associated with its use as a "negro spiritual." But while it is certainly true that films were sometimes altered on these grounds for certain U.S. markets, it seems a stretch indeed that this song would have caused problems, and, in any case, I received no indication from any of the people I polled in America of *any* familiarity with the "Sweet Cheerio" version at all. On the contrary, many have, in fact, pointed out that the very word "cheerio" is virtually unknown in American speech other than as the name of a breakfast cereal, and insofar as it is known at all is thought of as quintessentially British. (And even the cereal post-dates the film: it first appeared as "Cheeri-Oats" in 1941 and was changed to its more familiar name in 1945 after a knockdown, drag-out fight with the Quakers.)

The most likely answer, therefore, is that the "Sweet Cheerio" version was prepared for the British release. This is supported by the fact that in all the books I have read on the films, the only ones that mention the "Cheerio" version are British: Louvish, though he mistakes the "sweet cheerio" for a "wee" one, and Allen Eyles: "When the mock suicide of the author is staged, the executive regrets his attempts to halt the play as he looks at the body and Groucho and Chico sing "One last sweet cheerio" while Harpo brings in a wreath to lay on the corpse."

The only thing that slightly annoys me about this is that I just don't understand why they'd have bothered. I'm even mildly surprised by the notion that British audiences would have been unfamiliar with "Sweet Chariot" in the first place, but even if they were, so what? There must have been a hundred things a week in American talking films that baffled the British. (I have a 1931 British film almanac that has a lovely glossary of American phrases helpfully translated.) Would they necessarily know why Chico says, "E pluribus unum" directly before the song? It's certainly not going to affect their enjoyment of the film much, either way. So would it really be deemed problematic enough to justify rehiring the Marx Brothers, presumably at the same record-salary rates brother Zeppo wangled on their behalf, and an orchestra, and paying a lyricist/composer to come up with a satisfactory pastiche? And why alter the melody as well as the words? These are elements that remain mysterious, but for now it looks as though, in spite of all my reservations, "One Last Sweet Cheerio" was written and recorded and overlaid on the soundtrack purely to keep the British happy. The final irony is that I still prefer the "Sweet Cheerio" version. I like the words (the ones I can make out at least) and the altered melody is more haunting to me. In the original play they sing "Abide with Me," while in *Step Lively,* the 1944 musical remake of *Room Service* with Frank Sinatra, Gloria DeHaven, George Murphy and others, they sing "Auld Lang Syne" (perhaps because the frivolous use of a hymn was verboten).

Also "Sweet Cheerio" fans were the British rock band The Faces, who often performed it live *a cappella*. Meanwhile, Alice Cooper's 1969 debut album *Pretties for You* includes an ostensibly unrelated song called "Swing Low Sweet Cheerio," suggesting from the title at least that Cooper, a Marx fan and friend of Groucho's, may have been familiar with both versions.

71:25/74:28—"Yeah, man!"
71:32/74:35—"Sho 'nuff!"

Groucho's exclamations during the song reprise are carefully retained in both versions, though only really make sense in the context of "Sweet Chariot." But they're funny, either way.

71:52/74:56—Credit run

Oddly, this only features in the U.S./"Sweet Chariot" version of the film, and utilizes music heard nowhere else in the film. Only here are they credited individually: the opening titles just has them as "The Marx Brothers," so British viewers would have encountered the names Groucho, Harpo and Chico nowhere in the credits. These end credits retain the MGM billing order, with Chico listed second. (See *A Night at the Opera,* 0:09.)

9

At the Circus (1939)

Elephants! At your age!—J. Cheever Loophole (Groucho Marx)

"The next Marx picture," Robbin Coons told his readers in November of 1938, "will not be an adaptation of the most expensive stage play on Broadway":

> It will be a throwback to their own standard brand of comedy. It will be as different from *Room Service* as possible. *Room Service*, says Groucho, was an attempt to satisfy those who asked why the Marxes didn't tackle something different. As such, they're glad they did it. They'll be just as glad to get back in home territory for *A Day at the Circus*.

Not sure how glad they were, to be honest, but for certain it was an altogether less cocksure Marx Brothers that returned to MGM after *Room Service*. Most histories of the team note that it is at this stage that they (Groucho especially) start viewing their job as simply that, no longer as a source of enjoyment or fulfilment. They begin talking disdainfully of the material they are given, and enthusiastically of retirement. And not just privately, either. How MGM's publicity department must have winced, when interviews like this one with Robbin Coons started appearing in the columns:

> "When we get through this present contract," said Groucho, "we'll all be through. Three more pictures—one a year. By that time the public should be overly fed up with us. It will be amazing if they are not fed up with us before then. I myself have been fed up with myself for some time. A man, even such a man as I, hardened to most things, cannot keep on seeing himself on the screen without being violently nauseated. There is a limit."

It's usually put down to age, or crotchetiness, or to resentment of Louis B. Mayer's vindictive efforts to make things as difficult as possible for them, with no Thalberg to get in the way. But things begin to look a little different if you view their MGM career not as one episode, briefly interrupted by *Room Service*, but rather as two discrete adventures. First, there were the Thalberg movies: a deal for one film with an option, enthusiastically taken up, for a second. These completed, they were free to go where they wished, and RKO's *Room Service* offer was triply attractive: it was lucrative, it gave them the license to experiment with the fundamentals of the act, and there was a promise of two other equally idiosyncratic follow-ups. According to Arce, they made vague commitment to MGM of a future return (perhaps from residual loyalty to Thalberg) but not, it seems, a contractually binding one. Certainly the move to RKO was played by all parties as permanent, and a peevish MGM lost no time announcing they were replacing the uppity stars with a new team, consisting of Ted Healy, Buddy Ebsen and Buster Keaton! (Amusingly,

The legal eagle swoops: Groucho's missing first scene from *At the Circus*. Seated is Irene Coleman, Miss Chicago, 1931.

Paramount had attempted to keep the Marxes in line back in 1933 by spreading rumors they were considering replacing them with Healy and his Stooges.) But even when the *Room Service* experience began to sour with indecision, and with the prospect of *Of Thee I Sing* starting to slip away in consequence, why would they return to MGM? True, the studio's name was second to none in terms of prestige, but they must have known how limited their options would be there creatively. The answer, I suspect, is producer Mervyn LeRoy. My guess is that it was LeRoy personally who tempted them back to the old house, and not, as is usually perceived, with their tails between their legs, but because he made them an offer very much worth accepting. What may be significantly underestimated here is the extent to which he offered them a business-as-before deal; that is to say the extent to which he was a second Thalberg.

LeRoy was no MGM lackey: he enjoyed complete creative autonomy, acting as a vital buffer between studio and stars. He had arrived at Metro in 1936 from Warner Brothers already as an established maverick, and in a snowstorm of publicity that explicitly hailed him as their new Thalberg (indeed *Variety* claimed that Thalberg had been headhunting him personally). The *New York Post* in November of 1937 was one of many to make the comparison overt: "The signing of Mervyn LeRoy as a producer-director at MGM, upon completion of his current Warner Brothers film, *Food for Scandal*, has made MGM officials confident that they have at last culminated an exhaustive search for a successor to the late Irving Thalberg."

Alas, the troublesome experience of marshalling *The Wizard of Oz* seems to have turned him off the onerous duties of the producer and kindled a yearning to go back to good, honest directing. Otherwise, he would presumably have seen the Marxes safely through their next two pictures also, and we would now split their MGM work into the two convenient chapters of the Thalberg years and the LeRoy years.

Brief though LeRoy's association with the Marxes may ultimately have proved, the idea that they returned to the studio after Thalberg's death without a champion protector, and that at Mayer's mercy they were ill-used and even deliberately undermined, does not easily hold up. They were very much on LeRoy's team, and that counted for a whole lot in 1939. There seems little doubt that Mayer did dislike them, on screen and off, but even if he was silly enough to want to scupper the box-office potential of one of his own studio's films from so petty a motive (and does that really sound like Louis B. Mayer to you?) where is the evidence that he tried to? It's usually offered that he maliciously denied them the chance to test the new script in the form of a stage tour and left at that, but in fact a tour was announced as usual, and cancelled only because of scheduling difficulties (making it the second Marx film in a row to suffer that indignity. It's possible this may have been a complication arising from late script revision: as close to the wire as March of 1939 it was announced that the film "has been taken off the production schedule for a complete rewriting.")

And speaking of the script, it's also widely thought that screenwriter Irving Brecher was foisted on to the project by the front office, and disastrously obliged to write the script in isolation (without recourse to the productively combative input of other writers, as is necessary to achieve the correct rhythm and texture of a Marx script). In truth, Brecher was under personal contract to LeRoy, part of the package expressly brought to the project by him, and therefore likely fully endorsed by the Marxes as a good bet for snappy New York humour. (Also arriving at the studio under LeRoy's wing were Kenny Baker, the singing circus owner, and Lana Turner, briefly considered for the film also [see below, 2:31].) As to the matter of script collaboration: yes, the film would doubtless have benefited from a noisier and more competitive assembly, but it would be a mistake to read the credit as meaning the film is Brecher's sole and entire responsibility. After a first treatment by Ben Hecht, Brecher prepared a revision in concert with Arthur Sheekman, then a new draft, from which the finished script was essentially drawn, with Dore Schary. Still more chipped in with bits, including Buster Keaton, and the Brothers themselves according to the *Brooklyn Daily Eagle*: "Three secretaries sat on the sets throughout the picture jotting down the ad-libs of the Marxes between scenes and during rehearsals, and the best of these were juggled into the picture." (Any guesses?)

In script terms I see little to convince me of the *major* decline from the level of *Races* that many critics discern. The primary objection is that the circus setting is a mistake because the Marxes belong there, as opposed to, say, the world of opera, where they do not belong and in which their presence (and to which their relationship) can only be productively antagonistic. But even if it were true that they belong with the circus (and is it?) it surely must be added that the point of the ending is that they *bring* the circus to one of Margaret Dumont's high society, high culture soirees. The film builds to this crescendo just as *Opera* builds to that film's climactic orgy of iconoclasm, albeit, admittedly, to far less liberating effect. True, at Paramount no such script contrivances were necessary: all they had to do was turn up and the party was wrecked before it started. (They were plenty circus enough, all by themselves.) But still, the material is not the first problem here.

A much bigger issue than anything in the script, as far as I'm concerned, is the bizarre metamorphosis Groucho seems to have undergone. I don't mean that he looks different, though the truth is that he does, and not just because of that repulsive wig. (There's something strange all round about him, as if he had lost weight suddenly, or had plastic surgery.) Neither am I referring to scripted revisions of his established character, although there are plenty of those too, the biggest being that he is now possessed of a marked strain of comic cowardice, about which he explicitly jokes, very much in the Bob Hope manner. (The interplay with Goliath the strong man is the best and most often cited example, but it runs all through, and perhaps reaches its true nadir when he is frightened by a train whistle and rushes for safety to the arms of heroine Florence Rice. That one's especially unamusing if you come to it soon after a viewing of *Monkey Business*.) Likewise in error, I think, is the more general desire to get laughs by making him seem foolish, as when he emerges in costume in the Peerless Pauline sequence, and is then left whimpering on the ceiling at her exit, to be rescued only by Harpo's engineering of a demeaning slapstick fall. I'm not sure Groucho makes much sense unless he is fraudulently in control of every situation.

But these are all deliberate, exterior alterations to his character, and they don't get to the heart of the change he has abruptly undergone, which is a sudden and complete change in his *actual performing style*. He is giving a totally new and different performance to the one he had basically delivered, with superficial variation, over the course of eight previous movies. He's broader, louder, bigger, vastly less subtle. Indeed, what he resembles most acutely is a bad Groucho Marx impersonator. ("Irv Brecher, who wrote it, used to write for Milton Berle," recorded Hy Gardner, in a review describing the film as "only so-so", "and in some spots he's got Groucho doing Berle with a mustache.")

So far as I am aware, only Adamson among the major writers notices it—certainly he's the only one to observe that "Groucho is so chipper in in his first scene that his voice rises

At the Circus: (Left to right) Groucho, Chico and Harpo confront the 1940s.

several octaves", though it's not just this scene. And he also suggests what seems to me the most likely explanation: capitulation to over-emphatic direction from Ed Buzzell, who apparently instructed the Brothers to "really act" the scenes. ("Marx Brothers will do anything but act!" the *Brooklyn Daily Eagle* would have us believe Groucho retorted to one such exhortation. "If you want dramatics, use our stand-ins!") "Buzzell tried to graft his own personality on us and it just didn't work," Groucho confirms in one of his letters to his daughter Miriam in *Love, Groucho*.

The surprise is that Groucho would have so willingly gone along with his notions, not just because they were patently dud ones but also because Groucho just doesn't come across as the capitulating type. Here, I think we have to factor in the low professional ebb the *Room Service* debacle had left him at. Exactly as it had in 1933, when he found himself back at Paramount after a failed shot at independence and *Of Thee I Sing*, a big chance to break free and try something new had again rebounded, leaving him where he started and worse off than when he'd left. Not merely contemplating retirement but brazenly announcing it to the journalists tasked with making people want to see the movie, I think it's possible he'd have done whatever Buzzell told him. (And we should also remember that they *were* old pals: Buzzell was a former vaudeville star who had often worked with the Brothers, all the way back to Gummo days.) Neither was he helped, I suspect, by Buzzell's deliberately stone-faced attitude to their comedy, the purpose of which he explained to the *New York Times* (December 15, 1940):

> Personally, I think the Marx Brothers are among the funniest people in the world, but, like all laugh-seekers of their type, they are always "working" and if I was to prove a good audience to them during rehearsals and between scenes I would be sunk. So, I never laughed at their cracks and never tried to match repartee with them. I was the guy without a sense of humor.... Remember, I was once a comedian and I know how a comic goes berserk when he once starts cracking laughs out of an audience.

By far the easiest way to appreciate the extent of the transformation Groucho has undergone is to compare and contrast; to take any previous film, *Races* very much included, and simply alternate the scenes. Indeed, just compare the Dumont seduction scene here with any previous one. In the earlier films, his pacing is actually very deliberate, his intonation level and his body language very controlled. Though the overall impression is one of anarchy, the man himself is enigmatic, and his delivery is measured, the whole a kind of parody of gentility, and the point that you don't necessarily get the measure of Groucho straight away. (That, presumably, is how he ends up convincing her of his attainment and good intentions.) But this is an altogether zanier fellow; he seems to speak differently, move his body differently, there's a whole different timbre to his voice; he talks nineteen to the dozen in a constantly varying register. He moves funny: vastly more frenetic, he can't sit still for a second, darting here and there, flinging his arms about. He acts like an idiot.

The old Groucho had a challenging air of insouciance, as if he didn't much care whether you found him funny or not. His primary aim seemed to be to amuse himself, and if you didn't like it he'd probably enjoy himself all the more. This one wants you to think he's hilarious, and he's trying way too hard. He's knowingly and demonstratively comic—and for me at least, vastly less amusing in consequence, even when the lines are good. And more often than I remembered they actually are, in this film. But the delivery of them I find utterly grating.

Perhaps because of the brick wall response they were getting from the stars, the reports tended to focus more on the circus elements. (Reviewing the film, *Photoplay* magazine promised "plenty of circus acts, a midget, camels, elephants and a lovely gorilla.") At the production stage, article after article ignored the Marxes and expected its readers to be excited by lengthy descriptions of the circus tent MGM had specially made, which, they all agree, is "streamlined" and involves plenty of chromium. Whatever that means, it's a source of endless fascination to the columnists.

The same goes for the roll-call of real circus talent imported to bolster the efforts of the leads. Under the overall supervision of S.L. Cronin, manager of the Al G. Barnes Circus, the film allegedly found room for the Escalante aerial troupe, the Pena Family of acrobats, the Juggling Normans, a Cossack troupe of sixteen, and clowns Jack McAfee and Little Bozo. The seal who appears with Harpo was a seasoned professional called Slicker. Janet May ("the world's only upside-down walker") stood in for Eve Arden in the scenes where the latter appears to hang from the ceiling, using suction-cup shoes. (Despite not risking her neck in this way, however, the *Brooklyn Daily Eagle* does inform us that Eve "wore out twenty pairs of silk tights doing comedy scenes with the Marxes." Best not to ask.) But efforts to secure Bea, the baby elephant from the Tarzan movies, were supposedly denied on the grounds that it would be beneath her dignity to appear in a Marx film. (MGM's idea of publicity for the Marxes these days was to constantly reinforce how ridiculous they are.)

One of the more persistent claims in early publicity and magazine reports is that the film will feature Harpo conducting a symphony orchestra of monkeys. Here's the *Salt Lake Tribune*:

> Something new in symphony concerts is to be introduced by Harpo Marx in the new Marx Brothers comedy, *A Day at the Circus*. Heretofore, Harpo's musical contributions have been solo numbers on his harp. In *A Day at the Circus* he will be accompanied by a complete symphony orchestra. And all the players will be monkeys. Rehearsals with the monkey orchestra begin soon.

Sadly, it was not to be. Still, all in all and given the general emasculation and plodding literalism of the MGM approach to comedy, *At the Circus* strikes me as a fair half-success. Groucho's performance aside, it more or less manages to postpone, for *just* one more time, our having to acknowledge the decline of the Marx Brothers that had been in process since 1935. (And it contains one scene, in which Chico and Harpo search the strongman's room for evidence of wrong-doing, which can stand proudly with the best of Paramount.)

With *Go West*, you can't pretend it isn't happening any more. Here, if you screw up your eyes, and wiggle your fingers in your ears, you can *almost* hear the orchestra from *A Night at the Opera* tuning up, and see Groucho and Chico tearing up their contracts. In reality, they had just signed a new one for three more pictures, and it never got any better than this.

2:31 (NTSC)/2:37 (PAL)—"Step Up and Take a Bow"

A curious song number, performed by Florence Rice and a plainly unamused horse. Also, it would appear, a shadow of its originally intended self. The *Montreal Gazette* reported that eighteen girls had been selected ("from hundreds of applicants") to perform a "spectacular dance on horseback" at the culmination of the number. According to the report: "They had to be expert ballet dancers, have good singing voices, and they had to be able to prove all this by doing a toe-dance on a cantering bareback horse while singing in key." You can see the gals lined up behind Rice, which would seem to suggest the extra portion was shot and then cut, but it's hard to imagine the studio willingly dumping so costly and showy a sequence if they'd got as far as shooting it. It's more likely, I think, that the girls were worked into the visual design and left there for aesthetic value, but their real function was cut *before* shooting, victim of the cost-paring that would become epidemic on *Go West,* and shows how little MGM was willing to invest in the Brothers' productions from here on.

The *Brooklyn Daily Eagle* claims that Rice "was initiated into the Marx Leading Lady Club the first day of work when the comedians locked her in the gorilla cage and left her there an hour." According to other reports she was afraid of horses; unsurprisingly she was not first choice to play our equestrienne heroine. The *Philadelphia Enquirer* has Lana Turner originally in the frame: it's possible, as she was still doing unbilled bits in 1938, but got yanked to stardom—ie: out of the Marxes' league—very suddenly thereafter. Famously Turner had been spotted by the publisher of the *Hollywood Reporter* sipping a Coke in a drugstore; less well known is that the agent she was first brought to was Zeppo. An unsuccessful round of the studios ended when producer Mervyn LeRoy gave her an attention-stealing cameo in *They Won't Forget*. Zeppo instructed her not to tell Leroy she was fifteen until after she'd signed the contracts.

3:38/3:47—Goliath the Mighty

Welcome back to Nat Pendleton, our old pal from *Horse Feathers,* here as the circus's strongman with a mustache, a German accent and what looks suspiciously like one of Harpo's spare wigs. (See *Horse Feathers,* 8:45) He performs in a double-act with Harpo: an idea so alive with comic possibilities it seems a portent of doom indeed that their scene together peters out before it even gets going, after just a couple of seconds of pretty basic effects slapstick (Harpo fires a cannon ball too early and it hits Pendleton in the ass; Pendleton throws a lifting bar which Harpo catches and the weight makes him sink into the ground). And from then on there's no indication of the two of them having anything more than a passing acquaintance. The original point of teaming them was probably because Goliath's a brute, and it might make for an opportunity to work up a bit of cloying sympathy for Harpo, as with Lassparri. In the event, nothing is made of it because we never see them together after their opening act, so it is just left in the air as a strange, unfulfilled idea. Eyles even says that he is "roughly treated" by him "for an innocent mistake during a performance." This is either a missing or imagined scene, or he means the bit where Goliath throws the bar at him, in which case he's being blamed rightly, and the rough treatment comes more from the MGM junior special-effects team than from Goliath.

4:48/5:00—"Mister Carter! Mister Carter!"

Chico's first bit is pretty good, considering; asking people how they're doing and then refusing to listen to the answer because he doesn't have time. He looks interesting, too, in a long coat and sailor cap. And he scores yet another solid laugh by asking for the afternoon off because, following his divorce, it's the day he gets custody of his wife's parents.

Not at 7:15/7:34—The first Groucho scene

Groucho plays the shyster lawyer J. Cheever Loophole. (Incidentally, it is surely not coincidental that the financier who ousted the Laemmle family and took control of Universal Pictures in 1936, a move much resented in Hollywood, was called J. Cheever Cowdin.) It's at this point that we were once intended to watch a self-contained sketch, and Groucho's first scene in the picture. There's two ways of looking at the fact that we're not. On the one hand, any Groucho scene is worth keeping, and it's infuriating to know that this one wasn't just written but actually shot, and yet no footage of it seems to remain. (Whereas when you watch any of the MGM *That's Entertainment* films, they can't stop bragging about all the preserved outtakes they're going to include.) On the other hand, if we must be philosophical about it (and until someone finds the missing footage that's our only option), it has to be admitted that we actually aren't missing all that much. Showing Groucho, the lawyer, at work in court (and beginning with him asleep in the jury box), it makes its best 1939 stab at vintage Groucho wordplay, ranging from the not *too* inauthentic ("affidavit is better than none") to the positively torturous ("a woman has always been something to revere; my mother was a woman, granddaughter to Paul Revere, but that's a horse of another story"). It ends with the message we see Chico sending to him in the release version being delivered by a singing telegram boy. I think most fans would agree that, ecstatic as they would undoubtedly be at news of its recovery, it wouldn't be as exciting as the prospect of a fully restored *Horse Feathers,* even though the missing material there amounts only to a few snippets.

7:32/7:51—"Jeff Wilson Gives Up Green Backs For Bare Backs"

It must have been a slow news day. Here's the full text of the front-page news story for which the above is the bizarre headline:

> Jeffrey Wilson, nephew of the prominent New York socialite Mrs. Suzanna Dukesbury, is broke today! His aunt, Mrs. Suzanna Dukesbury, in a statement to the press, declared that she would not tolerate her nephew or any member of her family acting in a way to bring discredit to the family name.

And despite two huge portraits of the pair, that's it for the story. Love the exclamation mark, and the repetition of her name, Mrs. Suzanna Dukesbury, but there's no mention of why he's broke or how he's disgraced her, nor any reference to the circus beyond the hint in the headline. No Pulitzer for this one. An early report on the film published in *Silver Screen* (1939) includes a couple of details on this story that don't make it into the finished film, most notably that after disinheriting Kenny she "announces Lucius, her Pekingese pup, as her sole heir."

8:47/9:10—"Was I hearin' things, Julie? Did'ya really mean what'ya said?"

Once heard, this line can never be unheard, delivered as it is in a weird, strangulated yelp by Kenny Baker, our romantic lead in this movie. I am, to put it mildly, no advocate of the seemingly obligatory habit among Marx fans of mocking the straight guys and guffawing through the songs. And Baker's a nice enough little singer, with a personality that would probably play cute in other contexts. But it's hopefully not too unkind to say that the god who handed out magnetic screen presences made him a nice enough little singer with a personality that would probably play cute in other contexts. Certainly, he makes you think longingly of Allan Jones. Half an hour in, you'll feel like Rosa when she left him behind at the dock. More importantly, he has zero rapport (and virtually zero involvement) with the team: as a result this becomes the first time that the two elements—the comedy and the musical romance plot—seem rigidly compartmentalized, almost like in one of those Laurel & Hardy operettas.

He made an altogether stronger impression as the tenor on Jack Benny's radio show (preceding the much better-known Dennis Day, and playing a dopey kid not all that different from Day's character; he also appears alongside Benny, Harpo and many others in Stage Door Canteen [1943].)

Benny fans will recall that Baker was the only cast member to have a special credit at the end of every broadcast: "Kenny Baker appeared through the courtesy of Mervyn LeRoy Productions." LeRoy produced *At the Circus*, so it was the fact that Baker was under exclusive contract to him that landed him the role, ditto his song spot in *The King and the Chorus Girl* (1937), coincidentally written by Groucho but crucially again produced (and directed) by LeRoy. That this was a cosy arrangement is hinted by the constant joke references to it in the October 1939 *Silver Screen* article mentioned above, where almost every mention of Baker, or even his character Jeff in plot synopses, is followed with the note:"(courtesy of Mervyn LeRoy Productions)."

The duet **"Two Blind Loves"** comes in around **9:07/9:30**—you'll hate it; I'll concede it's forgettable. It's certainly a gutsy move, expecting us to sit through it this early in the film, when we still haven't seen Groucho and we've had one dopey song already. But I like the bit where he puts a doughnut on her finger. I think it's the only time I've ever seen anyone do that in a movie.

11:18/11:47—"Hey! Where's your badge?"

Set your disbelief suspension drive to baloney factor five, and ponder this claim in the *Milwaukee Journal* of July 22, 1939:

> Speechless Harpo Marx, whose voice has never been heard on the screen, has a speaking role at last. But his fans will never identify him because he appears as Chico, his brother, instead of Harpo. It happened during a night rain scene for *A Day at the Circus* on MGM's Lot 2. Escaping recognition, Harpo appeared earlier than schedule, perfectly disguised in the wig, make-up and wardrobe of Chico and his imitation of Chico's Italian dialect was flawless. Eddie Buzzell, the director, rehearsed Harpo believing him to be Chico three times with Kenny [Baker] and Florence Rice and then shot the scene. As the scene ended, the real Chico arrived. Befuddled, Buzzell called for a retake with the real Chico, then changed his mind. "If the director couldn't tell the difference, how can anyone else?" So Harpo speaks!

Yes, the incidental accuracy is unusual (it *is* a night rain shot), and that "Lot 2" touch garnishes the dish with the vinaigrette of authenticity, too. At a push, I'd be happy to accept that Harpo did actually pull this stunt one day on the set. Much harder to swallow is that this is what we are seeing in the finished film. Not only because, to fool Buzzell, Harpo would have needed not merely to do a flawless "Chico" in the take, but also a flawless Leonard on the set, through the rehearsal and before and during the shooting. Also, the scene is shot from a distance and through a studio rainshower: most likely the sound was re-recorded if it was ever recorded in the first place, which would mean getting Harpo to do the dubbing as well. And I don't care how well they could impersonate each other: that's Chico's voice. Meanwhile, however, the *Brooklyn Daily Eagle* (July 11, 1939) goes further, claiming that "for a gag in one scene" Harpo and Chico both exchange roles, and says that the Marx Brothers "defy the audience to pick the place where it happens." As do I!

11:31/12:00—Groucho

With his intended first scene in the dumper, this takes the Marx movie record for longest-delayed first Groucho appearance. Even *Duck Soup* didn't expect us to wait this long, and that at least spent most of the opening building up our expectations. This one takes twelve minutes just making room for him. The hat he's wearing delays the nastiest surprise, but the change in his performance I mentioned here is obvious from the first second.

11:48/12:18—"I haven't seen you since I stopped taking Scott's Emulsion."

Scott's Emulsion is a cod-liver oil preparation for children, available in orange flavor and original flavor (which presumably means cod liver flavor, about as euphemistic a use of the word "original" as can be imagined). Groucho's comment refers to the advertising, which depicted a fisherman carrying an enormous cod on his shoulder: Chico is keeping out the rain by wearing what looks like a fisherman's waterproof hat and coat.

12:18/12:50—"Oh, you mean my Lone Ranger badge? Sorry, they took it back, I stopped eating the cereal."

As many other writers have pointed out, this badge scene is pretty awful, in that it plays like a Marx Brothers scene written by people who have seen one or two Marx Brothers scenes but don't really have the first clue how they work or what's funny about them. It sort of sounds and moves like a classic Chico-Groucho duologue, but it's stupid. (Adamson notes, however, that the fault is not Brecher's: the script he submitted was very different and considerably better.) The mistake is to think that Chico behaves meaninglessly, whereas the truth is that he has his own anti-logic that is, on terms entirely incompatible with that of anyone else, rigidly logical. Here, his behavior is simply ludicrous, and the topper—where the badge he personally gives to Groucho he then rejects as if he had not done so—is mind-boggling. How could they have gotten it so wrong, and how could the two men—no matter how little enthusiasm they had—have performed it without protest? (You can imagine how keen Groucho in particular would have been to get it over with and get out of that studio rainstorm: according to press reports, he was wearing a rubber body suit under his clothes.)

Anyhoo, the line about the Lone Ranger and cereal refers to the Lone Ranger radio series that began in 1933, and pertaining to which various promotional tie-ins, including badges, were issued via the sponsor, General Mills, the guys and gals behind Cheerios, Wheaties, and Kix.

14:54/15:32—Chico's piano spot

Instead of playing for cute kids, he's got his preferred audience back here: a whole gaggle of adoring dames. One in particular stares at him the whole time, and when not responding to her he finds a moment to look directly into the camera and smile outrageously right at us: a striking reversal of the oddly sullen magnetism he projected in the earliest films. It's all very nice, but, as is the MGM way, only an insulting minute and a half in duration.

17:55/18:41—What is that thing on Groucho's head?

We got a glimpse when he fell over in the puddle at the end of his previous (and until now only) scene, but it's only here, in the merciless light of the studio train car set, that the full horror of Groucho's wig is revealed. It matters because there are ways you can tamper with Groucho's basic character and ways you can't, if you want it to retain any kind of meaning at all. Making him a "funny" coward, as I noted above, is a pretty bad idea that robs his persona of one of its unique qualities, but it is sustainable in context, just. But if Groucho is *anything* he is the enemy of pretension, affectation and vanity: he is, of course, the man who once actually grabbed a man's toupee and ran off with it, on the pretext that the Indians are coming. He just *cannot* wear a wig, and it only makes things worse that it's not something that's meant to be funny, not something we're supposed to even notice.

If it really was meant to be some new funny part of his character—if he had to keep holding it in place, say, in the Peerless Pauline sequence, adding to his embarrassment—I'd still be dead against it, but I'd be happy to debate the position with those who felt otherwise. But it's not supposed to be a wig, it's supposed to be his hair, and since it's not Groucho's own wig it must be there at the insistence of the studio, which is terrible. The most insoluble mystery of all, however, is *why* it's so bad. Bogart and Bing and Bud Abbott and many another star went to work rugged-up, as, of course, is Chico right here. But even Harpo's looks more realistic than this thing Groucho's got hovering on top of him.

17:58/18:44—"Well, after a fashion. And a pretty old fashion. And I wish I had an old fashioned."

An old fashioned is, of course, a whiskey cocktail, and according to some sources the first drink to be described as a cocktail, back in 1809. Shall we all go and have one now, and meet back at the P.T. Barnum joke, in, say, twenty minutes?

18:25/19:12—"Think you're the greatest circus owner since P.T. Barnum. Isn't it a P.T. we never met before?"

Everybody knows who Barnum was, along with all the famous things he probably didn't say, such as "There's a sucker born every minute" and "I don't get it; why would anyone pay a nickel just to see a short guy?" As to the line itself—I'm expecting dissent, but I think it's pretty funny, and made funnier still by Harpo's facial expressions. Too much of the dialogue in this film is just senseless wordplay (like "Either this coat's inhabited or I'm inhibited" at **8:43/19:31**, which doesn't mean anything at all). This, by contrast, always makes me chuckle, though others find it too silly. We have pretty much the same argument about "That's m'steak and I want it!" in *A Night in Casablanca*.

19:11/20:00—"Lydia the Tattooed Lady"

Well, this makes up for *a lot*. Even if they'd left the Hackenbush song in *Races* it would still be a revelation: the fact that they didn't makes it seem like a gift from realms uncharted. Suddenly, from nowhere, and just when you least expect it: the first original Groucho comic song since Paramount! This surprise reinstatement of the Groucho specialty number, and especially the reference therein to Captain Spaulding, is presumably what this bizarre publicity piece (from the *Los Angeles Times* of April 17, 1939) is getting at:

> The Marx Brothers' film *A Day at the Circus* will class as a musical before all is said and done, and will also reflect back on some of the earlier features in which the comedians appeared, like *The Cocoanuts* and *Animal Crackers*. The Marxes themselves have inspired a song called "Oh, the Elephant Never Forgets," which Groucho will either warble or chortle, while his brothers, particularly Harpo, carry on the tune on various orchestral instruments.

Publicity pieces like this are invariably confusing, but this one is especially so: all their films classed as musicals (unless they're thinking back no further than *Room Service*), so I can only assume what it means is that for the first time at MGM they will make their own musical contribution in the comedy scenes. As to the suggestion of a song called "Oh, the Elephant Never Forgets," I think that can be safely put down to Louis B. Mayer's short-lived decision to pay his publicists in the morning.

Whereas Kalmar and Ruby's lost "Dr. Hackenbush" was a somewhat stale rehash of earlier successes, this is something different, written by Harold Arlen and Yip Harburg, and a complete and confident success unlike almost anything else in the movie. (I especially like the joyousness with which it is performed, with all the extras joining in, Chico grinning from ear to ear, and Harpo leaping up and down.) As such it instantly became a classic of the team's repertoire, and has cropped up in a number of other interesting places, including almost immediately, in *The Philadelphia Story,* and much later, and definitively, in *The Muppet Show.*

Explaining all the references contained in this song would take up half the chapter: it's surely the most allusion-rich two minutes of the Brothers' entire careers. Not only that, in so doing I would be leaning entirely and unfairly on the research of two of my colleagues and passing it off as my own. Therefore, I have included their own essays on the matter as appendices, and invite you to turn first, now, to the concordance of references compiled by David A. Cory (Appendix I). The only one that has him stumped is the "little classic by Mendel Picasso." The only possible explanation we've been able to come up with—and I don't think it's good enough—is that it is a failed attempt to cram in an old joke: "I bought a painting by Picasso." "Pablo Picasso?" "No, Dave Picasso." The bathetic feel of "Mendel" supports the contention, but I just don't think the line conveys this meaning anything like clearly enough to satisfy songwriters capable of such sublimity: "She has eyes that folks adore so / And a torso even more so." (Incidentally, from childhood and until more recently than I care to admit cold sober, I had always heard those lines as: "She has eyes that folks adore, so annatour, so even more." What did I think "annatour" meant? I suppose I must have taken it for a French term for desirable, or seductive, or svelte ... though I'm not sure it's possible to have svelte eyes.) The only other likely possibility—that Groucho might have changed it randomly in the interests of incomprehensibility (exactly analogous to his "Thomas Lindbergh, mighty flier" [see *Monkey Business,* 19:26])—is, sadly, an exit that David already has covered: Yip and Harold definitely had it as "Mendel" from the very first. I'm also grateful for his more correct and contemporary explanation of "over on the west coast we have Treasure Island," which I always took to be a reference to the R.L. Stevenson one.

Then move on to Appendix II, where still another intriguing avenue as to the song's potential origins is opened and explored by the indefatigable R.S.H. Tryster. (My thanks to both gentlemen for allowing me to reproduce their work.)

Some final notes: Lydia is not the first person to have Washington crossing the Delaware tattooed on their body: Groucho claimed to be sporting the same design in episode fifteen of *Flywheel, Shyster and Flywheel,* way back in 1933. Originally the song contained the couplet "When she stands, the world gets littler / When she sits, she sits on Hitler" but it was deleted before shooting on the grounds that it might cause a second world war. The real tattooed lady at the 1939 World's Fair was not Lydia but one Betty Broadbent. Born in 1909, Betty quit a baby-sitting job at the age of seventeen to join the circus, married the ventriloquist, and then, after a brief stint having her head projected via mirrors on to the body of a huge stuffed spider, hit upon the gimmick that kept her in the circus business until 1967. She had Pancho Villa tattooed on her left leg and Charles Lindbergh on her right, among a myriad other Lydiaesque attractions. She became the first person to be honored by the Tattoo Hall of Fame in 1981, and died in 1983.

22:18/23:15—Gibraltar, the ape

Gibraltar is presumably so named in honor of the famous "apes of Gibraltar" (actually Barbary Macaques and therefore technically monkeys rather than apes), which live on the Rock of Gibraltar and constitute Europe's only colony of wild primates. Intriguingly, a "Mr. Gibralter" (*sic*) shows up in *Time for Elizabeth,* Groucho's stage-writing collaboration with Norman Krasna. Although it wasn't completed until 1947, accounts vary as to how long it took. The pair seem to have worked on it sporadically, with large gaps between stints (during one of which Krasna wrote and staged an entirely different play: 1944's *Dear Ruth,* loosely based on Groucho's own home life). In the Summer 1991 *Freedonia Gazette* Robert Bader quotes one Groucho letter from 1940 saying that he and Krasna are about to begin work on it, and another from the following year in which he describes it as "an idea we've had for two years." Krasna himself told Patrick McGilligan in his book *Backstory: Interviews with Screenwriters of Hollywood's Golden Age* that it took between ten and fifteen years. All of which is a long-winded way of leading up to the suggestion that Groucho might have whimsically carried over this extremely unlikely surname from *At the Circus,* while working on both projects.

25:44/26:50—"Patois!"
26:42/27:50—"Hors d'oeuvre!"

A pleasant enough innovation for Groucho: the exclamation of random foreign phrases as he embarks upon or compels a course of action.

27:20/28:30—"Maybe I'm Captain Flagg!"

Spoken by Groucho when his attempt to pull a handkerchief from his pocket results in yards of flags issuing forth (a further milking of the magician's coat gag). And as the DVD subtitles render the line as "Captain Flag" we might be forgiven for thinking it a reference to the comic book super hero of the same nomenclature. But as he made his first appearance in 1941 that would be impossible, to say nothing of unlikely, and personally I have my doubts. It seems certain, therefore, that what Groucho in fact says is, "Maybe I'm Captain Flagg!" as in Quirt and Flagg, the popular character played definitively, both in films and on radio, by Victor McLaglen.

29:29/30:45—"Who on this train smokes cigars—or heavy underwear?"

Now, this was a line that had baffled me for years, for two reasons. First, because I didn't have the first clue what "heavy underwear" was, and second, because whatever it was, I couldn't see how it could have any connection to cigars or smoking. Thanks to Joe Adamson, however, I am now up to speed. "Heavy underwear" is what we British know as "thermal underwear" (*Never heard of long johns?? what do you wear on cold days? or nights? And don't tell me being British doesn't help here!*—JA). And the idea of smoking them is intended to convey the fact that it's a bad cigar (*like referring to "El Ropo"*—JA). So there we have it: Even though in truth I didn't know what "El Ropo" meant either, I now confidently assert that heavy underwear is extra thick, warm, long underwear, and Groucho is saying that the cigar smells bad, like this thick cloth being burned. And there was no hidden meaning at all. (*Sheesh! It's an Irving Brecher line, not a George S. Kaufman line!*—JA.)

30:13/31:30—The cigar scene

"Because all midgets are supposed to smoke big cigars, Jerry Marenghi had to puff plenty," the *Brooklyn Daily Eagle* of September 6, 1939, informs us, "although he got sick after every cigar scene." Imagine his discomfort in this then, for entirely unconnected reasons probably the most controversial comic sequence in the movie.

It's usually criticized as (a) a misreading of the character and logic of the Chico-Groucho encounters (in that Chico's constant locating of one more cigar is just moronic rather than slyly irrational or absurd), and (b) not funny.

Sometimes the complaint is made as "(a) and additionally (b)," but usually as "(a) *therefore* (b)."

For myself, I must start by saying that the scene always makes me laugh, so I have to disagree with (b). I think I also disagree on principle with the logical necessity of the formulation "(a) therefore (b)," in that I think a thing can be (a) and not necessarily (b), though, of course, it might be.

If we're talking about the really great Chico-Groucho scenes, from "why a duck?" up to and including the contract-tearing scene, then I really do think it has to be conceded that the Tootsie Fruitsi Ice Cream routine also qualified as (a). I also think that most of the perceived flaws in Chico's behavior here could also be leveled at his almost malevolently obtuse reasoning in the *Cocoanuts* auction scene, which I'd certainly say is about as far from being (b) as is possible in this sad, imperfect world. Chico's certainly not behaving as impossibly stupidly here as he is with the badges in the first Groucho sequence.

It's not wildly inventive, of course, or an all-time classic scene. But still, I enjoy it, all in all; in particular I am amused by the sheer relentlessness with which he finds the cigars, the way Harpo produces the enormous box of matches and lolls about on the floor with them, and the way they bump their heads every time they stand up. I think the humor with the cigars is not so much in the fact that he keeps finding "just one more," though it's partly that; it's also that he keeps expecting Groucho to be pleased, no matter how often he has the true state of affairs explained to him (shades, now I come to think of it, of the soda fountain scene in Laurel & Hardy's *Men o' War,* a.k.a. the turkey-sandwich scene in Abbott and Costello's *Keep 'em Flying*). I like the comedy of repetition. If you like Laurel & Hardy's *Perfect Day* you should be okay here.

31:34/32:55—"Bad luck: three on a midget!"

As Chico rightly says, it's a superstisch: Groucho is, of course, referring to the old saw that it is bad luck to use the same match to light three cigarettes ("three on a match"). This is commonly thought to refer back to the First World War, because to keep a light burning for the length of time necessary to light three cigarettes would enable an enemy sniper to target you. In fact, its origins are slightly more mysterious, and its date of first use not conclusively known. It's also used as the title of a cracking movie from Warner Bros. with Bette Davis, Joan Blondell and Ann Dvorak thusly courting fate.

33:42/35:08—"No, but I'm getting tobacco heart!"

The term then in use for rapid irregular heart rate believed to result from heavy tobacco use.

33:52/35:19—"I told you to eat corn flakes for breakfast, not the goldenrod!"

Spoken by Chico to Harpo in response to the latter's violent sneezing. It's an edible wildflower, so Chico is presumably positing an allergic reaction to its pollen.

38:15/39:53—"There must be some way of getting that money, without getting in trouble with the Hays office!"

Groucho's rumination at the sight of Peerless Pauline secreting Jeff's stolen money in her bosom is probably the most famous joke in the film, which, of course, references the administration of the Hollywood Production Code by which films were censored, named after Will Hays. It occurs to me, though, that it was very sporting of the Office to let even *that* line pass: I can't see how it differs, in censorable terms, from the straightforward tit joke it pretends to be circumnavigating. If he had made any other comment about the task of getting to the money in its present location, they surely would have acted purely on the nature of the inference. So what's the difference? According to Joe Adamson, this scene was one of an indefinite number re-shot after close of production by a different director (see *Go West,* introduction). It can only be conjectured, then, if this line was the reason, and, if so, whether it was nearer or further from the knuckle in its original form.

43:32/45:24—"I guess Emily Post was right. A girl should never propose to a man."

This may be the only interesting thing Florence Rice says in the entire movie. Post (1872–1960) was an American famous for her writings on the subject of etiquette. Her 1922 *Etiquette in Society, in Business, in Politics, and at Home* is a classic of the "don't eat peas with a knife" genre, and has been updated several times, most recently in 2012, by her descendants. And still, via her institute, the work goes on.

44:45/46:40—"And yours truly, who could certainly use the money, for Jeff."

What is it about that "for Jeff" that makes the heart sink? After all, the Marx Brothers have been helping people out, and helping young lovers out, and catching villains out (all in their fashion, of course) since film number one. But there's something so craven about this; it's as painful, in its way, as watching Groucho leap with fear at that train whistle at **28:00/29:12**.

44:48/46:43—"Goodbye, Mr. Chimps"

Groucho bids adieu to Gibraltar by mangling the title of James Hilton's novel *Goodbye, Mr. Chips* (1934), the sentimental story of a beloved old English schoolmaster. It famously reduced to tears Harpo's normally waspish Algonquin pal Alexander Woollcott, who called it "a tender and gentle story as warming to the heart and as nourishing to the spirit as any I can remember." The joke also makes for a nice little bit of free publicity for another MGM movie of the same year, directed by Sam Wood (now well out of the Marxes' range, after their post–Thalberg prestige plummet).

45:24/47:20—Swingali

The film's most lavish production number, and a pretty shameless "they liked it once so give it to 'em again" carry-over from *A Day at the Races,* making room for a similarly large selection of MGM's black talent. Because the presentation of the acts is a stereotypical one the scene is controversial with modern audiences, but it went over like gangbusters in 1939, ironically in part by appealing to the same spirit of fraternity that has retrospectively outgrown its simple, patronizing efforts at inclusivity. (To which I will only add that audiences yet unborn might be just as baffled by our own comparable unconcern for the supporting cast of mournful elephants and confined, pacing tigers, and the three lions crammed into a single cage, forced to join Harpo and his friends in their antics. The point being that unless we genuinely scent malice, we should be as generously understanding of our grandparents' naiveté as we would hope our grandchildren will be of ours.) "Swingali" refers to Svengali, the Russian hypnotist of Gerald du Maurier's *Trilby,* the suggestion being that Harpo and his music have hypnotic powers.

46:35/48:34—"He waves that Toscaninian hand"

Acclaimed Italian conductor Arturo Toscanini (1867–1957) was at this time a household name in the U.S. on account of his work with both the Metropolitan Opera and Philharmonic Orchestra in New York and especially, from 1937, as music director of the NBC Symphony Orchestra. But for most of this scene, the story goes, Harpo isn't waving any kind of hand, Toscaninian or otherwise, because he was crippled with bursitis after falling off an ostrich. (Incidentally, Harpo had already been seen riding an ostrich in the 1936 Mickey Mouse cartoon *Mickey's Polo Team.*) But was he? Harpo's wife, Susan, places the bursitis episode at the time of *A Day at the Races.* True, that film was comparatively ostrich-free, but there are several reports of his being seriously hurt following a fall from a Shetland pony on the *Races* set that have a far more credible tone than the stories about his ostrich escapades on *Circus,* which are generally played for laughs. Further, while there are several accounts of the ostrich Harpo rides in *Circus* bolting with him on its back, and then with utmost unbelievability leaving the studio grounds and tearing down the street, they don't tell of subsequent injury. (The closest I could find was in an unrelated gossip snippet saying that Harpo has discovered if you hold an ostrich by the neck it lowers its head and pulls you off.) What I think we're seeing here, then, is the melding of these two very different stories, over time, into one anecdote, but the bursitis was probably the result of the pony fall in *Races,* and the runaway ostrich more likely bolted from the typewriter of an MGM publicity hack than it did from the set of the movie.

49:12/51:18—"Swing Low, Sweet Chariot"

This is a brief fragment of this famous melody for the second Marx film in a row—for American audiences, at least. This time, it *wasn't* inexplicably overdubbed so as not to confuse the British. (See *Room Service,* 66:19.)

52:13/54:27—"What a brawl that was. Well, here I am, after the brawl is over!"

Groucho is here referencing the popular waltz-time standard "After the Ball" by Charles K. Harris. Published in 1891, the sheet music sold over five million copies, making it the biggest selling song in Tin Pan Alley's history. Prior to this film it had been revived in two 1936 movies: *Show Boat* and MGM's *San Francisco*.

58:59/61:30—Searching Goliath's room

After "Two Blind Loves" gets a *second* working over from the gruesome twosome, we arrive at *the* classic scene of the movie. Let's not beat about the bush: this is the one sustained comic sequence that would not merely fit but still *shine* in any of their other movies, perhaps the only scene post-*Opera* that you could sneak into a newcomer's compilation of great Paramount moments and get away with it. Could it be that, because it was mainly business, Chico and Harpo were given the scenario only, and left to develop it themselves? By whatever fluke, here at last we have not just comic invention but true, liberating comic absurdity, whereby each funny idea not only tops its predecessor but also happily undermines it. The premise is that Harpo and Chico want to search the strongman's room for the stolen loot, but he's in there, asleep. So they have to search his cabin without waking him. The following elements all strike me as top-drawer Marx comedy:

1. Though the room is small, Chico suggests they look in different places, and meet up again in the middle of the room. Harpo marks a chalk cross on the floor for reference.
2. Though comic suspense is supposedly being milked from the prospect of Goliath waking and finding them, they pull him about with complete abandon, and when he does begin to stir, the sound of Chico singing "Rockabye Baby" in his ear *is* enough to send him instantly back to sleep, even when he's taken a pitcher of water full in the face.
3. Harpo, characteristically, is far more interested in amusing himself than performing the intended task, and when he accidentally turns on a fan and makes a snowstorm of some feathers from a shredded pillow, he opts to impersonate Santa Claus by stuffing a pillow up his sweater, making a beard out of a towel and loudly ringing a bell. This is already hilarious, given what he's supposed to be doing (and not doing) but the real masterstroke for me is that Chico, instead of angrily stopping him, capitulates likewise and instantly to the joy of the moment, and joins in with equal abandon. No longer merely making a noise sufficient to wake somebody, they are creating an almighty din through which it would be *impossible* for *anybody* to sleep. "Hey, Sandy Claus!" Chico shouts delightedly, "it looks like a white Christmas!"; all the while Harpo is grinning manically and clanging the bell. *Then* they suddenly remember what they're doing, and shush each other, and all is well.
4. After Harpo drinks the sleeping draught, Chico absurdly tries to wake Harpo *and* rockabye Goliath back to sleep at the same time.
5. The scene ends with the grotesque and strikingly non–MGM-ish final image of Harpo vomiting feathers.

Stills exist showing a presumably deleted continuation (or alternate conclusion) to this scene, showing Harpo standing up inside the mattress while Chico skulks mischievously alongside and Nat Pendleton and porter Willie Best look on as if terrified. My guess as to what's going on? Well, I'm thinking at some point Goliath awakens, only to find his mattress seemingly walking about the room. He's spooked, and calls for the porter, who gets even *more* spooked. It may well be that to do the traditional scared schtick was the reason Best was hired in the first place: in the film as it stands he is blatantly unused in what amounts to a pointless cameo. If my guess is right, this would have been an anticlimactic and very basic conclusion to what, in its present form, is one of the few undisputed highlights of their later career.

65:30/67:50—The "great scheme"

What is the plan, exactly? I don't really get it. Groucho has conned Dumont into thinking he is Jardinet's representative, so he can give Jeff the money to pay off his creditors. But how does bringing the circus to her party help? Why is that part of his great scheme? Or am I missing something?

66:56/69:48—The banquet scene

Not really a self-contained comedy sequence, but plenty of big laughs, I'd say, from the very start, as Groucho loudly counts the number of guests arriving and concludes, "They all showed up, looks like no second helpings." Probably as many good, funny Groucho lines here as in the whole rest of the film: "Good evening, frieeeeeends!"; "now let's lap up the vittles!"; "Elephants! At your age!"; "Can I quote you on that?"; "Mrs. Dukesbury's friends are my friends! I'll take care of him!"; "Take this bearded symphony down to the bandstand."

Then there's the downright jaw-dropping moment when a giraffe runs its long tongue up Dumont's back and she giggles on the assumption it's Groucho, and his superb method of stalling for time: making everybody wait while he has "another cup of coffee." A lovely shot of him taking alternating sips from a whole battery of cups, too, which is a good example of the visual extending/subverting the basic joke. Well done all round.

68:07/71:02—"I'm sure Marie Antoinette would like to say a few boring words"

There is no obvious reason for Groucho to liken Mrs. Dukesbury to the tragic wife of King Louis XVI of France, killed eight months after her husband, in October 1793. What the line is more likely recalling, therefore, is Norma Shearer's portrayal of her in the MGM superproduction released the year before, in which Chico's daughter, Maxine, had taken a bit part as a lady-in-waiting. As well as another reference to a recent hit movie from the same studio (see above, 44:48) there may also be a sentimental aspect to the reference: the film, like *A Day at the Races,* was initially planned and supervised by Thalberg, who died before it was completed. The line, therefore, is no insult to Dumont's character, but a veiled tribute to Thalberg, and to Shearer (a close friend of Chico's wife, Betty), making her first screen appearance after her husband's death.

72:10/75:15—"Jardinet's opening number will be Beethoven's somber and spiritual first movement of his Second Concerto...."

Though what we actually hear him playing as his first selection is the altogether more rousing Act III Prelude of Wagner's *Lohengrin*.

73:53/77:02—Step up again and take a bow again

And you thought Margaret Dumont getting turned on by a giraffe's tongue was unnecessarily kinky. Wait till you see your dismay at the prospect of this number also getting a reprise give way to fascinated horror as it is performed not by Florence with a horse but by Florence performing *as* the horse, with encouraging little taps from Kenny's whip. Hard enough to imagine what *we're* supposed to get from that, but what Dumont's guests are supposed to make of it, completely unfamiliar with the original routine as they are, is beyond supposition. (But they *do* love it; indeed they love the whole show. Those stuffed shirts may come out for Jardinet, but what they really want is a circus hosted by a loved-up pair of crooning S&M enthusiasts.)

75:51/79:05—"Suzie would like to mumble a little double-talk in Esperanto."

Or, in Esperanto: "Suzie ŝatus murmuri iom duobla-diskuto en Esperanto," Esperanto being an artificially constructed "universal language," invented in 1887 by a Polish eye doctor called L.L. Zamenhof and intended as a politically neutral, post-national aid to peace and understanding (it's hard for one nation to declare war on another when they're both speaking gibberish).

76:50/79:20—The circus finale

A further admission of the fact that the Marxes are now just another bunch of movie clowns: their first-ever pure, unambiguous slapstick climax. This includes reasonable trick-work and a few laughs, but it's all very anonymous. Groucho's running commentary is quite funny: "Keep calm, folks, it's all part of the show!" when it isn't and the people are in real danger. Likewise "Swing your lady!" and "I hope he's got two pair of pants with that suit!" are funny not because they are amusing in themselves but because they are his response to something that could easily result in multiple deaths.

77:19/80:37—"I hope he got two pair of pants with that suit!"

You know you're too obsessed with the Marx Brothers if your idea of a fun trivia game is: "Can you name four occasions on which the Brothers make a joke about two pairs of pants?" This is one; you can find the other three in the notes at the end of the book.

77:52/81:12—"And there goes Seabiscuit!"

A reference to America's most beloved racehorse, an icon of the mid–1930s. Why Groucho should evoke him when confronted by the spectacle of Margaret Dumont flying through the air is something about which you'll have to reach your own conclusions.

79:15/82:38—The End

The gorilla counts the money and confirms it's all there, and blissfully unaware that they are drifting farther and farther out to sea, Jardinet and his orchestra play on....

Who could have guessed that *At the Circus* would deliver the best ending of any Marx Brothers movie?

10

Go West (1940)

Rusty, I no like-a the west. All-a the people do is kill each other. I'd like-a
the west better if it was in the east.—Joe Panello (Chico Marx)

On December 16, 1939, alongside the news that MGM have acquired the screen rights
to *The Vagabond King* as a vehicle for Nelson Eddy, and that the search is on for a ten or
twelve year old boy to star in *The Yearling*, the *Independent Exhibitors Film Bulletin* made
the following announcement: "Marx Bros have asked for postponement of *Out West* (sic),
claiming lack of confidence in material."

Well, indeed. I could make a sarcastic comment here, but instead, I'll settle for a simple
admission: *Go West* strikes me as the thinnest and weakest movie the Marx Brothers ever made.
I like it less than *The Big Store* and *At the Circus* and even less than *Love Happy,* which shouldn't
really let us down because we should never expect much of it. Besides, it's got a funny penguin.

Indeed, so little do I find to appreciate in it that I feel the need to stress as clearly as I
can that the unavoidably negative tone of what must follow is not intended to reflect anything
more scathing than the fact that of these films that I love more than almost any others, this
is by some distance the one I love least. I'd rather see them in *any* context than not at all, but
if the gold standard is the team that made those five incredible films for Paramount Pictures,
it seems fair to say that they were never further from being that team than in *Go West.*

As desperate as the idea sounds, it had had a long gestation. A film called *Go West* had
originally been planned as far back as in the aftermath of *A Night at the Opera*, and a Kalmar
and Ruby script with the title duly prepared at that time. (It may or may not have contained
the lively Kalmar/Ruby number "Go West, Young Man" that Groucho performs, in his classic
Groucho make-up and costume for the last ever time on film, in *Copacabana*.) This original,
note, retained the contemporary setting of all other Marx Brothers films. The nineteenth
century setting they ended up with (which did little to affect units as hermetically sealed as
Laurel and Hardy, or Mae West and W.C. Fields) serves here to underline the feeling, first
sensed in *At the Circus*, that the Marxes are now officially "old time comedians."

An early announcement of the "new" *Go West,* with script credited solely to Irving
Brecher, returning from *Circus,* came in Louella Parsons's syndicated column in the Hearst
papers in September 1939. In addition to a generous dollop of publicists' moonshine ("Metro
Goldwyn Mayer is rounding up all the old-time cowboy heroes who are not under contract—
William S. Hart, Tom Mix, Hoot Gibson, Harry Carey, Buck Jones and dozens of others,"
an impressive none of whom appear in the finished film) comes the statement that "Sylvan

Groucho and June MacCloy cozy up in *Go West*.

Simon, who megaphoned *The Dancing Co-Ed* has been handed the directorial assignment."
Joe Adamson tells me that Irving Brecher told *him* that Simon ("regarded as the Garson
Kanin of the MGM lot," according to Parsons) had directed retakes for *At the Circus,* includ-
ing the "getting in trouble with the Hays Office" bit.

Buzzell had sailed off on the *Nieuw Amsterdam* for a doubtless much-needed vacation,
seemingly within seconds of completing the film, but he returned in time to pick up the

megaphone in place of Simon for the new film. Given the tone of his comments to syndicated columnist Robbin Coons it may have been with genuine reluctance. Calling himself the "two time loser," he opines that "there's no future in this picture. If it's good, the boys get the credit. If it's bad, it's Buzzell."

Is he just joking? It's hard to be entirely sure: "I pretended I wasn't here as soon as I heard they were looking for a director. I asked my agent to find me a picture somewhere else. The finger was on me. My past caught up with me." As if he didn't have enough to worry about, *Hollywood* magazine, as part of an on-set report that refers to Red Baxter as Red Taggart and to the film as *Way Out West* throughout, declared him "perhaps Hollywood's tiniest director."

First thing to note about *Go West* is its length: just 80 minutes, making it, apart from the more or less neck and neck *Room Service,* the shortest of all their post–Paramount films, and by a clear chunk the shortest MGM. It's suspiciously short, in fact, and the main reason seems to be the loss of an entire production number, still listed in the credits: "As If I Didn't Know," by Bronislau Kaper and Gus Kahn (who, by this time, seemed to have cornered the market in writing songs that get cut out of Marx Brothers films, having previously penned "A Message from The Man In The Moon," as not heard in *A Day at the Races.* They also wrote "You Can't Argue with Love" for this one, which by some oversight got left in.) Not only is there no hint of this song in the finished film, romantic lead John Carroll, a professional singer as well as actor, doesn't get a single solo number, and nothing approaching a love song, just the chance to share "Ridin' the Range" with the Brothers. But the studio call sheets list the names of Earl Covert, Phil Neely and Bob Priester for "specialty bits in the 'As If I Didn't Know' number," suggesting it was to be a far more significant musical contribution to the film than the relatively low-key "Can't Argue" and "Ridin' the Range."

The general consensus is that this sequence was never shot, rather than shot and cut, which leads to the inevitable suspicion that the post–Thalberg Marxes were being allotted an increasingly meager share of the studio treasury. (Note also in this light the unbelievably cheap and phony-looking "Dead Man's Gulch" set in the scene where Chico and Harpo are digging adjacent pits. You half expect Bela Lugosi to chase Louise Currie across it.)

An interesting sidelight on this matter can be found in a syndicated article by Paul Harrison published just before release that, unlike the usual kind of columnist's guesswork, makes several references that betray genuine knowledge of the finished film, not just aspects of the plot to a degree of detail I certainly couldn't have come up with without help, but also nice observations like the fact that Harpo is the only Brother who rides a horse in the movie.

But then, suddenly there is this:

> Harpo and Chico included their respective harp and piano specialties in every film except *Duck Soup* and *Room Service.* The omissions brought a flood of complaints from fans, so *Go West* has been given an extra quota of music. Romantic hero John Carroll has two songs, one with harmonica accompaniment by Harpo, the other with guitar plunking by Groucho.

Now, since he sings "Ridin' the Range" to the accompaniment of both Groucho's guitar *and* Harpo's harmonica, the two numbers being discussed here morph magically into one. But whence this talk of a second number which, after all, there is every reason to expect? Was it "As If I Didn't Know"—or still another absentee? And where did these songs go, and why? Whatever the motive, far from receiving "an extra quota of music," the result was to make this by far the least musical of all the MGMs.

It seems reasonable to speculate that the film had its budget cut very close to production, resulting in some drastic last-minute changes. Had these portions been shot and the film later cut for time, it would surely have been a comedy sequence to get the chop. And note that the article makes specific mention of the musical content of the film being beefed up, after complaints about its absence in *Room Service*. (I'm further impressed by the fact that the author also remembers *Duck Soup* as being light on toe-tappers, and so by extension this lovely aside about Groucho's guitar playing, which describes him as "a guitarist of concert skill," also seems to have the ring of truth: "He wasn't scheduled to play in this picture, but they finally let him when he began to grow pouty about it.")

Adamson notes that an executive producer had attempted to shave two hundred thousand dollars from the budget by cutting some of the more elaborate effects in the train finale, and was only talked out of it when Brecher, Groucho and Harpo objected in concert. Nice to see an executive producer taking notice of mere writers and stars: if the decision was taken *then* to cut the big singalong instead, all the more so. And it's odd how questions of budget seem central to discussions of the film from the start. That Louella Parsons piece made mention of the project being affected by the "wartime economy trend" and observed that "it is not estimated that it will be one of those lavish million-dollar spectacles." (She got that right: the budget of the finished film looks closer to ten dollars—probably Harpo's, on a string.)

What I suspect might be the final bit of evidence we need to straighten the story out is supplied again by Harrison, this time in his column of December 24, 1940: "The Marx Brothers got their usual $250,000 for *Go West,* and now have collected an extra $50,000 because their contract calls for that amount of damages if any of their pictures costs less than $1,000,000. Production figures on this one added up to $996,000."

Gotcha, MGM!

So how's this for speculation: penny-pinching MGM, with little remaining faith in a white elephant team it inherited from Thalberg, attempts to pare back the originally approved budget by chopping out at least one expensive production number, and by who knows what other corner-cutting dodges, only to end up getting stung by the Brothers for fifty thousand big ones ... and *that's* why *The Big Store*—in which they should logically have had even less interest and faith—has more money, bigger co-stars and proper musical numbers again!

This time round, at least, the schedules did permit a short pre-filming tour again, though with this material, and the team's evident lack of interest in it, you have to wonder just how important these excursions now were. (According to Chico's daughter Maxine in *Growing Up with Chico* Harpo and Chico switched roles on one of these dates: Harpo-as-Chico, in particular, is very hard to imagine.) Whereas the Broadway audience of the late twenties had shaped and moulded *The Cocoanuts* and *Animal Crackers* into things of ever more labyrinthine complexity and comic density, there was the sure risk that, by 1940, a tour of the outposts by comedians with their hearts elsewhere might well have the opposite effect, thinning out the sophistication and playing up the obvious and the physical.

An interesting interview published in May of 1940 in the *St Petersburg Times* states that the forthcoming five week tour will be taking in Illinois, Toledo and Detroit, but not (presumably) New York, and definitely not Los Angeles (the latter avoided, according to Groucho, so as to frustrate "those vultures who try to steal our best stuff and rush it into some other picture before ours comes out.") The report shows that one of the five scenes they roadshowed was the "robbing the safe" routine: probably much funnier on stage, with the two rooms split down the middle in the manner of a Kaufman adjoining doors sketch. Easy to imagine the opening sequence and the crowded stagecoach getting big laughs, too, in such a context. But it's harder to picture them roaring at the strange interludes, the left-handed moths, or Chico ruining the auction. Even if Brecher had written material of this standard, it may well have not survived the majority verdict intact. Groucho, at least, was losing his enthusiasm for the tours (if not, necessarily, his faith in their usefulness), telling John Chapman's "Hollywood" column: "It's the only way.... But I'm not going to do it anymore. Too tough a grind. It was all right when I was 14, but not now." Cecil Smith in his syndicated column "The Stage" seemed to sense their lethargy this time out:

> The present entertainment frankly confesses that its purpose is to obtain a preview of audience reactions to material proposed for the film. In the particular show I saw, things did not get going well until the last two scenes—an episode showing Harpo employing gargantuan methods of cracking a safe and an extremely funny scene in which the Brothers have fallen into the clutches of the Indians. Up to this point the material was scanty, and the labored ad-libbing of the stars, who may have been hungry at the 6:30 show, did not help much. If the producers share my opinion of it at all, they will start scurrying after a whale of a lot more good gags than they have now.

An article in *Motion Picture Daily* shows that this time they were also trying out something new:

> Previously the comedians have experimented with a series of personal appearances before making a picture. The idea has been to determine which gags are the best laugh-getters. This year, however, they are doing their checking of laughs and action in a new way. They are making 16mm films of the show and recording the audience reaction simultaneously. This filming of the act shows what action takes place while the dialogue is being read. In the past the comedians failed to remember anything out of the ordinary in action while reading lines.

The discovery of any of this footage would be, to put it mildly, a very big deal. Yet even with this extravagance the film came in cheaper than *At the Circus* or *The Big Store*.

But if you think that the shorter running time and comparative absence of music means there's less room for padding, let Leo the lion disabuse you from the outset: it's the Marx Brothers this film has least time of all for, even when they're on screen. Irving Brecher really is making bricks without straw here, even with the stage tour it has all of the faults of *Circus* and none of those occasional flashes of their former glory that partially redeemed it. Buzzell's re-engagement means Groucho's giving another fidgety, irritatingly high-pitched performance (though not to *quite* the same pitch, presumably because he saw it didn't work first time out); he's still wearing that awful wig; Chico's still a helpful dunce.

Perhaps its biggest problem is its reliance on "non-jokes": an energy-saving initiative that cuts down on the number of good lines needed for Groucho by the simple expedient of substituting lines that *sound like* they might be jokes, and which Groucho delivers *as if* they're jokes, with his customary rhythm and intonation, in the hope that half-awake audiences will assume that they *are* jokes. But they're not: "First business I've ever done with a dust storm!" "He's half Indian and half ostrich!" "Send for a St. Bernard dog, I'm snowbound!" Or even the oft-quoted: "I was going to thrash them to within an inch of their lives, but I didn't have a tape measure!" Sadly, the script rises above this level of invention in only the briefest of fits and starts.

There are also unmistakable signs here that the films are becoming much blander and simpler for the 1940s: long since stripped of most of their outrageousness and all but the mildest forms of absurdism, the film plugs the holes with garden variety "zaniness" (the cutesy Horace Greeley foreword), comic anachronism (telephones, Cadillac sedans, "I don't know why we don't sleep in a regular motel!") and intertextuality (Groucho's endless asides to the camera).

The latter are quite something. As well as the many lines explicitly said only to us ("At my age: corrected by an illiterate!" "You know, it's stimulating when two giant intellects get together" "You know this is the best gag in the picture?"), much of the dialogue Groucho delivers in conversation with the other characters is also performed with constant glances in our direction (in the first scene alone: "Not unless they're throwing a masquerade party out west" "The way he's dressed he looks like he was laying all over the streets" "Out west they shoot at anything that looks eastern" and "First business I've ever done with a dust storm").

I appreciate this distinction is subtle: Groucho has always done this from time to time, and from the very first; furthermore some of his most celebrated moments have been the occasions when he did ("I've got to stay here but there's no reason why you folks shouldn't go out into the lobby until this thing blows over," for instance, or "I might be the *News Weekly* for all he knows.") But these were all the funnier for being occasional, and were in almost every case toppers, that followed legitimate laughs, so as to create a kind of "second layer": "Well, all the jokes can't be good. You've got to expect that once in a while." As in that example, there is no actual relationship being established (or understood) between Groucho and us; he talks to us almost grudgingly, as if we were just one more problem he has to deal with. Here, these lines are operating on a different level. They are not commentaries on the script, written to sound like ad-libs; they *are* the script; they are comic asides that presume, in their frequency and confiding tone, a mutual familiarity and rapport. Accordingly, they come across as cutesy, almost obsequious. Most critics are in agreement that the film is a lesser effort, though few see it as the stand-alone bummer it seems to me. The general consensus is that it's a mush of nothing much, but bookended by two classic scenes: Groucho getting fleeced by his brothers at the start, and the train scene at the end.

Louvish goes so far as to say the opening scene "ranks as one of the Brothers' best." "No movie that starts with this scene can be *all* bad," says Adamson. Eyles calls it "the only memorable scene in the entire picture." My feeling is that it *is* one of the more watchable and professional scenes in the film—but that's very much a reflection on the film, not the scene. By the measure of any *other* Marx film, it strikes me as an almost complete squelch. Modeled transparently on the ice-cream scam from *Races*, it lulls us into pleasure with the spectacle of all three of the Four Marx Brothers charging on in the first scene, and with the pace and rhythm of its comic business. But look at it closely and it starts to slip away. First, there's little that's authentically Marxian about the con-job going on. Far from the logical swamp through which Chico drags Groucho in their classic encounters from *The Cocoanuts* to contract scene, it lacks even the residual absurdity of the Tootsie Fruitsie sketch. There, Chico's profusion of code-books and master code-books and his convoluted instructions for navigating a course through them were pleasingly ludicrous. But this is just slick mathematical flim-flammery that plays by ordinary comic rules: excepting Harpo's vintage dexterity with scissors and hat-switching, it could easily be an Abbott and Costello routine.

And for Groucho it's almost all non-jokes, like: "Oh, those are shoes! I thought that was fungus with buttons!" Or: "I'm not in business for love, you know. I was in love once and I got the business." They're conning us with these lines, as surely as Chico and Harpo are conning Groucho. Harpo blows dust off his purse, so it's the first business Groucho has ever done with a dust storm? This is to Groucho jokes what "la la la" is to song lyrics.

The train chase climax is a different kettle of fish: still atypical of the team and playing to none of their strengths (not even Harpo's really, except in flashes) it is at least amusing and exciting, with the nice basic idea of using the train to fuel itself. But that one pleasing absurdity is the only reason I can see why it is hailed as an authentic Marxian sequence by those who haughtily dismiss the stunt finales of the previous and following films as too atypical to accept. They're all exercises in studio resources, stunt men and special effects, and absolutely any screen comedians you care to name might be the stars. It just happens to be the Marx Brothers. And to be honest, I've never found it all that hilarious, even on its own terms. But it's a good, fun, well enough done little sequence, and God knows, in *Go West,* that's not to be sniffed at. The scene also contains most people's ironic choice of favorite line: "This is the best gag in the picture," said by Groucho as he gags and binds one of the engine drivers. The *Hollywood* magazine report mentions a gag not to be found in the film, which may have been cut because of its similarity:

> Groucho, during a chase scene in the new picture, passes a cemetery which advertises "Plots for Sale." Says Groucho with a leer, "That's the first time I ever had a plot in a picture of mine!"

Just happy to be here... (Left to right) Groucho, Harpo and Chico convey the sheer joy of making *Go West.*

Even the film's one and only innovation—to put them in a historical setting—seems, to me, a mistake from the get-go: given the sharply modern nature of their earlier comedies it is a sign of just how thoroughly MGM has tamed them that such an idea as this is even attemptable. Just seeing them come on in new costumes is a bit of a downer for me, and the film only very occasionally lifts my spirits thereafter.

Perhaps part of the problem is that it reflects the spirit of the team that made it. "They didn't have any enthusiasm at all," Eddie Buzzell recalled to Barry Norman in the late 1970s. "It was just a case of money. They took the money and they made the picture and that's all there was to it." As for Groucho in particular: "He was tired all the time. He'd come in in the morning and before he'd start work he'd sit down and smoke a cigar. Do you know how long it takes to smoke a cigar? He took all the time he wanted and then he'd put the cigar down and say, 'Okay, I'm ready for work,' every day for forty-five days." Not even his own cigars, either, according to Ed: Groucho would get the prop man to bring them to him. "Because he was cheap. He was really cheap."

"I'm not looking forward to it, but I guess it's just as well to get it over with," Groucho proudly announced to Arthur Sheekman before shooting commenced. "I realize I'm not much of a judge but I'm kind of sick of the whole thing ... I don't feel this way about all of our pictures: *A Night at the Opera,* for example, I always enjoyed looking at and, to a lesser degree, *A Day at the Races,* but the rest sicken me...."

This dourness is clearly apparent even in the generally light-hearted *St. Petersburg Times* piece about the stage tour: "Whole countries are being gobbled up in Europe this very minute," Groucho is quoted as observing, "yet here we are worrying whether Harpo should bust the next woman on the bean or on the bustle. It's a strange world."

0:43 (NTSC)/0:45 (PAL)—Musical Program

Note the retention of the lost Kaper/Kahn number "As If I Didn't Know" here: the fact that it made it as far as the credits would make me think it was shot and deleted in post-production, yet my earlier speculation above forces me to conclude it was cut for budgetary reasons just before. Confusing things further, the song *is* featured in the episode of the radio show *Hollywood Is On the Air* used to promote the film. Judging by the performance of "Ridin' the Range" in the same show, these are new vocal performances sung over the original orchestral recordings used in the film soundtrack, suggesting that "As If I Didn't Know" got as far as being sound recorded, at least. Since this program focuses heavily on the film's music it does not necessarily follow that its inclusion indicates it *had* been shot for the film, or even that it had not yet been cut. It may have been seen as a means of getting some value (ie promotional value) out of a piece of music they no longer had any permanent use for.

1:18/1:21—Groucho Marx as S. Quentin Quale

As is well known, this is a play on "San Quentin quail," i.e., jailbait. It's usually played up as a hugely near-the-knuckle bit of Hays-bashing, but the phrase seems to have been deemed pretty innocuous by this time. As well as Artie Shaw and his Gramercy Five's "When the Quail Come Back to San Quentin," there's a 1946 Merrie Melodies cartoon called *Quentin Quail,* about a quail who brings his baby a worm that looks like Frank Sinatra.

1:30/1:34—Foreword

An altogether too cute bit of new-fangled MGM tomfoolery, which seems in its punch-line to be consciously furthering the cause of reducing the Brothers from tameless spirits to wacky buffoons. I also don't like it because it is *the film itself* trying to be funny, rather than its stars. Horace Greeley, of course, was the celebrated newspaper editor, politician, vegetarian and slavery opponent, who remains the only presidential candidate in American history to have died before finding out how badly he did. The celebrated quote that the Marx Brothers would have made him sorry to have said is a controversial one, however, and debate rages as to whether he really said it, or someone else said it and he copied them, or someone else said it and falsely attributed it to him, or he only pretended to say it, or he only said it for a laugh, or he said it accidentally during a sneezing fit, or he only said it at night when nobody was listening. Given that historian Joseph Frazier Wall claims that Greeley himself denied making any such exhortation, and spent "the rest of this life vigorously protesting that he had never given this advice" it's safe to say the Marx Brothers taking him up on it would have been, at most, the bittersweet icing on an already ironic cake.

4:37/4:49—"This is the last hat of its kind. The beavers have stopped making them. They're all out playing football."

This is a reference to the Oregon State Beavers, a football team whose mascot is "Benny the Beaver." They first kicked a ball in 1893, making this another of Groucho's comic anachronisms.

9:27/9:51—The railroad meeting / important plot scene

Now, do please take the time to follow all this stuff about Cripple Creek and Dead Man's Gulch and the varying pros and cons of different routes that the prospective railway may take, because if you don't, you're simply not going to understand the plot from this point on. But while you're concentrating, take a moment to welcome our hero, Terry Turner.

Turner's played by John Carroll, and it's worth noting that he has less to do and makes less of an impression than just about any other Marx romantic lead. Seems like everything's cut back on in this film: the music, the comedy and even the romance. (How odd that he doesn't get to sing to Diana when he rides up on his horse.) He's completely inoffensive, but it's easy to overlook him, and very hard to remember what he looks like when he's not on. (Test yourself: does he have a moustache or not?)

And as the sneaky John Beecher we have an encoring Walter Woolf King. The former Lassparri makes a good foil for the team, being both menacing and buffoonish. He later moved into television: you can spot him in episodes of *The George Burns and Gracie Allen Show*, *Alfred Hitchcock Presents*, *The Munsters* and lots of westerns.

"Cripple Creek" is a locale so familiar from various westerns that I assumed it was strictly generic, but in *Groucho and Me* Groucho recalls appearing there as a boy singer. "We played Victor and Cripple Creek without getting killed," is his sentimental recollection of the place.

10:38/11:05—Dead Man's Gulch

This is, frankly, a pretty depressing scene. Opening with Chico and Harpo miserably shoveling dirt to a mournful, half-speed, clip-cloppy arrangement of "Oh! Susannah." (Harpo is dumping his dirt in Chico's pit, but Chico doesn't notice and get annoyed like he would at Paramount: his lack of progress just makes him even gloomier.) The extreme cheapness of the set has already been noted, and poor Chico is reduced to playing good Samaritan again, giving the old geezer the ten dollars they used to con Groucho with "no strings attached." Why they should feel instinctively generous towards this dilapidated old loser when poor Groucho got fleeced without mercy is attributable only to the fickleness of MGM morality. (Incidentally, the old man is that fine character actor Tully Marshall, one of the great supporting players of the silent era, here toiling for naught in an unbilled one-scene nothing part. But in a frequently reproduced still from this sequence the role is clearly being played by character actor Clem Bevans, presumably meaning Bevans was originally cast and replaced by Marshall at a later point. If so, it would be interesting to know why: Bevans was ideal casting for the role.)

All this, and you want comedy too? Well, fear not: at the very end of the sequence Chico pulls an Indian arrow out of Harpo's backside and his trousers fall down.

12:30/13:02—Eve Wilson

Our heroine is played by Diana "Mousie" Lewis, MGM contract player more famous for marrying the twenty-seven-years-older William Powell in 1940, a union that lasted until his death in 1984. She also cut some grooves as a golfer, and in recognition of her active support the Ladies Professional Golf Association has, since 1986, given the William and Mousie Powell Award to the female golfer "whose behavior and deeds best exemplifies the spirit, ideals and values of the LPGA." W.C. Fields fans should recognize if not her face then certainly her slightly squeaky voice from *It's a Gift:* in her screen debut she plays Miss Dunk, who drives Fields to despair by noisily debating the relative merits of ipecac and syrup of squill with her mother while, equidistant between the two, he is trying to sleep on his porch. She earned her nickname "Mousie" on account of her uncanny ability to impersonate Paul Garner.

13:22/13:56—Edward Buzzell's finest moment

It's the film's first clinch for the young lovers. John Carroll gallops up on his horse; Diana Lewis rushes to meet him. "Darling!" she calls. They rush into each other's arms and embrace ... whereupon Carroll's horse gets its head right between the camera and them, and stays there magnificently for four soupy, dialogue-crammed seconds, before the rein slowly tightens and a crew member pulls the scene-stealing nag out of shot. Now, this is a very hard moment to read. It looks like it could only possibly be an accident. But if it is, why didn't they re-shoot? I appreciate the fact that Mayer wanted to spend as little money on these boys as possible, but surely if anything demanded a retake it's this. Also, if the scene is set up to photograph the lovebirds, how lucky that the horse winds up in perfect sharp focus. Therefore we must accept the very strong likelihood that the effect is deliberate, and the moment at which the horse is pulled out of the way is likewise planned and timed. But, for the Lord's sake, why? Is it to conceal their first embrace, and thus plant the seeds of suggestion that it is far more passionate than the Breen Office would actually allow them to show? Or is it Buzzell's wry little comment on the value of the scene? Whatever the truth, it's hilarious to watch.

16:48/17:31—"Couple of tinhorns from the East."

Harpo and Chico at the bar, and yet another utterly joyless scene in which we get to see our heroes totally on their uppers without a trace of optimism, mischief or rebellion in their entire bodies. It's pointless, really, to compare scenes here to others with similar setups in different films. But still, how hard it is to watch the pair's desperate attempts to wangle a beer and then grovel their way out of the consequences, without the mind wandering wistfully to their audacity and arrogance in the speakeasy scene of *Horse Feathers*.

Anyway, you probably knew that a tinhorn was a braggart who comes on like a high-roller but has nothing to back it up (which means it is presumably being applied to this luckless pair of deadbeats ironically). But I never knew why: turns out the term derives from the horn-shaped metal can used by chuck-a-luck operators for shaking the dice.

20:08/21:00—The carriage scene

For me, this is the first time the film picks up. I quite like all that "We're here to meet ya, Mr. Beecher!" stuff when Lassparri comes on (especially as the film, at last, provides a character the team are given permission to irritate to death, the way they used to do to everyone without warning or motive at Paramount), and then we have the three Marxes together for the first time since the opener. Yes, there are some misfires (the "jerks in the carriage" joke), and another *truly terrible* Groucho non-joke ("Madam, it's none of my business but are you wearing a revolving door?") but on the whole, the invention, at last, *threatens* to outweigh the desperation. Note Harpo's relentless impersonations of Lassparri's facial expressions, his drinking the baby's milk in celebration, the way Groucho says "greasy fingers," and the oft-missed touch of his twice throwing Lassparri's pen out of the window. A brief flash of the real vintage Groucho, too, when Lassparri insults him to his face and he replies with a pointless "I heard that!" And it all leads to a bit of proper, funny, vintage business with the hats repeatedly going in and out of the carpet bag. True, none of it *builds* to anything, the way these things used to do with such impudent ease back in the day, and yes, it ends too quickly, just when it's getting going, really.... But if you're like me at least you're *laughing* now.

20:21/21:13—"How would you like to buy a diamond necklace that formerly belonged to the Czarina of Russia?"

A strange joke, given that the film is set in 1870, and will at other times attempt to make comic hay with anachronism: these references to early–20th century history are not, I think, intended to be funny for that reason, but purely on their own terms, exactly as if Groucho had said them in *Monkey Business*. (Which, incidentally, he easily could have: small indication that the writing is finally starting to come to life in this scene.)

As Lulubelle, to whom Groucho's question is addressed, we have June MacCloy. June came to the movies from Broadway, where she'd done duty for Earl Carroll, George White and Ziegfeld. According to legend she was removed from the 1928 *Vanities* by her mother, who objected to her revealing outfits. The deep and husky singing voice she displays in this film resulted in her oddest gig, and the one that did most to make her name: impersonating Harry Richman in the 1928 *George White's Scandals*. She was signed to Paramount in 1930, opening up the amusing possibility that she *could* have been teamed with the Marxes as early as *Animal Crackers*. In fact, Paramount did little with her: after casting her in the 1931 film of George Kaufman's *June Moon*, most of her subsequent work was in shorts. (Short films, I mean.) She retired to get married, and *Go West* was an attempt to make a fresh go of it. It actually proved her last film appearance, barring an uncredited bit in *Unholy Partners* (1941), an Edward G. Robinson meller. She nearly didn't get to be Lulubelle at all: she stepped in when none other than Marion Martin pulled out of the role due to pneumonia. June's memories of working with Groucho are worth recording as they paint a somewhat warmer picture of him than we tend to get at this stage in his career, when his impatience with the movies was beginning to make him testy and remote. She remembered him to her friend George Bettinger as thoughtful and kind, recalling that he would often visit her trailer to play his guitar and chat, and before entering would always knock and ask "Are you decent?" At a dinner party at his house, she accidentally dropped and broke an expensive crystal glass. Seeing her distress, he did likewise, to make a joke of it and calm her concern.

24:55/25:59—"Lulubelle, it's you. I didn't recognize you standing up."

A line that is very difficult to interpret in any way other than the obvious, and therefore a most mysterious (if welcome) bit of leniency from the Breen boys. (The only possible alternative spin I can put on it is that she was, for the most part, sitting down in the carriage scene, but she does stand up during the confusion over her bustle, so even that can't defend it from the charge of unambiguous salaciousness.) Despite this flash of comedic bravado, however, it's now a cowardly Groucho's turn to be demeaned: made a fool of in public by Baxter and Beecher, fumbling about like a complete moron with his gun belt at **25:55/27:01** and, of course, enduring the notorious humiliation dished out by Baxter from **33:31/34:57**.

24:59/26:03—"You should've been home. The *Pot o' Gold* called."

Another of those bang up-to-date jokes. *Pot o' Gold* was a radio quiz show that premiered in 1939 and instantly became the talk of the nation. The twist was that every episode a number was selected at random from the phone book, and whoever picked up was given the chance to answer a question and win a thousand dollars, hence Groucho's joke. It was such a smash that its origins were fictionalized for a sweet little 1940 movie of the same name, with Paulette Goddard, James Stewart and Charles Winninger. These days it's widely available in a variety of public domain formats, giving the lie to Stewart's claim that it was the worst film he ever made. To comedy fans, the premise may more readily recall the first scene of Woody Allen's *Radio Days;* it also inspired an amusing sequence in Abbott and Costello's *Who Done It?*

26:06/27:13—You Can't Argue with Love

Unquestionably, this all comes down to personal taste, and I'm *delighted* if anyone finds things to enjoy in this scene. But for me, Groucho's comic interjections in this number make for probably the low spot of their whole film career. Everything about this puts me on edge:

the awfulness of the lines themselves, his antsy, Buzzelled-up body language, and his heightened "new Groucho" comedy voice, never more annoying (especially on "You rotter! You scrounge!" and "How we laughed!" and "Goo! Let's braik clean!"). Line after line dies screaming, and falls so mockingly short of the *painfully* obvious intention: that each should build on the other, reaching such a crescendo of comic frenzy that the supposed topper of them all (the so-so joke about putting a lighted wick in Arthur Housman's mouth ... well, at least it actually *is* a joke) propels Groucho organically into the song itself at that point, on a wave of laughter.... Nothing, and I do mean nothing, in their work feels more forced or painful to me than this.

It's interesting to see Housman here. Though he doesn't, in fact, appear in *Way Out West* itself, his long association with Hal Roach in general and Laurel & Hardy in particular can't help but remind audiences of the connection between the two films. (Walter Woolf King, returning here after *Opera,* had also sung and fooled with Stan and Ollie in the interim.) Though he began his career in leading roles, by the thirties Housman invariably played either "drunk," or, as here, "drunk (uncredited)," with occasional chances to stretch his wings like "drunk wanting directions," "drunk who keeps turning off lamp" and "pickpocket posing as singing drunk (uncredited)." His characters rarely had names, so it's nice to note that in his very last film, *Escort Girl* (1941), he plays "Al the drunk." Unlike his fellow professional inebriate Jack Norton, who was teetotaler in real life, Housman was either Hollywood's first method actor or just someone who believed in doing a hell of a lot of rehearsal. This was one of his last film appearances: he died of pneumonia at age fifty-two the following year. Norton, born the same year, made it to 1958—so stay away from that bottle, kids. (Groucho's line about meeting Arthur in Monte Carlo "the night you blew your brains out" is presumably a reference to those who committed suicide after losing all at the gaming tables.)

29:58/31:15—Chico's piano spot

A good new touch where he plays piano using an orange, but as was now standard, the whole thing's over in a shameful two minutes flat. Compare it to the harp spot—not just the length of the number itself but of the preamble getting to it—and it really does seem mighty unfair. In keeping with the relentless modernity of reference that makes so odd a counterpoint to the unprecedented historical setting Chico plays "The Woodpecker Song," a 1940 hit.

34:16/35:44—Harpo squares up to Red Baxter
35:55/37:27—The Marx Brothers scare the heroine by existing

Harpo reclaims something of the team's surrendered dignity with this fine reminder of his old bravado, and ability to make the laws of the universe bend to his whim ... but we reach a new low soon after, as the mere sight of the three Brothers at her door causes Diana Lewis to slam it again in abject terror.

38:31/40:10—Robbing the safe

A comedy set piece, and the third in the film, after the opening scene and the coach ride. So how does this one shape up? Well, it's not a complete washout. The last thing to perish at MGM was the visual business for Harpo, not least because he was often entrusted to come up with his own, but the bit with the bureau drawers here shows how dry even *that* pot was getting. But I like the way he magically anticipates that a glass of mint julep will be abandoned and catches it in a bucket inside his hat, and removes a tiara with a huge magnet produced from nowhere. A lot of people don't like the way Groucho and Chico let themselves get drunk, however there is amusement in their repeated toasting of where the girls were born, as they endlessly get to their feet and bow; it's reminiscent of the Claypool-Gottlieb introductions, or the multiple Dr. Steinbergs, or the three hard-boiled eggs. Great screen floozy Iris Adrian plays Mary Lou. Writer Edward Watz met her at a party in 1987 and asked her what she remembered of the Brothers: "She said, 'They were all three horny! They all kept coppin' a feel!' I stammered something like, 'It wasn't just Chico?' She answered, 'No, that Groucho was the worst one!'"

38:47/40:26—"This is 1870—Don Ameche hasn't invented the telephone yet!"

This, of course, is a reference to Ameche's starring performance in *The Story of Alexander Graham Bell* (1939), fondly remembered for the moving scene in which Bell accidentally spills acid on his lap and Mr. Watson (Henry Fonda) is so excited at hearing his cries of agony over the phone that he rushes into the room with a big grin on his face, rather than the handful of ice cubes Bell was hoping for.

39:29/41:10—Groucho calls Harpo a "dope" and hits him on the hand with a hammer

The follow-up line—"That'll teach you: never trust me again!"—helps *just* a little, but *nothing* can fully dilute the shock of this sub–Three Stooges moment. Overlooking the playful mock-fighting Chico and Harpo occasionally demonstrated at Paramount, is there any other instance of physical violence between the Brothers anywhere in their work? If there is, I'm glad I can't think of it.

39:38/41:20—"That redhead's a demon!"
44:52/46:47—"The deed's gone: that redhead must have taken it!"

Strictly for those still diverted by the "Harpo—blonde or redhead?" debate. Even now, years after the apparently blonde wig has been substituted, screenwriters are still calling him redheaded of their own free will. Seems inarguable to me that it was light red, though I know it is just as inarguable that he is blonde in later color shots and public appearances. Oddly, it looked to be its darkest/reddest since *The Cocoanuts* in *At the Circus,* but this one seems much blonder again.

41:05/42:50—"You're a one-man fifth column"

Anachronism joke number 697. The term "fifth column," meaning those who seek to subvert or undermine from within, originated in a comment made in 1936 by General Mola during the Spanish Civil War, but it had become widely used in America around this time, as the prospect of entering or being dragged into a second European war grew ever more likely, to refer more generally to those in America acting against her inteests.

43:09/45:00—"I'm gonna sing you a song that I wrote myself with the aid of Stephen Foster"

Groucho's drunken revision of "Oh! Susannah" nicely name checks the original composer, the "father of American music," whose more than two hundred songs also include "Beautiful Dreamer" (warbled by Diana Lewis just before the Brothers turn up at her cabin and scare the life out of her) and "My Old Kentucky Home," interpreted memorably by the Brothers in *Animal Crackers*. This number, meanwhile, is also pastiched in *Duck Soup* and *At the Circus*. Despite his extraordinary productivity, Foster was only thirty-seven when he died in 1864. Curiously, none other than Don Ameche, mentioned by Groucho just a few minutes earlier, played Foster in the film *Swanee River*—also made in 1939—right before he invented the telephone.

44:54/46:49—The adjoining rooms

This is a film full of weird things, but this might be the most headscratching of all. Nearly seven minutes into the scene, the two rooms we have been cutting between throughout are suddenly shown alongside each other, with the wall between bisecting the image on screen. That means they must have deliberately built the sets that way, when it would be far easier not to. Groucho and Chico are in one room; Harpo is in the other, hiding. Beecher walks through from one room to the other trying to find Harpo and the missing deed ... It looks like the stage is set for a reprise of *A Night at the Opera*'s reprise of *The Cocoanuts*, and some scarcely inspired but at least amusing and well-staged dashing about between the two rooms.... But no. Harpo picks up the miniature cannon he used to open the safe and follows Beecher into the other room—and *that's that!* We never see the divided set again, and it's used to no essential purpose whatsoever.

46:24/48:23—"Ridin' the Range"

A charming little number, which reminds you just what a minimal role musical interludes have played in this film. (No water carnivals here!) Nicely shot not in the studio but on location in that wildest of frontiers, Red Rock Canyon Park, California, it opens with a lovely medley of shots: Harpo playing the melody on harmonica and lead horse; Groucho and Chico in the wagon, the former plucking his guitar, beautifully photographed in what looks by the long shadows to be the waning light of late afternoon. Groucho's "clippety clop" harmonies are really nice, and his Italian accent ("He shoulda shot at the stork-a when the stork he brought-a you!") is sweet too. No great shakes, but a highlight all the same. Groucho's line, "You won't like riding when you start riding but it gets you in the end" is probably a joke, on the theme of saddle-soreness.

49:09/51:15—The Indian reservation scene

It is folly to worry about the narrative trajectory of this film, but even if this scene was a scream it would seriously bog down a film that just started to get a feeling of momentum to it, with the bad guys racing to stop the good guys getting to the train in time to deliver the deed ... "Ridin' the Range" feels like a nice interlude before a frantic finale, but then we are plunked into this desperate sequence, obviously intended to be the film's fourth self-contained comedy highlight, but in which each line vies with the last to be clunkier and less amusing. The bit where Groucho goes into "My Bonnie Lies Over the Ocean," in particular, is excruciating, as is the Groucho-Chico exchange that ends with another of those characteristic non-jokes, this time from Chico: "Slot machine!" Harpo's harp solo comes in here; it's nice but it feels too late. The only bit that made me laugh in the whole scene was Groucho's "Well, why don't you open the window?" Mitchell Lewis, who plays the Chief, is also the Indian father who shows up in the bedding department scene of *The Big Store*.

50:02/52:10—"Are you the chief that runs from Chicago to Los Angeles in 39 hours?"

Another truly rotten joke, but the reference (obvious to American readers but *perhaps* not to all) is to the passenger trains of the Atchison, Topeka and Santa Fe Railway. Actually, Groucho is citing not the Chief itself (which, from 1926, took sixty-three hours to make the trip) but its replacement, the Super Chief, swanky new "train of the stars," which, from 1936, boasted of its luxury (and shorter journeys). A bit silly, really, in that the film is about the building of a pioneer line, but it scarcely matters by this time.

50:27/52:36—"He wants to know if you want starch in your shirts."

An enigmatic joke, this, which could easily mean nothing at all, but I remain convinced that Groucho says this because Chico's preceding attempt at authentic Indian dialect sounds Chinese.

53:01/55:17—"My Bonnie Lies Over the Ocean"

Groucho's unbearable parody of comic spontaneity references a traditional Scottish folk song, its specific origins and meaning unknown, that became extremely popular in America in the late–19th century. It also turns up in one of Abbott and Costello's few period films, *The Naughty Nineties* (1945), sung by Lou.

58:39/61:09—"Dante's Inferno."

That, at least, is what Groucho appears to say as he contemplates the train's furnace. But even in a script as uninspired as this one, would that really be anyone's idea of good enough to make a Groucho line? Isn't there the smallest chance it could be a pun we're not quite hearing? I suppose not. I suppose this film just has Groucho look at an engine and say "Dante's Inferno," because it can't think of a single damn thing funnier for him to say. It's more like a first-draft script note than a line: *NB—Insert Dante's Inferno joke here*. This then crossed through, and underneath: *Screw it. Just have him* say *"Dante's Inferno."*

67:46/70:40—"There goes our last chance to help-a those kids!"

No comment.

70:04/73:04—Harpo steps through one door of the moving house and out the other

As is well known, Buster Keaton worked as an uncredited gagman on the film; as is understandable, this is reckoned the moment that most obviously bears his fingerprints. You also won't need me to point up the superficial similarities between this scene and *The General,* nor note the fact that Keaton also made a movie called *Go West.* I did anyway, however, because I am incapable of taking a hint, even my own.

72:34/75:40—The final reveal

It may seem a silly point, but one reason why I really and truly never found the final shot of the train as funny as it should be is because it has so obviously been *built that way* by the prop department; the busted bits of wall have clearly been drawn that way and made that way, rather than reduced to that state by a rampaging Harpo. They lack anarchy and betray design.

72:50/75:57—The drummer puts his beater through a paper drum skin

Why? Who is he? This isn't some substitution Harpo has pulled to stop the opera. This character has never come into contact with the Marx Brothers. He has a "funny" drum for no reason connected with them at all, indeed no reason whatsoever. The only reason this happens is as a result of sheerest comic desperation.

73:25/76:33—Comic Golden Spike calamity

Recalling the famous occasion on May 10, 1869, when the Central Pacific Railroad from the West and the Union Pacific Railroad from the East met in Utah, of all places, and Leland Stanford ceremoniously hammered in the "golden spike" that united the lines. Here the task is entrusted to Harpo, who hits a man on the head with a hammer and the force of the blow sends him into a pit in the ground. Barring that crackerjack drum gag at the beginning, this moment at the very end is the scene's one joke. We've already seen the special effect, way back at the start of *At the Circus,* when Goliath threw the bar at Harpo. This time around it's the big climax. The three Marx Brothers then delightedly shake hands, and the film ends.

Horace Greeley's verdict: "This movie could have used a funny penguin."

11

The Big Store (1941)

Shall we bind the deal with a kiss, or five dollars in cash? You lose either way.
—Wolf J. Flywheel (Groucho Marx)

Some films lose stature by association, while others gain. Others can lose *or* gain, depending on what association you choose to make. Set *The Big Store* alongside *A Night at the Opera,* or any of the Paramount films, and it will come off looking like what it is: a film that never rises above nor plummets below a general level of easygoing mediocrity. But view it in correct sequence, after *Go West,* and you might find yourself wondering if it's not a return to old form.

It isn't, quite, but the MGM film it resembles most closely in style and feel is *A Day at the Races.* All it lacks is good comedy: there are no really strong sequences in it at all. But while there are few lines that will make you laugh, neither are there many that will make you wince. Points awarded straight away: Groucho has massively toned down the vocal contortions and tiresome freneticism of his performances for Buzzell, *and* lost that ludicrous wig. And the film isn't so silly as the previous two; it's less frantic, and mainly unburdened by those dreadful non-jokes with which *Go West* in particular had been filled. It doesn't try so much, and so it doesn't fail so much. If only they'd come up with just one or two great scenes it could have been a small favorite. As it stands, I'd cautiously nominate it as the best of their worst. True, it doesn't match the best moments of *At the Circus,* but neither does it sink anywhere near the depths of its worst ones—and it's better than *Go West* in every single way I can think of.

It was, it's fair to say, a movie that MGM wanted done and out of the way as soon as possible. The Marxes were tired, and the studio was tired of the Marxes. The public had moved on: I get the feeling they would have considered them old hat no matter how good the material. There seemed no point in making anything special of their films anymore, but when the studio tried to cut right back on *Go West* they ended up unexpectedly stung by the Brothers, who had a clause in their contracts entitling them to a bonus if the film came in shy of a million dollars. This time, therefore, they had to give them a full-scale production, but they took out insurance in two ways.

First they acquired Tony Martin as co-star. Even more than Allan Jones, Martin was an established name and a minor but certain box-office draw, and he is very much co-starring with the team here, not supporting them (see below, 00:15). Second, they decided to drum up a little more than the usual interest by splashily announcing it as the Brothers' last-ever

The Big Store: **Marion Martin and Harpo check their arithmetic.**

movie. The film was issued with a trailer fronted by actor Henry O'Neill at a desk, announcing that the Marx Brothers are retiring. Whereupon the three enter the room, confirm O'Neill's announcement and rush to the window to console stock footage of a seething crowd (supposedly protesting the decision in near-riotous fashion: at'sa some joke, eh boss?) by offering scenes from their "first farewell picture."

In a feature to coincide with the release, *Hollywood* magazine claimed that the Brothers "worked on the film for more than a year in an effort to make it an unforgettable one.... They wanted it to be their best picture because it is their last picture, and expect to be remembered for it." "The trouble is we've fallen into a groove," Groucho told the magazine. "We're in a rut and can't get out of it while we're the Marx Brothers, so we've decided to get out of movies altogether." Though few have much time for it today, original reviews were generally favorable to very favorable, a little sentimentally perhaps, given the occasion. Audiences liked it well enough, too. It was, in fact, the only MGM film other than *A Night at the Opera* to show a small profit at the box office.

According to *Hollywood* magazine, the Brothers marked the end of shooting with a solemn ritual:

> The last day of the picture, the brothers held a "wake" in memory of the comedy team that would no longer exist. A fire was built while the cast stood around it gloomily, waiting for the boys to toss in the trade-marks they had borne for 20 years as the Marx Brothers. Chico threw in his famous little hat. Harpo flung his blond wig into the flames. Groucho stood over the fire nonplussed. He had achieved fame through his moustache, but it was a penciled affair. He dug his hand into his pocket, took out a black make-up pencil and hurled it in.... The mood of the crowd suddenly changed to complete soberness. They knew the brothers meant it. This was movie history being unmade. The Marx Brothers slowly walked out of the studio as the Marx Brothers—for the last time.

I don't believe a word of it, either, and no, it's just that there's something in my eye.... Actually, if it *was* true, it might explain what the hell's going on with Harpo's hair in *A Night in Casablanca.*

While the film inevitably contains lots of music, original plans were for something in a more generic musical format: a second Latin American craze had hit movie town and the project got as far as being officially announced under the definite but unpromising title of *Argentina.* (It's just possible that this concept provided the entrée for the vocal group Six Hits and a Miss, who contribute significantly to the "Sing While You Sell" number, but had been seen to good effect the year before alongside Carmen Miranda in Fox's *Down Argentine Way.*) "The Marx Brothers become wild men of the Pampas," the studio told the trades in early September of 1940, at this point with Buzzell firmly penciled in to become their first-ever three-strikes loser. In the end, it wasn't just Buzzell who walked but the whole concept of *Argentina,* perhaps because the Ritz Brothers slipped out their *Argentine Nights* (1940) at Universal on September 6. If that *was* the deciding factor, it would likely account for the hiring of that film's writers and songwriters, Ray Golden, Sid Kuller and Hal Borne, for *The Big Store.* (I know what you're thinking, but, sadly, the dates seem to preclude the possibility that what became *Argentine Nights* actually *was* the original treatment for *Argentina,* taken to the Ritzes and Universal when MGM passed on it as a Marx project.)

It could have been a hit in Argentina, at least. According to Louella Parsons, "The Marx Brothers are extremely popular in South America with the movie fans because in most of their pictures Harpo chases a blond and they love it because to them it is a very funny and logical idea." But *Go West* showed how uncomfortable they seem in unfamiliar surroundings. Another anomaly may not have been a smart move, especially once it had been penciled in as their grand finale, and the reassuringly less colorful idea of *The Big Store* was born. (It was originally to have been titled "Step This Way" and briefly became "Bargain Basement" on its way to the present title; Groucho's preference, according to *Hollywood* magazine, was "The Philadelphia Store.")

Though the fact that *Go West* had been originally mooted in the wake of *A Night at the Opera* is well known, a tantalizing hint in the Louella Parsons column of April 21, 1936, whispers of an equally early genesis for this one. On the way to *A Day at the Races* the Brothers were having trouble coming up with their next screen story, she reported (with the team themselves favoring one about "an old time baseball team"), before making the claim that Kalmar and Ruby (whom, she rightly notes, worked on *Opera*, though the fact was little known) "have great ideas for a Marx comedy laid in a department store." (And back in 1935, *Variety* posted an enigmatic notice stating there was a delay in the "music for the department store idea.") Impossible to say if this was a coincidence or if anything of this notion got as far as submission, to then serve at least as germ for the present film. As far as the credits allow, this is the work of Kuller, Golden and Hal Fimberg, with Nat Perrin cited for the original idea.

Since Perrin is plainly the most promising name in that roll, it's worth pursuing that "original idea." The source was episode 15 of *Flywheel, Shyster and Flywheel,* Perrin and Sheekman's radio series. Groucho and Chico are called Flywheel and Ravelli as they had been on radio, but, frustratingly, only incidental details are carried over with the basic department store setting (the apprehension of a shoplifter who is then brought to Flywheel and the store manager, a mention of the sheet-music department, etc.). Even some of the film's titles show up in the dialogue: Flywheel explains that Chico should not visit the basement "because he's no bargain," while the final release title seems to be anticipated by this exchange between Chico and the store manager:

> MANAGER: Unless I can pay off my creditors by the fifteenth of the month, I will lose the store.
> CHICO: Hey! Dis is a big store. And if you do lose it you could find it again easy.

Sadly, the thing the film could have most usefully borrowed from the episode—its jokes—are left untouched.

Still, on the whole, this emerges, for me, as the most watchable of the last three MGMs. *At the Circus* and *Go West* were too often embarrassing exercises in attempting to make the Marxes relevant to a new comedy era, one that minimally shared their irreverence but knew nothing of their range or depth. There is a cold slickness and superficiality to those films, and a wholly unjustified feeling of self-regard. This is different: it knows it's nothing special and doesn't try to kid us otherwise. It is content merely to charm, and remind us of better days. (I like to think that's why *two* stars of the silent screen—King Baggot and Enid Bennett—are working in the store unbilled.) On reflection, I think they *should* have called it *Bargain Basement,* and sold it outright as a nostalgia piece, as suicidal at the box office as that may well have proved. It lacks the laughter of their best films, but it has more geniality than we'd seen from them in a goodly while. I find the more I see *At the Circus*, the more its bad points strive to outweigh the good. But the more I see *The Big Store*, the more it lulls me into accepting it on its own terms. It's happy. And it's warm. I have made a space for it.

Musically, at least, the film is full of innovations: a Harpo-Chico piano duet, a Harpo-Chico cameo in the big "straight" musical number, and a production fantasy for Harpo's solo spot. And yes, that brings us to "Sing While You Sell": the moment can be put off no longer. At least let us all acknowledge it's another pleasing first for the team: a great big proper MGM production number, with Groucho—not the romantic support—taking center stage. For that reason alone it has always had its supporters, but invariably the more serious a person is about the Marxes and their legacy, the less likely they are to appreciate it. For many, many, it is an object of seething hatred. Personally? I love it. I love almost everything about it. I love its happiness, its eagerness to please, its naïve lack of inhibition. I love the rhyming of "birdie" with "Verdi." I love the way Groucho seems to be genuinely enjoying himself—something I'd forgotten he was capable of since *A Night at the Opera*. Yes, at their very best, the Marx Brothers are oh, so smart, and this is merely oh, so pleasant. But just this once, I recommend pleasant.

You may quote me.

0:15 (NTSC)/0:16 (PAL)—"The Marx Brothers with Tony Martin"

For their farewell film, a casting first: The Marx Brothers partnered with an established name. All the other major stars in their films are accidental, just starting out when their

Close-out sale: Harpo (left) Groucho (right), and friend in *The Big Store*.

paths collided: Kay Francis, Ann Miller, Lucille Ball, Vera-Ellen, Marilyn Monroe. Here, the casting of Martin seems to deliberately announce that MGM no longer feels willing to commit to a project with the Marxes as sole attraction, hence the unique billing: "The Marx Brothers with Tony Martin in ..." The first (and only) time anyone but the Marxes had ever been billed ahead of the title in one of their films.

0:24/0:25—The big store

What seems a senselessly bland title is, in fact, a minor pun. "The big store" is a confidence trick where the scammers briefly rent or decorate an office or building to spuriously suggest authenticity and reliability. Though they are not *exactly* con-men per se, Groucho and Harpo's detective office, with its fake deliveries and messages and phony filing cabinets, qualifies as a semi-benign "big store" operation. (Wheeler and Woolsey fans will remember them doing something similar to convince Thelma Todd they are successful businessmen in *Hips, Hips, Hooray!* [1934], written by Kalmar and Ruby.) Author David W. Maurer, a linguistics professor fascinated by the language and mores of the underworld, wrote the definitive account of such techniques in his 1940 tome, *The Big Con: The Story of the Confidence Men and the Confidence Game.* One such enterprise he describes concerns the opening in a disused building of a "Dollar Store" with various items of merchandise in the window advertised at a dollar a piece. Once inside, the customer discovered a thriving gambling den. So successful were these that soon "dollar stores" were springing up all over America. According to Maurer, one such, in Chicago, eventually grew into a huge, legitimate department store, because the owner of the original building found that he could make more money offloading cheap merchandise than he could from gambling. Maurer does not specify whether or not the man's name was Hiram Phelps.

1:24/1:28—Ravelli

Chico's character, harder and harder to write for every time, accordingly grows more and more mysterious. Here, despite still dressing and talking like he's just got off the boat, he's the pal of the very much going places Tommy Rogers, and works at a music conservatory teaching kids to play piano like Chico Marx. He's also called Ravelli, which—were I in puckish mood—I might speculate is the same Ravelli who turned up at Mrs. Rittenhouse's party eleven years earlier, now mellowed with age and responsibility. After *A Day at the Races,* this is the second and final time that Chico's character is introduced first of the Brothers.

According to publicity releases, the four kids seen shooting the keys in the Chico style in the movie were found as a result of a nationwide search for children capable of mastering the style, and were coached in advance for a month by Chico himself. (A week to learn the piano moves, I'm guessing, and the rest to master four-handed pinochle.) One of the lucky ones was apparently a "12-year-old piano marvel, acclaimed by Leon Machan, pianist of the Cleveland Symphony Orchestra as a boy genius" named Richard Haydel. "Although he can't read a note of music, he plays like a concert artist and composes his own pieces. He also sings and dances, without having had a lesson until he signed his contract." He went on to appear uncredited in four more MGM films, but the big break didn't come. He died of acute respiratory infection in 1949, at the age of twenty-two.

1:54/1:59—"Who's Tommy Rogers?"

A fair question. One thing I can never decide upon in this film is just how famous Tommy is supposed to be. He makes the front covers of the papers on account of his stake in the department store, and as a musician has obviously been successful enough to get a band and a recording contract. The sheet music for "If It's You" has his big mug on the front and proclaims the number "Tommy Rogers' latest hit." Since Tommy describes himself in this scene as "a fella that's written a couple of songs and leads a corny little band" I always assumed the implication was that he had written "If It's You" himself. But we clearly see the sheet music crediting the piece to its real composers, Ben Oakland, Artie Shaw and Milton Drake. That would be a pretty big deal for a man in Rogers's position! Yet throughout the film characters don't seem to know who the hell he is, and he jokes with his girl about how selling two of his records is "a new high."

3:30/3:39—Meet the villains

Adding to the pleasingly retro feel of this film, here's a return appearance for Douglass Dumbrille (see also *A Day at the Races,* 8:00) as Mr. Grover. This time, however, he's more than merely shifty: in an effort to cover up his creative accounting as general manager of the Phelps Department Store he intends on murdering Tommy Rogers, the heir to the business, then marrying his aunt Martha when the deeds revert to her, then murdering her, too! Luckily for them and us, he has hired one of the stupidest murderers in history. Assigned to kill Tommy and make it look like an accident, this doofus opts to punch him in the head in the store elevator, thus merely knocking him briefly unconscious, and in the most public and least accidental of ways imaginable. Then he winks at Grover as if his job is done!

6:40/6:57—Finding Flywheel

Martha goes to the telephone directory to find a likely detective to assist in the protection of Tommy. Note that the supposedly impoverished Flywheel is one of only four on the page to have splashed out on a bold, highlighted and boxed entry ... and then forgotten to add any details like address or phone number. That Martha knows where to find him makes her no mean detective herself. Groucho told *Hollywood* magazine that Dumont's casting was a last-minute "old time's sake" gesture when the decision was taken to make this their farewell film (she was, of course, absent from *Go West*). "She's part of us," Groucho told the magazine. "Some people even refer to her as 'the Marx Sister' and she doesn't resent it. Such sacrifice must be rewarded. It's only fitting that she be with us in our last picture together." This necessitated the re-casting of Marion Martin who, odd as it seems now, was originally in the frame to play (a presumably very different) Martha Phelps.

7:03/7:21—Groucho and Harpo's detective agency

Not by any stretch a classic scene, but one of the best the film can offer; it's certainly charming and enjoyable. Yes, it shows an impoverished Groucho bending over backwards to ingratiate himself with clients, but that's been the MGM way for six years now and much of this scene is funny on its own terms, and ingeniously designed. As oft-noted, it's a very nice change to have Groucho and Harpo already teamed as the story begins. **Harpo's typewriter** at **9:05/9:28** gets my vote for biggest laugh of the whole picture. Like the best Marx moments it's funny twice: because while the noise it makes is so deafening that Groucho has to keep asking Dumont to repeat herself, Harpo himself is nonetheless contentedly typing *something,* and then also because it is so well done. When the carriage shoots off and Harpo catches it mid-air and drags it back, the effect is beautifully achieved.

And make of this what you will, from *Hollywood* magazine:

They started planning the picture over a year ago, but that didn't prevent them from changing it and writing it as they worked. One afternoon at lunch, for instance, Chico's coffee cup toppled into his lap. His pants were ruined, but an idea was born. It gave the boys a gag scene which they put into the picture that day. You'll see it as the scene where Groucho, a private detective without a client, is sitting in his office eating lunch. A customer comes in and Groucho hastily shoves the lunch into a desk drawer. The coffee container overturns and starts to leak through, dripping on his legs.

12:02/12:33—"That's strange. I could have sworn I shaved this morning."

Luckily, this is one of the few stupid *Go West*–style non-jokes this film has to annoy us. We'll allow them this one, but can anybody tell me what this could possibly mean?

12:50/13:23—"Welcome Home Admiral Dewey—Hero of Manila"

The point of this banner—a pretty funny touch typical of the film's wittier imagination compared with its predecessor—is that Groucho's car is very old. The Battle of Manila Bay was the first major engagement of the Spanish-American War in May 1898. Commodore George Dewey defeated the Spanish squadron, apparently earning the undying gratitude of detective Wolf J. Flywheel and his assistant, Wacky.

13:05/13:39—Mickey Rooney and Judy Garland

According to the marquee display (seen more clearly at **22:18/23:15**), the movie theater across the road from the Phelps Department store is showing "M. Rooney and J. Garland" in *Strike Up the Band*. It's one of three covert guest appearances the pair make: their faces can also be spotted on the rotating display of sheet music at **33:28/34:54**, while Virginia O'Brien references "FDR Jones" from *Babes on Broadway* in "Sing While You Sell." (*Babes* was directed by Busby Berkeley, one-time husband of Marion Martin, and also features Algonquin lynchpin and Harpo's pal and mentor Alec Woollcott.)

14:44/15:22—"We have the sheet music here"

A subtle in-joke here: sheet music from the MGM musical *Hullabaloo* of the previous year, featuring both Virginia Grey and Virginia O'Brien, is visible behind the close-up of the "If It's You" score (and again on the rotating display at **33:28/34:54**). The music shown is for the instrumental number "A Handful of Stars," which Virginia Grey whistles (dubbed, apparently, by Elvida Rizzo) while bicycling. Grey, our very likeable heroine, has appeared in a bewildering number of my personal guilty pleasures. Besides this: with Judy Standish in *Tarzan's New York Adventure* (the one where Tarzan leaves the jungle and puts on a suit jacket that rips right up the back); the lead in *House of Horrors*, trapped between Rondo Hatton and Martin Kosleck; one of a million delights in DeMille's delirious *Unconquered*; a lady in *The Bullfighter and the Lady*; a bullfighter in Abbott and Costello's *Mexican Hayride*. She's also in *Stage Door Canteen* along with Harpo.

15:00/15:38—"I'd be more than happy to make one for you personally"

We see dozens of people wandering about the store in the background as Tommy records "If It's You," none of whom seem in the least interested in the sound of his latest hit: they don't even look his way, much less come over and watch. I would, though not necessarily for the song alone: I've always been fascinated by this "home recording" machine that he uses. Did such technology really exist for sale, and could it have been that simple to operate? How did it filter out extraneous noise, for instance? The answers, it seems, are: yes, yes, and it didn't, so keep that baby quiet, mother. The machines used a blank disc, a cutting needle and a single microphone, and were used to make happy (now haunting) recordings of family events, parties, messages to relatives overseas, and pretty much anything else you can point a microphone at (including radio broadcasts that would otherwise be lost to us now). Perceived for decades as the very definition of ephemera, the thousands of discs that were made are at last being collected and preserved, and coming to be recognized by social historians as a peerless resource.

The old dear who is so excited at being given a unique recording of this slightly doleful number, and sits there casting sheep's eyes at Tommy throughout the performance, is played by Clara Blandick, Auntie Em in *The Wizard of Oz*. A friend of mine came up with a wonderful ending for the movie, which might potentially have been as great as Jardinet drifting out to sea in *At the Circus*: we don't see this woman again after this scene, and in all the excitement of Grover trying to kill Tommy and Groucho singing while he sells, we quite forget about her. But at the very end, after the plot is resolved and all walk off happy, we should cut to her sitting alone in her little parlor, excitedly putting the needle down on her treasured record. But the machine did not record it properly; there was a problem with the speed regulator, and the recording is slurring unbearably, and muffled by ambient noise. We briefly see the disappointment on her face as the camera closes in to a tight close-up of the rotating disc before, suddenly, we see the handle of her little umbrella come crashing down, reducing the record to a dozen fragments of useless shellac. Cue end credits and bouncy exit music.

18:08/18:54—Groucho meets Grover

Much like the film generally, because this scene isn't *great* in any objective sense it's easy not to notice how much *better* it is than any comparable scene in the last two or three films. Here we have the most authentic Groucho we've seen since the medical examination in *A Day at the Races*. Having obtained the contract to protect Tommy for no good reason other than that Margaret Dumont is a law unto herself, constitutionally incapable of seeing Groucho as others see him no matter what his guise, he swaggers into the office, throws his ridiculous threadbare fur coat on the sofa, flings his hat at the lights as if they were a hat stand, misses, steals a cigar, and strikes a match against his thigh to light it. (He does this repeatedly in *A Night in Casablanca*.) Then, as soon as he is introduced to Grover—that is to say long before he can have any reason to suspect his villainy—he begins insulting him for no reason, responding to his opening "How do you do?" with "That's rather a personal question isn't it, old man?" and immediately suggesting that he be fired. (Not only is this funny in itself, it pays off very nicely at the end, when Grover is finally revealed as a would-be murderer and Groucho says to Dumont, "I told you in the first reel he was a crook!") The gags here aren't great, but they're ten times better than anything we have any right to expect. There are dull stretches: the bit where Groucho and Dumont swap Byron and Shelley quotes never pays off, and the exchange between Groucho and Tommy, where Groucho fishes for compliments from him as if he were Thelma Todd or something, is just plain bizarre. Oddly, when the scene then picks up again (with Groucho yelling "Scram!" at Grover and the would-be murderer meekly obeying) it cuts, just as he and Dumont arrange themselves on the sofa in the classic herald of a vintage wooing scene. This doesn't actually happen until **58:22/60:52**, and it, too, is a good little unexceptional scene, short and sweet, with a nice punchline.

21:19/22:14—"I worked five years for Burma-Shave"

Groucho attributes his poetic prowess to his previous employment with the company that revolutionized advertising by using ditties displayed in sequential roadside signs, each containing a line of doggerel, so that the motorist reads the poem while driving along. A typical example being: "Your shaving brush.... Has had its day.... So why not.... Shave the modern way.... With ... Burma-Shave." Others are even better.

22:17/23:14—The fake fire hydrant

Not a bad little quickie gag that recalls *Horse Feathers* in two ways. First, because as in Harpo's opening scenes in that movie, he is operating in his own little plot thread, and will only later enter the "plot" proper; for the time being the film is content to cut to him occasionally and see what he is up to while the rest of the film proceeds elsewhere. Also, because it reminds us of the missing scene from the earlier film where Harpo makes equally creative use of a fake lamppost.

23:18/24:17—"He's all right, he's the detective here"

He is? Since when? Groucho has only just been appointed, after leaving Harpo at the car, so either the latter has been moonlighting as store detective for some time—making

Dumont's settling on Groucho even more coincidental than it already is (given that Harpo is the brother of the best friend of the man she is employing him to protect)—or the information has somehow already filtered down to some employees (like the guy at the lost and found department), but not to others (like the doorman or the other guy at the lost and found department) that the unspeaking oddball loitering outside is part of the new security outfit. But given his status, why then should the fact that the purse proves to be Dumont's suddenly make him a thief?

26:06/27:13—"Sing While You Sell"

The utterly joyful and vibrant Groucho song number, widely hated by killjoys. The excellently named Six Hits and a Miss join in and add to the fun at **26:26/27:34**, as do The Four Dreamers, in the first of only two feature film appearances, at **27:53/29:04**. By far the best guest performer here, though, is the delightful and spookily beautiful Virginia O'Brien, delivering her trademark deadpan in a rendition of "Rock-a-bye Baby" at **29:25/30:40**. I especially like her demonstration of "when the bough breaks," and frantic, spasmodic displays of cradle-rocking. Groucho's entrance in *Animal Crackers* is recalled when we see him in a sedan chair at **30:47/32:06**. He also does some great jitterbugging at **31:24/32:44**, and looks to be actually enjoying himself, for the first time since 1935.

28:36/29:49—"This is known as a California dress: on a clear night, you can see Catalina"

A phrase familiar to all who occupy or visit Los Angeles, and rarely off the lips of Los Angeles real estate agents, Catalina Island (more properly Santa Catalina Island) being a rocky outcrop off the California coast. The intermittent visibility is apparently a natural phenomenon. In the book *Fundamentals of Air Pollution* (Chapter 13: "Air Quality Criteria and Standards," Section IV: "Conversion of Physical Criteria to Standards"), author Arthur C. Stern, in jocular mood, waggishly notes:

> Between storms, even in unpolluted air, natural sources build up enough particulate matter in the air so that on many days of the year there would be less than ideal visibility. In many parts of the world mountains are called Smoky or Blue or some other name to designate prevalence of a natural haze, which gives them a smoky or bluish color and impedes visibility. When the Spanish first explored the area that is now Los Angeles, California, they gave it the name "Bay of the Smokes." The Los Angeles definition of the way it used to be before the advent of smog was that "you could see Catalina Island on a clear day." The part of the definition that is lacking is some indication of how many clear days there were each year before the advent of smog.

Strangely, however, he fails to add that when Groucho uses the phrase in *The Big Store* he does so only to indicate that in the correct lighting conditions it is possible to see the contours of the woman's undergarments through her dress.

28:50/30:04—"This is a bright red dress, but Technicolor is soooo expensive!"

Indeed, it was. From Gorham A. Kindem's essay *Hollywood's Conversion to Color* (in Thomas Schatz, ed., *Hollywood: Social Dimensions: Technology, Regulations and the Audi-*

ence): "Following the commercial success of Selznick's color feature films in the late 1930s, three economic factors continued to limit color feature film diffusion: (1) Technicolor's virtual monopoly over three-color services for feature films; (2) the high cost of color; and (3) limited markets for color ... it is not at all clear that Technicolor intentionally limited supplies of color to maximize its profits. In fact, evidence suggests that Technicolor's growth was hampered by wartime shortages of materials and supplies." According to *Film Daily* in March of 1941, the Technicolor company declared a significant loss in 1940. Doubtless the red they were in was vividly life-like, however.

28:50/33:32—"Oh, che-chawny, ain't I corny...."

An odd and near-unintelligible Groucho line that is, in fact, a phonetic rendition of the title of the old Russian ballad known in America as "Dark Eyes" ("*Ochi Chornyye*"). The song turns up in thousands of places: performed by Al Jolson in *Wonder Bar* and the Ritz Brothers in *On the Avenue;* a running joke in *My Man Godfrey,* written by Morrie Ryskind; spoofed by Spike Jones as "Hotcha Cornya"; and sung by Woody Woodpecker while ice-skating.

32:51/34:15—Marion Martin

Another of those duplicitous blondes that Douglass Dumbrille likes to call in to do his dirty work for him. Unlike Esther Muir, however, this one is after the hero rather than Groucho, and well aware that Grover has murderous intent. She's also rude and snobbish with the shop assistants, as if we need this extra excuse to cheer on Harpo when he cuts the back out of her dress while she's wearing it at **35:38/37:09**. Martin was originally cast as Lulubelle in *Go West* but had to pull out after three days' shooting because of pneumonia. As noted above (6:40), *Hollywood* magazine states she had originally been cast here in the Margaret Dumont role. Given that she was deliberately cast after illness forced her withdrawal from *Go West,* it may be that the present role was added just for her, after Maggie stepped into the one intended. She certainly has little impact on the plot—much less than she promises to, even—which may well suggest last-minute revision. She has one other interesting link with the Marxes, appearing in the fascinating 1934 short film *Mr. W's Little Game,* playing one of the word games so beloved of Alexander Woollcott, in the company of the man himself. If you've never seen Woollcott move and talk it's well worth seeking this out: believe me, he's *exactly* as you imagined him, his waspish put-downs given extra sting by his reedy voice.

36:51/38:25—The bedding department scene

The bedding department manager is tasked by Grover to get the Marx Brothers out of the bedding department. But how? Why, by starting a sale in the bedding department and driving them out, of course! "That's a great idea!" he exclaims with delight. It's certainly inventive, though hard to imagine why it would necessarily work, as indeed it does not. What follows is probably the weakest scene of the film, because it's the only part that really tries to be a big comedy scene, and fails. It also makes the elementary error of pairing the team with another comic, in the form of Henry Armetta. There's also some clumsy, odd trickwork involving the various "funny" beds. The whole sequence carries the strong whiff of that strange megalomania with which *Go West* is crazed: the certainty against all reason that bad material is great and that it's all building to an irresistible comic crescendo, when really it's making a sound like wet putty hitting a stone floor. All too easy to miss, then, that buried amid all the chaff is a pretty funny section, where Groucho tries to prove by logical argument that Armetta can't possibly have as many children as he thinks he does, and it momentarily convinces him—until he goes to his wife to repeat the line of argument, and receives a slap in the face. Also here is one of the film's funniest and most authentic lines: "get down and get him a bunch of grapes."

41:58/43:46—"Remember the Maine too, while you remember"

"Remember the Maine and to hell with Spain!" was the cry when an explosion sank the American battleship *Maine* in Havana harbor in February 1898, igniting the American-Spanish war. Oddly, the film's second arbitrary reference to this conflict, following the "Admiral Dewey" banner at **12:50/13:23**. Groucho also says "Adiós, Señor!" to Grover for no particular reason at **68:31/71:27**. Given the project began as a Latin-American extravaganza it's interesting to note these seemingly unconscious touches. The line also shows up in the Thelma Todd–ZaSu Pitts short *War Mamas*.

46:16/48:15—The Chico-Harpo piano duet

There are two ways of looking at this: either happily as a rare and unquestionably delightful chance to see the two brothers tinkling the ivories together, or crossly as a still-further diminution of Chico's one guaranteed moment to shine on his own. I lean towards crossly. First they cut his solos down to between one and two minutes while letting Harpo's wallow across a five-minute slot. Then they give Harpo a little piano spot in addition to the harp. Now poor Chico has to share his piano with him the whole time, and this despite the fact that MGM has pulled out all the stops to provide Harpo's most lavish harp sequence ever, immediately below.

52:29/54:43—The harp solo

An elaborate fantasy, where mirrors allow us to see a multiplicity of Harpos doing different things in 18th-century costume. Nicely done, and I suppose it's good that they could be bothered to come up with something different for him to do at this stage. Silly, though, that anyone thought it necessary for this to be "explained" by having it revealed as a dream. (That's "silly" spelled: M, G, M.) Glenn Mitchell, citing Allen Eyles, calls it "both unnecessary and undesirable," and all three of us are right.

57:43/60:11—The deadly camera

Grover continues his efforts to have Tommy bumped off in as subtle, non-incriminating and accidental-seeming fashion as possible, by having him shot during a press conference by a trick camera in which he's inserted a revolver without wearing gloves.

59:39/62:12—"The Tenement Symphony"

More than the chase finale, more even than "Sing While You Sell," this is the film's most controversial and divisive sequence. Some absolutely adore it; others loathe it with rare and nurtured passion. It's a lovely, big, silly, corny MGM prestige number—with a nice surprise when Chico and Harpo show up doing a solo—in which Tommy Rogers combines his musical prowess with lyrical nostalgia for his slum childhood of the sort often to be found in those who have most successfully gotten the hell out. The lyrics are clumsy, both in their complacent rose-coloring of the poverty, crime and ethnic tensions of the subject, and even more in their meaningless "anything for a rhyme" musical references ("Schubert wrote a symphony, too bad he didn't finish it / Gershwin took a chord in 'G' and proceeded to diminish it"). But it has a certain idiot charm and a plain sincerity, as well as an undeniable musical sweep, which makes it, for me at least, impossible to despise and easy to like. The reference to the Cohens and the Kellys ties in nicely with the "habeas Irish rose" joke in *Animal Crackers* (see *AC*, 83:01).

66:50/69:41—The incriminating photo

Hilarious supposed action shot of Douglass looking shifty as hell and dragging Virginia behind a curtain, while Groucho does nonchalant alongside. Great fun to imagine them posing for it; just about impossible to imagine (as the film demands) that any of the three were not standing stock still when it was taken.

66:59/69:51—"Grover Cleveland"

A silly but nicely placed joke reference to the only man to have been two separate American presidents.

67:01/69:53—"Why don't you assist Basil Rathbone and let me alone?"

A reference to Sherlock Holmes, played definitively by Rathbone on radio and in two 1939 films for Fox. The low-budget Universal series that cemented his association with the role was still to come, debuting with *Sherlock Holmes and the Voice of Terror* in 1942. This is one of two good Sherlock Holmes jokes in the film: earlier, when Groucho's description of himself as "the greatest detective since Sherlock Holmes" prompts Dumont to exclaim, "I'm *crazy* about Sherlock Holmes!" he shoots back with, "It won't do you any good; he's got a wife and three kids." Chico's daughter, Maxine, notes in her book that one of her most significant roles as a lead actress was in a radio Holmes show with Rathbone, while Groucho and Chico, at a temporary loose end in 1939, had shared the airwaves with him in the unusual radio series *The Circle*. Though aiming for an atmosphere of spontaneity the program was carefully scripted: according to Arce, Rathbone threatened to leave on account of Groucho's refusal to stick to his lines.

67:35/70:28—The chase

A special-effects finale akin to that of *At the Circus:* just simple, basic slapstick, without the narrative integrity of the pile-ups that concluded *A Night at the Opera* or *Go West.* To be honest, at this stage in their careers, I'm not going to be too worried about anything so long as it's at least amusing, and doesn't compromise their comic personas too grievously. So I can't dislike this the way so many seem to. My only real objections are to the persistent "funny music" (including an especially intrusive swanee whistle), the gratuitous presence of a "funny janitor," and some fairly obvious doubling. As well as doubles, there are other visible proofs of the effects work, notably the wire and harness on Harpo when he shoots through the roof of the elevator at **68:21/71:16**, and the rather charming Heath Robinson–style mechanism making the light bulbs fall from the shelf at **73:44/76:53**. (You can clearly see a wire raising the shelf and a rotating disc pulling the wire at top right.) The most interesting oddity is at **71:52/74:56**: look at the sign on the wall when Harpo roller-skates into the elevator. It's the store's floor guide, but the letters saying "Main Floor Directory" are mirror-reversed. This means that for some reason this shot has been printed back to front. (And note also Dumbrille's hair, which he is fortunately not wearing symmetrically. The parting is on the wrong side when he gets to the elevator and for an even briefer moment one sees that his boutonniere is also on the wrong side.) My best suggestion is that the direction Dumbrille is pointing in the previous shot did not match the elevator shot for editing purposes, whether this was because of an actual mistake in shooting or because of a change in the original plan of how the sequence was to be assembled. The longer shot was probably considered less problematic to reverse than the closer one, plus there was probably a general directional flow to that part of the sequence (basically right to left) to which they had to adhere. It's true that two shots previously, when Groucho says they have to get the picture to Tommy immediately, after he and Chico have picked up Harpo, they go more to the right, but the next shot, when Dumbrille says "There he is!" and points left, could have been shot for any part of the chase, to be inserted wherever needed, and may then have simply dictated the orientation of the next one (the shot it has followed is more of a stop-pick-up-start shot, but the Dumbrille and henchman two-shot reestablishes movement to the sequence, so flow may have been more important there, making it the "dictator"). The *Hollywood* article on the film's production hints at general difficulties and indecision with this scene broadly supportive of this account, notably a portion shot with Harpo "using the wrong stairway." Harpo, who had only just finished his seven years bad luck for breaking a mirror in *Duck Soup,* gets seven more at **71:38/74:42**. The shot of Groucho at **73:20/76:28** is equivalent to the one where, in the trailer, he delivers the line, "I used to do this in vaudeville!" which does not feature in the finished film itself.

Anyway, they save the day in the end, thanks to Grover telling everybody that there's a gun concealed in the camera. Then they all get into Groucho's car, and it is towed away, into—we assume—screen immortality.

But would they *really* never return to make another film? If so, the next couple of chapters are going to be fun.

12

A Night in Casablanca (1946)

I don't mind being killed but I resent hearing it from a character whose head comes to a point.—Ronald Kornblow (Groucho Marx)

The final two theatrical films the Marx Brothers made saw them allied with independent producers rather than any of the major studios. Luring a big name out of retirement is a popular tactic with independents, as it guarantees publicity and attention. In the mid-forties, David Loew, *A Night in Casablanca*'s producer (who, as we shall see, knew a thing or two about publicity), claimed to have signed both Garbo and Norma Shearer for comeback films that never emerged. He had more luck tempting the Marxes to go through their paces one more time. Lester Cowan, their second independent employer, for whom they made *Love Happy,* had big long-term plans for them and a whole raft of interesting ideas, but sadly, not very deep pockets. Loew's idea was simpler: to recreate one vintage Marx Brothers movie, no frills or deviations. Unlike Cowan, however, he had money, influence and a name that opened doors.

Loew was the son of MGM co-founder Marcus Loew ("the one who was neither Metro nor Goldwyn nor Mayer," as Simon Louvish observes). He was Hollywood royalty, but with the instincts of a maverick. The *Independent Exhibitors Film Bulletin* for 1946 declared its desire to "doff a respectful hat" to Loew for "working hard to make a worthwhile contribution to the industry in which his name has long been such an important factor," rather than sitting back and enjoying "the $15,000,000 inheritance from his father as well he might have." Producers are usually faceless men, bloodless, without story: the least sung and celebrated of the moviemaking pantheon. But Loew is going to become unusually important to this story, and he's a character worth getting to know. There's an intriguing thread to be unraveled here, that at one end takes us all the way back to 1933.

In March of that year, during the pre-production of *Duck Soup*, the Brothers left Paramount and formed their own company so as to star in an adaptation of Kaufman and Ryskind's *Of Thee I Sing*. In order to do so, they affiliated themselves with a new company, aiming to give stars the right to develop and produce their own material. Called Producing Artists, Inc., it was formed by Sam Katz, Max Gordon and Sam H. Harris. But by the end of June, according to the *Hollywood Reporter,* Katz had stepped down, and Producing Artists soon foundered, their demise perhaps hurried by the ill-will of the major studios whose stranglehold they threatened. *Of Thee I Sing* was never made, and the Brothers went back to Paramount like good little boys, to pick up where they left off on *Duck Soup*.

Of Thee I Sing seems to have been a project the Marxes could never quite shake, however.

Three kings return: (Left to right) Harpo, Chico and Groucho spend *A Night in Casablanca*.

Just as it seems to have been used, in part at least, to get Paramount's attention in 1933, according to Louvish it was again mooted as a potential vehicle during their flirtation with RKO in 1938, in part this time, perhaps, to force MGM's hand. Again, nothing more came of it, but we flash forward now to 1943, ten years after the Producing Artists announcement, and to some oddly familiar news reports. Hedda Hopper, on September 19, was abuzz with what she considered an inspired and radical new venture, the work of Hollywood agent Arthur S. Lyons and, making his first appearance in our story, independent producer David L. Loew:

"Loew and Lyons don't want to tie up stars, directors and producers to exclusive contracts. They merely want to fix it so these personalities will be worth more than ever, wherever they go. This is to be done by making each star his own boss. He will be the head man of his own subsidiary production company, operating within the parent framework." And what did they call this radically new yet oddly familiar parent framework? They called it Producing Artists, Inc.

Nowhere have I found any positive indication of an acknowledged link between the two companies, and all reports of the second speak as if the first had never existed. But how, then, to account for their overt similarities? The exact same name, and the exact same aims and methods: to unchain creativity from corporate accountability by serving as an umbrella organization that will, in exchange for a share of profits, finance independent productions by proven talent in a series of temporary companies. (There was no new "Marx Bros. Inc." this time, but "Jack Benny Productions" was formed under this Producing Artists' banner.) And here's where the loose ends get *really* itchy: according to *Billboard* magazine of June 17, 1944, they were shortly to film, of all things, a Technicolor version of the "George Gershwin oldie" *Of Thee I Sing*. Alas, I have found no evidence that the Marxes were ever in the frame this time (though I earnestly invite others more resourceful than I to keep looking). According to the *Motion Picture Daily* of February 14, 1944, Loew, Lyons and a third producer, Boris Morros (*The Flying Deuces* guy), had formed "Of Thee I Sing of California, Inc." expressly to make the film, and "it is understood" that *Jack Benny and Fred Allen* will co-star. (Let your mind wander over that!) Nonetheless it does seem to hint at a tantalizing bridge between the Brothers and Loew.

Unlike in the thirties, *this* Producing Artists did actually get some film exposed (though no frames of *Of Thee I Sing* were among them), though it, too, seems to have followed Producing Artists Mark 1 into oblivion within a few short years. But Loew was a man constantly popping up in charge of new and short-lived outfits, and he had seemingly taken to the idea of forming temporary production companies with before-the-camera personnel. It was against this background that Loew and the Marxes formed Loma Vista, and secured releasing through United Artists for a comedy to be called *A Night in Casablanca*.

As director they settled on Archie Mayo, a reliable artisan with an impressive pedigree stretching back to silent shorts and taking in *Night After Night*, *The Petrified Forest* and the Jack Benny version of *Charley's Aunt*. Groucho was at first very pleased with the choice ("he's no genius but he's far better than Buzzell," he wrote to his daughter Miriam), though his opinion would change substantially after completion. The original screenplay was by Joseph Fields, an old hand with vaudeville ancestry and a Ziegfeld pedigree. Groucho deemed it old-fashioned and inadequate; it was then tweaked and embellished by other writers, including Roland Kibbee (who had written for Groucho on radio and probably provided him with the best of the film's one-liners), and the up-and-coming Frank Tashlin (who devised some excellent visual bits for Harpo). There were others, too, though only Fields and Kibbee get screen credit. Then as always, this kind of layered collaboration was the best way of arriving at a good Marx script.

In another throwback to tried and proven methods (and at Harpo's suggestion), they even took some scenes on a brief stage tour prior to filming in order to polish them up for the screen. The motive this time was not purely in the interests of art: "memorizing dialogue becomes increasingly difficult as one gets older," Groucho admitted to Miriam. "We have scenes that I don't think Chico ever could have learned had we not played the stuff on the road." (And note that in the end credits the billing has returned to its pre–MGM order, with Harpo again coming second: see *A Night at the Opera,* 0:09.)

Consensus dictates that Chico was the motivating force behind the production: out of funds and badly in want of them after too many losing bets in dubious company, he needed his salary to pay off trigger-happy creditors. As a result, the film was mounted more or less as a necessity, with Groucho joining in reluctantly. (Eyles quotes Groucho: "Chico, Harpo and I wouldn't have teamed up again if Chico hadn't needed the money.") But Simon Louvish smells legend-building here and so do I. Of course he did need money, as he always did, and doubtless, too, was in hock to unsavory characters: that also came with the territory. But if Groucho and Harpo had no desire beyond avoiding reprisals against their brother, it would have been quicker and easier to just dip into their own savings than arrange, rehearse, tour and make an entire film! "Groucho, in particular, was aching for a return to movies," Louvish notes, and it is obvious from his letters to Miriam that he was at first excited and enthusiastic about the project. As for Chico, he had never wanted it any other way. "Why the hell should I want to quit?" he had told the *New York Post*'s Earl Wilson in a February 9, 1942, interview ostensibly plugging his touring swing band. "No, there's a certain little sadness in the breakup for me, and I hope that after Groucho lays off of that black mustache for a year or so, he'll get the urge to wear it again."

And speaking of legend-building, what are we to make at this distance of the epistolary spat between Groucho and Warner Bros. over the use of the word "Casablanca"? It's the thing everyone most remembers about the movie; you can find it in *The Groucho Letters* and just about every book ever written on the team and their movies. If you've not dipped into any of them or don't know the story by heart: Warner Bros. peevishly and absurdly objected to the title of the forthcoming movie, so Groucho wrote a hilarious letter spoofing their pretensions and questioning their right to call themselves Brothers, as the Marxes got there first. They replied even more officiously and without the smallest awareness they were being kidded, so Groucho replied even more sarcastically; they wrote again; he replied again.

All very funny. But is it true?

Clearly, the exchange was of enormous publicity value for the film, and was immediately utilized to that end: a larky announcement released to the trades claimed that the Brothers would shortly be seen in "*Adventures in Casablanca,* or *The Night in Casablanca,* or *A Night in Casablanca,* or *One Night in Casablanca,* or *It Happened One Night in Casablanca,* or anything the mayors of Casablanca [Warner Bros.] will permit!" But if they were *used* as publicity, could they have been *devised* as publicity? Remember, the official story is that the objection from Warners came first, and that Groucho merely responded. What actually happened was that the idea of a *possible* copyright violation was planted in the Hollywood gossip columns in a deliberate effort to get Warners to take the bait.

In a syndicated piece by Earl Wilson, published on June 3, 1945, Groucho uncannily anticipates, as if with second sight, the future course of events:

> Groucho said that inasmuch as Humphrey Bogart has already made a picture about Casablanca, he felt he should call himself Humphrey Bogus in his film. But maybe, he said, Warner Bros. will refuse to permit that. In that case, the Marx Brothers would have to ask the Warners not to call themselves Warner Bros. any more, as they would be usurping the word Brothers.

"Maybe," indeed. Exactly one week later it was, apparently, speculation no longer, as the *Montreal Gazette* and others announced: "Battle Over Name *Casablanca* Causes Flurry in Film

Capital." Now, it was claimed, the "latest developments" in the affair "were being watched by the entire motion picture industry," and Loew is quoted as saying, "There is no logical reason why Warners can claim for all time the exclusive use of *Casablanca,* just because it was fortunate in having a picture by that title at the time the Allies staged a conference in that city."

Another piece syndicated in November claims that "an arbitration board" (nice and specific!) has ruled in Loew's favor, and here again is what it generously calls a "facetious crack" from Groucho (already facetiously cracked and published at least once earlier in the year, and, says the legend, already the signed and delivered text of a facetious letter): "I'll sue Warners and demand that they desist from calling themselves brothers on the grounds that the Marxes established prior rights to that title." (The *Motion Picture Daily* of November 15, 1945, likewise reporting the victory, has it decided by "an arbitration board sitting in New York." Don't these boards have names?)

But the sharp-eyed might spot that these reports all have one striking thing in common: *none contains so much as a breath of a statement, or even acknowledgment, from Warners themselves.* As Groucho confessed in a letter to his friend Dr. Samuel Salinger, who had remarked upon one such story around this time: "We spread the story that Warners objected to this story purely for publicity reasons. They may eventually actually object to it, although I don't think so.... At any rate, the publicity has been wonderful on it and it was a happy idea. I wish they would sue, but as it is, we've had reams in the papers."

So instead of an out-of-the-blue communication from a humorless Warners stooge, what we may actually have is a studio carefully targeted and goaded into response. And if they did, this could well have been *after* the first Groucho letter. The first need not be read as a response to a prior communication: it might just as easily have been sent unprompted, in spurious response to these reports of Warners' displeasure that the Marxes and Loew had themselves cooked up and planted in the papers. Whereupon Groucho could have proceeded as planned, firing off a series of facetious letters to which Warners responded uncomprehendingly.

But what if even *that* sober reduction of the legend is too generous? What if those uncomprehending Warner replies never did arrive as hoped for, and claimed? What if there was, at most, one perfectly reasonable request for clarification—*or even none at all?* (The third Groucho letter certainly reads as if there had been no response to the previous one, beginning, "Since I last wrote you....")

Note that all the books that quote Groucho's supposed responses at considerable length only ever paraphrase the replies from Warners, and incredibly vaguely at that. The source of the information they all rely upon seems to be *The Groucho Letters* itself, where they are also paraphrased. So where are these letters now? Who signed them? Do Warners still have copies in their files? Why aren't they reproduced, even in extract form, alongside Groucho's contributions to the debate in *The Groucho Letters?* Or anywhere? Ever? (And the only reason I'm consenting to ambivalence about the possibility of there having been even *one* letter from Warners is because although the fact that it, too, is never quoted is *most* likely because it never existed, I suppose it *might* also be that the quoting of the one would make it even more obvious that nobody was then quoting the non-existent others.) Do we even know if Groucho's letters were sent to Warners, rather than just to the papers on that pretext? They are, you'll notice, the only missives in the entirety of *The Groucho Letters* not to be dated. Why, it's almost as if they were never *really* sent....

I have one other reason for not believing one damned word of this saga, and as hinted earlier it concerns the mystery man of our story, producer David Loew. I don't know if Loew was a genuine rogue or not, but the more I have looked into his career the more I am convinced of this: he was a showman prankster worthy of comparison with Kroger Babb, William Castle or P.T. Barnum himself.

Those familiar with the background to *A Night in Casablanca* will recall the popular story that Harpo was offered $55,000 to say the word "Murder!" in the film, but with admirable professional integrity turned down the whopping sum. Though taken seriously in most accounts of the film, this was a wheeze entirely typical of its author. Loew's *outré* publicity schemes were many, but perhaps by virtue of his MGM royal blood, nobody seemed to connect the dots between them, and he appears never to have acquired any personal reputation as a flimflam man.

I've added a few general examples of his inventive publicity stunts to the notes section at the end of the book, but the important thing to note as far as *Casablanca* is concerned is just how many of them involve Loew seemingly being compelled to respond to complaints, petitions, and threats of legal proceedings.

The all-time classic in this regard must be the "strip picket" affair, which unfolded before a rapt Hollywood in November of 1940. On the afternoon of November 25, a little known actress called Gerta Rozan, who had been hired to appear in one scene of a Loew epic called *So Ends Our Night* and had supposedly discovered at a preview the weekend before that her scene had been cut, startled passers-by outside the office of Loew and his then-partner Albert Lewin by calmly removing her blouse. She returned the following day, before a loitering crowd and several lanes of stalled traffic, and removed her skirt. "Today, her slip is scheduled to go," hyperventilated the *Victoria Advocate* on the 27th. A placard that she carried with her read: "DON'T SEE 'SO ENDS OUR NIGHT'—LOEW-LEWIN UNFAIR TO GERTA ROZAN." "She intends to remove an extra layer of clothing every day until her part is restored," explained Frederick Othman—with great beads of perspiration forming on his forehead and dripping on to his notepad—in the *Milwaukee Journal*. "And if this doesn't take my face off the cutting room floor then I'll just take off some more tomorrow," added Rozan (in "her flimsiest chiffon brassiere and laciest panties"). Quite coincidentally, of course, it "was the sexiest love scene in the picture." What were the odds! Loew carefully fanned the flames, somehow keeping a straight face as he complained that she was "heaping ridicule upon the producers of a serious and profound motion picture." On the third day, supposedly unable to take any more provocation ("We're not getting our work done," Loew complained to the credulous pencil-chewers), Loew and Lewin put a coat over her and took her inside, promising to either restore the scene or give her a part in their next picture, or both. For three days, Loew had achieved saturation coverage, got the name of his forthcoming film seen in every paper, and spread the word that it would now include *for certain* a hot love scene featuring a girl the nation had just seen parading in her underwear. A pretty girl holding a banner saying "*See So Ends Our Night*" might have secured a little coverage on a slow news day. Loew had the banner say "Don't see *So Ends Our Night*"—and owned the papers for three days running.

The publicity value of creating a phony complaint and then defiantly addressing it seems suddenly to have become a preoccupation of Loew's in 1945, beginning in June with the staging of Warner Bros.' objection to *A Night in Casablanca*.

To be the victim of one legal challenge against a seemingly innocuous Marx Brothers film may be unfortunate; to incur a second looks like carelessness—or contrivance—but that's what Loew would have you believe happened. At one point in the film, Groucho and Lisette Verea blow smoke at each other (in what future generations may need convincing is only a slight exaggeration of a once genuine courtship ritual). The result, Groucho opines, is "like living in Pittsburgh." According to the *Gettysburg Times,* William B. McFall, president of the Pittsburgh Chamber of Commerce, and F. E. Schuchman, president of the Civic Club of Allegheny County, officially petitioned Loew to have the line removed. United Artists released a fatuous statement ("If they feel that Pittsburgh is a smoky city, it's not only their right but their bounden duty to say so"), and to nobody's surprise the newspaper's headline was: "WISECRACK WILL REMAIN IN FILM." A pattern seems to be forming here....

Then we have Loew and Albert Lewin's production of *The Private Affairs of Bel Ami.* This one attracted the supposed wrath of America's womanhood in December, on account that it threatened to be the third George Sanders film (after *The Moon and Sixpence,* also from Loew and Lewin, and *The Picture of Dorian Gray,* also from Lewin) to feature the actor dispensing a stream of misogynistic bons mots. Loew's would-be nemesis this time: Mrs. J. D. Cahn, president of the New York City Associated Women's Clubs. "We have all intentions of boycotting the film," she wrote, "should the original plan of slander upon women be continued," but Loew, as ever, bravely held firm. Actually, he and Lewin had already used the "annoying women" tactic on *The Moon and Sixpence* in 1942 ("*Moon and Sixpence* Angers Women But They'll Like Film, Say Authors" was the headline in the *Miami News*), but that time they hadn't gone so far as to goad (or load) some likely dupe into making an actual complaint. As always, the headlines did the job.

The odd one out among these is Loew's apparent battle over the partial banning of his production of Jean Renoir's *The Southerner,* because it's almost impossible to believe it wasn't genuine. Lloyd T. Binford, head of the Memphis censors board, had long enjoyed a reputation—without any help from Loew—for banning outright or drastically cutting Hollywood movies so as to protect the delicate sensibilities of the South. ("Mostly," as *The Age* noted in 1953, when the now 86-year-old Binford was still very much at it, he "cracks down on pictures that attempt to show racial equality.") *The Southerner* was just one of many to have incurred his displeasure, this time because it "pictures the Southern farmer as squalid, ignorant white trash," and he declared it banned in August. Loew issued his usual challenge, and Binford seemingly backed down. It's hard to believe this one was set up, given Binford's uncompromising nature, though the coincidence in that case—given that it occurred after *Casablanca* and before *Bel Ami*—would be extraordinary. Somehow, I wouldn't put it past him (and I've tentatively developed one possible argument for concluding that this was indeed another scam in the notes section).

You'll notice that in most of the above cases, real people with real names are cited, and their co-operation presumably secured. But it was much harder—and riskier—to play a presumably one-handed game against a behemoth like Warner Bros. If he was making allegations of belligerence that were not true, that would surely be to risk serious repercussions if they decided to call his bluff.

And why, for that matter, didn't they? I don't know. All I know is that another of those odd little coincidences happened next.

With *A Night in Casablanca* in the final stages and Loma Vista ready for dissolution, Loew turned his attention to the forming of his next fly-by-night outfit. Announced to the press in March of 1946, Enterprise Productions was still another collaboration of disparate types, including David Lewis, former personal assistant to Irving Thalberg, and the usual surprise name from in front of the cameras (in this case, actor John Garfield). By August they were announcing the coup of having lured Norma Shearer from retirement (presumably at the inducement of Lewis). As usual, that was the last anybody heard of that. Their big premiere release, *Arch of Triumph* (1948) was released through United Artists, which declared it "probably the greatest commercial failure in the history of motion pictures," despite some typical Loew moonshine before release about the studio having to fight off efforts to tone down the sizzling love scenes. By August of 1948 (according to the *Montreal Gazette*) Enterprise had dropped their lease on the studio space they had been renting, and released a statement announcing that they would not be releasing statements announcing anything much for the time being. And by November, Hedda Hopper is speaking enigmatically but somehow tellingly of "the late, unlamented Enterprise Studios." Why "unlamented"? Was the Hollywood grapevine getting wise to the ways of its head honcho and tiring of being played like the proverbial flute? Just as intriguingly, David Loew, she tells us, has "one plan for the future—to lie Loew." Thus, the short life and quick death of a typical David Loew production outfit.

But what has this to do with *A Night in Casablanca*? Well, back when Enterprise was new and the reports positive, much of the press interest had surrounded the fourth main player in the outfit after Loew, Lewis and Garfield. According to Loew's carefully managed reports, he struck up a conversation with one Charles Einfeld at a party, and they hit it off.

"Why don't we go into business together?" asked Loew.

"Why not?" replied Einfeld.

And it all happened as simply as that, if the *Spokane Daily Chronicle* et al. are to be believed. Well, maybe it did. But remember, *A Night in Casablanca* fans, this is all happening in the early months of 1946. What had Charles Einfeld been doing hitherto? What secure position was he willing to throw away, just to enter into uncertain partnership with Loew, so impressed with him had he been after an evening's chat at a Hollywood party? Turns out he was vice president in charge of advertising and publicity at Warner Bros.

Might he have been the source of that one possible communication from the studio asking for clarification over copyright? Or might Loew have even courted him from the first, tempting him to go along with his publicity caper, and not spoil it all with counter-claims and calls for retraction, even if annoying the studio with whom he would, in any event, soon part company, only to magically reappear as a key player in Loew's latest enterprise? It's all credit to David Loew that even after I've chased him around the historical record everywhere I could find him, following this project here, that company there, down each and every rabbit hole of distraction and obfuscation.... I still wouldn't like to say for sure.

Before we leave this slippery web, one final bit of wild conjecture that for once does not directly involve the mischievous Mr. Loew. Could there have been a secondary motive to all this on the Marxes' part, besides publicity? Note first the curious coincidence that within the year Chico would be suing Warner Bros. for real, claiming that he had been "deeply humiliated" by having his name used without permission in the film *Rhapsody in Blue*. According to which report you want to go with, he was particularly hurt either because "he was quoted in the picture as endorsing certain piano-playing techniques which he did not approve," or because "the film gave the impression that he once played piano in a theatre in a cheap neighbourhood." (The very idea!) According to the *Independent Exhibitors Film Bulletin* of March 18, 1946, he was also claiming Warners owed him $100,000 for "services rendered," something of which the studio had "no recollection." Either way, he was intent on sticking it to them for two hundred thousand big ones. In February of '48 a court duly awarded him ten thousand dollars, which was likely on Sun Up's nose by the following morning, but by April some pesky Sig Rumann of a judge ruled the evidence insufficient and ordered a retrial. When the *Bulletin* pondered if the suit might be "a return" for Warners' unhelpfulness over *Casablanca* it made the mistake of not realizing just how beneficial that episode had been (the key to understanding its true nature) but in raising the general issue of revenge, it may not have been barking up the wrong tree after all. Note this revelation from an interview with Bob Thomas in the *Reading Eagle* and elsewhere of April 5, 1946:

> Harpo tells me that two or three years ago Chico was playing a Warner Brothers theatre in Pittsburgh when he fell ill. Harpo flew from Hollywood to fill out the engagement. Nevertheless, says Harpo, Chico was fined $2,000 by the theater for not filling the date. So when Harpo heard Chico mentioned in *Rhapsody in Blue* he persuaded his brother to sue for damages because Warners did not get permission to use the name.

So, given all that, might the phony Casablanca war, too, have been, partially at least, another front in the same campaign, its purpose primarily to keep the gossip columns singing the Marxes' tune, but also to annoy Warners, make them look foolish and, if possible, goad them into wasting money on a futile breach of copyright suit?

Whatever the truth of the matter, the last laugh was ultimately on everyone: copyright being a fickle limpet, the film is now issued on DVD by—yes, madam, you guessed it—Warner Bros.

That just leaves Harpo seemingly without a *Night in Casablanca* myth to be punctured. Worry not, and no, I'm not going back to that hooey about him being asked to say "Murder!" Instead, we now come to the Strange Affair of the Augmented Hair. If you've been reading this book cover to cover, a) well done, and b) you'll have noticed I've dwelled somewhat morbidly on the question of Harpo's wig color. Is it red? Is it blonde? Is it red just once and blonde thereafter? Or is it never truly blonde, just varying degrees of red? Or any and all of these things, constantly varying from film to film? Muddied further by conflicting testimony, and the monochrome ambiguity of the films themselves, it's a vexed and complex matter. But if these questions already inspire endless confusion, debate and dissension—and let's face it, they don't really—they are as nothing to the intellectual heat generated by the man's coiffure this time out.

No doubt as to the color, at least: with questionable aesthetic bravado, it's a piercing, glow-in-the-dark peroxide white. Take your sunglasses if you're going to see it on the big screen. But is it a wig? Instead of his usual style—full, rounded and soft—it seems to be small, tight and close-cropped on the sides. The official story to account for this is that it was not a wig at all, but Harpo's own hair dyed and permed, hence the pinched look. But this cannot possibly be. Harpo's hair was thinning even in the 1920s: though he may not have been quite the proverbial cueball by this time, the suggestion that this mop could have been found growing naturally on the Arthur scalp is a plain non-starter. The bizarre truth seems to be that they bleached and curled whatever of the real Harpo remained (basically the back and sides) and filled the wide-open spaces with specially prepared fluff of the same consistency and hue. It sounds complicated and time-consuming, and vaguely icky, and the end result is, in any case, unsatisfactory to say the least. Why on earth did they bother? What was wrong with the wigs that had stood by him for twenty years, and indeed would come out of the mothballs again for *Love Happy*? (I am irresistibly reminded of that publicity story about him putting them on the fire at the end of *The Big Store*.) And just imagine what he looked like with only those curly patches of real hair when the piece was removed, as presumably it was, every evening. Like an electrified Larry Fine is my guess.

But enough of such frippery—what of the film? The news is happy. It emerged to good reviews and better business; indeed financially it was the biggest first-run hit of their careers. True, it's a touch slow to start, and it runs out of steam by the end, but for the most part it's well paced and it's funny and it has charm, and it benefits from a better script and—very usefully—a more intimate production than any of their later MGM vehicles.

There is plot, and young lovers, and the film does expect us to be vaguely interested in them, but overall they are far less intrusive and centralized than we've lately been accustomed. They vanish almost entirely around the middle, the point where at MGM they traditionally take over; instead it's more or less one comedy scene after another. Admittedly these are

"The only reason I'm making this picture is because in five years I had forgotten how miserable it could be." Groucho (center) with Chico (left) and Harpo (right) during production of *A Night in Casablanca*.

largely recycled: Groucho as the waspish hotel manager insulting his guests, the Harpo-Chico miming sequence, Chico interrupting Groucho's tryst with Beatrice, the scene with the packing and unpacking of Sig Rumann's trunk, and the very funny scene in which Harpo and Chico fill the hotel dance floor with tables and chairs, are all to a greater or lesser extent based on earlier hits. But who cares so long as it's funny? Groucho, in a white linen suit and fez, looks great and seems rejuvenated. The five-year break may have aged the team but it also invigorated them, and it gave audiences a chance to realize what they had been missing.

There's even a contribution from Kalmar and Ruby—sort of. The low budget precluded any original songs, so the one and only number featured is the old Bert and Harry classic "Who's Sorry Now?" (Making the most of what it's got, however, the film has it performed twice, in separate nightclub scenes with the audience all joining in, as well they should if they have to hear it every night.) The dialogue, even without their assistance, is often very good indeed, easily the best the team had been given in a decade:

> GROUCHO: Since when were you a bodyguard? I thought you were in the camel business?
> CHICO: In the daytime I'm in the camel business. At night, I'm a bodyguard.
> GROUCHO: I see, well suppose I get killed in the daytime?
> CHICO: Well, then I give you a free ride on my camel.

As well as plenty of good, typical Groucho material, as he crassly woos Beatrice and insults pompous guests (the "Smythe" scene is a recognized classic), there's also an abundance of fresh, surprising, funny lines emerging legitimately from the situations. That's a good test of a Groucho gag, actually: the ones in *At the Circus* or *Go West* were obviously pre-written out of context and inserted at random, or else, when genuine responses to the actual situations, weren't funny. But there are *dozens* of good ones here, and it's a measure of their effectiveness that when stripped of context they don't mean a damned thing: "You haven't got another stick of gum on you, have you?" "Yes, but think of the fun!" "That's quite a trick, you try that sometime!" "How are things down the other end?" "That reminds me, I must get my watch fixed." "You can hardly notice it unless you're looking for a plate of soup." "Speaks excellent German." "Bring this lady a cheese sandwich." "I wonder if it gets crowded in here on New Year's Eve." "Excuse my ashes." "Well, I'm all ears. Pretty near, anyway." "That's m'steak and I want it!" "Wouldn't it be great if they ate each other?" "You sound like a motorboat." "Keep your medals on, fat boy."

Nonetheless, the production was accompanied by the predictable rumors of imminent re-retirement. "It's just too much work," Harpo told Bob Thomas in his column of November 14, 1945. "We started on the story of this picture last January, and it will be a year by the time of the final preview."

"The only reason I'm making this picture is because in five years I had forgotten how miserable it could be," contributes Groucho.

"I like making pictures," adds a rueful Chico. "I like everything that has to do with show business. But if Harpo and Groucho don't want to work, what can I do?"

Perhaps because his hopes going in were so high, Groucho professed himself hugely disappointed by the end product, and laid the blame squarely at the director. After seeing the first preview he wrote to Miriam: "I was terribly depressed at the preview. We had worked so long and hard on this, and thought we had it so solid and tight, and then to see reams of it emasculated by that fat idiot Mayo, well it was heart rending."

But on most audiences, I'm pleased to say, the film has the opposite effect: it's a delightful return to form.

0:50 (NTSC)/0:52 (PAL)—Musical Score by Werner Janssen

One of the problems Groucho had with the finished film was with the music. Conducting the Janssen Symphony Orchestra of Los Angeles (I'm guessing the name isn't a coincidence), Werner surely has come up with a pretty uninspiring main theme. It doesn't sound much like the music to a Marx Brothers film. But elsewhere his touch lightens and his effectiveness improves.

1:35/1:39—Sig and Lisette

These two shifty-looking characters will be your villains for tonight. The vampish Beatrice is played by Lisette Verea, a Romanian cabaret star of the thirties in the second of only two film appearances (the other was a 1933 Romanian version of *The Ghost Train*). All the more pleasant to note, then, that she's extremely good, and spars splendidly with Groucho as a kind of composite Margaret Dumont and Esther Muir. Mitchell notes that she was customarily a blonde, but had her hair dyed red specifically for the film. According to Sheilah Graham, in her syndicated column of November 3, 1945, she wore her own dresses and jewels in the film, the latter "mostly loot gathered by Lisette when she was engaged to a prominent Egyptian prince."

And though he seems to have lost a considerable amount of weight, there's no mistaking our old pal Sig Rumann next to her, making his record-breaking third appearance as a Marx villain. And this time he really *is* a villain—a renegade Nazi, no less—who has Harpo for a manservant and, in an uncomfortable borrowing of the Lassparri scenes from *A Night at the Opera,* beats him when in bad humor. Sig is best as blustering authority figures and pompous asses, so while it is unquestionably great to have him back, his effectiveness, and our pleasure, is diminished here by his overt cruelty and reprehensibility. As well as for achieving the hat trick in the first place, Sig is also notable for having different billing in each of his three Marx appearances: Siegfried Rumann in *Opera,* Sig Rumann in *Races,* and Sig Ruman here. Had he appeared in *Love Happy* he would presumably have been billed as S. Rum'n.

1:45/1:49—Dan Seymour

Wary as I am of endorsing *any* claim made about this movie that has the people who made it for a source, it *appears* as though Joseph Fields's original, largely jettisoned script had been much more overtly parodying of the Warners Bogart movies. Very little explicit reference remains (luckily) in the finished film, but one sly nod may well be the casting of Seymour as the Prefect of Police. Seymour had appeared briefly in *Casablanca* and played a role similar to this one in *To Have and Have Not.* Other hints include Groucho's Lauren Bacall homage ("You don't have to sing for me, just whistle") at 22:03 and, I suppose, Seymour's line "Round up all likely suspects" at 2:24. (The latter seems to have been dubbed over a slightly different line, and it is at least possible that he was, as sometimes claimed, originally saying the correct *Casablanca* line, "Round up the usual suspects." But was that a "classic" line already by this time, as indelibly associated with the film as it is today—or as "You know how to whistle, don't you,

Steve?" was with *To Have and Have Not* even at the time—to the extent that an effort needed to be made in post-production to avoid direct quotation?) There are a couple of other minor echoes. Director Mayo, of course, had been responsible for *The Petrified Forest.* Romantic lead Charles Drake had been an underused Warners contractee with several Bogart connections, appearing unbilled in *The Maltese Falcon* and *Across the Pacific,* and securing credit and a significant supporting role in *Conflict.* (Leading lady Lois Collier had no Bogart pedigree, but it would be sheer negligence not to point out that you can also catch her in *Slave Girl, Jungle Queen, Jungle Woman, Cobra Woman, Weird Woman, Miss Mink of 1949* and *Flying Disc Men From Mars.*)

2:36/2:43—Holding up the building

This is probably the most famous moment in the film, widely credited to (the uncredited) Frank Tashlin. One also suspects his hand in the brain-twisting reversing waistcoat at **6:26/6:43** and the moment where Harpo eats a candle, after first removing and retaining the flame, at **38:18/39:56**. Tashlin's training in animation made him an ideal source of Harpo material, and while all of these moments have the feel of animated cartoon gags, they are impressively realized in live-action form. Perhaps no small thanks to Tashlin, Harpo is in splendidly inventive form throughout the film—the only thing that slightly undermines him is discussed immediately below.

5:21/5:35—"Rusty, you schweinhund!"

Sig Rumann insults Harpo with the classic German curse, little used in Germany itself but rarely off the lips of Germans in Anglophone movies. Based obviously on Harpo's opening scene in *A Night at the Opera* we again have him as valet to the principal villain, allowing his impish curiosity to supersede his duties, and being rewarded for his invention with a nasty beating. Consistent with Rumann here being a Nazi and not a snooty opera singer, the level of cruelty towards Harpo will go much further than it did in the first film, with correspondingly more depressing results for the movie. There's no point enjoying watching him put Rumann's cane down the back of his jacket and perch his hat on top if you know that he's then going to pull it out and wallop him savagely with it. It's an unfortunate error, because Harpo's business is of a very high standard in all these scenes. It has the most unfortunate effect on the duel scene (see below, 15:35).

9:34/9:59—Chico's enormous bow-tie

Chico's in fine sprightly form here, too; the one odd touch is this strange addition to his otherwise usual costume.

10:20/10:47—The new manager

It's almost the longest delayed Groucho appearance: only *At the Circus* tops it, and that's because an earlier scene was cut. In fact, the same thing happened here. The film had some twenty minutes cut from it after the first preview, including Groucho's first sequence, showing him receiving the invitation to become hotel manager. The scene can be read in Louvish's *Monkey Business,* or, if you're after a more evocative version, it's included in the novelization. Yes, I did say "in the novelization": this is the only Marx Brothers film to have been so honored, and the book—surely the oddest spinoff of any Marx production—now goes for nifty prices on the collectors' market.

15:35/16:15—The duel

Another example of the error in tone discussed above (5:21). This scene, in which Rusty manages to casually humiliate "the finest swordsman in Bavaria," is crammed with wonderfully magical, fearless Harpo touches, but soured almost entirely by Rumann's sinister ringside observations: "Cut him up a little, Kurt. I shall enjoy watching. It will soothe me to see someone in pain…. I would like to see a little blood!" And this was a scene that could have used an extra-light touch anyway, given that it began with Rumann calling Harpo an "inferior ape." (Note the return appearance of the curtain-ring gag at **17:59/18:45**, a variation on equivalent jokes in *Monkey Business* and *Duck Soup*.)

19:42/20:32—"This is like living in Pittsburgh—if you can call that living!"

A reference to Pittsburgh's reputation for smoke pollution, caused by its mining industry. The town had been associated with smoke and grime since the early 19th century: Anthony Trollope called it "the blackest place which I ever saw." But it wasn't until 1941 that a smoke-control ordinance was passed, and then only to be postponed for the duration of the war. The legislation was finally enforced in 1946, adding extra topicality to Groucho's joke. It also inspired Loew to pull his least-known publicity stunt of the picture, detailed in the introduction.

24:19/25:21—The vanishing dance floor

Interesting that, of all the other things MGM did to Chico to spoil his character, they never made him rescind his penchant for larceny. True, the targets had to be seen to be deserving (or Groucho, or both) but it remained a part of his make-up till nearly the end. Here, of all places, we see the first-ever definite renunciation of his wicked ways. Like a good MGM Chico he needs money to help Pierre (our hero, in case you're wondering). He makes a comment that suggests his own dishonesty, but then checks himself and exclaims, "Hey, what I say? I'm a–crazy!" Then when Harpo slips his hand into a rich man's pocket in customary fashion, Chico admonishes him, "Hey, not-a that way!" Worry not, though, for this newfound honesty serves as lead-in to the film's funniest scene, as the pair fill the dance floor with tables and chairs, forcing Groucho and the other patrons to negotiate their maneuvers in an ever-shrinking space. Yes, it's inspired by the stateroom scene in *A Night at the Opera*, but it's hilarious, all the same. ("What a great place to squeeze an orange!") The Harpo-Chico miming scene that follows is another case in point: a direct lift from *A Day at the Races* and a dubious innovation in any case—but still beautifully done and irresistibly funny.

48:14/50:18—"Well, I could pinch-hit for the count"

Yet another baseball term, this one meaning a substitute batter. It is also used in cricket, but there refers to a lower-order batsman promoted to the head of the batting list in order to score quick runs.

49:10/51:16—"The Blue Danube" waltz

It's honest, at least.... This scene advertises its indebtedness to the "thenk yo!" bit from *A Day at the Races* even to the extent of beginning with the same background music. (But as with everything else here, what follows is no less funny for being secondhand.)

55:25/57:47—"Remember what happened in 1929!"

Here we have a sporting Groucho reference to the stock market crash that wiped out most of his savings and investments. (See also *Animal Crackers* 22:10, and *A Day at the Races* 18:28.)

55:39/58:02—"Goodbye, Mr. Chips!"

This makes Groucho's second onscreen pun on the title of this popular novel and film. For more information, see the first: *At the Circus*, 44:48.

56:47/59:13—"You ask-a me how? It's all-a your fault!"

Am I mistaken or is this the only time Chico ever genuinely loses his temper in a film? *Certainly* it's the only time he shouts at Groucho.

57:47/60:15—"Her name's Rembrandt"

Take another look at that painting, folks, and tell me again that's a Rembrandt! It's not even a Charles Laughton.

58:14/60:43—"He's dreaming of a white Christmas"

The Brothers' amusing, near–Paramount vintage plan to break out of jail. First make it look like Harpo has somehow contracted rabies. Then, get the guard's attention by yelling, "Mad frog, er, mad dog! Get a dog doctor!" Then, when he comes and asks the matter, Groucho delivers this obstructive line, in vague reference to the fact that by some means Harpo's mouth has been slathered with white foam. Nobody needs to be told what the line refers to, but its presence here may be due to the fact that Bing Crosby's original recording had topped the Christmas charts in 1945, despite having been recorded back in '42.

60:06/62:40—The packing scene

What Leslie Halliwell calls "the kind of scene you want to sit through again, even if you miss the last bus" is, it's only fair to point out, the same sequence Adamson says "is performed so slowly that it reminds us less of Henderson's scene in *A Night at the Opera* than of those Abbott and Costello scenes where there is a gorilla in the room and nobody seems to notice." Most fans, I think, will lean more towards Leslie, though perhaps not quite to the extent of willingly walking home for it. It's a kind of compendium of similar moments from several films, not just *Opera* but *The Cocoanuts* too, and the simultaneous packing and unpacking from *Room Service*. It's one of those rare and cherishable ensemble scenes that we simply don't have enough of for which to be ungrateful, where not only are the three Brothers together but acting in perfect physical concert, a single machine, with Harpo in the control box and Groucho and Chico as satellites. No matter what any one of them does, no matter how arbitrary or *outré* the decision any third part of the machine makes, so fine-tuned is the circuitry that the other two-thirds will grasp it instinctively and know how best to respond, or even anticipate it and aid its progress. In such moments they become a true team, as opposed to a conglomeration, and a kind of private voodoo animates and protects them. Villains and buffoons are not merely frustrated into defeat, they are humiliated into compliance: Rumann and his ally are reduced to becoming cogs in the same works, as everything they do to extricate themselves from the path of Marxian determinism merely drags them further into its inviolable programming. By the end, five men seem to be performing some arcane ritual, of the sort that a whole team of anthropologists would take ten years of study to make more obscure and less explicable. As a sequence, it is idea and design and enactment in perfect synthesis, and perhaps the most striking thing about it is that it's not anywhere near the best thing the Brothers ever did. This is what they pull out of the hat when they're not even trying too hard.

The actual big stunt finale that follows seems doubly unnecessary after this certain climax, especially since the production values aren't quite equal to the task, the pacing is awry, and the musical score hasn't been let in on the joke. There's a little doubling for the Brothers here, too, though it's less obtrusive than in *The Big Store*, and, because he's wearing a full wig, there is the unintended side effect of the Harpo double coming off looking more like Harpo than Harpo does. It's nothing special but no matter—think of it as an unrequested extra: a free Limoncello after your penne con radicchio e mozzarella affumicata. You didn't order it, but it slides down easy enough, and you've already had a good night.

13

Love Happy (1949)

I'm going to cover you with sardines—that's how much I love you!
—Faustino (Chico Marx) to Madame Egelichi (Ilona Massey)

Producer Lester Cowan told *Showmen's Trade Review* in 1948 that "the day of the loony comedy is really just dawning, and box office charts will show an increasing swing toward laugh-provokers." Accordingly, he had high hopes for *Love Happy*, which he felt would be just the ticket "in a world in which the threat of war, depression and other nightmares is growing constantly."

But for many involved in the production, *Love Happy* soon became a nightmare all its own. The story of the film, and how it ended up the way it did, is convoluted. It begins with *Copacabana* (1947), Groucho's first effort to carve a career for himself in the movies, without his brothers. The film paired him with Carmen Miranda, and the general feeling was that a solo Groucho was a more or less viable proposition. (Not that prior uncertainty on that score doesn't permeate the finished product: it even finds room for Groucho to perform a Kalmar and Ruby number, "Go West, Young Man," in his traditional costume and greasepaint moustache. And according to an interview with Groucho published in November 1946, this sequence was to have included "a quick gag scene in which he turns to the audience and says, 'I wish Harpo and Chico were here,' whereupon Harpo and Chico run through the scene.") For Groucho, this was a modest but encouraging step in a new direction. In a letter he sent to his daughter Miriam, Groucho says he accepted it because "it was the only (film) offered to me, except for making a Marx Brothers picture, something I have no more desire for nor interest in."

Harpo wasn't too keen on another group venture either. But he did have an idea for a solo picture that he and Ben Hecht had been toying with: in fact, he'd been telling interviewers about it since 1944. (Hecht had been long acquainted with the Brothers—he even had a hand in an early draft of *At the Circus*—but he and Harpo had recently become closer friends via their mutual involvement in the Hollywood Zionist movement.)

The pair seemed to find an encouraging ear in Cowan, but the alliance was a lopsided one from the start. For Hecht and Harpo, the producer's value was probably located in his recently formed production arrangement with Mary Pickford, which augured well for United Artists distribution. For Cowan, far more interesting than the actual property Harpo had brought to him was the chance it offered to get all the Marx Brothers back together again: the very thing Harpo did not want to happen. As Harpo's son Bill recalled: "Dad was lied

Whose picture is this anyway? Groucho (center) guests and Harpo (right) stars in *Love Happy*. Ilona Massey looks on.

to by the producer and it was an awful experience for him, but he had to do it because he was under contract." All the time he was supposed to be developing *Love Happy*, Cowan was busily courting Groucho and Chico, and announcing a plethora of other vehicles for one or more of the trio to the trade papers. These were so numerous that it is difficult to sort the bona fides from the flotsam, and the different projects from the same ones differently named. (*Love Happy* itself was variously identified as "Blondes Up," "My Blonde Heaven," "Hearts and Diamonds," "Diamonds in the Basement," "Diamonds on the Sidewalk," "Side-walks of New York" and "The Sidewalk.")

Though Harpo himself spoke hopefully of a second solo vehicle called "The Clown," to be shot in France and co-starring Glynis Johns, the majority of these projects, all announced between the middle of 1947 and the end of 1949, were surely nothing more than column-filler. For instance, there was Bob Thomas's claim that Cowan was in London scouting locations for a film with Groucho as a Scotland Yard man: "It's supposed to be a thriller." According to others, it wasn't a thriller but a Scotland Yard burlesque, teaming Groucho with Sid Field. ('Who's Sid Field?' many American readers will doubtless wonder, even as British comedy fans weep at the prospect of the single unfulfilled Marx project they'd happily give up *Humor Risk* and the *Horse Feathers* off-cuts for.) Then the Scotland Yard idea became but one third of a film in which all three brothers would appear separately, to be set in England, France and Italy. Sheilah Graham quoted Cowan: "I want Groucho to play a Scotland Yard detective in London, Chico to play an Italian guide for tourists in Rome and Harpo for a 'French-type movie' in Paris." (Obviously there's a strong chance that this "French-type movie" was, or became with the other two segments dropped, "The Clown.")

Back in America, Dorothy Manners, standing in for a vacationing Louella Parsons, told Louella's readers that Cowan was so pleased with Ilona Massey's work in *Love Happy* that "he plans a series of comedy detective movies to star Groucho and Ilona." The opener would be titled "My First Murder," and would be a mix of "zany detecting and dazzling musical numbers—or as dazzling as numbers can be in these days of cutting down."

Hedda Hopper, meanwhile, had the two starring in something called "Treasure Hunt," to be shot "when producer Lester Cowan gets around to it." While we were waiting, other sources pinned Groucho in a romantic comedy musical with a Honolulu background, with Dick Haymes and Joan Caulfield supplying the love interest. That's unless Haymes was being partnered with Chico, in what the *Showmen's Trade Review* called "a hard-hitting western" to be called *Dusty Trail*. Or perhaps Cowan was dispensing with the Brothers entirely, and instead reteaming *Love Happy*'s three female leads, Vera-Ellen, Ilona Massey and Marion Hutton, in something called "The Customer is Always Right." And on it went.

But by far the most persistent rumor (and the only one the Brothers themselves acknowledged as a serious possibility), was a biopic of their own lives, to which end Cowan had somewhat oddly purchased cinematic rights to Alexander Woollcott's famous obituary of their mother, Minnie. It was officially announced to the press in 1947, and still very much on the table as *Love Happy* was taking shape. According to reports, the Brothers were to play themselves, presumably in contemporary linking scenes, with flashbacks to actors playing them in their youth and prime. ("All we have to do now is find four Larry Parkses," Groucho told Bob Thomas.)

This raises so many pertinent questions and opens so many tempting avenues of speculation: Would Zeppo have returned? Would Harpo have spoken? Did we really come that close to seeing Gummo in a movie? We can only imagine, but Chico told a New York press conference during shooting of *Love Happy* that the biopic would immediately follow. Bob Thomas, in a syndicated column from April 30, 1948, "Marx Brothers Plan Retirement," announces the forthcoming "Hearts and Diamonds" and adds: "Brother-manager Gummo says they'll make one more film after that and it will be the life of the Marx Brothers." Sadly they never did, and though the announcements continued to lard the gossip columns for some time, none of the Brothers darkened Cowan's towels again, almost certainly because of the considerable difficulties during the shooting of *Love Happy*.

Cowan and Mary Pickford had merged properties and formed their own independent concern, Artists Alliance, in September 1946. Seemingly troubled from the first, the company had already been disbanded *and* reformed by December, and a year later nothing had been produced, despite regular announcements: "This unit just keeps on scheduling, but never producing, it seems," noted the *Independent Exhibitors Film Bulletin* in April of 1947.

Though work *had* in fact begun on *Love Happy* by this time, its course was constantly diverted in unpredictable directions. The following April it was announced that production would move to England, as part of United Artists' "new British production program"; by

June the *Bulletin* announced with surprise that Cowan had "evidently changed his mind on release plans" for what was then being called "Hearts and Diamonds": "Originally set for United Artists distribution, Cowan is now dickering with Eagle-Lion for release of the film."

In the event, UA did confirm their decision to handle the project the following month, but money was scarce and elusive from the first. Like the stage struck heroes of the film's own plot, Chico and Harpo received no payment up front for their performances, settling instead for a percentage share of profits while, in a decision that would shortly turn around and bite him, Harpo gave up all rights to his scenario for a flat fee of $10,000. (One wonders if they knew about the studio's plan that "Chico, Harpo and Ben Hecht will be approached with a view of reducing their percentage" if the budget exceeded $750,000.)

Chico was "all for making pictures in which they own a share," according to the *Showmen's Trade Review*, which quoted him claiming breezily: "It's the first picture where we've never taken a dollar in advance." But Chico being Chico, the truth was slightly different: he was *officially* receiving only a percentage share, but Cowan had in fact loaned him $8,500, to be paid back from his percentage payment once received. (For him, at least, pay day was also pay-up day.) This was one of a number of financial discrepancies spotted by I. H. Prinzmetal, eagle-eyed (and Grouchoesquely-named) attorney at law in July 1948:

> Dear Lester,
> I was quite appalled when I was informed that you had executed a check on the account of Artists Alliance to your own account in connection with expenditures ... for your personal attorneys, expenditures to Chico Marx which are not covered by any of our agreements, and other expenditures which are not properly obligations of Artists Alliance. As a member of the Board of Directors of Artists Alliance and as an attorney for this company, I must notify you of my objection to this action and must insist upon an accounting by you of these expenditures and an immediate repayment to Artists Alliance of the amounts which cannot be properly charged to them. From a personal point of view I must confess that I am particularly shocked and greatly disturbed...

Timely intervention by Pickford, and Cowan's promise to reimburse the absent funds, smoothed over this particular episode, but it spoke clearly of a production that was financially undernourished and out of control. The stage was set for the crucial development that Cowan had probably been angling for from the start, and which Harpo least wanted to hear: that it be converted into a full-fledged Marx picture, nominally at least, by getting Groucho to appear in a wraparound narrative.

In a letter to Miriam from June of 1947 Groucho mentions a film that Ben Hecht is making "with Harpo and Chico," showing that at that stage at least he had no notion whatever of what was around the corner. But with Cowan's assurance that only he could guarantee the production's future, plus the promise of $25,000 for just a few days' work, he finally consented to the inevitable and signed on. (He had to take Cowan to court before he got paid, however: he was awarded $42,726 in April of 1951.)

The exact nature of his involvement remained indefinite at this early stage, and Harpo missed no opportunity to play it down. By September of 1947 columnist Leonard Lyons was ready to announce that all three Brothers "will return to the screen in a Ben Hecht story produced by Lester Cowan" but that "Harpo and Chico will do the comedy routines while Groucho will be the narrator." In October, Hedda Hopper's column carried a short interview with Harpo that, following his lead, still pointedly refers to "the picture he and Chico will make for Lester Cowan," and stresses that "Groucho will do the narration for the picture but *won't* act in it." Move on a year to the *Deseret News* of September 8, 1948, and Groucho *will* be appearing on camera, though all of his scenes will be shot "in a mere four or five days." Harpo, for all his defiance, must have seen the writing on the wall: "I've always been just an extraneous character before. I've never been woven into the story. Groucho has always been the important one. This time he knows he's not going to be important in the picture. He's doing it as a compliment to Chico and me."

Bill Marx, who was twelve at the time and a regular visitor to the set, recalls it as "a difficult film for Dad to do. Originally it was going to be his movie. But in order to get financing, the producer had to write Chico and Groucho into the story. So the final film was nothing like Dad originally had in mind." Forced to watch their cherished project being slowly dismantled and reassembled as a cynical commercial proposition, Hecht (who had cared enough to write the final draft from his hospital bed, after having his gall bladder removed) took his name off the film and stomped away. And in Harpo, an animosity towards Cowan was fomented that led to his being one of the very few human beings to have reduced the mild-mannered clown to an apoplectic profession of hatred. (This by his own admission, according to his wife Susan.)

With Hecht gone, the script was handed over to a fascinatingly mixed bag of other writers, among them George Panetta, Otto E. Englander, William Alland, Chas. L. Issacs and Manny Mannheim. In the event, only two received screen credit: Frank Tashlin (returning after valuable but unbilled contributions to *A Night in Casablanca*) and gagman Mac Benoff, who signed on after most of the film had been shot "with little continuity and much mish-mash." (This would seem to imply that he was responsible primarily for the expanded Groucho sections, and their integration with the extant remainder.) Curiously, Benoff recalled Chico being recruited first:

> Lester Cowan, the producer, was a real promoter. Groucho and Harpo turned him down flat. But Cowan was a smart man. He got Chico, who always needed money. Then Harpo, being a pushover, agreed to do it in order to help out Chico. Then, having the two of them, he got Groucho.

Though by his own admission he joined late, Benoff's chronology does make sense. It might conceivably have been only when Cowan came back to Harpo after a first rebuff, this time with Chico in his pocket, that Harpo recognized the chance to convert a *fait accompli* into the solo vehicle he had long nurtured, albeit with Chico nominally on hand as well. (In contrast to his determination to underplay Groucho's involvement, Harpo would graciously call Chico's peripheral role "a bigger part than he's ever had before.")

For a time, though, it looked as if Chico might not be joining the party after all: in late March 1947 he suffered a heart attack while performing in Las Vegas, and impulsively instructed his management to announce his retirement. But scientists know there are only two immutable laws: energy does not create itself and Chico Marx does not retire, and with the scare over and the heart attack officially diagnosed as mild, it took just one day for him to take to the wire, from his bed, to announce that he hadn't authorized the reports of his retirement, he felt fine, he didn't even have a heart problem, Harpo couldn't speak in real life, he was a real Italian and Margaret Dumont didn't get the jokes. (Only a few years before he had faked a heart attack to get out of a Las Vegas nightclub contract; now he was faking not having one, to stay in a contract.) He was suffering, he said, from "roulette fever" (that much was true), and took the opportunity to add that he was "going back to Hollywood" where "we have some plans for independent movie production." The *Love Happy* insurers were presumably appeased, and after the briefest permissible convalescence the fatal gambler made his weary way back to the cinematic tables.

Meanwhile, his producer kept on maneuvering. A neat portrait of Cowan the showman emerges clearly in this letter to Gradwell Sears, UA's vice-president in charge of distribution, written in tones more akin to a press release than a private communication:

> With everybody in the industry running for cover and planning to make cheap pictures, it looks like the big new opportunity for the independent studio is to do the opposite. Am sure you would rather have a *Red River* instead of a Joel McCrea western... This is why I have been trying to build up my Marx film instead of seeing how cheaply it could be made. For example, I have added 3 sock dancing spots—two by Vera-Ellen and one by Paul Valentine and a solid song spot by Marion Hutton. These plus Harpo's number and a three and a half minute piano number between Chico and Leon Belasco which Chico says is the most effective number he has ever done on the screen. These features were not contemplated in the original script or the original budget and hope will help make the picture more attractive to women as well as kids and men who have predominated the Marx Brothers fans... Result I need about $100,000 to finish the job bringing my total expenditure on the film to $935,000 which is certainly not out of line. I can get this money on the outside by giving away only 10 percent to Standard Capitol for $150,000 secondary money. Certainly would rather give UA much greater share than to any outsider for the obvious reasons...

He also mentions "the big secret stunt" he has up his sleeve for the picture. This was his most audacious (and lasting) innovation of all: to sell off advertising space in the film to a variety of companies whose neon logos would be clearly displayed behind Harpo in a rooftop chase finale. This late interpolation into the screenplay necessitated the re-shooting and restructuring of the already-shot Groucho material, totally changing his personal relevance to the plot (exactly what Harpo wanted to avoid).

The extant Italian trailer still features shots of Groucho frisking Harpo and Ilona Massey in his office rather than on the rooftop, and Marx expert Mikael Uhlin has shrewdly suggested that it is therefore likely all of Groucho's appearances had originally been confined to his office set, but when the rooftop chase was devised it became necessary to bring him into it too. (This may well further account for the now-pointless appearance of the great Eric Blore as Groucho's virtually non-existent assistant Mackinaw—perhaps he featured more prominently in the original, office-based ending.)

Bob Thomas in a February 1949 column noted that the Brothers had been called back for retakes, but added that Chico, by this time performing with his band in England, couldn't make it: "So Harpo will double him in the scenes." Needless to say, there is nothing suggestive of the latter in the film, but it does look as though the shots of Chico in the finale have been shot separately. This would account not just for his limited presence generally but also, crucially, for the fact that only Harpo and Groucho join Ilona Massey at the very end of the sequence: the natural and obvious place to bring the three brothers together. Chico and Groucho never encounter each other on the roof top, and while they appear to share the final scene, it's likely the shot of Chico playing cards with the dog in Groucho's office was shot elsewhere and cut in: the two are not shown together in the same frame and give the impression of performing separately, with Chico's total appearance being that one tightly-framed shot. I would suggest that the sole reason for this shot, and for Faustino and Grunion seemingly having joined forces (what happened to poor Mackinaw?), is to make up for Chico's abrupt disappearance from the end of the roof scene, and his absence from what should be the full Brotherly reunion that ends it. (Harpo's presence in at least one still with Chico and the dog adds further weight to the suggestion that it was separately shot, probably at the same time as the Harpo-Chico cut-ins on the roof scene.) Apart from Harpo and a short, self-contained moment with Massey, Chico never shares a shot with anybody (unless his or their faces are obscured) from the beginning of the roof sequence on: for the most part, the film cuts to him, and away again.

As well as hinting about his "big secret stunt," and asking for more money, Cowan had also told Gradwell Sears that he had "8600 feet of cut film ready for preview." Sears took him up on his offer and the results were not joyous, at least not in the opinion of lawyers O'Melveny and Myers, who wired Pickford in May of 1949 in a mood of staccato melancholy:

> None of us have seen picture. Can't judge independently on soundness of Mr. Sears' comments.... Picture may not be as bad as he indicates. On other hand Sears may be correct. Serious situation if picture met with strong exhibitor antagonism. Risk to your guarantee to Bank of America.... Your suggestion—having picture viewed by impartial man with industry experience—is a good one. If merit in Sears' views—problems. If editing needed—have to get finances to do so. Cowan making deals with advertisers to pay part of expense. We must ascertain facts— but insoluble problems ...

Meanwhile Cowan continued to dicker with the idea of further reshoots— and struggled to pay his lab bill. The latter fact came to the attention of UA Director Paul O'Brien in June:

> *Love Happy* has been delivered to United and two actual engagements have been played. However United only has four prints ... cannot secure more from lab because of indebtedness of producer to lab. Also Lester has been talking about making a new ending ... all of this seriously impedes distribution of picture.

Cowan gave his assurance he was "making arrangements to pay lab bill" in a terse one-sentence telegram sent a few days after O'Brien's, but still no resolution had been achieved by September. By that time, Pickford had reached the end of her ringlets:

> Today Wallich of Standard Capital discussed with me your failure to raise funds to release negative of *Love Happy* and stated there is no alternative but for Nassers to put up the completion bond which would subsequently wipe you and me completely out of profits in this picture and also deprive us of a very valuable asset of the sliding scale. My attorneys advise this procedure would result in bankruptcy of Artists Alliance, lawsuits and serious loss of face. You already know how far I was willing to go in granting your many requests and exacting demands in order to bail out moneyed and other interests than myself. The fact that I have now been home six days without word from you is unpardonable under these grave circumstances.

No doubt at this point she remembered she had once written a book called *Why Not Try God?*

Somehow, a preliminary edit was cobbled together in time for a limited release in the Great Lakes region of the U.S. in October, before a final, tightened version was officially unleashed in March of 1950. And there the matter rested until 2004, when attentive fans noted that a new, unheralded DVD issue of the film was of an entirely different cut to the one previously seen, and some six minutes longer. This proved to be that original cut prepared in 1949, prior to the assembly of the generally released 85-minute version from 1950.

Several of the differences plainly support this history, most obviously the fact that the shorter version uses a superimposed sign in the roof chase, beneath which the original sign, seen throughout the longer cut, can occasionally be glimpsed. It also tidies up some moments in the original that are slackly edited (for instance, the Harpo gag where he reverses the mirror he is using to see the back of his head is shown twice in the long cut, as if we're going to laugh at it even more a second time; he's also forced to smoke rope twice as long in the torture montage).

But the DVD also threw up a couple of mysteries, foremost among them being the fact that so much of the variant material involves Groucho. Given that he is there because his presence was deemed essential, and that he remains, even in the 91-minute cut, a commodity in very short supply, why remove so many of his lines? Several funny jokes are to be found only in the long print—not only in the narration but with Groucho actually seen in the shot—while the dialogue with Ivan, the assassin, at **67:42/70:35** is the sort of thing most audiences have been waiting the whole film for him to deliver.

And not all the missing material is to be found in cuts anyway: the scene of Chico arriving at the theater is present in the eighty-five-minute print, but *without* Groucho's voiceover. The Groucho version is scored to a piano version of the main theme whereas the short cut has different boogie-woogie music, over which Mike's tap shoes, muted in the other cut, can be heard. *This* would suggest that it is the shorter version that features the original soundtrack, Groucho's material was then added, necessitating the removal of the original soundtrack ... but then, for some reason, it was deleted again, and the original soundtrack restored.

The explanation lies in the Brothers contractual stipulations, and specifically in Harpo's determination that Groucho's appearances should not be allowed to change the film's essential focus, which was on Harpo the tramp. Accordingly, Groucho's maximum screen time was prescribed in the negotiations at the time he was first signed. This full allotted presence had been accounted for in the script he was originally given, but the restructured ending pushed him over his agreed-upon screen time, hence the subsequent deletions both of scraps of easily removed voice-over and the most self-contained of his scenes on camera.

Prior to his agreeing to an extra two days of shooting in February of 1949, all three Brothers signed an agreement confirming the possibility that to make room for the new material, some "photography and soundtrack made to date of Groucho Marx will not be in the picture as finally released" and that "the portions thereof marked with an 'X' will also come out if Groucho performs on said dates."

Accordingly, Groucho's parts of the roof scene were filmed separate from the bulk of it and very carefully rationed. More so even than Chico, he tellingly takes no active part in the action or antics, and until meeting up with Harpo and Ilona at the very end is only ever seen alone, in a series of silly cutaways showing him sneaking about, going in and out of doors and peering out from inside a steam funnel.

It seems fair to assume that all Cowan ever really wanted was a Marx Brothers picture. Perhaps deliberately luring Groucho with fancy talk of Honolulu musicals and Scotland Yard burlesques, he went along with Harpo's solo idea as the only alternative to not securing his services at all. But it's unlikely he ever greatly cared for "Diamonds in the Sidewalk" and always intended sneaking Groucho in: if true, and Harpo cottoned on, that may go some way towards explaining the unprecedented rage Harpo claimed to have displayed towards him. Harpo pointedly ignored the film in his autobiography, and just about the only positive thing he took away from the experience was the contractually-established ownership of any gags he helped devise that were not used in the final cut. (These enticingly include "the seltzer bottle gag, all gags and business in the wedding sequence, the skating routine and gag, the dog gag, the eye gag where he falls asleep, the popcorn gag, all business with bending telescope, the wire with sliding Chinaman routine, and all gags in the dream sequences where Harpo dreams and thinks he is singing.") Nonetheless, according to the *Motion Picture Daily* Cowan eventually hosted a cocktail party for Harpo in Hollywood, the night before the latter took the SS Queen Mary to London for the premiere. All in the interests of business, no doubt, but call me a sentimental old fluff, I still like to think it implies they had patched things up a little.

Though not without its defenders (and what film is?) *Love Happy* has a terrible reputation. It is generally considered not merely the worst Marx Brothers film, but on an entirely different plane far beneath the rest. This seems unfair for two reasons: first, and most importantly, because it is silly to judge a film by the measure of what you and Lester Cowan wanted it to be (a Marx Brothers film), rather than what it sets out to be (a Harpo film with Chico and Groucho in support). Second, because audiences who *do* approach it in the right spirit often find far more to enjoy in it than they had expected, or had earlier perceived.

It's a fragile thing, with little that sticks in the mind the next day, but I can't say it ever strikes me as a chore to watch. (When the lights went up after its screening during the National Film Theatre's 2004 retrospective, there was a palpable feeling of happy surprise that it was as *easy* to enjoy as it proved; "I *liked* that!" the man next to me said, as if startled by the revelation.)

Despite the financial problems that plagued it, it feels a lot less cheap than *A Night in Casablanca*. For one thing it has original song numbers: something way beyond *Casablanca*'s budget. "Who Stole That Jam?" may divide opinion, but we should all agree that the title song is very nice indeed, and there's a lively and effective music score throughout. (The composer tasked with "writing music to accompany leaps on a swinging pendulum, gadgets zooming at a smoked ham, and pipes giving out with wolf whistles" was Ann Ronell, former Gershwin protégée, co-writer of "Who's Afraid of the Big Bad Wolf?," used in *Duck Soup*, and Cowan's wife.) Vera-Ellen is a sweet heroine, Ilona Massey a fun villainess, Melville Cooper a perfect bumbling foil, Leon Belasco a splendid stooge for Chico—whose piano spot, incidentally, is his best in years.

All it really lacks is the kind of comedy one expects of a Marx Brothers movie, though Frank Tashlin certainly devised some effective gags for Harpo (including a classic where he attempts to hide behind the back row of the theater and instead knocks over the collapsible seats, which knock the row in front, which then does likewise to the one in front of that, and so on, domino-fashion, until the entire auditorium is razed).

The rooftop chase, too, usually draws grudging respect for some of its actual gags, if not their cynically commercial inspiration. Such nice ideas as having Harpo ride the Mobil horse and exhale smoke from the cigarette of the Kool penguin were, unsurprisingly, the work of Tashlin rather than Cowan. "In *Love Happy* I had the chance to write the chase sequence I've been wanting to do for years," Tashlin told *Showmen's Trade Review*: "I used my past experience as an animator to devise the scenes in which Harpo is chased over the New York skyline by the villains. The idea of combining animated signs with human characters is a sure-fire laugh-getter, as proven in our sneak preview."

Put that way, it doesn't seem quite so crass a marriage of art and commerce after all.

NOTE— I deliberated as to which edition to use in the guide, but eventually opted for the longer cut, since I think it will come to be seen as the standard version, even though the shorter cut is the more official and at time of writing remains the more ubiquitous. (The extended cut is also vastly cleaner and sharper in both image and soundtrack than even the better examples I've seen of the eighty-five-minute one; most DVD editions, including the one in the official Universal UK box set, have an ugly splice at the beginning of the theme song, so that the first time we hear the title in the lyrics it sounds like "L'y," and are further scarred by scratchy visuals and several jumps and sound drops.) There are many minor differences between the two; in the guide below I will mention the most significant, and I thank Steven R. Wright for allowing me to lean on his pioneering work in this regard. In stout defense of the principle that somewhere there is an example of literally anything, Steven is the world's only bona fide Love Happy *expert.*

0:00 (NTSC/PAL)—Groucho's prologue

Groucho plays Sam Grunion; a grunion is a type of sardine-sized fish found only in

Harpo and Vera-Ellen in a "write your own caption" shot from *Love Happy*.

California and Mexico. (There's a reference to them in Scott Fitzgerald's *The Last Tycoon*.) Note that Groucho is here appearing on screen with his real eyebrows and moustache for the first time. (Before you wake me up in the middle of the night and scream, "What about *Copacabana*!" into the phone: nope, that was a fake moustache too.) In fact, he very rarely had a real moustache until this time, and it was only with the televising of *You Bet Your Life* that he accepted it as an essential part of his persona. This is a nice enough little intro, but it does reflect the rather slapdash nature of the enterprise generally. Note the delay at **0:11/0:11**, after Groucho says, "The Royal Romanov diamonds are missing," and then mugs helplessly in anticipation of the dissolve that eventually comes in six agonizing seconds too late. It's also fairly obvious, if you follow Groucho's eyeline, that he is reading his lines. (Watch him scan the room in the passage beginning "Scotland Yard was baffled..." at **0:38/0:40**.) I doubt very much he would have needed assistance of that sort: more likely there just wasn't time for him to learn them. There's the chance of some good laughs here, but he's too hesitant and laid back–seeming to get them. For instance, consider the lines: "I am Sam Grunion, private eye, at your service. Secrecy is my motto. I never tell. You will notice even my business card has nothing on it." Groucho was the world's master of making lines play funnier than they read, but this is a rare indeed case of the opposite. On paper it looks like a good joke, and if you haven't seen the film you can more easily imagine him delivering it at the uninterruptible pace of Mr. Hammer or Captain Spaulding. Here, he kills the laugh by putting an inexplicably long pause between "business card" and "has nothing on it."

This pre-credits scene is basically identical in both versions, except for the fact that the longer cut has, for some unknown reason, what Steven R. Wright calls "strange, Morse code dihs and dahs" added to the soundtrack at the beginning, that gradually become louder and more unpleasant until they fill the soundtrack, entirely replacing the instrumental effect that accompanies the shot of the diamonds in the short cut.

0:54/0:56—"... round the Cape of Good Hope and into Gimbels' basement"

This is one of the film's smaller mysteries. Non-American readers should know that Gimbels was the largest department store chain in America. (It opened in 1887 and went into liquidation exactly a hundred years later.) Now, given that when we first see the diamonds they are indeed in the basement of a large store—and, as Groucho goes on to say, "From Gimbels' basement the trail led me to a group of struggling young actors..."—we might be forgiven for thinking this is where our story begins. But the diamonds are not in the basement of Gimbels, but that of a fictitious food emporium called Herbert & Herbert ("the finest food for the finest people"). Now, under normal circumstances, one might suspect that the original intention was to set it in Gimbels but the chain objected to the use of the copyrighted name, and (given the more slaphappy than love happy nature of the film) the earlier scripted reference got overlooked and left in. Remembering the film's pioneering relationship with advertisers, however, it's tempting to posit the exact opposite: the scenes with Harpo showing the fictitious shop front had already been made and could not be reshot, but a last-minute tie-up with Gimbels resulted in the change to Groucho's monologue—which had either not yet been shot or could certainly be reshot very cheaply at short notice. (If the latter, this might well explain Groucho's unfamiliarity with the lines.) And then, hopefully, we won't even notice that the store is, in fact, called Herbert & Herbert's.

1:31/1:35—"starring The Marx Brothers"

This opening credit is the first of two surprises in the titles, since a great deal of contractual steam was expended behind the scenes to ensure that the relative importance of the three would be reflected in their billing. The final agreement, signed by all three, allowed for the film to be "advertised and billed as a Marx Brothers picture," but only on the strict understanding that "in all screen credits Groucho shall be separately mentioned as a narrator or commentator, and Groucho's billing shall be below that of Harpo and Chico, preferably at the bottom of the credits." This is exactly how the end credits are arranged: first Harpo, then Chico, and with Groucho last (as "Sam Grunion, the narrator of our story"). UA's lawyers spotted it, and warned that the collective opening credit constituted a contract violation in a memo sent in July 1949: that nothing was done may be simply down to the fact that pretty much everyone was past caring by that stage. The other surprise in the credits is that Mary Pickford's name appears: she had expressly asked that it should not. "Actually, I think this will not harm but rather help the picture," she noted wryly in an undated memo, "as those who remember me on the screen do not constitute the Marx Brothers audience."

2:52/2:59—"That's Mike Johnson"
3:02/3:10—"That's Maggie Phillips"
3:20/3:29—"This is Maggie's best friend, Bunny Dolan"

Paul Valentine, as Mike, is "introduced" in the credits, like Marilyn and Bruce Gordon. In truth, it wasn't the first film for any of them (though it was Gordon's first credit). Valentine had had three decent credited roles previously, beginning with Jacques Tourneur's noir classic *Out of the Past* back in 1947. Far from having the desired effect, his lead here proved one of his last screen roles: he jumped ship to TV shortly after. Fascinating and somewhat poignant to see Vera-Ellen here, an incredible dancing talent on the brink of great things, with *On the Town* and *Three Little Words* just around the corner. Sadly, just around the corner also was anorexia, not a diagnosable condition at the time, but one that by 1954's *White Christmas* had left her unrecognizable as the voluptuous, fresh-faced starlet we see here. Bunny Dolan is played by Marion Hutton, the sister of Betty Hutton. There's no mistaking the kinship, but if, like me, you regularly suffer from nightmares in which you are trapped in a broken cable car with Betty Hutton, Martha Raye and Joan Davis, be reassured that she is not quite so maniacally intent on delighting you (or else) as her sister. She'd previously co-starred with Olsen & Johnson and Abbott & Costello, but this was the last of her five film appearances. Her solo number, "Who Stole that Jam?" is fairly good fun (and note the extra lines introducing it in the longer cut). The longer version of this scene ends with an extra moment of Groucho: the image freezes on Mike's dance routine, whereupon Groucho fades in, peering over his glasses and asking, "Is there a band-aid in the house?"

3:50/4:00—The strolling delicatessen

Harpo's introductory scene is far happier than Groucho's. He's back in a proper wig, looking at least three years younger, rather than older, than the man we saw in *A Night in Casablanca* (the wig isn't as dark as the one in *The Cocoanuts*, but is, I think, fairly obviously red. It has been said that he had also had minor cosmetic surgery before production began). He's an unapologetic thief again, relieving shoppers of their purchases with dexterity and ingenuity; he lights a man's cigar with the flower in his lapel; he terrifies a yapping dog with a truly classic Gookie (in glorious close-up, and well worth freeze-framing). Then, in a great moment, he catches the tins of sardines that Melville Cooper flings in all directions with impossible yet casual skill. Cooper, incidentally, gives a very good performance—as, it has to be said, do most of the cast. He shared billing with the Brothers again (but no more screen time than they do with each other) in *The Story of Mankind*.

12:38/13:10—Faustino the Great

We've long since ceased to entertain any hopes of Chico being given great material, but with that much clearly understood and allowed for, he's in pretty good form in this film. He plays "Faustino the Great," the most unknown actor who never appeared on Broadway. His first appearance in the longer version is accompanied by some amusing Groucho narration missing in the short cut: "Here's another Broadway hopeful, Faustino the Great. For twenty years he was an organ grinder with a monkey. Then one day the monkey went on strike. He wanted shorter hours and longer bananas. Now Faustino is a mind reader—if he only had a mind."

15:51/16:32—"Have you seen any funny-faced tramps with bushy hair?"

The actor playing the policeman who delivers this line, and later brings Harpo to Madame Egelichi, is Edward Gargan, a familiar face in over three hundred movies, often as Irish cops. He appeared with most of the major comedy stars of the thirties and forties, perhaps most memorably in the excellent tit-for-tat sequence in Laurel & Hardy's *The Bull-fighters*. ("Fellow bricklayers...") This is his second appearance in a Marx Brothers movie: he's also the railway ticket seller in *Go West*.

16:44/17:27—Harpo and the bull

This is the first piece of Harpo material to appear only in the longer cut. After he arrives with the food and ends up crushed against the wall, we see him being approached by the pantomime bull. He produces a string of fake sausages from his coat and inserts it in the bull's nostril, where it is sucked inside. He then goes to the back end of the bull and considers inserting a tin of sardines. Acknowledging the impossibility (even if it was a French picture he couldn't do it) he instead pulls the bull's tail, which makes the noise of his bulb horn. The pompous British actor (who is later to be heard suggesting they put on the play without scenery or costumes) emerges from the end of the costume and rejects the offer in grandiose fashion. Harpo instead offers a ham, and points to the actor to suggest a resemblance.

18:32/19:19—Tootsie-fruitsie ice-a cream

Harpo and Chico's first scene together is unbearably charming, and its mood of nostalgia is enhanced by this certain reference to glories past. It's often hard to know if the Marx Brothers are referring to past hits or not ("Sweet Adeline" and "on the mezzanine" in *Room Service*, "Home again!" in *A Night in Casablanca*), but this, like Lydia's tattoo of Captain Spaulding, seems definite.

24:57/26:01—"She's giving him the whammy!"

Note the heavy shadow over Ilona Massey's breasts in this scene: a clear attempt to minimize the inflammatory potential of her cleavage, apparently during production. (At least, it doesn't look like an optical—but, having said that, why not just dress her in something else in that case?) There seems to be no particular rhyme or reason to this: sometimes they are shadowed, and at other times we get a good clear eyeful. It also sits oddly with the later moment when we see her figure through her back-lit dress, and Chico's hat erects. (The film was singled out by the Legion of Decency for its "suggestive situations, costuming and dancing.") Perhaps Ilona's mother had a hand in the production? According to the *Evening Independent* back in 1939 (September 7): "When Ilona Massey's mother, who lives in Hungary, saw the actress in *Rosalie*, she dispatched a worried letter to her daughter disapproving of the low cut of her gowns..."

26:07/27:14—Searching Harpo

This sequence, in which Egelichi's goons attempt to search Harpo for the sardines and instead produce a bewildering variety of items from his coat (including a barber's pole, a dog, two plastic legs and a huge block of ice, perhaps left over from *Horse Feathers*) is a nice reminder of his ability to store and produce anything, a gift rarely exercised to anything like its full potential since Paramount days. Nonetheless, the moment is usually criticized for two reasons. First, because it is all too obviously engineered, with Harpo standing tight against the wall and the items being passed through a hole, which is fair enough. And second, because the search comes to an end, suggesting that the number of unlikely things he has in his possession is finite, which takes something of the magic away. This seems to me less fair: it's always looked to me as if the villains simply give up, in the specific realization that they *won't* ever reach the end. This is a permissible reading: there is never any explicit confirmation that the coat's secrets are now exhausted. One of the items produced is a mailbox with the name "Moss Kaufman" written on it: a reference to the greatest of Marx writers George S. Kaufman and his playwriting partner Moss Hart. They had written *The Man Who Came to Dinner*, which includes a character named Banjo, an acknowledged Harpo surrogate.

29:20/30:35—Groucho and Egelichi
29:47/31:03—Chico and Lyons

A big chunk of material only present in the longer version, beginning with the most unfortunate absence of all: Groucho's account of his previous attempts to apprehend Egelichi in various disguises; as he tells us he shows us a series of photographs showing the two of them in various outfits and compromising positions. In the final one they are both in bathing suits, hers sexy and his comical. It's hard to imagine any editor willingly excluding this material from a print of *any* required length, showing again that that the rationing of Groucho was contractual rather than creative in origin. This leads directly into another sequence unique to the long cut, showing Chico attempting to forestall the withdrawal of Lyons, the unwilling backer, by showing him a parade of what Groucho's narration calls "tempting inducements"—various luscious chorus girls, which Groucho amusingly describes as "a dozen harmonicas, a solid mahogany lamp table, a sterling silver trash basket, a set of the *Encyclopaedia Britannica...*" before concluding: "But Lyons was no dope—he selected the blonde on the end." It's very dimly possible this deletion was made in the name of the Breen office; more likely for the same reason as the one preceding.

30:39/31:58—The Sadie Thompson number

Sadie Thompson is the lead character of W. Somerset Maugham's short story *Rain* (originally *Miss Thompson*), much-filmed under a variety of titles, and detailing the effect on a small South Seas island inhabited only by natives, uptight missionaries and American Marines of a visiting prostitute/showgirl (delete according to strength of Hays Code influence at time of production). Gloria Swanson, Joan Crawford and Rita Hayworth are her most memorable interpreters. There are a few extra inconsequential lines of dialogue in the longer version, just before this number begins (Mike tells the actors they are playing Marines who haven't seen a woman in months, "So look hungry").

35:04/36:34—"Madame Egelichi, wearing the pants of the dreaded cat woman...."

Until anyone can show me otherwise I am forced to override my gut instinct and conclude that this *is* a reference to the *Batman* villainess. I'd have thought that in those days children's pop culture simply was not the instantly comprehensible reference point to all that it is today, but the reference seems too specific to be an allusion to a cruel, feline type of villainess in a general sense. Time-wise it fits: the character first appeared in comic form in 1940; although initially known simply as "The Cat," she was named "Catwoman" by 1942.

35:11/36:41—Torturing Harpo

Never a sure-fire recipe for fun, and for much of this scene the weird factor is ramped up still higher by giving Harpo a horrible straight, wet wig (perhaps the same one he wore while shaving the aviators?) which really does make him look like a non-comic lunatic. Likewise add to the "strange ideas" file the decision to use the sound of a squealing cat to suggest Harpo's stomach noisily registering its hunger. The ninety-one-minute print has even more torture for your money: the rope-smoking shot goes on longer, and there is an all-new sequence in which Harpo is put in a washing machine. For this sequence, Raymond Burr retains the bizarre "torturer's outfit" that in the shorter print is only briefly glimpsed during the Hungarian rope torture: a silky black smock with gloves and what looks like a skull motif on the front. He also behaves differently in these two sequences, more overtly maniacal, where he is elsewhere stone-faced. Immediately before and after these two sequences he is his usual self, and wearing a normal suit. The saving grace here is that it gives Harpo a chance to show his insane fearlessness (when an apple is placed on his head for deadly target practice, he ravenously eats it).

41:47/43:34—Chico's piano spot

This is a little treat. For Chico's most dignified piano sequence in nearly fifteen years he adapts a routine he regularly used on stage in his nightclub act, here with Leon Belasco accompanying on violin. (According to Louvish, the germ of this routine had been in his kit bag since 1911.) This lovely sequence lasts for some five minutes: long enough to include his last three MGM solos put together, plus change.

60:59/63:35—Harpo's hut

In perhaps the film's oddest scene, we get to see inside the shed that Harpo calls home. Here he keeps not just his beloved harp but also a musical water cooler made from a tuba and a live penguin dressed as himself. The penguin's voice sounds to be pretty obviously human speech speeded up. Unfortunately, slowing it down is no use: it isn't Groucho propositioning Marilyn, or Harpo saying, "My name is Harpo Marx and this is my real voice," or the three greatest aviators in the world auditioning for a part in *A Day at the Races*. It seems to be unintelligible gibberish, and it sounds like a voice played backwards no matter which way you play it. There's a lot of echo, which doesn't help. It might, at a push, be a foreign language. Or it really could be what penguins sound like when they're talking to one another. So assuage your disappointment with the last-ever harp solo, attractively shot against a moonlit sky.

66:28/69:18—Mackinaw

The character portrayed by the excellent Eric Blore, Hollywood butler par excellence, as what Groucho calls "my faithful operator." Presumably, he is meant to be a kind of Dr. Watson, of the Nigel Bruce school, hence the wholesale-quantity Englishness he is required to convey in his one line of dialogue: a completely unintelligible "How jolly!" (It sounds like "Olloy!") He *must* be a victim of reshooting and editing, supporting the suggestion that an original ending in Groucho's office was replaced after the initial shooting with the rooftop chase. In the film as it now exists he disappears almost as soon as he is introduced, after his pipe registers its approval of Marilyn.

67:42/70:35—Groucho and Ivan / Marilyn

We begin with a few seconds of dialogue present only in the long print: again, not the sort of thing I would want to excise were I holding the scissors, especially since it contains three pretty authentic Groucho jokes in quick succession. This leads directly into the bit everyone remembers: the brief appearance of Marilyn Monroe.

"Some men are following me," she says.

"I can't understand why," Groucho replies.

"Someone I met at a lunch counter told me they were making retakes on a movie called *Love Happy* and needed a girl for a bit part," Marilyn later told Ben Hecht. She was apparently then taken to meet Cowan (who she recalled as "a small man with dark, sad eyes") and Groucho (who smiled at her "as if I were a piece of French pastry"). In interviews Groucho often claimed he chose Marilyn from several girls auditioning for the part. (In *The Marx Brothers Scrapbook* he evocatively, if a touch mysteriously, recalled her wearing "this dress with bare tits.") Though she only appears for a few seconds in the film, she figured extensively in its promotion. It seems Lester Cowan recognized her potential early on, and employed her specifically to publicize the film, sending her on a nationwide tour (during which she saw New York for the first time) at a hundred dollars a week for five weeks, plus cash to spend on new outfits. She also posed with Harpo and Chico for a series of charming "Flip-o-Vision" flip books that are among the most worthy of all Marx movie tie-ins. "I have just signed a girl who is a real find," Cowan wrote in a letter in November 1948. "She has the Lana Turner/Ava Gardner type of appeal. She sings and dances better than Betty Grable." Indeed, Cowan was still trying to think of new things for her to do in the film virtually to the last minute, writing to Pickford in June of 1949: "I would like to change ending using a gag which I have in mind for Groucho and Marilyn. If we shoot gag in Hollywood we will subject ourselves to heavy tax liability, as tax collector would claim film not completed and shipped March 1. I'm hoping Groucho may come to New York and I could shoot gag there." (It's not entirely clear whether he means he wishes to slightly alter the extant Marilyn scene, or add her to the very end of the film: either way this idea seems to have gone no further, which is where Cowan's ideas usually went.)

Love Happy's director, David Miller, claimed it was Johnny Hyde, a vice president at the William Morris agency (who was taking a personal and not entirely professional interest in Marilyn at this time) who had specifically brought her to Cowan's attention, which would make Groucho's story of picking her out of a lineup somewhat suspect, dress with bare tits or not. However, given that Miller also recalled Harpo coming to him after commencement of production to ask if it would be possible to fit Chico into the picture (Chico was in fact hired for the film before Miller) I'm happy to believe Groucho on this one. Recalling the film and the tour for the magazine *Modern Screen* in January 1951, Marilyn reminisced: "Groucho chased me across a room, and I was on the screen less than sixty seconds, but I got five weeks work out of the part by going on the PA tour which promoted the film in eight major cities. I felt guilty about appearing on the stage when I had such an insignificant role in the film, but the people in the audiences didn't seem to care."

71:42/74:46—The miming routine

This is now the third time we've seen this, but better a Marx Brothers reprise than another Mike Johnson dance number. It's still pretty funny. The only problem is that it doesn't really make any sense anymore: as Chico acknowledges in some guilty lines of dialogue, there really should be no need for this torturous translation of gestures now that he can read Harpo's mind.

76:28/79:44—The rooftop pursuit

A game effort to recreate not merely the physical exuberance of earlier stunt finales but also the genuine physical invention of *A Night at the Opera*, boosted by some imaginative use of the product-placement signs: as impressive a case of making a virtue of necessity as low-budget cinema has offered. The pacing and editing show the difference between Thalberg's resources and Lester Cowan's, however, and some of the effects are a little basic, but on the whole, it's not bad. The longer version has a couple of extra Harpo gags: a not too effective one where he falls into a vent while shrouded in superimposed smoke, and a better one where he makes music with some steam pipes. But the most interesting thing to look out for is the sign Madame Egelichi walks in front of at **85:10/88:48**, causing Chico's hat to become tumescent. It's for Baby Ruth candy in the eighty-five-minute version, but GE Lamps in the long version. The fact that the spikes of the latter can be seen when Chico walks past the sign even in the shorter version (at **73:57/77:06** in the short cut; **83:02/86:35** in the long cut) proves it was GE originally, with Baby Ruth substituted later. There's also an accidental clear shot of the GE sign remaining in the eighty-five-minute print at **68:45/71:41**, equivalent to **76:43/79:60** in the longer print. While the geography of the rooftop seems to be fudged here, unless Harpo has somehow doubled back on himself, the shorter version nonetheless cuts a couple of seconds of Harpo's pursuers following him, presumably to remove the greater part of the shot showing the GE sign. Note also in the short cut the very slight upward movement of the superimposed Baby Ruth sign uniform with the camera rather than the rest of the background at **68:43/71:39** (when it lights up again after Throckmorton says, "There he is!") showing clearly that it is superimposed. The basic fact of the switch in sponsors between the two versions is in itself a mystery, however: even if Baby Ruth came in late and stumped up some extra cash, why would that negate the need to acknowledge GE's contribution? In odd addition, GE lamps *did* do a promotional tie-in with Groucho's previous film *Copacabana*: Groucho appeared in magazine ads pretending to put a bulb in a reading lamp, and looking, as he so often did when posing for publicity shots, as if he'd sooner be in a neck brace.

90:56/94:49—End credits

Shown against a plain background in the long version, but the same shot of the actors rehearsing used for the opening credits in the shorter.

14

The Incredible Jewel Robbery (1959)

Run for your career, boys. A new monster has arrived scaring the daylights out of actors, producers, theatre owners, sports promoters and sponsors. According to some of the prophets, within six months most of the theatres, nightclubs and sports arenas will be dismantled and converted into parking lots. We may not even need the parking lots, because no American with a television set is ever going to go outdoors again.
—Groucho Marx in the *Hollywood Reporter,* April 28, 1949

Groucho did very well by what termed the "squint-eyed hermits" of the home-viewing audience. His quiz show *You Bet Your Life* jumped from radio to TV in 1950 and soon became one of the best-loved shows of all time. (As early as 1930, in an article discussing the rise of talking pictures he had prophesied: "I look forward to the day when I can sit back in my easy chair, drop a nickel in the slot of my television set and see a gorgeous revue.") So successful did the show make its host that he soon became associated with it first and foremost in the public mind; his films of two or more decades before were—briefly—almost an afterthought.

Chico and Harpo also made their share of TV appearances. But by far their most important work for television was the comedy special *The Incredible Jewel Robbery,* shown as part of the anthology series *General Electric Theater.* And because Groucho also makes a small appearance at the end, *The Incredible Jewel Robbery* represents the last time the three brothers appeared together, and has a fair claim to being considered their final film.

After all, what is a movie, really? More specifically, what are the differences between a film and a TV show, and how fundamental are they to our right to compare and contrast them on equal terms? I fancy our divisions will seem entirely arbitrary soon, when neither the movies nor TV as we know them will exist anymore. Experts and historians may want to keep note of whether a piece was originally intended for the small screen at home or the big one in the high street, but the distinction will be ultimately as academic as the people drawing it.

A more lasting signifier of difference—and one which cuts across the movie/TV divide anyway—might be whether it is shot on film or video, though when both formats likewise give way entirely to newer technologies even this distinction will blur. Future film historians will look back at our Hitchcock filmographies, and the thousands of critical studies, and wonder with genuine bewilderment how we could have been so silly as to not give equal consideration to such masterpieces as "Revenge," "Breakdown," "One More Mile to Go,"

"Wet Saturday," or any of the other short classics he personally directed, on 35mm film, in exactly the same conditions and with many of the same crew as *Psycho* ... but "only" for his TV series *Alfred Hitchcock Presents* rather than the cinema, automatically consigning them to secondary status in our eyes. By then, maybe, they will also be calling *The Incredible Jewel Robbery*—likewise shot on film by a great movie director—the fourteenth and final Marx Brothers movie.

Though Chico's *New York Times* obituary would surprisingly hail its "expert comic pantomime" and call it "grossly unappreciated," critical reaction to the production was gen-

The last hurrah: Harpo (left) and Chico (right) arresting themselves in *The Incredible Jewel Robbery*.

erally cool, at best. United Press syndicated columnist William Ewald called it "a little like trying to set Donald Duck down inside *Bicycle Thief*" which, though surely among the more incomprehensible observations anyone has ever made about anything, is just as surely not complimentary. But while it is clearly not perfect, and indeed could and should have been better, it is certainly underrated.

Here's one possibly helpful way of looking at it. Unlike the majority of great screen comedians, the Brothers only ever appeared in feature films. I've long been fascinated by the thought of what their short comedies would have been like, if only they had made any. Surely they were ideally suited to the form? Imagine the concentrated madness they could have distilled in a twenty minute movie, with no need to worry about plot, motivation or resolution! Well, *The Incredible Jewel Robbery* is the closest we'll get to realizing that fantasy.

Clocking in at a snappy 24 minutes, it is basically an extended sketch in three acts, each "explaining" the one before, that works somewhat on the principle of a shaggy dog story. Writers Dallas Gaultois and James Edmiston were usually to be found in the credits of TV westerns, but two other names on the roll afforded greater hope for optimism. Producer Harry Tugend was a Brooklyn-born former vaudevillian with a writing pedigree in radio comedy, the Ziegfeld Follies and Bob Hope movies. He was also a good friend of the team, and went on to produce Groucho's most interesting TV film: the 1964 adaptation of his play *Time for Elizabeth*. (He also claimed to have been the man who told Groucho to grow a real moustache in the late forties.) Director Mitchell Leisen, though sadly only to be found working on TV by this time (he directed six *GE Theater* productions in 1959 and 60), had graduated from being Cecil B De Mille's costume designer to a director with a notably light touch in the thirties and forties. He had good visual ideas and an eccentric imagination, and his many fine films included *Murder at the Vanities* (a pre–Code murder mystery musical, with Kitty Carlisle), and the *Big Broadcast*s of 1937 and 38. Quite accidentally, the Marxes had been landed with probably their best and most suitable director since Paramount days.

We begin by watching Chico and Harpo, as two suspicious characters ("Nick" and "Harry," respectively), robbing a variety of premises to acquire a confusing assortment of seemingly unrelated items, and stashing them in their cars. (Both Harpo and Chico spend much of the film behind the wheel of their automobile. It seems strange, somehow, to witness them not merely in casual mastery of the art of driving but also conforming to its myriad rules and conventions; the **shot of Chico cruising** at **10:31/10:58** being especially amusing for the incongruously cool assurance of his facial expression. I was tempted to assume we had seen neither do anything of the sort before but this is not so, of course: Harpo was Groucho's driver in *The Big Store*.)

We see **Harpo's final Gookie** at **5:57/6:12**, one of a number of classic Harpo tricks, some not seen since the earliest films, making their farewell appearance here. (He blows **smoke bubbles** at **3:21/3:30** and throughout, and **hands Groucho his leg** at **25:23/26:28**.) The Gookie takes a worthy last bow, as he pulls the face in imitation of a bizarre portrait hanging on the wall of the paint shop he is robbing. (It's a ridiculous painting, amusing in that it is so obviously contrived to facilitate the joke, and captioned underneath "Our Founder': a little grandiose for what looks to be a pretty ordinary, fairly shabby paint store... Was it saved? Is it even now hanging on someone's wall?)

Harpo wears an overcoat and battered hat (with the unusual addition of a bow tie).

It's an outfit seemingly designed to evoke his classic screen look without actually duplicating it. A happy moment, then, when we first see **Chico** at **6:47/7:04** and find him attired exactly as we had hoped he would be, in the classic felt hat and jacket.

Our confusion as to why they are stealing such an odd assortment of things, including a salami sausage and a doughnut, is explained when they pull up their car in a deserted spot and use their swag to painstakingly convert it into a police car. (They use the sausage as a template for the "City Police"insignia on the side, and the doughnut to dot the "i.") Their plan, we next learn, is for Harpo to rob a jewelry store, whereupon Chico, in stolen police uniform, will rush in to "arrest"him and drive him away. Probably the film's biggest laugh, nicely underscored by Elmer Bernstein, comes when we first see **Harpo's disguise** at **19:22/20:12**: that of the popular comedian Groucho Marx. Playing the store manager, first seen at **19:03/19:52**, is **Benny Rubin**, who had been a tap-dancing vaudevillian in the twenties, star of a string of Vitaphone shorts in the thirties, and had more recently appeared in over fifty episodes of *The Jack Benny Program*. The robbery goes to plan, though Chico's bumbling inefficiency when trying to apply the handcuffs leads to Harpo obligingly offering him assistance. Their getaway is then delayed when they stop to take a pregnant woman to the maternity hospital. Alas for them, while they are waiting at traffic lights, a real police car pulls alongside, and the driver notices that they have painted their insignia white on black, instead of black on white... In the subsequent police line-up, the jeweler is unable to identify Harpo as the man who robbed him, and instead fingers a more likely suspect: the one, the only Groucho himself. "We won't talk until we see our lawyer!" Groucho exclaims, in **the film's only line of dialogue** (at **25:21/26:26**). With that, they shake hands, Harpo gives Groucho his leg, Chico takes Groucho's, and **the *You Bet Your Life* duck descends** (at **25:27/26:32**) bearing the legend "**The End.**"

One clever touch is the fact that it is not a "silent movie," merely a movie that is silent: though the characters do not speak we presume they *could* at any point, instantly bursting the illusion. But for various amusingly contrived reasons they do not, until gloriously at the end.

The interlude with the pregnant woman makes sense when viewed in this light, providing two scenes, first when they are flagged down and then subsequently in the hospital, where realism would seem to demand speech so strongly that it is as if the film is challenging itself to put up or stop shutting up—either drop the pretense, or admit to it and start using title cards. But in both cases we are given a deliberately coincidental reason why the ambiguity is maintained without interruption. In other words, not only is it a film with silent movie jokes, the fact that it plays as a silent movie is a joke in itself. Groucho's line is therefore the very funny topper to a running gag.

Like much else in the film, that all could have been made clearer, and should have been made more of. Certainly there are obvious ways it might have been improved. The first half is a touch too leisurely, the second a tad too rushed. The scenes of them acquiring the various items could have been done as zippy montage, and their choices might have been generally more bizarre and seemingly unrelated, allowing for greater absurd invention as they put them to use, in the manner of the sausage and the doughnut. The realization that they have made an elementary mistake painting the car is beautifully done, but it seems to be leading towards an absent finale, perhaps a pursuit with inventive sight gags, rather than straight to the coda. And, needless to say, the laugh track is obtrusive throughout.

The overall feeling I take away from it, however, is that of an inventively-devised, well-told smoking room story. There are several good laughs, and for that matter a small handful of real knockouts, especially the Groucho disguise, the handcuffs, and the beautifully played moment as Chico's face slowly registers his realization of what the two cops alongside his car have just realized for themselves... Best of all is the joyous ending, with Groucho, Chico and Harpo together again, for one last sweet cheerio.

It shouldn't have been their last combined appearance—nor even, for that matter, their next one. Sheilah Graham told her readers in November of 1956 that the Marx Brothers biopic idea, first mooted around the time of *Love Happy*, was again a going concern. This time it was to be called *Minnie*, with Groucho, Harpo, Chico and Zeppo all appearing. Harold Heffernan suggested the following March that Groucho, Chico, Harpo and *Gummo* were set to appear as themselves, and that Zeppo might "possibly" join them. As before, a search ("so far unsuccessful") was underway for youthful lookalikes to play them in the main sections of the film. (Groucho's suggestion that they cast "four beautiful girls and let me be the director" was, apparently, not acted upon.) Sol Siegel was to be the producer, and a script (now called *Minnie's Boys* but unconnected to the later stage play) was duly completed, only to be followed by the usual sound of doors firmly shutting. Joe Adamson read the script a decade later and found little to get upset about: "Their lives were seen in flashback and Groucho, at least, was seen in the present day, recollecting stuff and discussing it with his daughter Melinda. I didn't like it."

Then in 1957 Groucho, Harpo and Chico all appeared in *The Story of Mankind*, a kind of fake-epic from producer Irwin Allen. Groucho had been recruited first, to play Peter Minuit in his familiar style, and wangled in-jokey supporting roles for Harry Ruby and for his wife, Eden. ("She plays an Indian chief's daughter and she's very good," he told columnist Joe Hyams. "She ought to get a lot of offers from Indians.") A slot was even found for Melinda, though in a different scene, as an early Christian. ("An early Christian is a Jew who gets up at 5 a.m.," Groucho explained.)

That Harpo and Chico should sign on too was most likely an idea that suggested itself naturally to Allen once Groucho's involvement had been secured. Traditionally, Groucho was the hardest of the three to tie down to a project, but he and Allen had been friends since the latter produced his two solo films, *Double Dynamite* and *A Girl in Every Port*. (Groucho told Hyams he was doing the film "as a favour to Irwin Allen. He's a crook.") But though they were indeed soon added to the roster, each of the brothers ended up appearing separately, and Harpo (who plays Sir Isaac Newton in pantomime, with harp and a glorious red wig) was not brimming with enthusiasm. "The only reason I took this job was that it required only one day's work," he told the *Yonkers Herald Statesman*. "One day's work is about my limit." As usual it was Chico, the keenest to appear, who got lost in the shuffle, scarcely even noticeable as a monk warning Christopher Columbus that he'll sail off the end of the oith. Writers have traditionally had great sport laughing at Irwin Allen for the short-sightedness of deciding to keep the three apart, but have we any evidence to show, or even suggest, that the decision was his? Isn't there a chance the deciding voice was Groucho's?

Subsequent reunion plans all came to nothing. There was the suggestion in 1958 that they were interested in securing film rights to George Panetta's off–Broadway success *Comic Strip*. (Panetta had also contributed to the script of *Love Happy* and written Chico's sweet

TV show *Papa Romani*.) Then there was talk of them all being wooed by Jerry Lewis for a film called *Crazy House* (set, according to Hedda Hopper, in "a boarding house for vaude-villians" and unappetizingly described as "a slapstick to end all slapsticks") and by Billy Wilder for a satire called *A Day at the United Nations*.

That Lewis's idea sounds pretty horrendous we can hopefully all agree, but there is a tendency to view the Wilder project as an altogether more regrettable near-miss. According to Maurice Zolotow in *Billy Wilder in Hollywood*, it was fully worked out by Wilder and I. A. L Diamond and sold, on the assurance that "Groucho loved it" and "if Groucho loved it, then Harpo would do it for Groucho," to an "ecstatic" Mirisch Brothers:

> Groucho Marx is the brains behind a heist mob. Their scheme is that since the New York police are so occupied with protecting the United Nations delegates, the rest of Manhattan is unguarded. They plan to pull a Tiffany caper! Chico would play the strong-arm guy of the mob. Harpo would be the safecracker. One scene would show Harpo unable to open a can of sardines. Using sewers as a passage, they blast their way into Tiffany's and steal four suitcases of dia-monds. They plan a getaway on a tramp steamer going to Brazil. At the docks, there is an anti–Communist picket line. The police think the Marx Brothers are the Latvian delegation....

And so on. I could continue—Zolotow does, if you're keen—but I'm guessing that's plenty enough to help you resist the temptation to overly mourn this one. And anyway, the record shows that the Marxes, like most great comedians, did best by directors without strong comic personalities of their own, especially one as fanatically protective of his scripts as Wilder. According to an interview published in the *Florida Sunday Independent* of Christmas Day, 1960, it was Harpo who pulled the plug on this one, citing lack of energy and a reluctance to be away from home for up to a year.

Finally, immediately after *Jewel Robbery*, they were signed to appear in a TV series called *Deputy Seraph*, in which Harpo and Chico were to portray trainee angels being sent to earth to do good works by Groucho, their boss. Once on earth they would assume other physical forms, thus Harpo and Chico would only actually be seen in the wraparound sec-tions: there was simply no way that they could have stood up to the rigors of a weekly series otherwise. As it proved, however, even involvement that limited was too much of a risk for Chico's insurers, and the series was cancelled after some intriguing footage, the last ever shot of the three brothers in concert, was taken for the first show. Chico's health worsened rapidly, and he became the first of the team to pass into full-time immortality in 1961.

Alas, poor Chico—oldest, smartest and most beloved of Minnie's five boys. "That's right, folks!" he had cheerily exclaimed, endorsing Groucho's announcement of their retire-ment in the trailer for *The Big Store*, before ominously adding: "but where do we go from here?" Groucho thought he knew exactly where *he* was going: to pastures new, where he could rely on his wit alone, with neither brothers nor greasepaint moustache to trap him in any kind of showbiz yesteryear. And Harpo, for his part, had a blissful home life that more than made up for the reduced professional opportunities, and enough in the bank not to worry. It was Chico who was left most resoundingly in the lurch. Yes, he needed money to feed his gambling, but there was more to his sadness than that: he genuinely loved show business. His only option, to become a bandleader, led to at best limited success. When the *New York Post* wondered what had prompted their retirement in 1942, his reply was entirely to the point: "Why the hell should I want to quit?"

The truth is this: the Marx Brothers *did not* retire in 1941. Rather, Groucho left the act, knowingly forcing his brothers' hands. We have seen how even as early as the pre-production of *At the Circus* Groucho was making plain to journalists that he was fed up and would be bowing out after the next three MGM films. For all his breezy talk of the three of them going their separate professional ways on an equal footing, he must have known that Chico's options were always going to be vastly more limited, and would invariably come back to the Marx Brothers, sooner or later. ("I think I can make good as a bandleader," he told *Billboard* in 1942. "If I don't, I can always go back to selling tootsy-frootsy ice cream.")

The sheer number and frequency of the news reports in the years after *The Big Store* announcing reunion projects suggests that some at least *must* have been genuine, yet all but two went nowhere, and chasing them through the news archives is often a labyrinthine chore. For instance, in 1944, Louella Parsons announced that the Ritz Brothers were planning a musical called *The Barber of Brazil*. Whether she meant Marx all the time and said Ritz by mistake, or if the Ritzes passed on the idea and it got floated around, by the following year she's telling a different story, first that the Marxes are in talks with Paramount about a new movie, and incidentally that Chico "has a deal on the fire on his own—the Ben Bogeaus movie *The Barber of Brazil*." It's possible that Chico had talked Harpo and Groucho into expressing an interest too, since by 6 May Sheilah Graham is claiming that "The Marx Brothers and Abbott and Costello are having a spot of trouble because the Marx boys are making a movie called *Barber From Brazil* and A and C are planning their version of *Barber of Seville*, which Costello sold to Universal for $25,000." If Chico *had* turned a solo project into a group one, the effort rebounded: like all the rest, no more was heard of the Barber of Brazil. The same fate befell a very intriguing suggestion that turned up in the *Saratogan* in 1951: "Broadway producer Lee Sabinson's whooping offer to Groucho Marx to re-team with Chico and Harpo for a musical stage version of Moliere's *The Doctor in Spite of Himself* was flatly nixed. The boys vow they'll never work together again." And Dorothy Kilgallen told her readers in 1954 that "Harpo and Chico are said to be pressuring Groucho to yield to offers for a television comedy series," but if so, the old boy remained implacable.

"Times have changed, and styles in comedy have changed, too," he told an interviewer in 1958. "It would be unwise to bring back that act. It could be disaster. If the memory of the Marx Brothers is good and if people remember them fondly, that's good. Let's keep it that way—a pleasant memory. Besides, I couldn't do that stuff again. Anyway, I wouldn't."

Saddest of all the potential revivals was suggested in Aline Mosby's "Among the Stars" column, in which she describes Marx reunions as "one of the annual false alarms of show business" before adding that "Chico hopes it actually will happen on TV this year."

Chico revealed Monday the team may yet reunite during 1956 in a color spectacular based on their famous movie hit *Animal Crackers*. The oldest of the Marx Brothers announced this hope as he sat on the living room couch of his small Brentwood home he's lived alone in for the past twenty years, since he and his wife separated....

"The music was good, the jokes up to date, only the costumes would have to be changed. It wouldn't be tough. We even remember the episodes. Remember the scene about the painting missing from the house? I said we'll search the house next door. Groucho says there isn't a house next door—so I say we'll build one and I get out the plans," and he lapsed into a perfect representation of everybody's dialogue....

Inevitably, he is again asked why they split in the first place.

"We just got tired of making pictures, it got boresome. Not to me, but to Groucho. Harpo was non-committal," he said.

Apropos of seemingly nothing at all, Groucho got on the wire in 1952 just to tell columnist Erskine Johnson that the act was permanently finished:

Groucho Marx tells me that offers have been pouring in but he won't be teaming up with madcap brothers Harpo and Chico for a TV comedy series designed to revive the zany Marx antics. The mad-eyed, sharp-tongued Groucho will roll along with *You Bet Your Life* and an occasional movie role because "this gives me all the work that I want to do."
"We made fifteen movies together and that's enough," Groucho says.

Of course, the mad-eyed, sharp-tongued Groucho owed Chico nothing; even so, it's hard not to imagine his feelings as he reads that reference to offers "pouring in"—pouring in and then dropping dead, at the doorstep of the brother Minnie had always called "the jealous one."

Meanwhile, the silent one had been busier than he seemed. His autobiography *Harpo Speaks!* appeared in 1961 and was instantly recognized as a classic. Despite Groucho's relentless efforts to be seen as the book-writing brother, it is Harpo's memoir (written up from his recollections by Rowland Barber) that remains the one Marxian artifact fully as essential as the films, and like the films, still delighting each new generation that stumbles upon it. Harpo recalls their New York childhood with an astonishing vividness (and, of course, a wealth of great stories, many of them true), and goes on to provide an equally evocative account of his friendship with Alexander Woollcott and the members of the Algonquin Round Table.

Its publication spurred him to a welcome round of promotional appearances on TV, but ill-health was catching up on him also, and after an ill-advised experimental heart surgery he died in 1964.

The three remaining Brothers were left to enjoy the great Marx revival and reap the fruits of icon-status while still alive, even if the greater public remained somewhat in the dark as to who this fifth brother called "Gummo" was, exactly. He sometimes liked to joke that he wasn't too sure either. By the time he died in 1977, Groucho was too ill to be told.

The former Captain Spaulding had spent the greater part of the decade acting out a fantasy with an adoring world, whereby he would pretend he was still the comedian he had been forty years before and they agreed to do likewise, to their mutual reassurance. He had also found himself a hero of the counterculture following the Marx revival on American campuses, and like many another old man before and since who wakes to find himself an idol of youth, he clearly found it intoxicating. It was seductive incentive to become what they wanted him to be, even without the possibility that bullying and coercion may have played a part too, as many who were closest to him alleged. Entirely up to you whether you want to believe the "real" Groucho was the one who hung out with rock stars and advocated the assassination of Nixon, or the one who preferred an atmosphere of calm, at home, reminiscing with his dwindling peers, with those he loved and understood. But I trust you'll enjoy, either way, these reflections from the seventy-nine year old Groucho in 1969, mere moments before his new constituency showed up:

I don't know what the problems of today's kids are. I'm sure we had problems too, but we didn't burn down the schoolhouses to remedy our complaints. I'm not in much sympathy with the kids. I sympathize with the parents. I happen to be one, and I think it's nonsense to blame the parents when kids take LSD. Kids today are detestable, and thank God mine are grown up.... By and large the parents are superior to the kids they're spawning. You couldn't give me another one. And it's no good saying that the ones you read about are a minority. They're not a minority if they're all yours, and you have to wait for the car to get home to know your daughter hasn't got pregnant, or leprosy. I never thought the time would come when I'd be rooting for Nixon, but it's better than obliteration.

His 1970s one-man shows, the unforgiving recordings of which now sound unavoidably depressing, were sell-out affairs that caused genuine delirium and delight, and if the story behind the scenes at this time (a sorry tale of exploitation too well rehearsed elsewhere to need elaboration here) was much less jolly, at least the public man seemed not quite to have lost the true professional's ability to make reality seem irrelevant, even suspect, for as long as the show was running.

But in 1977 reality finally claimed its fee, and there was something almost Faustian in the way Presley stole the headlines. "You only live once, despite what Jesus or somebody once said," he had wistfully observed in that 1969 interview. "Harpo and Chico promised me if there was anything to that bit they'd get in touch with me. I haven't heard from them. Go out to the garden and tear a flower in four. It won't be a flower again."

Zeppo, the youngest brother who never got to dance in his own spotlight, was now the elder statesman at last. This poignant, unexpected seniority ran out in 1979—then, only the movies were left.

And that, as the couple sat behind you in the cinema used to say, is where we came in.

Epilogue

I know that Rembrandt was deaf (no, that was Beethoven). I know that Van Gogh got hungry one day and cut off his own ear and that Toulouse Lautrec walked around on his knees. And that's about it.

—Groucho

Were they artists?

Surely they were nothing further removed. Just fortunate beneficiaries of the American dream who rose from poverty to success simply because they were lucky enough to have funny bones, and extroverted enough—and hungry enough—to put them on the market?

No, I would argue that the work they created *is* art. It is art of the best and most useful sort: that which engages the mind and enriches the spirit simultaneously. Like Chaplin, they helped define their times and are yet whole enough to speak to all times. For those who love them, they have the very rare gift of becoming a lifelong influence and touchstone.

And they have endured.

The pity is that Groucho, in particular, honestly thought his art was ephemeral. Chico and Harpo doubtless thought so too but didn't care so much: to them comedy was just a job, and they had all that laughter (and in Chico's case, nothing else) in the bank.

Groucho liked to imply as much, but in truth he was highly sensitive about his status in the industry and the popular imagination. Robert Bader's compilation of his published writings abounds with rebuttals to the perceived professional slights of columnists, and he promoted *The Groucho Letters,* his volume of published correspondence, with extraordinary zeal, so keen was he to be perceived as a literary man.

Only towards the very end of his life did he realize that the films he had dismissed decades earlier as turkeys were going to be his ticket to perpetuity: listen to him being interviewed in the fifties and sixties and it is clear that he really did think his quiz show *You Bet Your Life* was the most important thing he had done, simply because of its enormous popularity.

"A lot of water has gone over the dam since I last wrote you," he wrote to Norman Krasna in 1956. "And, if this were *Animal Crackers,* I would then say, 'A lot of dam has gone over the water.' But times and humor change, and what was gold in 1930 turns out to be nothing but dross in '56."

How wrong he was.

It wasn't *Animal Crackers* that was doomed to history, it was 1956. Within a decade and a half those films were back, playing to capacity crowds, and they've never really gone away since.

The reason for their uniqueness and longevity may perhaps be found in their mix of rare comic intelligence and moments of sheerest nonsense, of physical abandon and mordant wit, of disarming silliness and daunting erudition. Their appeal extends equally to children too young for their sophistication and adults too sophisticated for their immoderation.

Other comedians achieve our sympathy and acclaim by first attracting the attentions of, then getting the better of, life's bullies. The Marxes, at their best, never attract our sympathy because they basically *are* bullies, but, wonderfully, they secure our acclaim because they are bullies who target the strong.

Comedy is, or should be, universally self-deprecating, and it should be *fair*. It is one of the great things humanity invented to set against its arrogance, its ignorance, its destructiveness and its self-regard. And the Marx Brothers exposed all these flaws as no other act quite did: with acid disregard for pretension, delusion and duplicity—and at the same time with joyousness, with innocence, and with the certainty that the exposure of injustice can be a pleasure as well as an obligation. All those things that indict us as a species they took on, pierced, made small, and rose above. They pointed a route out of our confusion, and towards clarity. They made us laugh by showing us how serious we are, and how ridiculous that makes us.

They are as important as Goya, or Mahler, or Dostoyevsky, and funnier than all three put together.

Appendix I: Lydia the Tattooed Lady, Uncovered

David A. Cory

Groucho's performance of "Lydia the Tattooed Lady" is a classic, but the Internet abounds in multiple copies of a mistaken transcription of Groucho's introduction to "Lydia."

What shows up in this transcription is:

> My life was wrapped around the circus. Her name was Lydia. I met her at the World's Fair in 1900, marked down from 1940. Ah, Lydia. She was the most glorious creature under the sun. Guiess. Du Barry. Garbo. Rolled into one.

As Nick Markovich (administrator/archivist of the Yip Harburg foundation) explains, when Groucho lists the three beauties that were all rolled into Lydia, the first is Thaïs, the Athenian courtesan who allegedly convinced Alexander the Great to burn the palace of Persepolis. Jules Massenet wrote an opera called *Thaïs*. The Scottish soprano Mary Garden made her American premiere in the title role. The other two women were Madame du Barry, mistress of Louis XV, and famed actress Greta Garbo. Interestingly, Yip Harburg also wrote lyrics for a song ("Salome") which was sung by Virginia O'Brien in the 1943 movie *Du Barry Was a Lady*.

The joke about the World's Fair in Groucho's intro refers to the *Exposition Universelle* in Paris in 1900, and the New York World's Fair, 1939–1940.

There are many historical and topical references in the song itself:

Battle of Waterloo—Napoleon's final defeat by the Duke of Wellington.

Wreck of the *Hesperus*—a poem by Longfellow, based on events that occurred during a blizzard off the East Coast of the United States in 1839. In the poem, a sea captain's daughter is tied to the mast of a ship to keep her from being washed overboard during a storm, but both she and her father die.

Kankakee—a town in Illinois.

Paree—the one in France. You've heard of it—it's been in all the papers.

Washington Crossing the Delaware—the famous painting by Emanuel Leutze of the beginning of the surprise attack on the Hessians in Trenton, New Jersey, December 25, 1776.

Andrew Jackson—colonel in the Tennessee militia in the War of 1812 and later President of the U.S.

Mazurka—a Polish dance.

Niagara—the Falls: you know, the big ones between New York and Canada.

Alcatraz—the island in San Francisco Bay that used to be a prison.

Buffalo Bill—William F. Cody, of Wild West Show fame.

Just a little classic by Mendel Picasso—This is the most puzzling phrase in the song, and one for which I can't find an explanation.

Captain Spaulding—Groucho's character in *Animal Crackers.*

Godiva—the lady who, according to legend, argued with her husband, Lord Leofric, about the oppressive taxes he levied on the citizens of Coventry in the 11th century. He challenged her to ride naked through town, and promised to lift the taxes if no one looked at her. She rode, no one looked, the peasants cheered, and the taxes were lifted—or so one version of the legend goes.

Whalen unveilin' the Trylon—a great turn of phrase. Whalen was president of the World's Fair Corporation, which planned and built the 1939 World's Fair on the site of what was up to that time an ash dump in Flushing Meadow. The symbols of the fair were the Trylon and Perisphere—a big pointy tower next to a big round building.

Treasure Island—another topical reference. Treasure Island is an artificial island in the San Francisco Bay. It is connected by a small isthmus to Yerba Buena Island. It was created out of fill dredged from the bay in 1936 and 1937 for the 1939–1940 Golden Gate International Exposition.

Nijinsky a-doin' the rhumba—Russian ballet dancer and choreographer doing "the dance of Latin romance."

In their book, *Who Put the Rainbow in the Wizard of Oz? Yip Harburg, Lyricist,* Harold Meyerson and Ernie Harburg point out a couple of interesting facts about "Lydia." The song was censored and in order to get it into the movie, Yip Harburg had to add the last stanza:

> She once swept an Admiral clear off his feet
> The ships on her hips made his heart skip a beat
> And now the old boy's in command of the fleet
> For he went and married Lydia

I guess the censors could accept the rest of what they considered a risqué song as long as Lydia became an "honest woman" and got married in the end. Myerson and Harburg also point out that Yip tried his best to make "Lydia" sound like Gilbert and Sullivan, because Groucho was a big fan and would have parties at his house where he would play recordings of Gilbert and Sullivan operas and sing along with them. The one mystery that remains unsolved is the name Mendel Picasso. It seems safe to assume that this is a reference to Pablo Picasso, but although he painted in a number of different styles, it's unlikely that he was a tattoo artist. As far as I can tell, he never depicted Buffalo Bill in any medium. And what of the first name? Picasso's given name was Pablo Diego José Francisco de Paula Juan Nepomuceno María de los Remedios Cipriano de la Santísima Trinidad Martyr Patricio Clito Ruiz y Picasso. That's quite a mouthful, but I don't find anything that looks like Mendel in there.

I have consulted no less an authority than Ernie, the son of lyricist Yip Harburg. Ernie didn't know, but said he would put out feelers to see if anyone does know. So far, no one has come forward with an answer. But through intensive research (i.e., typing "Mendel" in the Google search box), I have learned that in Yiddish, Mendel is the pet form of the Hebrew name Menahem. So, was Yip somehow implying that Picasso was Jewish? Well ... it's not impossible.

Apparently, there is some speculation that Pablo Picasso's maternal grandmother was Jewish. In a speech made by Gary Schwartz at the opening of the exhibit, "The 'Jewish' Rembrandt" at the Jewish Historical Museum on 9/11/2006:

Not long ago I was surprised to read the following sentence about Picasso's grandfather in John Richardson's monumental biography of the artist: "Next to nothing is known about this bizarre gentleman ... beyond the fact that he married a plump young woman from the province of Málaga, Inés López Robles, rumored to be a Maranna (of Jewish descent)" (p. 22). This was thus Picasso's mother's mother. If the rumor about Inés López Robles were true then even the great goy Pablo Picasso was in fact Jewish according to Jewish law.

Rumors about a woman who lived a couple centuries ago aren't much to go on, but then, wars have been launched on less substantial evidence. In the end (or at the end of the day, as the talking heads on TV are so fond of saying these days), it really doesn't matter. Maybe Yip just threw Mendel Picasso into the song because it sounded funny, or because he knew it would drive people like me crazy through the ages, and that's good enough for me. I am reticent to pursue this topic any further for fear of being classified as that most unamusing of writers: the "humor analyst."

Sing along with me now:

> La la laaa
> La la la
> La la laaa
> La la la

Appendix II: Lydia the Tattooed Lady, Exhumed

RODNEY STEWART HILLEL TRYSTER

How often does it happen that one of a world-famous performer's favorite party pieces is one best known for *not* being showcased in one of his films?

Of course, it happened to Groucho Marx, who loved singing the song "Dr. Hackenbush," which had been written for *A Day at the Races.* In his next MGM film, *At the Circus,* he would sing one of his most popular ditties, "Lydia the Tattooed Lady," but in *A Day at the Races* he didn't sing at all, unless one counts "By the Old Mill Stream," a few words of which accompany the hand-washing interludes in the big examination scene, and a single line, just before the fade-out, of yet another song that didn't make it into the finished picture, "A Message from the Man in the Moon." Bizarre as it may sound, what these next few paragraphs will examine is the question of whether, by singing "Lydia the Tattooed Lady," Groucho was receiving a message from the man in the moon.

To achieve this feat, it is perhaps best to go back to Berlin.

In the Marxian world, Berlin is usually taken to mean the man who had no hits in *The Cocoanuts,* or, as Groucho once put it in a letter, "Irving, not Hitler." But in the capital of present-day Germany, in mid–2013, it was hard to walk around without seeing a poster on bus stops, part of a campaign to raise money for a memorial to Dr. Magnus Hirschfeld.

Hirschfeld (1868–1935), succeeded like no other prominent Berlin figure of the 1920s in combining at least three of the main elements the Nazis wished to purge from society: he was Jewish, socialist and homosexual.

He was also an empiricist and founded an "Institute for Sexual Research," as well as what may be considered the world's first gay rights movement. It is not surprising that Hirschfeld's institute and its library were among the earliest targets of the Nazis after they achieved power in Germany. It was ransacked on May 6, 1933, and most of its contents "starred" in the great public book-burning that took place four days later, the bonfire topped off by a bust of Hirschfeld.

Among the witnesses to these events was Christopher Isherwood, whose first permanent lodgings in Berlin had been an apartment attached to the institute. Hirschfeld himself was absent at the time and instead of returning home from his travels, he ended his days in France.

Hirschfeld was a very well-known figure indeed and his nickname was "*Tante* [Aunt] Magnesia." So much had he become a part of the culture that one even discovers a late–1920s solo cabaret act featuring the actor Wilhelm Bendow as a character called "Magnesia the Tattooed Lady."

"So what?" I hear you snort. Tattooed ladies were a staple of a certain kind of entertainment back then. Why should one in 1920s Berlin be relevant to our story, especially if she wasn't even called Lydia?

Ah, but she was....

The character that eventually morphed into Magnesia the Tattooed Lady began life as Lydia Smith the Tattooed Lady in the literary-political cabaret "*Die Wilde Bühne*" ("The Wild Stage") that opened in the basement of Theater des Westens in September 1921.

The actress Trude Hesterberg was behind this venture, on borrowed money (her artistic co-director was Hans Janowitz, best-remembered for co-authoring the screenplay of *The Cabinet of Dr. Caligari*). Among the talents involved were later legendary names like Friedrich Holländer and Kurt Tucholsky.

The Tattooed Lady sketch was not a song, however (though Mischa Spoliansky and Kurt Schwabach had the previous year written "*Das Lila Lied*" ["The Lavender Song"], dedicated to Magnus Hirschfeld). Tucholsky and Bendow were the credited authors of the monologue during which Bendow used the illustrations on his torso suit to comment on events of the day.

What is presumably the first script of this act has been published, with topical jokes relevant to the concerns of 1921. Bendow, however, seems to have gone on with the character till at least the end of the decade, by when, as noted above, she had been renamed Magnesia, a nod in Magnus Hirschfeld's direction that seemed to have required no explanations (Bendow's own nickname was "*Lieschen*").

Nobody claims to know how much of the act was written by Tucholsky and how much by Bendow, though it may not necessarily be the case that Bendow was responsible for more of the material as the years went on. One can read descriptions of Bendow and Tucholsky sitting together many an evening in order to update the act. Not many holds were barred in terms of content and Bendow not infrequently got in trouble with the police.

The act was in two parts, one for mixed audiences and a raunchier finale for which Bendow asked the ladies to leave (this is in the script; it is by no means clear that ladies in the real audience were actually expected to exit). Bendow would introduce himself as coming from the state of Orania, having been born a little behind South America in the city of "New-Popel" (i.e., "New-Snot").

He then explained that most of the political illustrations were to be found on his breast. Here one could formerly have found the Kaiser and his family, now erased. A blank space is explained as waiting for the man who will bring order to Germany's finances. The right breast showed the king of Greece being bitten by a wild monkey (this was true and had been fatal in 1920). Movie star Fern Andra was in the portrait gallery on his back, part of which had, he said, been confiscated by the censor (this part was "anders als die anderen"—different from the rest, an obvious reference to Richard Oswald's 1919 film of that title about homosexuality). Nearby was Herr Lubitsch, seen filming "Sumurun, the Oyster Princess of du

Barry" (three Lubitsch titles in one—du Barry was to pop up in Groucho's introduction to the 1939 song).

The show business jokes continued: the director of the Lessing Theatre was seen at a table counting out and paying entertainment tax to the Berlin municipality; the table was too long to fit in the area available for the illustration and would be continued, Bendow said, on his sister's body. Two honorary members of the film-extras union were named: Emil Jannings and President Ebert. Bendow apologized for an unsightly spot where the tattoo artist's hand had trembled: "In Munich I call the spot an Expressionist painting. Nobody notices." The first half came to an end with Piesecke, described as a lunatic and the only man in Germany who hadn't gone on strike, and, underneath him, the only living creature in Kattowitz that would vote Polish in the Upper Silesian referendum: a louse.

The second half included Adam and Eve (the apple, Bendow claimed, was drawn from life) and nude dancer Celly de Rheydt in her work clothes ("not even a bonbon in her mouth"). Bendow described parts of his body that had not been approved by the police for exhibition in public; there one would otherwise have been able to see Germany's independent party after its split, the Siamese twins ("partly going for a walk, partly on the road to sin") and a circumcision celebration in southern Madagascar.

In other accounts, presumably of later versions of the act, this appears to have evolved into "the tribe of wild horsemen, the Goyim, celebrating Ludendorff's circumcision." (World War I military commander Ludendorff was allied with Hitler during the 1923 attempted coup, the "Putsch." Apparently partly due to his wife's influence, Ludendorff hated Catholics as much as he hated Jews, and Hitler's refusal to join him in the former hatred brought about an estrangement between the two.)

In writing a song about a tattooed lady in the late 1930s, Arlen and Harburg weren't breaking new ground; World War I soldiers had sung "The Tattooed Lady" to the tune of Harry Von Tilzer's "My Home in Tennessee," with lines both suitable and unsuitable for publication at the time (and rhyming "hips" with "battleships" into the bargain).

One published source tries to make a connection between the Bendow act and Groucho's song, but it seems highly speculative. In Ethan Mordden's *Love Song: The Lives of Kurt Weill and Lotte Lenya* (2012), Bendow's act as Lydia is mentioned as part of a description of early 1920s Berlin cabaret and a footnote goes on to inform us that "somebody at MGM took note of Lydia, because the Marx Brothers film *At the Circus* (1939) offered Groucho in a number by Harold Arlen and E.Y. Harburg, 'Lydia the Tattooed Lady.'"

The footnote also points out how much tamer the MGM version was than Bendow's original. Bendow's Lydia was around before MGM was founded, but could still be seen for a few years after that event. The footnote unfortunately conjures up the unlikely vision of an early '20s talent scout standing at the back of the "*Wilde Bühne*," scribbling in his notebook: "Use Lydia character for song after Marx Brothers become famous on Broadway and are finished at Paramount."

However, the mere fact that someone has already gone into print linking the two Lydias is certainly a reasonable excuse to dig around a bit more.

Was Groucho's tattooed lady called Lydia for any other reason than her convenient near-rhyme with "encyclopedia"? Whether Harburg intended anything more than that is surely very hard to know with any certainty today, but it is perhaps worth asking how likely it is that he knew of the tattooed lady of Berlin cabaret.

Bendow's Lydia/Magnesia character seems to have been very well known locally, but how would the news have reached the USA? Or, more specifically, Harburg? By the late 1930s there were many talents in the USA who had seen better days in Berlin, but if one looks at the chronological list of Harburg's songs, he seems to have collaborated only once with one of them, Franz Waxman (as former pianist for the Weintraub Syncopators, Waxman could easily have been a source of information about Berlin cabaret from the late 1920s on, but can't we do better than that?)

Harburg's schoolmate and good friend Ira Gershwin collaborated with Kurt Weill more than once, but not before Harburg had written the song in question. Weill was apparently not very enthusiastic about George Gershwin, but his relationship with Ira seems to have been excellent. Ira and Weill had met no later than the Gershwin brothers' arrival in Berlin in April 1928, when Bendow's tattooed lady character would still have been a staple of his cabaret turns.

However, much more useful than the chronology of Harburg's published songs is the chronology provided by the Kurt Weill Foundation for Music, where one can read: "March–June 1937: Begins working with Sam and Bella Spewack, and E.Y. (Yip) Harburg on a musical play ('The Opera from Mannheim') about German refugee actors. Unfinished lost."

So we do know that Harburg actually spent a lot of time with Weill before working on *At the Circus.*

In his letters to Lotte Lenya, Weill refers to Harburg as brilliant, as well as mentioning that working with him every morning is "a lot of fun," so they probably talked about more than just the show they were working on (and the show they were working on had, in any case, relevance to pre–Nazi German theater).

Although it's highly unlikely Weill didn't know about Bendow's Lydia, can we be absolutely certain he did? We can actually get very close, because at the "*Wilde Bühne*" in January 1922, shortly after the Lydia character was launched there, a piece of theater history took place, for a total of six evenings: the only appearances as a performer on the Berlin cabaret stage by Bertolt Brecht. If that doesn't clinch it, nothing will.

Of course, the preceding was just a little game, in order to demonstrate how straight a potential line drawn between the two Lydias could theoretically be.

Plenty of people who must have known Bendow's version were in Hollywood in the 1930s: "*Wilde Bühne*" composer Friedrich Holländer was around as Frederick Hollander; Marlene Dietrich was there, having shared bills and cast lists on the German stage and screen with both Bendow and Trude Hesterberg. Ernst Lubitsch, a comedy specialist, cannot have been unaware that he was allegedly depicted on Lydia's body. In fact, there were probably enough people in the know to justify Harburg's having used the name deliberately as an in-joke.

In the very unlikely event that Harburg's lyric was really a coincidence, it is almost inconceivable that quite a few people didn't tell him about it afterwards. Exactly when Wilhelm Bendow gave up his tattooed lady is unclear, though Magnesia could not safely have appeared after the Nazis had had their way with Hirschfeld's institute. Despite his apparently open homosexuality, Bendow continued to appear on stage and screen in the Third Reich, though there was a little gap towards the end of the war. He was sentenced to six months in a labor camp for having ad-libbed a line in a shipwreck sketch: he had answered his sketch-partner's cry about salvation upon seeing an island with a drily intoned "Yes, can there be any salvation for us anymore?"—and everyone knew what he meant. (If Bendow spent six months in a labour camp for ad-libbing one line, what would the Marx Brothers have been sentenced to? The Marxes' propensity for ad-libbing begs the question and yet it seems horribly flippant in light of what would probably have happened to them had they been in Germany at that time. And that in spite of the fact that Hitler—the suppressed couplet about whom returned to "Lydia" when Groucho performed it during the war—was alleged to have liked them. In December 1937 this preference and those of other world leaders were reported in the American press, giving the French film magazine *Cinemonde* as the source. The previous month's issue of *Photoplay* had contained an article on the same subject by Cornelius Vanderbilt, with an overlapping but not identical list of celebrities. In his discussion of Hitler, Vanderbilt wrote "I'm told, though I have no proof for this statement, that the Marx Brothers are his favorites...." Is this a case where disclaimer had mutated into fact within the space of a few weeks?)

By the time Wilhelm Bendow was punished for his morale-damaging indiscretion, the biggest production with which he was ever associated had already been released: Goebbels' answer to *The Thief of Bagdad*, the color fantasy epic *Münchhausen*. Bendow had the small but showy part that must be mentioned if the lead-in to these lines is to make any sense: The Man in the Moon.

Notes and Sources

It will be observed that many of the contemporary news reports cited come from obscure and/or provincial newspapers like the *East Somerset Hill Farmer's Gazette and Breeding Guide* or the *Next Street From Yours But One Bugle*. It should be noted that the material in most cases comes from syndicated columns published in many sources, hence the frequent use of phrases like "and elsewhere" and "among others" when quoting them. I mention the exact paper in which I saw the piece, with date, merely to prove that I didn't just make it up to support some spurious point or other, not to imply that I am quoting content unique to or originating from the cited source.

Unless otherwise stated, any citing of Joe Adamson, Richard Anobile, Simon Louvish or Glenn Mitchell in the main text refers to their books *Groucho, Harpo, Chico & Sometimes Zeppo, The Marx Brothers Scrapbook, Monkey Business* and *The Marx Brothers Encyclopaedia*, respectively. Given that Allen Eyles, the other essential source, has written two books on the Brothers, I will indicate which one I'm referring to below, though much material is common to both.

Introduction

The James Agee quote pops up all over. It's from his review of *A Night in Casablanca* in *The Nation*.

Chapter 1

Humor Risk's year of production has been variously claimed as 1920, 1921 and even as late as 1926, but production announcements in contemporary newspapers seem to confirm 1921. The *New York Clipper* on March 9 states that production on the film was now beginning, and the Brothers wrote to *Film Daily* (under their company name of Caravel Comedies) on April 11 to announce it had been completed. The earlier report names John William Kellette as prospective director. Kellette had form in comedies for Fox and Paramount and was also a scenario writer, though his most lasting bequest to popular culture was as a songwriter. His "I'm Forever Blowing Bubbles" remains widely - familiar, and was much performed by Harpo in his later career. In common with consensus, however, the Caravel announcement claims Dick Smith as director. If Kellette had indeed been originally assigned it is just possible he may have had to pull out due to ill-health: he died in 1922, following what the *Variety* obituary (August 11) calls "a lingering illness." ("Kellette died a poor man," the report adds. "He had been ill for months," confirmed the *Washington Times* of August 8.) The Caravel report also names A.H. Vallet as photographer, and promises two swift follow-ups, to be titled *Hick Hick Hooray* and *Hot Dog*. Groucho expresses his desire to see the film again in the *Marx Brothers Scrapbook*. In *Hello, I Must Be Going*, Chandler has him saying "I'd give fifty thousand dollar for a print," but implies he is merely underlining how unlikely a contingency that would be, rather than expressing any actual desire. Harpo's more sincere offer of a reward for a copy was reported in the *Brooklyn Eagle*, 12 December 1945. The United Artists movie offer is in Mitchell. According to *Variety* (April 27, 1927) that one actually got as far as a screen test. As well as these near-misses, the *New York Evening*

Post (February 25, 1928) reported that the Brothers "have been offered a staggering sum by a moving picture company to appear in a screen burlesque on the life of Napoleon Bonaparte," with Harpo as Napoleon, Groucho as Wellington, Chico as Blucher and Zeppo as King William of Prussia. Alas, they "are said to have refused the offer, at least for the time being." In addition, in 1925, both Zeppo and Harpo made film appearances ahead of *The Cocoanuts*, the former in the now lost *A Kiss in the Dark* and the latter, in an amusing featured cameo, in *Too Many Kisses*. Paramount's *Behind the Front* (1926), however, featured what may well have been the first sighting of an authentic Marx routine in the movies, and it didn't involve any of them. As *Variety* noted on March 3, 1926: "One of the laugh hits of the picture, where the pick-pocket drops a lot of knives and forks from his sleeves has been taken bodily from *I'll Say She Is*. It's a Marx Brothers bit." The set report in *Variety* was by Ruth Morris and published on March 15, 1929. A few more on-set observations of their first movie: the *Queens Daily Star* (July 18, 1929) records Harpo worrying that "his beloved pickpockets stuff might be mistaken for trick photography," Groucho unhappy with the early hours and Chico tentatively predicting a future for the team in films, but insisting that they will always need to test the material in front of an audience first. *Standard Union* (February 23) notes the auction scene being one of five that had to be reshot because of bystander laughter on the soundtrack, and spots Harpo between takes "entertaining groups of the little dancing girls with a green wooden snake joined on a strip of rubber." *Huon Times* (September 10) states that takes being spoiled by laughter was such a regular occurrence that auditioning extras were first shown some of the scenes to make sure they were capable of keeping a straight face before being employed. Though the laughs were clearly still as fast-flowing as ever, the topicality of the piece may have faded a little. Alexander Woollcott, announcing the arrival of the play in Los Angeles in 1927 (*Yale Buffalo Courier-Express*: December 21) observed that Florida real estate was "a topic which you might think of as long since exhausted. But it is probably still a laughing matter in California." The Paul D. Zimmerman quote is from his book *The Marx Brothers at the Movies* but I saw it in *Halliwell's Film Guide*. The Eyles quote is from *Complete Films*. Strangely, Groucho sings a few lines of "When My Dreams Come True" in an early draft script of *Monkey Business*. The Andrew Sarris quote is in Byron & Weis. The original playscript is included in Kaufman: *By George*. With regard to Mr. Hammer's sewer pipe samples: a chap called Dennis P. de Loof has argued (according to Eyles in *Complete Films*) that all of the references to sewer pipes in *The Cocoanuts* are examples of phallic symbolism, and the suggestion seems to be catching on. For my dollar there is no hidden meaning to it at all: Groucho is expecting Mrs. Potter to be interested in his sample of sewer pipe as if it could be any kind of an incentive to get her to purchase his real estate (so likely an incentive that he carries it about with him). It's a typical, wonderfully absurd Kaufman-Groucho joke, and the absurdity is the point. There are probably very few occasions when you can say that the whole point of a joke about sewer pipes is that it *isn't* an example of phallic, or any other, symbolism, but here I confidently assert is one of those few. And it is in this rare example of a joke relying for its effect on the absence of phallic symbolism that Dennis P. de Loof discerns phallic symbolism. The *Educational Screen* quote is from the September 1929 issue. **8:37**—Information on *Business is Business* from the *New York Times* (June 6, 1925) and *Variety* (June 10). No copies survive according to Marion Meade: *Dorothy Parker: What Fresh Hell Is This?* (London: Heinemann, 1988). **12:59**—The Dumont interview appeared in the *Poughkeepsie Eagle News* (December 20, 1935) and doubtless many another sheet. **20:27**—An additional note of confusion: Harpo apparently drank ink in the Brothers' live show *Spanish Knights* (or *Spanish Nights*), presented in 1928 between the stage versions of *Cocoanuts* and *Animal Crackers*, suggesting that this, at least, was his own innovation rather than Florey's (*Variety*, April 11, 1928). **26:39**—The story of the Prince of Wales going to see Harpo while in mourning appears in Harpo's autobiography *Harpo Speaks*. According to Harpo it took place during an official MGM-funded solo tour of Europe to promote *A Night at the Opera* overseas in 1936. Harpo details anecdotes from the Italian, French and English leg of the tour, yet oddly I have been able to find no record of it whatsoever anywhere else, nor in fact any indication that he visited any of these countries in a professional capacity at that time. Returning to the Prince, Harpo further states that on an earlier occasion he had been so amused by Harpo and Chico's "flash, flush, flute (etc.)" sketch that he sent Harpo a "velvet-lined hamper" containing all the listed items. **29:53**—The Kaufman anecdote is from Meredith. **31:06 and 62:03**—The Jewish daughters anecdote is in Cavett. The *Animal Crackers* playscript is included in Kaufman: *Kaufman & Co.* **41:10**—Gilbert Ryle popularized the term "category mistake" in *The Concept of Mind*. The Eyles quotes are from *Complete Films*. **51:49**—The material on twenties advertising in general and Listerine in particular is taken from Moore. **56:55**—The manner in which Harpo's vocal ambiguity solidifies into certain inability at MGM has much exercised Marx fans, but Glenn Mitchell has made the thought-provoking point that in his subsequent television appearances Harpo seemed willingly to embrace the limitations we prefer to think of as studio imposition, "rather than seeing it—as we, with the benefit of perspective, tend to do now—as a weakening of his persona." **60:36**—A further reflection on the meaning and effect of the lolly moment, again from Glenn Mitchell: "For me, Harpo's blank expression suggests a detached lack of comprehension of the emotions being expressed—he only senses that something's wrong and offers comfort, as for example a dog might do, without knowing the full circumstances. The offer of a lollipop is a child's approach to making the other person feel better—the lollipop offering no solution to the dilemma but being something a child knows makes people feel better generically, not appreciating that it will make no difference." **71:30**—*Variety* (December 18, 1929): "Mexican cigarette habit is especially strong among ... musicians who claim the weed gives them an extremely sensitive touch and ear."

Chapter 2

The Benchley quote is in *Benchley at the Theatre*. Comparisons between film and play use the script included in Kaufman: *Kaufman & Co.* **1:34:** A questionable speculation on the cutting of the songs: It's very slimly possible that they were removed not solely for time but because there was felt to have been a public backlash against musicals in 1930. As the 1931 *Kinematograph Year Book* noted, looking back at the year just gone, one of its most significant developments was "the great recession of interest in 'musicals'": "For some reason which now seems quite illogical, the industry, in the first flush of the sound revolution, decided that the fate of the strange new thing was somehow hinged pretty largely on music... This cycle definitely wore itself out, before the producers realized it. Consequently, some of the most expensive productions of 1930, which were 'musicals,' did not get very far at the box office, and some of them were total failures." So seriously was this taken that at least one 1930 musical (*Maybe It's Love*: see *Horse Feathers*, 16:00) was issued in America with its songs cut. Most likely, though, it happened the way Arce says: Heerman simply couldn't understand why comedy scenes should have to be jettisoned in favor of songs, and over-rode the objections of almost everyone (including the Marxes) by arranging a test-screening of a compilation of comedy scenes, to see if audiences grew restless and called for music: they did not. The DuBarry scene was cut on the understanding that it would be "saved for another film" (if only!) as the picture was already over length without it. **3:51**—Lillian was Groucho's guest on *The Tonight Show* on August 21, 1962. Thanks to W. Gary Wetstein, Steve Garland and Patrick Barr for enabling me to hear the soundtrack. **4:16**—Ann Roth's appearance in the film is mentioned in *Motion Picture News* (May 7, 1930) and confirmed in Arce. **5:55**—A little more on the earlier Captains. There is also a George Spaulding billed by *Variety* in May of 1914 as "Captain Spaulding." This one seems to be some sort of bandleader or musical impresario who, as we join the story, is presiding over a successful vaudeville show in Honolulu. There are quite a few George Spauldings around in entertainment about this time, including a Hollywood actor and a celebrated composer; my guess would be that this is neither of them. The reason why the seemingly elusive fire-eating Captain is not as regular a presence in the record as he should be is that he seems to have used the name only occasionally. His real (or at least usual) name is W.S. Le Compt: in a 1909 ad he is billed as "Le Compt—The Man That Eats an Arc Light Every Show" (with the bizarre testimonial: "Satan said: He has fooled me for forty years and got me guessing yet"). The *Lewiston Evening Journal* in October 1909 prints a terrifying story of him proving his gift genuine by putting a blacksmith's iron in his mouth, then taking a mouthful of hot lead, all under the close supervision of baffled medicos. No wonder the paper reckons his performances are not to be missed, accompanied on the bill as they are by the comparably irresistible "Funniest Donkey in the World." As simply "Le Compt" or "The Great Le Compt" he figures often in the trades through the first decade of the new century; it is in September of 1910 that *Variety* notes with interest that he is "working under the name of Captain Spaulding" while performing in London (having told us in June that he would be travelling there, still as Le Compt, on the Lusitania). Perhaps he retained the name from then on—several references to "the Mysterious Capt. Spaulding" or "Capt. Jack Spaulding," sometimes sharing a bill with Houdini, post-date this engagement—but I have been able to find no explanation of the name's origins or the reason for the switch. The *New York Clipper* announced his death ("suddenly last Saturday") on December 6, 1916: "He was seventy-two years old and had been in the theatrical business for more than fifty years." *Variety*'s obituary notice referred to him as "W.S. Le Compt/Spaulding." **Not at 8:04**—Consensus insists this cut was made for a Code-era reissue. I've always taken the unpopular position that it was deleted for its original appearance (my guess would be an eleventh hour snip made after assembly, possibly even after premiere, but before general release), a view shared, so far as I know, by Glenn Mitchell alone. It is certain that the cut was *requested* at the time of original production, along with several others that were not actioned. These latter still remain in the print we have now, which means that even in the Code era a lot of obviously risqué material, objected to even in 1930, still slipped through. Perhaps there was simply too much to catch. The Irish censor reported back after a viewing: "I'm afraid I must see this entire film again, as there are so many gags and so much objectionable business that I find it difficult to define them." **12:48**—Interestingly, in 1961 Phil Silvers (standing in for Dorothy Kilgallen in her *Voice of Broadway* column, e.g. in *Jamestown Post-Journal*, July 13) recalled this line as an example of something that was funny simply because it sounded funny, even though "nobody could ever explain why." Goldstein says Kaufman once whimsically took credit for inventing the Fig Newton (and pledged to sell the idea to "some biscuit concern or other") after he claimed to have been struck by a fig falling from a tree and "that made him think of gravitation." **20:28**—The Benchley review is included in *Benchley at the Theatre*. **22:11**—The Harry Ruby anecdote is in Mitchell. **24:23**—I've only found two sources that correctly identify Abe. The *Animal Crackers* script in *Kaufman and Co.* casually pins him down in a footnote, seemingly unaware of the fog of mystery it is so blandly penetrating. And more oddly, Wes D. Gehring's *The Marx Brothers: A Bio-Bibliography* correctly notes Abe's true cartoon identity, yet still somehow thinks Abie the fish man is revealed as "Abe Cabiddle," and the name is only "a comic reference" to Kabibble. The cause of all the mischief is simple: Kaufman and Ryskind and/or Chico opting lazily to call the fish peddler "Abie" too. If they had only called him Janek the Fish Man there would have been neither ambiguity nor confusion. **30:16**—Goldstein states with certainty that the ad libs were scripted from the start; I'm increasingly inclined to believe the same. **30:54**—Further (and subsequent) to these suggestions, I've been alerted to an alternative definition in *Safire's Political Dictionary*. This claims that the "boys in the backroom" are "political bosses," a usage it traces to 1879. The illustration it offers, however, merely uses the word "boys," which is in fact the terminology under discussion: the further extrapolation that these boys are the ones in the backroom may be true but is not illustrated or supported (neither does it account for the currency of "see what [they] will have" as a fixed use). **34:03**—All the stuff about the rules of bridge is thanks to W. Gary Wetstein: I'm bluffing like crazy throughout. The Groucho anecdote is from Stuart; the Chico anecdote is from Gummo's interview in *The Marx Brothers Scrapbook*. **40:15**—Bob Gassel suggests that the reason "Flitz" is blacked out the second time and not the first may not be because it's a brand name (and the first time it had simply been overlooked), but to discourage imitation, given that Harpo is this time using the spray with potentially fatal irresponsibility. Not sure, but worth repeating, I thought. **40:48**—Barry Norman's Zeppo interview was conducted for his television series *The Hollywood Greats* and a transcript was later printed in the *Freedonia Gazette*. The section cited is also in his book *The Movie Greats*. Heerman's cutting down to size of the jail cell legend is quoted in Arce and Kanfer. My feeling is that when you add the cloudy passage of time to a great story that it's in everyone's interest to perpetuate, informed denial counts for more than cheery endorsement. So, given that all those who claim the story to be true add that it was done at Heerman's instigation, Heerman's own dismissal has to carry the most weight. What is certain is that the press loved the story and ran with it, so obviously hokey additions began to pile up all around (like a sign on the outside of the cell saying "Marx Brothers hoosegow," according to *Motion Picture News*, May 7 1930): I'm putting my money on the Heerman version. Harpo's and Chico's medical problems were widely reported, e.g. in *Hollywood Filmograph* (July 10, 1930); that they delayed reshooting is in *Film Daily* (June 23) and *Variety* (July 2). The electrical storm was reported in *Yonkers Statesman* (November 13) and *Brooklyn Daily Star* (October 24).

Information on the use of stand-ins in the film culled from *Film Daily* (May 5, 18 and 22) and *Motion Picture News* (May 31). *Variety* (November 12, 1930) on the Zeppo-for-Groucho stage switcheroo: "With Groucho in the Michael Reese Hospital with appendicitis, and Zeppo wearing his mustache and clothes, the performance of the brothers lacked spirit. Zeppo was adept at the substitution and when the boys know where they stand it will be okay. At the first show they were inevitably rather listless, uncertain, and didn't do well." One last morsel about stand-ins: according to *Variety* on August 29, 1933, the stand-in Groucho was then using quit his job in order to double his salary at RKO by becoming stand-in to both Wheeler *and* Woolsey! **44:58**—*Cocoanuts* playscript in Kaufman: *By George*. **75:50**—I don't know why Alvin Kelly was known as "Shipwreck." **76:44**—The stolen Beaugard, incidentally, is not the only notable painting to be titled *After the Hunt*. American artist David Dalhoff Neal produced another in 1870: an interior, and with fewer dogs, but recognizably in the same ball park. It's possible it provided the inspiration, however tacitly, for "the famous Beaugard." **83:01**—The material on *Abie's Irish Rose* makes use of Benchley, Meredith, Adams and Ford.

Chapter 3

Robert E. Sherwood reported on the premiere in his "Moving Picture Album" column of August 9, 1931, published in the *St Petersburg Times* and elsewhere. As to the possibility of their returning to Broadway, Glenn Mitchell reminds us that they "seemed consistently to ponder a return to Broadway, if only perhaps as a lever in disputes with film studios." There's even reports of a return to Broadway being planned after *The Big Store* and their supposed retirement that, according at least to the *Brooklyn Eagle* (August 8, 1941) might even have found room for Zeppo "for sentimental reasons." Groucho and Norman Krasna were supposedly co-writing the book for that one, but *Animal Crackers* remained their Broadway swansong. Norman McLeod's praise for Zeppo is from a studio release published in the *Schenectady Gazette* and elsewhere in late '31. After steering Fields and the Marxes to certain glory, McLeod went on to direct Burns and Allen, Charlie Ruggles and Mary Boland, Leon Errol, Danny Kaye, and Bob Hope five times. His films tapped perfectly into the commercial mood of their times, which is why they were usually popular then, are often forgotten today, and frequently have incredibly evocative titles like *Redheads on Parade*, *Swing Shift Maisie* and *Never Wave at a WAC*. (The "Z," incidentally, stands for "Zenos.") This is technically the first of his three Marx directorial assignments, not two: he later directed a 1963 edition of *Celebrity Golf*, featuring Harpo. He also co-directed (with Norman Taurog) a film called *Finn and Hattie* the same year as *Monkey Business*: this Paramount comedy starred Leon Errol, ZaSu Pitts and Mitzi Green, and was based on a novel by Donald Ogden Stewart, but its main point of interest here is that it re-uses the *Monkey Business* ship set. Mankiewicz's views on comedy and his writers are in Meryman. That Perelman and Johnstone did not hit it off on a personal level was told me by Johnstone's great-granddaughter Meg Farrell. The Sherlock Holmes quote is from *The Hound of the Baskervilles*. My speculation that "the gags-used to gags-written ratio must have been more wasteful here than on any other film in history" is amply confirmed by a perusal of the early script credited to Johnstone, Perelman and Sheekman, and dated April 11, 1931. While, tellingly, the lines given minor characters often read like a transcript of the finished film, barely one line in twenty of Marx dialogue has survived intact. Sometimes the changes are wholesale, with the loss often to be regretted; sometimes they are organic, and usually improvements: Groucho's response to Thelma Todd's enquiring what he is doing in her closet ("Nothing—come on in!") was originally "Nothing—but it's not a bad idea!" When Chico claims that his father and Columbus were partners, Groucho's protestation that Columbus has been dead for four hundred years was originally met with a simple joke: "That's why they split up!" Much better the imponderable logic of, "Well, they told me it was my father." In these and many similar moments we clearly see the Marxes testing, rejecting and improving, just as they had done on Broadway and would do again in the Thalberg live try-outs. **1:31/9:46/27:42**—The Glenn Mitchell quotes are from personal correspondence. The result of the Olsen & Johnson lawsuit was reported in the *Berkeley Daily Gazette* of January 5, 1932. There are references to the film being called *Pineapples* in, among others, *The New York Sun* (January 26, 1931) and *Film Daily* (January 28, 1931); Groucho explained the meaning of the title in *Western Mail* (May 21). **7:34**—Innocence is further established by the presence of the joke in the April 11 script draft. **9:00**—When they performed the sketch in London, Chaplin (or, in some sources, Jolson) imitations were substituted for those of the unknown Frisco. That the immigration line is not in any of the incomplete surviving original *I'll Say* scripts was confirmed by Noah Diamond, who has painstakingly pieced the work together (and patched up the holes) in order to at last bring it back to the stage, with spectacular success. **12:17**—I have been unable to find the identity of the unseen puppeteer in any official or contemporary source; nonetheless there seems little serious doubt that it was Albert Levinson, aka Al Flosso, identified by *Variety* (November 13, 1937) as one of the very few notable exponents of the art in America, and to be found taking out ads as a Punch and Judy performer in *Variety* in the late twenties. It is stated as certain fact in Flosso's biography *Coney Island Fakir* by Gary Brown. Interestingly, there was already a link between Flosso and the Marxes: his father-in-law Pop Krieger (whom he first met and associated with as a boy) was a famous Punch and Judy man and a friend of the Marxes' grandfather, and Flosso himself had known the Brothers growing up in the same neighborhood. Magician Ben Robinson was told by Flosso's son that his father was without doubt the elusive puppeteer in this scene, and further notes the telling similarity between the unusual puppet heads seen in the film and those which survive among Flosso's effects. I suspect the Billy Barty sequence was deleted for time, since the Punch and Judy scene was far more rudimentary in earlier scripts and was probably built up on set. This meant it swelled to fill the available slot and made the subsequent material with Barty unnecessary. **16:00**—For the same reason, I imagine, we only briefly meet former vaudevillian and Hal Roach regular Rolfe Sedan (you've seen him a hundred times, often as a waiter, all the way from *Trouble in Paradise* to *Young Frankenstein*) as the genuine ship's barber. According to a report in the *Philadelphia Inquirer* (June 28, 1931) this was originally a featured comic role. Most cast lists also place him under the whiskers as one of the aviators in *A Night at the Opera*. There is another connection with *Road to Rio*, less relevant but worth noting all the same: the presence of Harry Woods, as Alkie Briggs in one and ship's purser in the other. **17:57**—The Thelma Todd interview appeared in, among others, the *Salt Lake Tribune*, July 31, 1932. The April 11 draft script describes Thelma's character as "a dumb, sexy, tart-type." **19:26**—The Thomas Lindbergh line is present and correct in the April 11 draft. **27:42**—Joe Helton is for some reason "Joe Farina" in the April 11 script. The name change may be taken to suggest the mutation into the urbane, more sophisticated figure we see in the film (perhaps an effort to null the implications of the Marxes aligning themselves with a gangster). Certainly in the earlier draft he is a much more typical gang boss, and far less affectionate to the Brothers, who rib him as mercilessly as Groucho does Briggs. One excellent lost sequence at Farina's house begins with Chico's superb conversation-opener: "Nice house, but you're burning too much coal." Groucho then shifts into Mr. Hammer mode, producing a lump of coal from his pocket and attempting to sell it to Joe on the grounds that it doesn't burn at all: "No trouble with ashes, no lame backs from shovelling, lasts a lifetime, and best of all there's no heat." When Joe crossly explains that they burn oil rather than coal, Chico produces a can of oil and begins oiling Joe's joints, whereupon the former gangster takes a swing at Chico! "I don't blame you," Groucho continues, producing a can of oil from his own pocket. "Now here's an oil that's right up your alley—and that's where I got it from." **40:17**—Harpo's use of a gramophone is not to be found in the April 11 draft. Here, after the other three have attempted to pass themselves off as Chevalier in the established way, Harpo uses different passports to claim the identity first of a Chinese passenger called Charlie Hipsing, then a bearded Russian called Alexia Valeska. "Well, at least you didn't say you were Maurice Chevalier!" says the inspector, whereupon Harpo also produces Chevalier's passport, but merely whistles the song. **46:25**—As expected, the April 11 script shows the post-shipboard sequences to have been considerably longer and more elaborate, beginning the day before the party and containing much more detail during it. As well as for the reason I suggest—the shift in primary focus to the scenes on the ship—I wonder if the more general abbreviation that becomes apparent from a reading of the draft may be due to its having been written to fit the more leisurely 90 minute frame of its two predecessors, rather than the streamlined contours that were ultimately imposed on the three Hollywood Paramounts? **51:19**—The Kaufman anecdote is told by Dick Cavett in his foreword to *Kaufman: By George*. **54:03**—The joke is more simply stated as "You must have been a baby when you got married" in the April 11 draft. **58:27**—*Cocoanuts* playscript in *By George*. **63:88**—No old barn in the April 11 script: instead the climax takes place in the waterfront warehouse that hosts Briggs's bootlegging operation. Another example of the toning down of gangster elements in this (and their subsequent) film.

Chapter 4

One question still dangling over *Horse Feathers* is the extent to which it does or does not derive from an oft-mentioned early project provisionally entitled *The Marx Brothers at Yale*. This may well have been just a fall-back title with no particular concept attached, something to dangle to inquisitive journalists when there was nothing more concrete in the offing; nonetheless, it was dangled often. One of the most intriguing sightings was in a 1927 edition of Alexander Woollcott's *Theatrical Stitches* column (e.g. in the *Yale Buffalo Courier-Express*: December 21), where he claims it is one of the two projects being considered as the team's forthcoming stage follow-up to *The Cocoanuts*. (The other, "a farce dealing with Long Island life and called *While London Sleeps*" is recognizably the winner, notwithstanding the provisional title that would be plenty inexplicable enough even if it hadn't just served duty as the title of a Rin Tin Tin movie.) Even odder is the suggestion made a year before in the *Times Recorder* (Zanesville, Ohio: October 31) that it will shortly begin production as the team's first film (with George Kaufman in place to write it, yet). Oddest of all is the claim apparently made by Harpo in *The New Yorker* prior to the filming of *Monkey Business* (July 4, 1931; thanks to Glenn Mitchell) that their next film would be "a college picture" to be entitled *The Marx Brothers at Vassar*. Whether a joke on Harpo's part or an amusing mishearing on the part of his interviewer, the disguised title surely points to the same project. If it is true that the original plan for a follow-up to *Monkey Business* was something in the nature of a direct sequel, and that it was nixed owing to studio nervousness over gangster subjects, it's possible that the old "stand-by" idea was again picked up, but on this occasion, with time running short, was developed into one of their most celebrated and perfect films. Here's some ballast for *Horse Feathers*-as-genre-parody, from the *Argus* (November 7, 1932): "Surely, after this, the American producer will never dare to make a college picture again? The Marx Brothers have laughed it off the screen in *Horse Feathers*. The professorial bluff, the blonde and beautiful co-eds, the big shots of the campus, and the heroes of the football field, taken seriously by the camera for three years, are rolled into pantomime." Some indication of what the original "burning college" ending was like can be gleaned from the description lazily retained in the studio's promotional materials, and even more lazily quoted in contemporary reviews: "That night the Huxley students celebrate with a huge bonfire. But Harpo decides the bonfire isn't big enough for such a sensational victory and sets fire to the college. Suddenly, the word comes that the villainous gambler Jennings (David Landau), the Marx-men's arch foe, is trapped on the third floor. Groucho cigar and all, runs into the blazing building, amid cheers. He returns unexpectedly and hands a bystander his cigar. "There's no smoking in the corridors," he explains, and rushes back into the building. He reappears— not with Landau, but with a diploma for Zeppo. "I'll bet that'll burn Jennings up," he remarks as he retrieves his cigar butt." On the lost material: Perhaps my comment that censorship cannot account for the cuts is a tad too strident. The records of the Irish film censorship board, at least, do confirm that among the cuts demanded were the "lamp post incidents," while "a lot of mauling" in Thelma's room "should come out." **2:27**—*Cocoanuts* playscript in Kaufman: *By George*. **8:45**—Several sources, including Eyles, Louvish and the IMDB, name Pendleton's character "MacHardie" but contemporary trade magazines, based on official studio releases, confirm it as McCarthy. It would seem later (largely British) ears have been led astray by the hardboiled American pronunciation of the name given by the film's characters. Thanks to Glenn Mitchell for alerting me to this! According to a profile of Pendleton published in *Picture Play* in 1937, he was from "one of the oldest Yankee families" and, despite being "usually cast as a stupid character," was in reality "an intelligent, well-read and brilliant scholar" who "speaks French, Portuguese and Spanish as fluently as a native." **9:13**—I found the line about Chico boring holes in cakes of ice in several papers, including the *Reading Eagle* of September 24, 1932. Andy Marx told the story about the Lindbergh kidnapping during his introduction to a screening of the film at the Aero Theatre in Santa Monica in January 2013. It's also alluded to in Kanfer. Nat Perrin's observation concerning *Monkey Business* is confirmed by a reading of the draft script dated April 11, 1931 (see note for Chapter 3, 63:88, above). **15:50**—Fleischer cartoons, being released through Paramount, often feature Paramount music. Variations on "Whatever It Is, I'm Against It" and "I'm Daffy Over You" also show up in Popeye cartoons. **21:05**—Other comedies in which Tong wars are depicted include Keaton's *The Cameraman* and Langdon's *Feet of Mud*. **22:32**— Robert Greig interview in *Schenectady Gazette* (September 2, 1930) and doubtless elsewhere. **52:46**— Chico's accident was extremely serious, and held up filming for three months. According to the *Vidette-Messenger* (June 22, 1932) his knee was "broken in six places" and "mended with silver wire while Chico stayed for weeks in a hospital." While the film was on hiatus, according to *Modern Screen* (July 1932), "the director took a European vacation, Groucho took to polo, Harpo went to the beach and Zeppo picked up some extra change from a radio broadcast. In fact, everyone is having a swell time—except Chico. Says he's going to try eating worms."

Chapter 5

British readers may remember sitcom couple George and Mildred doing a variation on "his Excellency's car" during their opening credits. The Marxes' explanation of the title *Oo La La!* is in *Variety*, October 11, 1932. The details of their lawsuit against Paramount are from *Hollywood Reporter*, January 24, 1933. Two somewhat tall claims were added to the Marx Brothers Inc. saga by *Variety* on April 18, 1933. First, that Groucho and Chico were about to travel to New York to work with Kaufman and Ryskind on the *Of Thee* screenplay; second, that the Brothers planned a further six films under Producing Artists, but not as stars: "However, one of them might function as a director." Which one, I wonder? Harrison Carroll's syndicated *Behind the Scenes in Hollywood* column suggests that in addi- tion to *Of Thee* and *Grasshoppers* ("the story that the comedians were supposed to do at Paramount") the team was considering "a burlesque of *Quo Vadis*" as independent producers. We also get an indi- cation of how they might have been slotted into *Of Thee*: "Groucho will play the president, Harpo the apologetic vice president whom everyone ignores, Chico the French (or possibly Italian) ambas- sador and Zeppo the president's secretary." (*San Matteo, California Times*: April 11, 1933.) Louvish quotes McCarey's *Cahiers* interview. The addition of James Parrott to the writing team (to provide "additional comedy") is in *Film Daily*, July 31, 1933 and *Hollywood Filmograph*, August 5th. A few observations on the extant draft script (credited to Kalmar & Ruby and Grover Jones) in which Zeppo plays Bob Firefly (and Vera, posing as Trentino's niece, is referred to throughout as "Vera Trentino"). It's very different from the version we know, with even the most recognizable scenes still comprised of largely different jokes and dialogue. Much of the second half is entirely different. As expected, most of the additions that smack unmistakably of McCarey are nowhere to be seen; the same goes for the excellent radio-derived material supplied by Perrin and Sheekman. A few further observations: There is free use of the word "dictator" in approving contexts: "You must indeed have great faith in your new dictator to give him such a magnificent reception," one of the dignitaries says to Dumont in the opening scene. Firefly is revealed as "an agent for the Eureka Ammunition Company." There are two hilarious Groucho-Zeppo letter dictation sequences, modeled transparently on *Animal Crack- ers* ("Take a letter" "Who to?" "None of your business!") that have been gutted to make room for anonymous slapstick. The slight jumps in "Wait Till I Get Through with It" mark messy and regret- table cuts in the negative, presumably for the same reason, since there is nothing censorable in the vanished portions. The same filleting process has afflicted almost all the dialogue routines. The initial conversation between Firefly and Chicolini wallows gorgeously over several pages, with room for some authentic "why a duck"–style material (Groucho asks why the dog is not in a pound; Chico replies he only weighs ten ounces) and this irresistible gag: Groucho: "What do you call your dog when you want him?" Chico: "I don't want him." It is also in the middle of this blizzard of sublime nonsense that Chico, not Zeppo, tells Groucho that the way to annoy Trentino is to insult him, and not to get him to leave but specifically to get him to start a war, so that Groucho will get a sale for his ammunition. (The supposedly satirical elements of the scenario are much more overt throughout.) Chicolini and Pinky are cousins. The last scene has another lengthy musical number, and Firefly declared king. Some regrettable lost gags in the battle scene, too, especially this glorious exchange: Groucho: "How're ya fixed for cavalry?" Chico: "I've gotta five thousand men but no horses." Groucho: "That's funny, we've got five thousand horses but no men." Chico: "That's all right—our men can ride your horses." Groucho: "Not a bad idea. If our horses get tired they can ride your men for a change." The material on the "dictator craze" movies makes use of Doherty and borrows the phrase from him. The NRA is of course the National Recovery Act (i.e. the "New Deal"), not the National Rifle Association. The material on fascism, the New Deal, Iron Pants Johnson and Jacob Maged makes use of Jonah Goldberg: *Liberal Fascism* (London: Penguin, 2007) and Robert O. Paxton: *The Anatomy of Fascism* (London: Penguin, 2005). Worth a mention that Robbin Coons (e.g. in *Niagara Falls Gazette*, August 11, 1933) says the original idea of doing a comedy about a dictator was Groucho's. If the Ruritanian elements of *Duck Soup* take your fancy, the essential next port of call is *Million Dollar Legs* (1932), again from Paramount, and with W.C. Fields and Jack Oakie—temporarily considered as *Duck Soup* replacements when the Marxes upped sticks and tried to go independent. Also in the cast: one Susan Fleming, an actress whose beauty stood out even in a town that farmed for that commodity, and who eventually became Mrs. Harpo. About a mythical country that decides to enter the 1932 Olympics (rather than wage a war, losing it vital satire points), it is hilariously funny. Herman Mankiewicz produced from brother Joseph's script. Also running along similar lines was Wheeler and Woolsey's *Diplomaniacs* (1933), again by Joseph Mankiewicz, and with support from *Duck Soup*'s Edgar Kennedy and Louis Calhern. (William Seiter directed.) Such were the similarities, according to Ed Watz (*Wheeler and Woolsey: The Vaudeville Comic Duo and their Films,* McFarland, 1994) that Paramount went so far as to unfairly accuse Mankiewicz of plagiarizing *Soup* (or *Cracked Nuts* as it still was at that point). The *Sydney Morning Herald* review of *Horse Feathers* is from December 2, 1932. "They'll piss!" is in Adamson. The Harold W. Cohen review appears in the *Pittsburgh Post-Gazette* of November 18, 1933, among others. **1:08**—The Margaret Dumont interview is from *Modern Screen* Magazine, January 1934. Amusingly, the *Albany Evening News* (September 11, 1933) carries a mention of Groucho enjoying head massages from Raquel Torres on set. Presumably not at the same time that Maggie was scratching his leg: that would be sheer decadence... **2:51**—Back when it was still called *Cracked Ice*, it was announced that a certain Patricia O'Roark had been given a starring role (e.g.: in *Hollywood Filmograph*, November 19, 1932) and she was (presumably) still in place in March of '33, when *New Movie Magazine* published a (presumably) silly piece claiming that she won the part while she "tramped wearily day after day from studio to studio looking for a job as a stenographer." Then, while she was "sitting in the waiting room at Paramount wondering how long a girl can be expected to go between meals" she was spotted by "a couple of half-familiar men" who turned out to be Marx Brothers and offered her a role on the spot! (It doesn't say which two...) This suggests serious studio publicity build-up, yet Miss O'Roark disappears completely from the record from this point on. "The *Jaws* of its day" is from *Halliwell's Film Guide*. Glenn Mitchell warns: "You can't discuss Raquel Torres's film career without mentioning *White Shadows in the South Seas* (1928)..." so consider that a mention. **3:34**—Michael J. C. Taylor, who has spent many years researching Zeppo's individual life and career, has suggested that the fourth brother's contribution to the film was considerably larger not just in earlier script drafts but even in the original shoot. Though it is well known that he was downgraded early on from being Groucho's son, Bob Firefly, to merely his secretary, Taylor claims that in the original shoot he is a Freedonian spy, romancing Raquel Torres (and performing an intricate dance number with her) for reasons of political subterfuge. Further, he states that he had been told by Paramount and Universal archivists that this material still exists. (Needless to say, that would be some big deal if it ever saw the light.) Taylor speculates that the loss of these scenes was directly linked to Zeppo's retirement: either that it proved the last straw and prompted it, or that he had already made his intentions clear and its retention was therefore deemed unnecessary. Whatever the truth about his retirement, it certainly wasn't sudden or unexpected. *Variety* reported it as imminent in 1928 (October 31), and still further back, during the stage run of *The Cocoanuts* in 1926, the *Times Recorder* (Zanesville, Ohio; October 31) announced that the Marxes were poised to bring their act to the movies as a threesome: "Groucho, Harpo and Chico are to say goodbye to Zeppo, who is to desert the song and dance stage for the legitimate, devoting his time to the lighter plays." And in 1932 (the year that, according to the *Niagara Falls Gazette* [February 22], it "now seems certain" the whole team will go their separate ways to pursue solo interests) he appears to have been acting on a desire to become a screenwriter. *Variety* (October 11) claims that Universal is expressing interest in a script he has penned entitled *Muscle Bound.* It's a story that cries out for skepticism, but it would seem the script really was written, and is preserved among the Groucho Marx papers held at the Smithsonian. An odd claim that shows up a few times—and seems so inconsequential as a publicity squib that it's most likely true—is that Zeppo personally came up with the title *Cracked Ice* (e.g.: in *Hollywood Filmograph,* September 10, 1932). It's a good title, too good to waste even, perhaps explaining why it was immediately appended to the sixth Paramount vehicle that both studio and stars fully expected to happen (announced in *New Movie Magazine,* October 1933). **6:08**—As the variant performance of this scene preserved in the extant radio promos reveals, it changed notably on the studio floor: the sequence we see is likely therefore a patchwork of more than one recording on different days—still no excuse for so blatant a continuity gaffe, however. **22:10**—Nat Perrin recalls Chico bringing a dog to script conferences in *The Marx Brothers Scrapbook.* The story about Groucho naming a dog Chico is definitely in the book *Brothers: On His Brothers and Brothers in History* by George Howe Colt, but it's also in one of the main Marx books, as an example of Groucho's occasional mean-spiritedness towards his brother. I'm pretty sure it's the *Scrapbook,* but I didn't make a note when I read it and now I can't find it again. **34:14**—Andrew Smith mentions the dark keys in *Marx and Re-Marx.* **39:17**—All but impossible to imagine what they had in mind for this extra sequence, but the *New York Sun* is one of several to state unequivocally that Groucho will play the wolf and the other brothers will play the pigs. **42:32**—As far back as 1925, *Variety* (November 11) carried a story about vaudevillian Fred Schwartz suing Fox because of its use of the mirror routine in the film *In Hollywood.* Schwartz claimed the routine was invented by his father. **52:52**—In fairness to McCarey, my subsequent reading of the earlier Kalmar/Ruby/Jones draft shows this scene embryonically present and correct, and though the details are entirely different, they are equally witless. Nonetheless, Leo must retain some measure of responsibility even if he contributed none of the material in the finished film personally, simply for opting to retain it when so much wonderful dialogue was cut. And thanks to Glenn Mitchell for reminding me that the "funny" music at the end of this scene is "The Old Grey Mare Ain't What She Used To Be." Speaking of McCarey, let's close on some wild speculation. The *Cumberland Sunday Times* (September 3, 1933), in a tantalizing snippet, refers to McCarey "donning make-up for a scene" in the film. Now, even if true, there's no reason to think he will be clearly visible, or even if his appearance made it to the final cut. Nonetheless, the very blandness of the news item, the way in which there is no elaboration of any sort to make it an amusing anecdote, suggests accuracy to me, and McCarey certainly had enjoyed doing unbilled walk-ons in earlier films with Charley Chase, and would again in *Make Way For Tomorrow* (1937). So, if he's doing it for fun he'll want to be visible in some way even if not distracting; he's not likely to be in a line-up of identically dressed soldiers, or part of a distant crowd. He's also not likely to be in any of the big ensemble sequences, which are so carefully choreographed and spatially arranged (and probably would have meant hours, likely days, stuck on the set). So I think if he's here at all, he'll pass through or by. So here's where the speculation gets wild. Modern cast lists do an admirable job of naming the uncredited actors playing various unnamed party and reception guests. But there's one walk-on character that nobody seems to be able to put an actor to, and it's a surprise, because he's both showy and named: the Honourable Pandooh of Mufhtan. From the little we see of him, he seems to be an ordinary white guy in a big fake beard...

Chapter 6

The Louella Parsons quote is from her syndicated column of September 11, 1934. Although MGM seemed oddly reticent to admit to Zeppo's departure, it was already widely known. There may have been a degree of wishful thinking in this release, which appeared in *Photoplay* in June of 34: "Those who have worried about Zeppo Marx's abandonment of his three other brothers to turn agent, will be glad to know that it won't be the 'Three Marx Brothers' but still a quartet. Zeppo's parts in the insane operas were never enough to take too much time, so to keep the professional name intact he'll do a walk-in-and-out at least in future pictures." It suggests that someone felt strongly either that Zeppo accounted for a significant portion of their popularity or, at the very least, that the name "The Four Marx Brothers" was not to be given up lightly. *Variety* announced his departure on March 27, and again suggested that continued film work is not to be ruled out entirely, but added pointedly, "he says if he is too busy in the agency business he can phone his part over to the studio as they have screen images of him to dub in the sound." The quote about Thalberg is from Loos. The E.V. Lucas quote is included in Dilys Powell (Ed): *Punch at the Cinema* (London: Robson, 1981). Though the film's brilliant title must have greatly stoked audience expectation, it is worth noting that a few papers (e.g. *Motion Picture Herald* of June 1, 1935) announce the forthcoming production as bearing the much more Paramountesque title of *Raspberries*. Groucho's comment to Paul Johnson is recalled in the latter's *Brief Lives* (London: Hutchinson, 2010). Harpo rhapsodized about the pre-filming tour in the *New York Times* of November 17, 1935. Chico adds his view via *San Diego Union* (May 9). Further testimonials from the latter source, from Morrie Ryskind: "Far more important than the individual triumph of each Marx Brother during this personal appearance is the fact that they will return to Hollywood with a picture scenario 100 percent funnier, 100 percent more sure-fire as to its laughs than was the same story which we had originally planned to produce in the usual old-fashioned way." And Sam Wood: "The tour was a remarkable proof of the psychological fact that nothing builds laugh situations better than actual audience applause.... (We) dropped out of the story several situations that had been pets with all of us in the conferences. They had sounded funny to us, but by a public en masse their reception was only mild. They were immediately deleted and substitute material inserted. Several substitute gags of this sort, of which we didn't think so much ourselves, absolutely wowed every audience to hear them. Needless to say, these gags will be in the show." Kaufman on trying to get out of the assignment is from the *Philadelphia Inquirer* (December 1, 1935). According to the *Perth Sunday Times* (February 23, 1936) his first draft included the direction "Chico plays 'Pagliacci' with his right hand and 'Stars and Stripes Forever' with his left. (Let the so-and-so try this one.)" It feels genuine, except, perhaps, for the "so-and-so." A slight spanner in the works with regard to my (generally accepted) account of the film's origins is the fact that the early draft script of *Duck Soup* mentioned above features a strikingly prescient late scene in which the team cause chaos at the opera, in the stalls, a box, and on stage. ("I'm sorry, gentlemen," says an usher to Chico and Harpo, "but you have the wrong seats." "That's all right," says Chico. "We're not enjoying ourselves anyway.") This makes it somewhat hard to swallow that Kalmar and Ruby contributed merely an early draft to *Opera*, after Thalberg and McGuinness had devised it, rather than cooked up the original idea themselves from the leftovers of this abandoned scene. Dumont is even given the line: "If his Excellency doesn't get here soon, he'll miss the whole performance." ("He's-a not missing anything," Chico replies. "He's in the dressing room with Vera Trentino." "In her dressing room?" asks Margaret. "Why, what could he be doing there?" "He could be playing solitaire," Chico replies, "but I don't think so.") Groucho says that Kalmar and Ruby's work on the film "wasn't any good" in *The Marx Brothers Scrapbook*. He implies their services were no longer required after this; Adamson more convincingly suggests a prior engagement: the songs they were hired for never got written either. The Gloria Swanson quote is from her autobiography *Swanson on Swanson* (London: Hamlyn, 1981). Sam Wood explained why making them less funny would make them more popular to the *Buffalo Courier-Express* and others on November 3, 1935. The *Rochester Democrat and Chronicle* (June 27, 1935) makes the interesting claim that Wood—at odds with his generally perceived reputation as almighty overlord—frequently deferred to Kaufman on set ("he gives the official orders but at the conclusion of every take he talks to Kaufman"). Kaspar Monahan's review is from the *Pittsburgh Press* of November 23, 1935, among others. **1:20**—The material on Mussolini, the film's reception by Italian censors and Hollywood's attitude towards Italy and Italians makes use of Peter Bondanella: *A History of Italian Cinema* (London: Continuum, 2009), R.J.B. Bosworth: *Mussolini* (London: Arnold, 2002), Gian Piero Brunetta: *The History of Italian Cinema* (New Jersey: Princeton University Press, 2009), Nicholas Farrell: *Mussolini: A New Life* (London: Phoenix, 2003), Michele Sarfatti: *The Jews in Mussolini's Italy: From Equality to Persecution* (Wisconsin: University of Wisconsin Press, 2006) and David Welky: *The Moguls and the Dictators: Hollywood and the Coming of World War II* (Baltimore: Johns Hopkins University Press, 2008); also Higham; that the Alfieri Law "pushed American producers out of the Italian marketplace" is in Brunetta; "the temporary withdrawal of MGM... from Italy" is in Bondanella. Louvish notes the "can't Mussolini all of us!" line in *Chaplin: The Tramp's Odyssey* (London: Faber, 2009). Further cultural sensitivity was deployed pre-production, at least according to the *Milwaukee Sentinel* (April 15, 1937), when the production heads vetoed Harpo's suggestion that there should be a cutaway in the film to a shot of Verdi turning in his grave. "We had to think of the

Italians," Harpo is quoted as reflecting. "Too bad." Just a joke, of course, but jokes are rarely formed in vacuums: this one seems reflective of certain currents genuinely in the air. Ditto a curious report in *Motion Picture Daily* (July 21, 1935) of Louis Geller, an exhibitor in Jersey City, taking to a New York arbitration board his case against United Artists for demanding a $60 rental fee for *The Affairs of Cellini* which he considered "impossible for him to show" in his neighborhood without offending the "Polish and Italian element": "Geller claims that under an announcement made some months ago by the Hays office, an exhibitor does not have to play a picture if a particular community takes offence." Thomas Rácz, who first discovered the Hungarian print, got in touch with my website in 2010: "I have to say that the situation is not that easy. There are a lot of legal issues we have to consider. The people at the archives were helpful, but they are afraid of the copyright committee which has the power to fine them or shut them down. I am doing the best I can..." **2:25**—Marx-brothers.org quotes this line as an earlier version of the milk-fed chicken gag; Louvish has it in an early version of the stateroom scene. Quite probably they are both correct, with the line moving about and being tried out in different places during pre-production and tour. **5:35**—The Eyles quote is from *Their World of Comedy*. **11:34**—Kaufman's contributing to *Face the Music* is in Goldstein. **13:53**—The quote from *Socratic Dialogue* is in Goldstein. The quote about Sheekman's perennial involvement is from Stuart. There's been a lot of confusion about when the unbroadcast "Hollywood Agents" pilot was recorded. My CD claims 1933, which is impossible, given the presence of "Cosi Cosa" and "Alone." Wes Gehring's *The Marx Brothers: A Bio-Bibliography* puts it at 1938, a date disproved by Mitchell, who suggests 1936 on account of a reference to Jean Harlow (who died in 1937); other sources modify this to 1935 via the additional argument that singing newcomer Hollace Shaw, plugged on the show as the Marxes' own discovery, was a regular on CBS's *Saturday Night Serenade* by 1936. In fact, it was recorded on January 15, 1937, as announced in the radio section of *Motion Picture Daily*. This puts it safely clear of Harlow's death by nearly half a year, while it was actually in February of 1946, not 1936, that Hollace Shaw took over from Jessica Dragonette on *Saturday Night Serenade*. **21:45**—According to *Picture Play* (June 1935) Lawrence Tibbett was originally sought for the lead singing role, or at least a story had gone round to that effect, as a result of which the Marxes "got nicely snubbed." Perhaps his experiences with Laurel and Hardy in *The Rogue Song* (1930) had soured him of comedians? The magazine explained that "he is determined to make his return to the screen in the most dignified manner possible." An even weirder follow-up to all this is the claim in *Motion Picture Herald* (November 23, 1935) and *Variety* (November 6) that the film was promoted in Baltimore by a stunt that involved planting three men dressed as the Marx Brothers in a box during a Tibbett concert, and having them disruptively applaud and call out before running up and down the aisles "in the manner made famous by the brothers." *Variety* goes so far as to claim that the management of the theatre, entirely unaware of the stunt, sent for the police, who chased the interlopers from the building, and that several of the patrons could be heard opining that it was the genuine Marx Brothers who had caused the disturbance. If these stories are true one pictures Tibbett exploding in fury and having to be scraped off the proscenium, and rightly so. **31:42**—Last I knew, Billy Gilbert was still playing both parts in the official BFI listings. **36:09**—Material on Balbo makes use of Christopher Duggan: *The Force of Destiny: A History of Italy since 1796* (London: Penguin, 2008) and David Gilmour: *The Pursuit of Italy* (London: Allen Lane, 2011). Allen Eyles quote from *Complete Films*. That Balbo was indeed the inspiration for the aviators is asserted without qualification in Claudio G. Segrè: *Italo Balbo: A Fascist Life* (California: University of California Press, 1990). **48:48**—There's vague ballast for the suggestion that the rocking cabin may have been built up on the tour and then reduced again for film from the *New York Times* (August 30, 1936). The subject is the *Races* tour, but it may nonetheless illustrate established procedure: "They accumulated truckloads of props as they went along, their technicians building them as they were needed. Sometimes these were discarded after one appearance, and as a result four trucks were needed to cart the abandoned stuff back to the studio." Of the cartoon butterfly Derek Malcolm asks, "What is this if it isn't surreal?" in his book *A Century of Films* (London: I.B. Tauris & Co, 2000). It's a fair question, but it should immediately be noted how unusual, even unique a moment it is in the Marx canon. More than 'anarchic,' which merits a limited application in their very earliest films, 'surreal' is perhaps the most problematic of the adjectives regularly applied to the team's work, while the actual Surrealists' history of infatuation with the Brothers is basically a lively comedy of epic point-missing. While superficially both Marxes and Surrealists deal with the overthrow of restraint and the celebration of the irrational, Surrealism dresses its revelations in the lead-lined overcoats of the Freudian unconscious, Jungian dream analysis, Marxist dialectics and similar barriers to intellectual clarity: any true Surrealists in a Marx movie would be played by Sig Rumann and repeatedly locked in wardrobes. The Surrealists thought they wanted to destroy reason but didn't realize that an anti-system is still just another system, and abandonment is still conformity if everybody's doing it. The Marxes reject all systems a priori, as much from ignorance as discernment, but their revolutionary tendencies go only as far as deflation: outright destruction would take their playground away, and them with it. The Surrealists were for the most part a singularly humorless bunch, never more so than when they were trying to be funny. Nonetheless Salvador Dali felt sufficient sympathy to write an entire script for them that, with conspicuous generosity, I have refrained from mentioning anywhere else in the book. **52:07**—The alternate extract from the *Animal Crackers* playscript is included in Kaufman: *Kaufman and Co.* **70:11**—Don on Jack quote found on www.jackbenny.org. **76:38**—Now that I've been tasteless enough to sing the praises of the film's straight opera moments, let me record that the bulk of the non-comic footage was shot by a second unit at the New York Metropolitan Opera with Cesare Sodero ("radio maestro") conducting, under the supervision of Herbert Stothart and George Schneider of the MGM musical staff. Footage of the Brothers themselves, where needed, was shot separately and integrated in the editing room (*Variety*, July 17, 1935).

Chapter 7

The Marxes' original contract with Thalberg was for one picture with an option on a second, not for two pictures. So it was a measure of his satisfaction with *A Night at the Opera* that he immediately acquired them for the follow-up, and of theirs with him that they turned down a juicy offer from Sam Goldwyn and United Artists (according to *Variety*: July 17, 1935). In the account books, however, the film did not actually break even until a 1948 reissue; indeed the only of their MGM movies to show a profit on first run was *The Big Store*. This surprising pair of facts, and the losses on *A Day at the Races* quoted in the chapter, are in John McElwee: *Showmen, Sell It Hot: Movies as Merchandise in Golden Era Hollywood* (Pittsburgh: GoodKnight, 2013). This book is much recommended, and I find many of its attitudes toward received wisdom, Marxian legend and the sixties university prism most congenial. Groucho said the try-out show wasn't funny in *Elmira Star-Gazette* (July 14, 1936) and elsewhere. Some further improbable claims for the scientific precision of the road tour method, from the *New York Times* (August 30, 1936): "The Marx Brothers have returned from their tour with some interesting statistical information.... Irving Thalberg, their producer, sat through eleven shows on Saturday and Sunday, during which all the gags were tried out and those to be used in the film were determined. During six weeks on the road the Marxes used 600 comedy situations. By the trial and error method, they selected 175 as those which audiences enjoyed the most, and 75 of those, with the highest laugh rating, will be used in the picture." The *Rochester Democrat and Chronicle* published an eyewitness account of the final live show in San Francisco (August 1936) that I ardently hope is accurate: "Every chorus girl came on with a painted mustache similar to Groucho's, Chico played Groucho's part, Groucho played Chico's part, and Groucho's daughter Miriam played Harpo's role. Harpo came on the stage while the picture, *Devil Doll*, was on the screen, attracted the audience's attention by whistling, and then proceeded to do a pantomime act with the flicker. When an actor on the screen started to eat, Harpo would try to grab the food from him. Harpo also tried to make love to the girls on the screen." The film is legendary for the amount of material created for it that didn't make it to the final version: the elephantine venture relentlessly hemorrhaged both comedy and music, from stage version to script, from script to shooting script, from shooting script to film, and from film to final cut. Mitchell details some of the most interesting deleted material in his entry on the film in the *Encyclopaedia*. Passing reference to further bits and pieces could fill a book by themselves. I'll content myself with noting my one favorite, from *North Tonawanda Evening News* (August 25, 1936): "Only the restrictions of a budget will prevent the Marx Brothers from including a live skunk as a member of their company when they go on the road with the stage version of their new comedy *A Day at the Races....* The trainer refused to rent the animal unless he went with it. For this he wanted an additional $12.50 a day. Result, the play-going public will see a stuffed skunk in the show." Groucho's dismissal of geographical variation in audience response is from the *Evening Independent* of July 1, 1937. Goldstein has George Kaufman wanting to direct the movie on the first hand word of Samuel Marx. The material on the aborted pre-film Broadway version from *Variety* (August 7, October 9 and November 13, 1935) and *Motion Picture Herald* (November 23, 1935). The Seaton/Pirosh interview was published in the Florida *Evening Independent* among others on May 31, 1937. The plagiarism lawsuit is reported in *Motion Picture Daily* (August 26, 1937). A later report on March 12, 1938 confirms the suit was successful, to the tune of $10,000. **2:10**—Maureen's interview published in *Rochester Democrat Chronicle* and others through 1937. **8:00**—The story about Dumbrille's marriage is from Wikipedia, but don't let that put you off. **9:08**—The Hackenbush number would have been the only time a Marx Brother had burst into song at MGM without ambient justification. Later numbers like "Lydia" or "Riding the Range" are being performed *as* songs *by* the characters, with visible instruments, and even "Sing While You Sell," which comes closest to the effect that "Dr. Hackenbush" would have had, is partially rooted in reality in so far as it is *about* the virtues of singing and dancing while at work. But for a Groucho character simply to start singing in the middle of a scene would have been to assume a liberty afforded only the romantic leads at MGM, and revert to a distinctly Paramount freedom. Though I've no evidence to support me, I can't help wondering if this, rather than merely time constraints and an odd sense of priorities, was a contributory factor in the song's excision. The *Brooklyn Eagle* (April 9, 1942) and *Showmen's Trade Review* (May 2) explicitly state that Groucho performs "I'm Dr. Quackenbush" in *Screen Snapshots*. Tony Slide and Annette D'Agostino Lloyd catalogued the series in 1998: prior to that the entries had been so ill-preserved that Leonard Maltin was unable even to supply a list of them in his book *The Great Movie Shorts*. Annette has confirmed that this edition is indeed missing from the official archive, but it could easily be lurking somewhere. **9:30**—Groucho takes personal responsibility for saving the professional dignity of the nation's Dr. Quackenbushes in *Chicago Tribune* (June 1, 1936). *Variety* (July 1, 1936) reported on the coincidence credit, naming *Bullets or Ballots*, *Fury* and *San Francisco* as the first beneficiaries of the new nervousness. The disclaimer was noticed sufficiently to be spoofed by the likes of Laurel and Hardy in *Blockheads* and the Stooges in *You Nazty Spy! Variety* also informs us (on July 8) that the Beagle lawsuit, which may have been the main cause of the Quackenbush retreat, not only persisted after the switch to Flywheel but had only just been settled—and in the Marxes' favor! It also seems to be saying that the plaintiff wasn't even called Beagle after all, but rather "Morris Beegel." **16:18**—Groucho quoted in Hubbard Keavy's column in *Elmira Star-Gazette* (July 14, 1936) and elsewhere. **43:51**—The Esther Muir interview is in the *Pittsburgh Press* (May 23, 1937). She also appeared alongside Keaton and Andy Clyde, and Wheeler and Woolsey (again) in *On Again—Off Again*. **66:52**—Mags did the examination scene in the live tour: *Variety* (July 22, 1936). A report that appeared in *Screen and Radio Weekly* further affirms eyewitness certainty of the lady herself taking the full punishment on set. **85:44**—The Halliwell quote is from *Halliwell's Film Guide*. He's the only person I've ever read ardently defending this anti-climactic catastrophe of a sequence, but he does so even more forcefully in *Halliwell's Hundred*: "I'll never forget the elation with which it was received one Saturday in 1947 in Edinburgh.... I thought the building would disintegrate around me, so loud were those Scottish laughs." Of the film's more negative reviews, my favorite is the *Chicago Tribune* (July 4, 1937) attributing the script to "the type of gag writer who thinks only in terms of two pigs under a gate making more racket than one." One last oddity: According to the normally scrupulously reliable *Caldwell News and Burleson County Ledger* (March 11, 1937), Harpo's wife Susan is somewhere to be found in this film. The paper claims she arrived on the set to meet her husband for lunch and "the director" decided she was just the girl he was looking for and insisted she appear. Hmmm. If you spot her, let me know....

Chapter 8

The *New York Post*'s account of its RKO visit was published on June 22, 1938, but likely took place a significant while before. Comparisons between *Room Service* play and screenplay make use of Murray/Boretz. Ryskind's hiring to write the screenplay was announced in March of 1938. The *New*

York Times (March 9, 1938) claimed that the Marxes had been dropped by MGM following a dispute; this surprising suggestion is backed by the *West Australian* on May 20, which also states that they left MGM "last summer, after a disagreement over money." This presumably refers to the exorbitant inducements the studio would have had to have offered to keep them from RKO and the promise of a fresh start on *Room Service*. That their MGM association was deemed permanently over, rather than on hiatus (despite the possible handshake agreement to return mentioned by Arce), is stated in several accounts (e.g. *Schenectady Gazette*: 23 June 1937); Chico also stated this under oath, as a witness at the 1941 trial of Joseph Schenck and Joseph Moskowitz for tax irregularities. MGM threatening to replace them with Healy, Keaton and Ebsen is in Arce. That the RKO deal was for three films is in *Film Daily* (October 2, 1937), *San Diego Union* (October 10), *New York Times* (October 10) and elsewhere. Among the papers that mention *Of Thee I Sing* being revived as a project for RKO at this time is *The News* of October 18, 1937; it's also stated in Louvish, Arce and Eyles (*Complete Films*). Eyles further states that RKO went stale on the idea after the problems with *Room Service*'s production and Zeppo instead lined it up as an MGM project, but they likewise pulled out when *Room Service* was released and judged a curate's egg. Something similar to this appeared in the *Philadelphia Inquirer* (August 27th, 1937): this has RKO's *Room Service* offer still in the fire, with MGM simultaneously set to go on *Of Thee* (having paid Kaufman $100,000 for the adaptation) and likewise courting the reluctant Marxes. (Clear winner of the award for weirdest project announcement of all from around this time, however, is the claim in the *Plattsburgh Daily Republican* [August 17, 1938] that the team "in all seriousness want to do a dramatic picture" and "are negotiating for the purchase of the screen rights to *The Brothers Karamazov*.") The Republic offer is in the *Syracuse Journal* (August 17, 1937). Arce also claims they received firm offers at this time from Columbia and—imagine it, imagine it—Paramount. Oddly enough, Chico also confirmed he had made overtures to TCF while standing as a witness at the Schenck trial. Chico's admission was published in the *Motion Picture Daily* of March 12, the day after the same paper reported Harpo taking to the stand and swearing that "although he had been friendly with Schenck for fifteen years, the latter had at no time sought to bring him under contract to Twentieth Century–Fox." *The Three Musketeers* was still being mooted as a forthcoming Marx production as late as March 10th, 1938, when the *Adelaide Chronicle* told its readers it will follow *Room Service* into production. These near-collisions between the Marxes and the Ritzes are becoming prolific. As well as this we have the Marxes abandoning *Argentina* after the Ritzes' *Argentine Nights* (but making use of the regular Ritz writing team for its replacement, *The Big Store*) and the odd affair of *The Barber of Brazil* detailed in Chapter 14. The *Buffalo Courier-Express* of July 12, 1941 carries a report that not only Jimmy Durante but also Harry Ritz was being tested for the role of Banjo in the film of *The Man Who Came to Dinner*, after Harpo had turned it down. No wonder one so often finds idle publicity pieces in the papers claiming that plans are afoot to team the two acts, such as in the *Showmen's Trade Review* (November 8, 1941): "Columbia is reported to be debating the idea of starring the Marx Brothers and the Ritz Brothers in the same picture. If true, Harry Cohn and Company may go into the straight-jacket business in a big way. What a sweet directorial assignment for some Samson." However fanciful, there are repeated follow-up reports on this bizarre suggestion in the trades. Additional material on the bidding war came from Milly S. Barranger: *Audrey Wood and the Playwrights* (London: Palgrave-Macmillan, 2013). Two oddities relating to RKO's bid: Though the biggest handover for film rights to a play that year, it was not—despite the general understanding—the biggest of all time, that being (according to the *Film Daily* report) the $300,000 Paramount forked out for our old pal *Abie's Irish Rose* in 1928. And while this same source explicitly denies the quoted figure of $250,000, nonetheless this (or more commonly $255,000) remains the generally-understood sum paid in just about every other contemporary and later source. The earliest linking of the Marxes to the project I have found is in *Variety* on July 7, 1937. Director William A. Seiter notched up over a hundred credits in a career stretching back to 1915 and ahead to the middle fifties, when he switched to TV and enjoyed several more productive years. (Seasoned in comedy, he directed the Ritz Brothers, Wheeler and Woolsey, Abbott and Costello and Laurel and Hardy, the latter in by common consent their best feature film *Sons of the Desert*.) When a child star, Mitzi Green impersonated the Marxes, and did a Maurice Chevalier so good she might even have got away with stealing his passport; a startling George Arliss, too. (You can see her as the Marxes in *Little Orphan Annie*

[1932].) Maxine, Chico's daughter, got to know her in the thirties and in her book *Growing Up with Chico* recalls an amusing occasion on which she stayed at their house specifically so as to perfect her impersonation of Chico: "There's nothing I can grab a hold of!" she exclaimed after multiple frustrated attempts. Getting ready for bed, Maxine saw her applying a heavy cream to her face, and asked her what it was. Green replied that it was a freckle remover. Maxine asked if it worked: "'It hasn't yet,' she replied, rubbing it in diligently, 'but I keep hoping.'" With Chevalier, Lillian Roth and almost all the other great talent Paramount had ropes around in 1930, she appears in the revue film *Paramount on Parade*, in which the Marxes' presence was so temptingly announced, yet so frustratingly not to be. Cancer took her in 1969 at forty-eight years of age: she had been a professional entertainer for all but three of them. Her unfulfilled RKO schedule was announced in *Miami News* of April 2, 1938. Milton Berle's participation, though hard to imagine, was seemingly seriously intended, and was widely announced, for example by Louella Parsons in the *Pittsburgh Post-Gazette* (November 4, 1937), and *Film Daily* (October 11) which calls it "an important part." These are all definitely referring to a role alongside the Marxes; the runt of the litter therefore is *Long Island Daily Press* (September 6), which suggests Berle may be in line for the lead "now that the Marx Brothers-RKO deal looks sour." Walter Winchell had a go at *Room Service* in, among other places, the *Palm Beach Daily News* of March 22nd, 1938. By very strange coincidence, it was in exactly this period (between *Races* and *Room Service*) that Maxine Marx (in *Growing Up with Chico*) recalls Winchell, "brimming over with spite and gossip" (and referring to himself as "we"), being invited to dinner with Chico's family. She recalls that they all "took an instant dislike to him" and he left early, whereupon Chico observed: "That's the kind of bastard who can make or break a career." Oddly, the *Brooklyn Daily Eagle* of 25th September and the *Reading Eagle* of 29th September both seemed to think the abandoned pre-filming tour had gone ahead as planned: "the transcontinental tours of the waggish trio, with constant alterations of a gag from city to city and from section to section, were used to advantage by them in helping the play to be translated to the screen," claimed the former; "fourteen days was all that was required for the final lookover and pruning," added the latter. Presumably a case of old press releases being taken on trust. Plans for Harpo to talk and Groucho to wear a real moustache from *Salt Lake Telegram* (April 4, 1938), *Maitland Daily Mercury* (April 6), *LA Times* (June 5), Sheilah Graham in the *Sunday Morning Star* (June 19) and *Winnipeg Tribune* (June 25). The team's fear of jokes being stolen in rehearsals and try-outs and used by others from *Salt Lake Telegram* (June 23) and *Adelaide Mail* (September 3). Groucho's obsession with pre-production secrecy takes on an appropriately neurotic tinge in this context, but was nonetheless a constant and well-known issue. He would use it as an explanation for why the *Go West* tour didn't play Los Angeles, and was still griping about it to a set visitor at the time of *Night in Casablanca*: "You can't print any of the gags ... I'll hear 'em tomorrow night on my radio" (*Independent Record*, August 31, 1945). In 1937, according to the *New York Times* of February 8, the situation had become so grave that an entire sequence from *A Day at the Races* had to be eliminated, after its jokes, "recorded in their film only two days before," were "being told in millions of homes through a network program originating in a Los Angeles station... The estimated cost of that one revision alone, a studio executive said, would be about $10,000." (The studio's solution, according to the piece, was to hire 'gag policemen' to hang about on the lots and "mingle with workers and visitors on the set, and woe betide the suspect who happens to lead the gag policeman to the lair of a radio comedian.") Al Boasberg, the gagman who contributed greatly to *Opera* and *Races* during their live tours, vented his wrath at "gag pirates" in an interview published in the *Albany Evening News* (July 20, 1936), in which he remembered that the sanity clause line from *Opera* "was stolen and was all over the world before the picture was released. The gags from (*Races*) will be stolen like that... " The newspaper goes on to tell of "a New York snooper columnist" who visited a *Races* show rehearsal, heard and published the "my watch has stopped" line and "was coldly received" on a return visit. "Do you know your lines yet?" he allegedly asked the Brothers, to which Groucho replied, "Not as well as you do." Earliest reference to all this stuff that I've found is in *Silver Screen* way back in June of 1932, which claims that the *Horse Feathers* set is "boxed in and closely guarded" because the stars "suspected all visitors of purloining their gags." Ironically, Meryman says that one of the reasons new lines were constantly demanded on *Horse Feathers* was because Groucho himself was "using jokes from the script to amuse his friends at the comedians' table at the Hillcrest Country Club." Mankiewicz got wise to it, and "began saving the best jokes until the very last minute." Sheilah Graham reported on an unenthusiastic on-set Groucho in the *Utica Daily Press* and elsewhere on 30th July, 1938. **50:40**—In the original show the theatre is not part of the hotel. In the screenplay Ryskind *had* attempted to open out the action a little prior to this moment: the film had begun with Harpo outside putting up posters advertising the play, and there was a funny scene in which a cleaner entered the ballroom early in the morning only to find, and be terrified by, the entire cast of the play asleep, dressed as miners. Like most of Ryskind's new ideas, these were cut from the film itself. **66:19**—The Eyles quote is from *Complete Films*. Ryskind's screenplay confirms that "Swing Low" is the intended song. To some degree, the musical remake *Step Lively*, made by RKO six years later (notable for its immortal publicity tagline: "It's fun"), plays rather more as one might have expected the Marx version to turn out, with songs, less reverence for the original, more movement between smarter and more interesting sets, lots of gals and gams, and quite a bit more pizzazz in the production. (Note that "Godspeed," the title of Davis's play that was supposedly changed to "Hail and Farewell" in *Room Service* on the strict orders of the Breen Office, makes it through without difficulty this time round.) Some may object to Brown and Carney's, of all feet, being slipped into the still warm shoes of Harpo and Chico, but the truth is they do so ably; George Murphy, too, is a fun and energetic Gordon Miller. That The Faces were fans of both film and song was confirmed by keyboardist Ian "Mac" McLagan, who got in touch with my website to explain further: "'One Last Sweet Cheerio' from *Room Service* is a favorite of mine and Ronnie Wood's. We had 3/4 inch reel-to-reel black and white video machines back then, and had every Marx Brothers movie that was available. We used to be able to quote pages from each film." Ian passed away in December, 2014, just before this book went to press. Possibly the Monkees were also keen on the movie: certainly the episode from their series entitled *The Monkees in Manhattan* is one of the most brazen bits of plagiarism it's been my pleasure to encounter.

Chapter 9

Robbin Coons recorded Groucho announcing his retirement and his philosophical take on *Room Service* in the *Warren Times Mirror* of November 9, 1938 and elsewhere. Suggestion that LeRoy was courted by MGM at Thalberg's own suggestion in *Variety* (March 11, 1936); general perception of LeRoy as MGM's replacement boy wonder in *New York Post* (November 27, 1937 and March 19, 1938), *Variety* (December 15, 1937), and *Utica Observer-Dispatch* (August 21, 1938: "They have never reopened the office of the late Irving Thalberg since the death of that youthful Hollywood wizard, but the other rooms of his bungalow on the MGM lot now are occupied by filmdom's other wonder boy, Mervyn LeRoy"); general perception of *The Wizard of Oz* as cause of his disenchantment with production duties in *Buffalo Courier-Express* (August 19, 1939). The announcement of production being postponed while the script is rewritten appeared in, among others, the *Ironwood Daily Globe* of March 30, 1939. The pre-filming tour is announced in the *New York Times* of November 11, 1938 and elsewhere. Chico mentions that there hadn't been enough time to do it in an interview for Eileen Creelman's "Picture Plays and Players" column in the *New York Sun* some time in 1939, whereas in the *Brooklyn Eagle* (November 12, 1939) he blames a more familiar culprit: "We made this decision because the elapsed time between the personal appearances and the picture's release was too long. In previous pictures many of the gags no longer were new stuff. They had been grabbed by radio acts and other laugh-hunters. We wanted the gags in this picture to be as fresh when they reached the screen as when they were written into the script, for we believe they are the funniest and most original we have had in any of our pictures or stage comedies. Yet, who knows?" The other screenwriters and order of drafts and revisions are as laid out in Louvish. Mention of Marx script input, Groucho's "use the stand-ins" quip, Eve Arden's cavalier profligacy with silk tights, the bit about the baby elephant (all September 6, 1939) and Hy Gardner's bit about "Berle with a mustache" (October 29) all to be found in the *Brooklyn Daily Eagle*. Readers appreciative of the news that the seal was named Slicker may be further gratified to hear that his pun-servicing counterpart from *Horse Feathers* was called Lucille, if *New Movie Magazine* (June, 1932) is to be believed. The *Salt Lake Tribune* on July 29 was one of a good many to report excitedly on the monkey orchestra. **2:31** - More elaborately staged version of "Step Up and Take a Bow" described in *Montreal Gazette* of January 2, 1940; baloney about them locking Florence Rice in the gorilla's cage described in *Brooklyn Daily Eagle* of September 6, 1939. Snippets from the Lana Turner story as told by *Modern Screen* in September 1938 and again in August 1951. **3:38**—The Eyles quote is from *Their World of Comedy*. **19:11**—To my great surprise, we've turned up a little more on "Oh, The Elephant Never Forgets": "All three of the brothers are musical and have written songs of their own, but never before as a collaboration. The tune is based on a song their mother used in the Marx Brothers' act more than 25 years ago, when they were the Three Nightingales in short pants. She got it from her mother, who was a harpist. The lyrics are typically Marxian, and are appropriate since they mention the hippo, rhino, leppo, zebro and chimpo." (*Buffalo Courier-Express*: April 30, 1939.) The early Kalmar/Ruby/Jones script of *Duck Soup* that I can't stop going on about has Groucho say to Harpo, "I'm glad I didn't ask you for Washington Crossing the Delaware!" during its (long and not very funny) embryo version of the scene in which Harpo displays his tattoos. Thanks to R.S.H. Tryster for alerting me to the story of Betty Broadbent. **22:18**—Patrick McGilligan interviews Krasna in *Backstory: Interviews with Screenwriters of Hollywood's Golden Age* (California, University of California Press: Revised Ed, 1992). **29:29**—The Adamson quotes are from personal correspondence. **33:52**—Goldenrod has exactly this effect upon Sneezy in *Snow White and the Seven Dwarfs* (1937). **38:15**—Adamson on retakes is from personal correspondence. Mark A. Viera suggests in *Majestic Hollywood: The Greatest Films of 1939* (Philadelphia: Running Press, 2013) that Buzzell refused to shoot the Hays Office joke on the grounds that it wouldn't be understood, whereupon LeRoy gave him a day off without pay and hired Simon specifically to shoot this moment. The general understanding—that it was a retake after principal photography and after Buzzell had left the country—seems to me more likely. The source of the confusion might be Brecher, who in Mike Sacks's *And Here's the Kicker: Conversations with 21 Top Humour Writers on their Craft* (Writers' Digest, 2009) says that "the director was replaced" for the line, but not, I think, meaning to imply Buzzell was taken off, only that it was a second director who actually shot it. In this lively interview, Brecher also blames Buzzell for the film's reinvention of the Brothers' screen personae, which he sums up as having them "mincing around acting cute." He does not, however, waver from the Thalberg line in favor of the Paramount ethic: he stresses that "you need that romance... you also need a villain" and that the Marxes "have to act altruistically," but argues that Thalberg "cast very good actors and actresses for the romance portions" of *Opera* and *Races*, whereas "what I got was garbage." As to how the Hays Office joke got past the Hays Office, Glenn Mitchell in personal correspondence wondered if they simply "enjoyed the ego-massage of a name-check to the extent where they'd pass a line with those sort of implications." Though a big hit at the time, and one of the film's more popular and oft-quoted moments today, the line is pure Bob Hope and further evidence of how the film is trying to re-shape the team for the coming decade. Variations on the moment occur in several other films; perhaps the least expected is at the end of the Monogram mystery *Murder by Invitation* (1941): the hero and heroine end the film in a clinch, whereupon the comic relief suddenly looks to camera and tells us, "The Hays Office ain't gonna like that long kiss!" **46:35**—Susan's version of the bursitis story is in Adamson. Pony fall in *Milwaukee Sentinel* (April 15, 1937: "He fell on his shoulder—a distance of about four feet—and was so badly hurt that he was confined to his bed for two days") and elsewhere. A typical account of the ostrich story: *Reading Eagle* (November 8, 1939). Glenn Mitchell has reminded me that the comedian Billie Ritchie really did sustain injuries falling from an ostrich, to the extent that his death has been attributed to its long-term consequences. **68:07**—Maxine Marx discusses her mother's friendship with Norma Shearer and her small role in *Marie Antoinette* in *Growing Up with Chico*. **75:51**—Simon Louvish reminds me that Esperanto is also the language used in the street signs of the Jewish ghetto in *The Great Dictator*, perhaps because of its association with its universality and fraternity, or maybe (Louvish speculates) because Chaplin feared that Yiddish, with its Hebrew characters, might reinforce an undesired sense of difference between the audience and the characters, and risk alienating them. **77:19**—You are officially too obsessed with the Marx Brothers. Unless you knew the answer without even having to check here, in which case, though you won't be hearing it from me, you probably know that already. For the record: in *Monkey Business* Chico is caught trying to steal a passport, and explains to his victim that he thought his hand was in the trousers of his own suit, accounting for the fact that another man is wearing them by observing that the suit in question had two pairs of pants. Then in *Horse Feathers* he acquires a co-ed with two pairs of pants, and in *Duck Soup* illicitly obtains a war code with two pairs of plans. This latter joke, for all his pontificating about gag thieves, was used by Groucho ahead of time in a newspaper article in which he expressed disapproval of the New Deal because he's "against any code without two pairs of pants." (*Brooklyn Daily Eagle,* November 10, 1933.) And honorable mention, of course, to whoever it is that has four pairs of pants, lives in Philadelphia, and it never rains but it pours.

Chapter 10

Joe Adamson has read the original Kalmar & Ruby script, and tells me that the basic plot was about the map to a gold mine, in comparison to which the occasionally mentioned rodeo elements didn't play that much of a part. Eileen Percy wrote in the *Milwaukee Sentinel* (May 5, 1936) and elsewhere: "Although the plot is being carefully guarded, I understand it has a western locale, in one of those divorce resorts, to be exact. Groucho is a shyster lawyer..." Sounds like *Peach-O-Reno* to me... Joe Adamson's anecdote concerning Irving Brecher and Sylvan Simon is also from personal correspondence. Buzzell explained how he tried to get out of the job in the *Corsicana Daily Sun* (May 14, 1940) and elsewhere. *Hollywood*'s report on the making of "Way Out West" is from December, 1940. Kaper and Kahn also wrote unused numbers called "There's a New Moon Over the Old Corral" and "I Can't Get Along with Horses" for the film. Bob Gassel planted the thought in my head about the potentially adverse effects of the stage tour. Mitchell notes that this time Nat Perrin went along to help beef up the gags: the extent to which he contributed is uncertain, but it's worth noting there is a surviving copy of the script for the opening scene (in the Smithsonian Groucho collection) that lists as its authors on the cover "Nat Perrin and Irving Brecher." Groucho told Chapman he was getting too old to tour in in the *Buffalo Courier-Express* (August 29, 1940) among others. Cecil Smith put the boot in in *Chicago Tribune* (May 15, 1940) and elsewhere. The filming of the live shows is in *Motion Picture Daily* (May 6th, 1940). The Eyles quote on the opening scene is from *Complete Films*. Buzzell is quoted by Barry Norman in *The Movie Greats*. The letter to Sheekman is included in *The Groucho Letters*. **0:43**—Studio publicity, pressbooks and posters made reference to the song right up to the film's release (and even in rereleases), supporting the conclusion that it was not excised willingly: it's almost as if they are *pretending* it's still there... a puzzler, indeed. **12:30**—The explanation of how Diana Lewis got her nickname is a lie. **20:21**—June MacCloy's recollections of Groucho were shared with me by George Bettinger in private correspondence. **38:31**—The Ed Watz quote is from personal correspondence. **67:46**—No note.

Chapter 11

My certain nomination for funniest news report about this movie is won by the *Hollywood and Broadway* column, as it appeared in *Rockaway Beach Wave*, apparently the name of a real newspaper, on August 28, 1941: "Groucho and Chico are trying to persuade the silent member of their provocative family to go 'brunette' in *Step This Way*, the new bit of Marx madness now being 'shot' at Metro. For years, Harpo has worn an orange-colored wig which photographs like a dizzy blonde. Now the other brothers want him to dye it black and part it in the middle." No explanation attempted as to why they should want him to do any such thing, let alone why he should dye his "orange" one, rather than just get a new one in their preferred hue. MGM publicity at its most desperate. The issue of *Hollywood* magazine quoted throughout this chapter is from August, 1941. First run profitability confirmed by John McElwee in *Showmen, Sell It Hot* (see notes for Chapter 7). Nat Perrin was writing the scenario for *Argentina*, according to the *New York Times* of March 22, 1940. Louella Parsons on South American blonde chasing from *St. Petersburg Times*: October 12, 1941. *Variety* reference to the "department store idea" from August 28, 1935. As well as *Step This Way* and *Bargain Basement*, Hedda Hopper has *Gin Rummy* as another provisional title, but I don't recall hearing of it elsewhere (*Pittsburgh Press*: May 5, 1941). **1:24**—The stories relating to the search for the four junior Chicos and Richard Haydel appear in the *Pittsburgh Press* among others (April 11 and June 5, 1941). **15:00**—British comedy fans will doubtless recall Norman Wisdom putting on record that he loves you loves you loves you, using similar technology in a similar setting, in his debut feature *Trouble in Store* (1953).

Further reflection on these wonderful machines, from Glenn Mitchell: "Home disc recorders were indeed available and had been for some time, but were beyond most people's means. I recently transferred to CD some discs for a now-elderly friend whose uncle had such a machine and recorded her doing songs and recitations when a small child, around the beginning of the 1930s. It was also common for stores—particularly, but not exclusively, record shops—to offer a disc recording service for people who wanted to record messages to send to loved ones, and so on. The Beatles, in their very early days, cut a demo disc using precisely such a service." **28:36** and **28:50**—For more on the hesitant march of Technicolor, Kindem's essay and some other relevant material is in Schatz (ed): *Hollywood: Social dimensions: Technology, regulation and the audience* (London: Routledge, 2004). For more on smog, fog, gas and particulate matter, along with unsparing consideration of the effect of atmospheric pollution on rubber, paint and large commercial animals, see Stern/Wohlers/Boubel & Lowry: *Fundamentals of Air Pollution* (New York, Academic Press: 1973). Order both books at the same time and they might give you a discount. Tell them Groucho sent you. **59:39**—Tony Martin recalled the film in a 1991 interview with R.S.H. Tryster: "We had the preview of the picture. They didn't run it at UCLA, where people understood jokes. Instead they previewed it at Santa Monica, and all the old Jewish people came, who didn't understand it. But I sang a song in that called 'The Tenement Symphony.' And they thought that was sensational. And all the cards in the lobby said: 'More Tony Martin!'" **71:52**—I drew a complete blank on the reverse printing: this speculation masquerading as my own is in truth entirely R.S.H. Tryster's. (No wonder Tony Martin called him "pretty sharp.") But while the haphazard assembly of the scene may have passed you and I by at first, it was no match for the sharply professional eyes at *American Cinematographer* magazine's July 1941 issue: "It is all well enough to assume that fast-paced zany comedy is nonsense and needn't be too logical, but that is not enough excuse to allow for the complete lack of coherence and continuity shown in some of these cuts. They would be deemed inexcusable in an amateur film: what excuse is there, then, for their appearance in a professional one?" Oddly, the film's editor, Conrad Nervig, was the first-ever winner of an Oscar for editing (for *Eskimo* in 1933).

Chapter 12

The forming of Loma Vista was announced in May of 1945. One possible means by which the Marxes came within Loew's field of vision is suggested by the announcements seen often throughout 1943 that they were due to return in a Technicolor musical for producer Hunt Stromberg (e.g. in *Film Daily* of June 3 and September 21, *Motion Picture Daily* of August 9 and 17, and *Motion Picture Herald* of August 17 and 21). Stromberg and Loew (and Lester Cowan) were all independent producers who distributed through United Artists, and fraternized at UA business and social functions. Likely, the opportunity to do *Casablanca* for Loew emerged from the collapse of Stromberg's project, which is played up in the trades as a definite goer for a time. The Groucho interview about *Copacabana* appeared in the *Milwaukee Journal* among others on November 29, 1946. The letters about the making of *Copacabana* and *Casablanca* are in Marx Allen. The Eyles Groucho quote is from *Complete Films*. The Groucho letter confirming that the Warners controversy was instigated as a publicity gimmick is in Kanfer, frustratingly undated. Strange how often this sort of nonsense followed the Marxes around even without Loew to fashion it: see also Beagle to Flywheel, Quackenbush to Hackenbush, and the story reported in *Film Daily* (October 26, 1933) that the Mayor of Fredonia, NY, asked the Brothers to change the name of *Duck Soup*'s locale. A typical example of the press reports claiming the phony Warners objections are genuine is in the *New York Times* of May 20, 1945; there are many others. A few other examples of David Loew's publicity stunts: He announced a search for "six startling beauties" in July of 1945 to star alongside George Sanders in *The Private Affairs of Bel Ami*: "startling," that is, in the proportions of their busts, as the leg fad was now over, and returning GIs rarely look below the waistline. ("It wasn't too easy to find enough actresses who were honest-to-goodness built that way," co-producer Albert Lewin gallantly informed the *St Petersburg Times*.) In May of 1946, Loew claimed to be shooting two versions of the film, one of them daring to break the long-standing injunction against showing a couple together in a double bed, the other maintaining established order for the benefit of "England and other places." This was a spin on an earlier caper pulled when he and

Lewin were collaborating on *The Moon and Sixpence* in 1942, and Loew claimed to have cast two women in the role of Sanders' Tahitian lover: "Deva Wani, Japanese dancer" for territories happy with authenticity, and Elena Verdugo for "communities where marriage between a Polynesian and an Englishman is not acceptable." And in 1943 he claimed to be about to produce the first film with an unwritable title. "That old familiar two-tone whistle a drugstore cowboy uses admiringly every time a shapely slick chick trips past a windy corner," as syndicated columnist Ted Gill put it, had supposedly been registered as a title by Loew and his then-partner Arthur Lyons. "We describe the title officially as being composed of two enthusiastically whistled notes, the first being on an ascending scale, and the second on a descending scale," Loew helpfully explained. Gill's report goes on to preposterously assert that Loew and Lyons "were gambling a cool million on this two-note title," calling it "the first and only all-sound-and-no-sight picture title ever used." Needless to say the accompanying *film* was never described, nor made. Making the case for Loew's prior involvement in the banning of *The Southerner* seems a forlorn endeavor, given censor Binford's busy track record before and after. But I was struck by the assessment of the film in Martin O'Shaughnessy's study of its director (*Jean Renoir* [Manchester: Manchester University Press, 2000]). The author notes how the film's subject seems to promise a serious examination of "the dark side of America's origins" but instead seems consciously to avoid doing so: "after its initial hint of doing something very different, *The Southerner* reinvigorates American myths in a conservative manner; the conquest of a wild land by the small farmers whose independence and strong-mindedness made them the backbone of American democracy; the centrality of the family as foundation of society; the goodness of small rural communities; the key role of religion." Specifically, he claims, any consideration of the black experience that might be considered an essential component is notably marginalized. It sounds rather like the sort of thing Binford would thoroughly approve of—so perhaps he did. There is certainly an unusually non-specific quality to his objections. Maybe Loew, aware of his reputation and of the value of harnessing it to the cause, was able to induce him to feign an objection that he would later withdraw, once Loew had made the necessary fuss? The reports of Pittsburgh's objections to the smoke joke, and United Artists' statement of response, are from the *Gettysburg Times* (April 16th, 1946) and the *Milwaukee Journal* (April 17, 1946). The reports of Chico's lawsuit are from *Spokane Daily Chronicle* (Jan 28, 1948), *Deseret News* (Feb 4, 1948) and *Milwaukee Journal* (April 1, 1948). Harpo's hair? Well, you must form your own conclusions there. But note that as early as 1941 the *Poughkeepsie Star-Enterprise* was moved to note: "His hair is so thin that his forehead extends almost to the back of his neck. This condition, he says, is the result of wearing a hat while playing poker." *The Saratogian* (August 29, 1945) is just one of many to spread the rumor that his hair is all his own, permed to match the look of his usual wig. As Leonid Kinskey would say: "Phooey!" That the film was their all-time box-office champ is still another useful surprise to be learned from John McElwee's *Showmen, Sell It Hot* (see notes for chapter 7). Stated in the small print on the back of the DVD, but unnoticed by me until pointed out by Glenn Mitchell, is the fact that copyright on the film was renewed by Gummo in 1974. **5:21**—Sig follows "Schweinehund!" with "You blöder Hammel!" This is essentially "stupid sheep" (though "Hammel" is also mutton and a castrated male sheep, neither of which is the gist of this insult, which is more general). "Whether the ovine reference has any linkage to Harpo's ersatz thatch must remain speculation," notes R.S.H. Tryster, who speaks excellent German.

Chapter 13

Much of the material on the production and pre-production history is from the Mary Pickford collection, housed at the Academy of Motion Picture Arts and Sciences' Margaret Herrick Library; thanks to Chuck Harter for digging it out. Additional and supplementary sources as follows: Lester Cowan opined that *Love Happy* would help promote world peace in *Showmen's Trade Review* on September 18, 1948. Groucho recalled *Copacabana* for *Radio TV Mirror* in 1954: "I got a lot of fan mail about it—all threatening." The letters to Miriam are included in Marx Allen: *Love, Groucho*. Ben Hecht's involvement in the early stages of *At the Circus* is in Louvish. According to some sources he also contributed rough draft material to what would become *Monkey Business*. Bill Marx recalled Cowan's treatment of his father in Nick Thomas: *Raised by the Stars: Interviews with 29 Children of*

Hollywood Actors (McFarland: 2011). The reference to *The Clown* is in Mitchell: he says Harpo told British reporters about it in June 1949, the date thus proving that it was not yet another title for *Love Happy*, as has elsewhere been suggested, but an entirely separate project. (It's likely what the *Philadelphia Inquirer* as late as January 19, 1953, is intriguingly referring to as "a clown picture with Irving Brecher," adding even more intriguingly that "Harpo WILL talk in the flick.") The list of Cowan's other announced Marx projects uses material from the syndicated columns of Hedda Hopper (May 1947 and May 1949), Louella Parsons (July and September 1948), Bob Thomas (January 1949), Harold Hefferman (May 1949) and Sheilah Graham (October 1949), and issues of *Showmen's Trade Review* (May 1948 and February 1949) and *Motion Picture Daily* (May 1948 and June 1949). The Groucho quote about four Larry Parkses, referring to the star of *The Jolson Story*, was published in the *Milwaukee Journal* among others on December 12, 1948. Chico announcing the biopic at a press conference is in Eyles: *Complete Films* and the *Showmen's Trade Review* of October 16, 1948. Some of the material on the Lester Cowan-Mary Pickford alliance comes from the *Independent Exhibitors Film Bulletin* in 1946 (September 30, October 11 and December 9) and 1947 (April 14), *Motion Picture Daily* (April 1948) and *Film Daily* (October 10, October 14, and November 4, 1946); the suggested switch to Eagle-Lion distributors is in the *Bulletin* (June 21, 1948). Chico boasted about not being paid in *Showmen's Trade Review*, October 16, 1948. A small account of Groucho's lawsuit against Cowan appeared in the *Spokane Daily Chronicle* of April 28th, 1951, and doubtless elsewhere. According to the *New York Post* (August 21, 1944), Harpo and Hecht were so intent on getting the project going, even at this early date, that Harpo turned down a mysterious $100,000 offer from RKO. Doubtless with tongue in cheek, the *Post* claims they had titled it *Harpo's Bazaar.* Hecht wrote the final script in hospital according to the *San Diego Union,* September 26, 1947. ("Mary Pickford and her partner, Lester Cowan, didn't dare hope that this comedy, which stars the Marx Brothers, would be written, with Ben so ill.") Groucho refers to this in his letter (June 20, 1947) to Miriam: "Ben Hecht, who is doing the picture with Harpo and Chico, is dangerously ill in a New York hospital. He has been getting transfusions and all those things and it's quite serious." Harpo's tirade at Cowan is in Adamson. The uncredited writers: George Panetta would go on to write Chico's TV show *Papa Romani*, and the play *Comic Strip* that some sources claimed the Brothers were interested in filming in 1958; Otto E. Englander was story writer on many of the classic Disney animated features; William Alland was the guy who spends the whole of *Citizen Kane* trying to work out what "Rosebud" means and before long would be the producer of a plethora of fifties monster movies; Chas. L. Isaacs is probably Charles Isaacs, another graduate of late 1930s radio, in Hollywood by the early 1940s and chief writer for Jimmy Durante's show by the 1950s. The most interesting name here for our purposes is Manny Manheim (or Mannheim). He co-wrote the famous 1947 radio sketch with Groucho and Bob Hope that descended into a riot of inspired ad libs and gave John Guedel the inspiration that would eventually lead to *You Bet Your Life.* Manheim's AP obituary says he got his start writing a radio sketch for Groucho and Chico (one wonders if this could be the fairly undocumented "Hollywood Agents" show, or it might just as likely be a misremembering of the Bob Hope sketch); also that Groucho "once credited Manheim with helping him launch his television career on the strength of Manheim's *You Bet Your Life* scripts": again one wonders if what this really means is that Manheim helped *inspire* the show (and on radio, not TV) by giving him the chance to shine in the Bob Hope sketch, or if he really was a writer on *You Bet Your Life.* (Though it's breaking no confidences to admit that the program was by no means as spontaneous as Groucho liked to imply, it's a definite stretch to say the shows had *scripts.*) His oddest Marx-credit is on the Groucho solo movie *Double Dynamite*: "based on a character created by Manny Manheim." Perplexingly, the film gives no indication of which of its many characters Manheim created, and given Manheim's history as a radio writer for Frank Sinatra the obvious guess is his—but to what extent could it possibly be deemed a characterization borrowed from elsewhere? He plays a regular Joe with no distinguishing characteristics of any sort. So since Groucho's splendidly named Emile J. Keck is the only character *with* much of a character, all likelihood points there. But if so: created when, and to what purpose? In the early forties, when he was head writer for Milton Berle, he hired Groucho's son Arthur as a junior gag-man because, according to Arce, he owed Groucho a favor. Arce has this association ending in 1942, but they maintained contact and in the late fifties began collaborating on scripts: they co-wrote an episode of *G.E.*

Theater called *Do Not Disturb* and a play called *Everybody Loves Me*; the central character of the latter was generally considered an acidic portrait of Groucho. The Mac Benoff quotes: "little continuity and much mish-mash" is in Mitchell; "a real promoter" is from the article "The Final Marx Brothers Flick?" by Burt Prelutsky, published in the *Toledo Blade Sunday Magazine*, and probably elsewhere, shortly before Benoff's death in 1972. Harpo played up the importance of Chico's role in the *Deseret News* and elsewhere, September 8, 1948. Chico announced his retirement in the *Reading Eagle* and elsewhere on March 25, 1947, and denied it in the *San Jose Evening News* and elsewhere on March 26. Cowan's letter to Gradwell Sears is dated November 7, 1948. Bob Thomas's claim that Harpo will double for Chico in the retakes appeared, among other places, in the *Reading Eagle*, February 19, 1949. (And there's more: "Harpo tells me he might also go to England to star in a movie mystery. He's waiting for a script." He's still waiting.) I was alerted to the limited 1949 Great Lakes premiere by Joe Adamson in personal correspondence. Thanks to Steven R. Wright and Mikael Uhlin for the material on the alternate versions and Italian trailer. Marxbrothers.org has a complete list of variations in the longer and shorter versions of the film. Harpo's contractual stipulation that Groucho's appearances should be limited is also mentioned in Arce. The Cowan/Harpo cocktail party is in *Motion Picture Daily*, May 20, 1949. Ann Ronell described the peculiar challenges inherent in writing music to accompany gadgets zooming at a smoked ham to columnist Lucia Perrigo in October 1950. The Tashlin quote is from *Showmen's Trade Review* of March 5, 1949. **3:50**—Harpo's plastic surgery is mentioned in Kanfer. **67:42**—The material on Marilyn's promotional efforts draws on Anthony Summers: *Goddess: The Secret Lives of Marilyn Monroe* (London: Gollancz, 1985), Donald Spoto: *Marilyn Monroe: The Biography* (New York: Cooper Square Press, 2001), Ted Schwarz: *Marilyn Revealed: The Ambitious Life of an American Icon* (Maryland: Taylor Trade, 2008) and Lois Banner: *Marilyn: The Passion and the Paradox* (London: Bloomsbury, 2012). The David Miller story and quote from Cowan's letter comparing her to Betty Grable is in Banner; Marilyn recalling the production to Ben Hecht is in Schwarz. Miller's claiming that Harpo asked him during production to work Chico into the script is in Mitchell.

Chapter 14

The film was originally announced (for example in the *Niagara Falls Gazette* of January 19, 1959) under the title *The Best Laid Plans*. The *Hollywood Reporter* Groucho quote is included in Bader. The second Groucho quote is from *The Chicagoan*, February 15th, 1930, included in Harris. The anecdote about Harry Tugend and Groucho's moustache is from Chandler. The timecodes presented a problem here. As my decision elsewhere was that if it was authentic to the original release it should be included, so I have reluctantly used the timecoding of the Shout Factory DVD version, and thus included the Ronald Reagan introduction and the utterly senseless pre-credit extract of a random part of the later film. The film itself begins at 2:03, and that is where I urge viewers, and newcomers to the film especially, to begin watching. Obviously commercials are not included or allowed for. With regard to the areas in which I suggest the film could be improved: interestingly, the silent, one reel condensation of the film that was issued for home viewing on Super–8 addresses some of these problems, robbing the soundtrack of the canned laughter and squeezing the opening section into a much tighter three minutes. Unfortunately, it also loses most of the really funny bits, even from sections that it does retain: the Gookie, the smoke bubbles, Chico with the handcuffs and, most perversely of all, the jewelry shop manager's fingering of Groucho for the crime, who now just enters at the end for no reason at all. The elimination of Harpo putting his hands up when he backs into an effigy means the source of the policeman costume is now hard to discern, and the loss of the scene where Harpo robs the novelty shop also gives us no reason to presume they aren't using real guns. Joe Adamson's comments on *Minnie's Boys* are from personal correspondence. Groucho's novel casting idea for *Minnie's Boys* is from Hedda Hopper's column (e.g. in *Buffalo Courier-Express*, October 31, 1955). His interview with Joe Hyams about *The Story of Mankind* appeared in the *Deseret News* of February 15, 1957, and elsewhere. The Harpo quote is from the *Yonkers Herald Statesman* in 1956: the piece also claims that Harpo is set to play not Newton but "Darwin, father of evolution"—perhaps suggesting a late revision to avoid any ruffled feathers in the Bible belt; most likely a simple error. The plan to film *Comic Strip* was mentioned in the *Philadelphia Enquirer* of July 21, 1958. Hedda Hopper's nightmare of a Jerry Lewis slapstick vehicle for the team is from her syndicated column of April 11, 1961. Chico asked Earl Wilson why the hell he should want to quit in the *New York Post* of February 9, 1942, and spoke of the possibility of a return to ice cream in *Billboard* on March 28. Louella Parsons referred to the mysterious *Barber of Brazil* in her columns from October, 1944 and March, 1945. *The Doctor in Spite of Himself* is mentioned in *Saratogan* (November 26, 1951). Dorothy Kilgallen suggested an aborted TV series in her "Voice of Broadway" column in the *Jamestown Post-Journal* (January 25, 1954). Chico told Aline Mosby about the TV *Animal Crackers* in the *Grand Prairie Daily News* of January 26, 1956, among others. Groucho said times had moved on in *Sunday Herald* (August 3, 1958), nixed future reunions in Erskine Johnson's "In Hollywood" column (e.g. in *Panama City News-Herald*: February 24, 1952), and dissed da kids and reflected on the afterlife in the *Milwaukee Journal* (April 11, 1969) and many others. The older Groucho, torn between living up to the demands that the most demanding fan base in the world demanded, or relaxing in an atmosphere of calm and nostalgia, is beautifully if heartbreakingly evoked in Charlotte Chandler's memoir *Hello, I Must Be Going.*

Epilogue

The Groucho quote is in one of *The Groucho Letters*. The letter to Krasna is one of *The Groucho Letters.*

Bibliography

In this list of primary sources cited and consulted, I have given the exact edition I used. Where different, original year of publication is given parenthetically. Secondary sources are cited in the Notes and Sources section. Try saying that after an afternoon with Herman Mankiewicz.

Adams, Samuel Hopkins. *Alexander Woollcott: His Life and His World*. London: Hamish Hamilton, 1946.
Adamson, Joe. *Groucho, Harpo, Chico and Sometimes Zeppo*. London: WH Allen, 1973.
Anobile, Richard J. (ed.) *Why a Duck?* London: Studio Vista, 1972 (1971).
Arce, Hector. *Groucho*. New York: Putnam, 1979.
Bader, Robert S. (ed.) *Groucho Marx and Other Short Stories and Tall Tales: Selected Writings of Groucho Marx*. London: Faber, 1997 (1993).
Barson, Michael (ed.). Flywheel, Shyster & Flywheel: *The Marx Brothers' Lost Radio Show*. New York: Pantheon, 1988.
Benchley, Robert. *Benchley at the Theatre: Dramatic Criticism 1920–1940*. Massachusetts: Ipswich Press, 1985.
Byron, Stuart, and Elisabeth Weis. *The National Society of Film Critics on Movie Comedy*. New York: Grossman, 1977.
Cavett, Dick. *Talk Show*. New York: Henry Holt, 2010.
Chandler, Charlotte. *Hello, I Must Be Going: Groucho and His Friends*. London: Robson, 1979 (1978).
Classic Film Scripts: The Four Marx Brothers in Monkey Business *and* Duck Soup. London: Lorrimer, 1972.
Crichton, Kyle. *The Marx Brothers*. London: Heinemann, 1951.
Doherty, Thomas. *Pre-Code Hollywood*. New York: Columbia University Press, 1999.
Donati, William. *The Life and Death of Thelma Todd*. Jefferson, NC: McFarland, 2012.
Eames, John Douglas. *The MGM Story* (Revised edition). London: Octopus, 1982.
Edmonds, Andy. *Hot Toddy*. London: Macdonald, 1989.
Epstein, Lawrence J. *The Haunted Smile: The Story of Jewish Comedians*. Oxford: Public Affairs, 2002 (2001).
Eyles, Allen. *The Complete Films of the Marx Brothers*. New York: Citadel Press, 1982.
_____. *The Marx Brothers: Their World of Comedy*. New York: Barnes, 1969 (1966).
Eyman, Scott. *The Speed of Sound: Hollywood and the Talkie Revolution, 1926–1930*. Baltimore: Johns Hopkins, 1999 (1997).
Ford, Corey. *The Time of Laughter: A Sentimental Chronicle of the Twenties, the Humor and the Humorists*. London: Pitman, 1970 (1967).
Goldstein, Malcolm. *George S. Kaufman: His Life, His Theatre*. Oxford: Oxford University Press, 1980.
Halliwell, Leslie. *Double Take and Fade Away: Halliwell on Comedians*. London: Grafton, 1987.
_____. *Halliwell's Film Guide* (7th edition). London: Paladin, 1989.
_____. *Halliwell's Harvest*. London: Grafton, 1986.
_____. *Halliwell's Hundred*. London: Granada, 1982.
_____. *Mountain of Dreams: The Golden Years of Paramount*. New York: Stonehill, 1976.
Harris, Neil (ed.). *The Chicagoan: A Lost Magazine of the Jazz Age*. Chicago: University of Chicago Press, 2008.
Higham, Charles. *Louis B. Mayer: Merchant of Dreams*. London: Pan, 1994 (1993).
Kanfer, Stefan. *Groucho: The Life and Times of Julius Henry Marx*. London: Allen Lane, 2000.
Kaufman, Beatrice, and Joseph Hennessey (eds.). *The Letters of Alexander Woollcott*. London: Cassell, 1946.
Kaufman, George S. *The Cocoanuts* (1925), included in Donald Oliver (ed.). *By George: A Kaufman Collection*. London: Angus & Robertson, 1980 (1979).

Kaufman, George S., and Morrie Ryskind. *Animal Crackers* (1929), included in Kaufman and Co. New York: Library of America, 2004.

Loos, Anita. *Kiss Hollywood Goodbye*. London: WH Allen, 1974.

Louvish, Simon. *Monkey Business: The Lives and Legends of the Marx Brothers*. London: Faber & Faber, 1999.

Marx, Arthur. *Groucho*. London: Gollancz, 1954.

Marx, Groucho. *Groucho & Me*. London: Virgin, 1994 (1959).

Marx, Groucho, and Richard J. Anobile. *The Marx Brothers Scrapbook*. New York: Harper & Row, 1989 (1973).

Marx, Harpo (with Rowland Barber). *Harpo Speaks!* London: Robson, 1976 (1961).

Marx, Maxine. *Growing Up with Chico*. New York: Limelight, 1986 (1980).

Marx Allen, Miriam (ed.). *Love, Groucho: Letters from Groucho Marx to His Daughter Miriam*. London: Faber & Faber, 1997 (1992).

Meredith, Scott. *George S. Kaufman and the Algonquin Round Table*. London: Allen & Unwin, 1977.

Merryman, Richard. *Mank: The Wit, World and Life of Herman Mankiewicz*. New York: William Morrow, 1978.

Mitchell, Glenn. *The Marx Brothers Encyclopedia*. London: Batsford, 1996.

Moore, Lucy. *Anything Goes: A Biography of the Roaring Twenties*. London: Atlantic, 2008.

Murray, John, and Allen Boretz. *Room Service* (1937). New York: Dramatists Play Service Inc., n.d.

Norman, Barry. *The Movie Greats*. London: Hodder & Stoughton, 1981.

_____. *Talking Pictures*. London: Hodder & Stoughton/BBC, 1987.

Perelman, S. J. *The Most of S. J. Perelman*. London: Methuen, 1979 (1959).

Robinson, Jeffrey. *Teamwork: The Cinema's Greatest Comedy Teams*. London: Proteus, 1982.

Roth, Lillian. *I'll Cry Tomorrow*. London: Arthur Barker, 1957 (1953).

Schatz, Thomas. *The Genius of the System: Hollywood Film-making in the Studio Era*. London: Faber, 1998 (1989).

Schulberg, Budd. *Moving Pictures*. London: Penguin, 1984 (1981).

Sheekman, Arthur (ed.). *The Groucho Letters*. London: Michael Joseph, 1967.

Smith, Andrew T. *Marx & Re-Marx: Creating and Re-Creating the Lost Marx Brothers Radio Series*. Albany: BearManor, 2009.

Stuart, Gloria. *I Just Kept Hoping*. New York: Little, Brown, 1999.

Yagoda, Ben. *About Town: The New Yorker and the World It Made*. London: Duckworth, 2000.

Zolotow, Maurice. *Billy Wilder in Hollywood*. London: WH Allen, 1977.

Index

Numbers in **_bold italics_** indicate pages with photographs.